2016 UNITED STATES EQUESTRIAN FEDERA

The National Equestrian Federation of the United States a membe
the United States Olympic Committee.

THIS BOOK SUPERSEDES ALL PREVIOUS EDITIONS

THE RULES PUBLISHED HEREIN ARE EFFECTIVE DECEMBER 1, 2015 UNLESS OTHERWISE SPECIFIED AT
THE TIME OF THEIR ENACTMENT AND REMAIN IN EFFECT EXCEPT AS SUPERSEDED BY RULE CHANGES
ENACTED BY THE BOARD OF DIRECTORS AS PUBLISHED ON THE FEDERATION'S WEB SITE AT www.usef.org
OR BY SUBSEQUENT EDITIONS OR SUPPLEMENTS TO THE RULE BOOK

Published by United States Equestrian Federation, Inc.
4047 Iron Works Parkway
Lexington, KY 40511
859-258-2472
Fax: 859-231-6662

THE SPORTSMAN'S CHARTER

That sport is something done for the fun of doing it and that it ceases to be sport when it becomes a business only, something done for what there is in it;

That amateurism is something of the heart and spirit - not a matter of exact technical qualifications;

That good manners of sport are fundamentally important;

That the code must be strictly upheld;

That the whole structure of sport is not only preserved from the absurdity of undue importance, but is justified by a kind of romance which animates it, and by the positive virtues of courage, patience, good temper, and unselfishness which are demanded by the code;

That the exploitation of sport for profit alone kills the spirit and retains only the husk and semblance of the thing;

That the qualities of frankness, courage, and sincerity which mark the good sportsman in private life shall mark the discussions of his interests at a competition.

UNITED STATES EQUESTRIAN FEDERATION, INC.

(the Federation)

THE NATIONAL
EQUESTRIAN FEDERATION, INC.
OF THE UNITED STATES
4047 Iron Works Parkway
Lexington, KY 40511

(859) 258-2472
Fax: (859) 231-6662

NOTICE: Verbiage in red text indicates new or revised rules approved to become effective December 1, 2015, unless another date is specified. EFFECTIVE dates for new rules are listed and these dates do vary.

The Rules published in this Rule Book are subject to additions or revisions pursuant to Chapter 1, Sub-chapter 1-B of the Rules. Please see the Federation's web site at www.usef.org for any changes subsequent to the publication date of this Rule Book.

While every effort has been made to avoid mistakes in this publication, the Federation does not assume any liability to anyone for errors or omissions. Corrections and additions are published on the Federation's web site at www.usef.org

BYLAWS

GENERAL RULES

CHAPTERS 1-13

BREED/DISCIPLINE CHAPTERS

Which pertain to the classification, conduct and operation of competitions and to general matters affecting Exhibitors, Judges, Stewards and Competition Officials.

A knowledge of the rules of any sport is required of each participant and the
exhibitor at a Licensed Competition is in no way exempt from this responsibility. A complete knowledge of and compliance with the rules are essential and the exhibitor must be fully cognizant of all the rules as well as class specifications in the Divisions in which he or she shows.

It is obvious that however complete rules may be, they can never cover all possible situations which may arise. If a matter cannot be solved by interpreting the rules to the letter, the solution to be adopted by those responsible should lie in a principle which follows as nearly as possible the spirit of the rules.

PLEASE READ ALL CROSS REFERENCES CAREFULLY, AND REFER TO THE FEDERATION'S WEBSITE AT www.usef.org FOR OFFICIAL CHANGES AND THE MOST UP-TO-DATE VERSION OF THIS RULEBOOK.

UNITED STATES EQUESTRIAN FEDERATION RULES
The term THE FEDERATION when used herein refers to and denotes only the United States Equestrian Federation, Inc.

SPONSORED BY HAGYARD EQUINE MEDICAL INSTITUTE || © USEF 2016

CHAPTER 1 DEFINITIONS

SUBCHAPTER 1-A DEFINITIONS

GR101 Adult or Senior (Individual)

GR102 Age (of Equine)

GR103 Age (of Individual)

GR104 Agent

GR105 Amateur

GR106 Amateur Classes

GR107 Clients

GR108 Coach

GR109 Commencement and Completion of Classes

GR110 Comparable Dates

GR111 Competition Dates

GR112 Competition Staff

GR113 Competition Officials

GR114 Competition Terminology

GR115 Competition Year

GR116 Competitor

GR117 Disqualification

GR118 Elimination

GR119 Excused

GR120 Exhibition (Class or Demonstration)

GR121 Exhibitor

GR122 Falls

GR123 Family

GR124 Gender

GR125 Hand

GR126 Horse

GR127 Junior

GR128 Ladies' Classes

GR129 Lessee

GR130 License Rights

GR131 Licensed Competition

GR132 Licensee

GR133 Local Classes

GR134 Longeur

GR135 Maiden, Novice, and Limit Classes

GR136 Not in Good Standing

GR137 Open Classes

GR138 Opportunity Classes

GR139 Owned by Him or Her

GR140 Owner

GR141 Owner's Classes

GR142 Para-Equestrian

SUBCHAPTER 1-B ADOPTION AND AMENDMENT OF FEDERATION RULES

SPONSORED BY HAGYARD EQUINE MEDICAL INSTITUTE || © USEF 2016

CHAPTER 1 DEFINITIONS

SUBCHAPTER 1-A DEFINITIONS

GR101 Adult or Senior (Individual)

1. An individual who has reached his 18th birthday as of December 1st of the current competition year.

    a. For competition purposes, in the Dressage division, competitors shall compete as Adults from the beginning of the calendar year in which they reach the age of 22.

    b. For the Eventing Division, see EV104.

    c. For Paso Fino Division, see PF106.1.

    d. For the Arabian Division, see AR110.

    e. For the AMHA Medal Classes, see MO165.

GR102 Age (of Equine)

1. For competition purposes any horse is considered to be one year old on the first day of January following the actual date of foaling.

    a. Exception: In the Paso Fino Horse Division, a horse's age is determined by the age it is on the first day of January during the twelve month period September 1 through the following August 31.

    b. Some breed/disciplines may, for purposes of eligibility to compete, use the actual age of the animal (of foaling date).

2. A mature horse is one that is over four years of age.

3. A junior horse is one that is four years of age or younger. Exceptions:

    a. Junior Breeding or In-Hand classes are open to horses two years old and under. Junior Horse performance classes held in the Arabian, Friesian, National Show Horse, and Western Division(s) are open to horses five years old and under. Senior Breeding or In-Hand classes are open to horses three years old and over.

    b. Friesian: six and older.

    c. For Andalusian/Lusitano, see division rules.

GR103 Age (of Individual)

1. The age of an individual on December 1st will be maintained throughout the entire competition year.

2. Persons born on December 1st will assume the greater age on that date.

3. If a competition is in progress on any November 30th, an individual's age at the start of the competition will be maintained throughout the competition.

4. Exceptions: see GR149, EV104, DC912, DR119.3, RN104 and PF106.1-.4.

GR104 Agent

Any adult or adults, including but not limited to any groom(s), veterinarian(s), coach(es) or other persons who act on behalf of an exhibitor, owner or lessee of a horse, trainer, rider, driver or handler at or in connection with a Licensed Competition.

GR105 Amateur

See GR1306 and GR1307.

GR106 Amateur Classes

1. Every contestant must hold amateur status. See GR1306 and GR1307.

2. Amateur classes may be restricted to riders, drivers or handlers who are no longer eligible to compete as a junior exhibitor. In the Dressage or Western Dressage Division, individuals are only eligible to compete as amateurs from

the beginning of the calendar year in which they reach age 22. See DR119.3.

GR107 Clients

1. As used in GR1304, GR1039 and GR1012.4, "client" and "clients" of a judge, steward or technical delegate shall include:
   a. any person who has received, or who has a member of his or her family who has received, horse training or instruction in riding, driving or showing in hand or in halter from the judge, steward or technical delegate or from said official's employee, whether or not remuneration has been given or received, and whether or not such training or instruction took place at a Licensed Competition
   b. any persons who pay horse board (excluding stud fees and broodmare board) to the judge, steward, or technical delegate, or to a member of his or her family and
   c. any persons entered in a Licensed Competition as rider, driver, handler, exhibitor, owner or lessee, and members of the family of the foregoing, on an entry blank signed in any capacity by the judge, steward or technical delegate or his or her agent, employee or member of his or her family, whether or not remuneration has been given or received.
2. The conducting of clinics or assistance in group activities such as Pony Clubs, unless private instruction is given, will not be considered as instruction, coaching or tutoring.

GR108 Coach

For purposes of these rules, a coach is defined as any adult or adults who receives remuneration for having or sharing the responsibility for instructing, teaching, schooling, or advising a rider, driver, handler or vaulter in equestrian skills. See also GR906.4 and GR908.

GR109 Commencement and Completion of Classes

1. Refer to GR829.
2. In classes where horses compete collectively, a warning is issued and the in-gate must be closed two minutes after the first horse enters the ring.
   a. Judging must not commence until the gate is closed or at the end of the two-minute call. An official timer must be appointed to enforce this rule.
3. Exception: Dressage or Western Dressage division.
4. For Paso Fino, see PF102.7.
5. In a class where horses compete individually, a class is considered completed when all horses have completed the class routine as designated by the rules.
6. In classes where horses compete collectively, a class is considered completed when the class has been judged in accordance with the rules and the judge(s) submit their cards to the ringmaster or announcer.
7. None of the above applies to the Jumper division. Refer to Chapter JP.

GR110 Comparable Dates

1. For competitions with a start date of December 1, 2008 or later, the following provisions will be in effect:
   a. For the 2009 competition year and therafter, comparable dates will be based on competition's 2006 dates using the Memorial Day Date Rotation Axis. Under the Memorial Day Date Rotation Axis, all USEF competition dates rotate in conjunction with Memorial Day.
   b. For the 2009 competition year, any competition that did not hold a license for the 2006 competition year, but received a license for the 2007 and/or 2008 competition year, will have priority over new competitions requesting dates. However, competitions with licenses for the 2006 competition year will have priority over any of the above

mentioned competitions.

c. For purposes of determining mileage between competitions, quarters will be defined as follows: first quarter - December through February; second quarter March through May; third quarter - June through August; fourth quarter - September November. The first day of a competition is the date used to determine the mileage applied to the entire competition.

GR111 Competition Dates

A competition or competition date begins at 12:01 am on the calendar date on which the first class (or Horse Inspection, if applicable) is scheduled and ends at midnight on the calendar date on which the last class is scheduled.

GR112 Competition Staff

Includes and refers to the following persons: Gate Attendants, Ring Clerks, Farriers, Timekeepers, Announcers, Ringmasters and other persons engaged directly by the competition.

GR113 Competition Officials

Includes and refers to the following persons: Directors, Officers, Chairman of the Show Committee, Manager, Secretary, Judges, Stewards, Technical Delegates, Veterinarians, and Course Designers.

GR114 Competition Terminology

1. For the purposes of USEF rules, the following definitions apply to USEF licensed competitions.

    a. Rated class - any class held on a licensed competition date that counts towards the division or section rating. (See Chapter 3)

    b. Unrated class - any class held on a licensed competition date that does not count towards the division or section rating, or any class held at an unrated licensed competition. (See GR301.4)

    c. Recognized class - any class held on a licensed competition date for which there are USEF division rules. (See GR305 or GR902.3)

    d. Unrecognized class - any class held on a licensed competition date in accordance with the requirements of GR305.1 or GR902.3. (See GR902.2)

    e. Division - group of rules pertaining to a specific breed or discipline (i.e. Morgan, Jumping)

    f. Section - group of rules within a specific breed or discipline division that pertains to a type of class (i.e. Working Western Section within the Arabian Division)

GR115 Competition Year

1. For the purposes of these rules, the competition year is defined as starting December 1st and ending November 30th.

    a. The Paso Fino competition year is defined as starting September 1 and ending August 31.

    b. A USHJA Hunter or Jumper Zone may define its competition year as starting October 1st and ending September 30th, providing it makes this determination prior to June 1st of the year preceeding the new competition year. If a Zone elects to change its competition year it must keep that change for a minimum of three (3) years.

GR116 Competitor

The horse, rider (handler, driver) or horse/rider combination being judged depending on the judging specifications for a particular competition.

GR117 Disqualification

1. To exclude a competitor or horse, for cause, from participation in a given class, division or competition.

2. Competitors may be disqualified by the Licensed Competition.

3. If a competitor is disqualified following the completion of a class, for the purpose of

determining the number of horses which have been entered, shown, and judged, said competitor's performance shall count. If the competitor received an award, the award must be forfeited. A competitor disqualified in this manner may not use this class as a qualifying class for a Championship (see also GR809.2.).

4. Competitors have the right to contest any action taken pursuant to this Rule by filing a protest or grievance pursuant to Chapter 6 of the Rules for hearing and determination by the Hearing Committee.

GR118 Elimination

1. See also GR1305 and specific division rules.

2. To exclude a competitor or horse, for cause, from judging consideration in a class.

3. A competitor who is eliminated is ineligible to receive an award regardless of the number of competitors in the class.

4. If an eliminated competitor completes a class, in accordance with GR116 and GR117, for the purpose of determining the number of horses which have been entered, shown, and judged, said competitor's performance shall count.

5. None of the above applies to the Jumper division. Refer to Chapter JP.

GR119 Excused

1. To have a judge(s) grant permission to, or request that a competitor leave the class.

2. A competitor who is excused is ineligible to receive an award.

3. None of the above applies to the Jumper division. Refer to Chapter JP.

GR120 Exhibition (Class or Demonstration)

1. An Exhibition may be held as a recognized but unrated class or demonstration, as required by division rules. See DR136 for rules pertaining to exhibition classes and demonstrations at Dressage Competitions.

2. Exhibition classes must be advertised in the prize list and may be judged and ranked. At any USEF licensed competition, Exhibition classes may not be restricted to Friesians.

   a. However, results may not be counted for high score awards or championships.

   b. If published, the rankings report must be clearly separated from competition results and noted as being from an exhibition.

   c. Judges for breed, hunter, jumper, or Western exhibition classes held at Licensed Competitions are not required to be licensed by USEF.

   d. Judges for Western Dressage exhibition classes must be licensed as described in WD123.1.

   e. At Federation licensed Hunter, Jumper or Hunter/Jumper competitions, only one exhibition or demonstration class may be held per licensed competition day and the results of such classes cannot be counted for Federation or Federation affiliate awards.

3. Exhibition demonstrations may also be held using horses individually, in groups or in entertainment acts. Such demonstrations cannot be held as a class.

4. Horses used in exhibitions, demonstrations, and retirement ceremonies are subject to the provisions of GR839, but are exempt from the dress and saddlery rules of the competition.

GR121 Exhibitor

1. The owner or lessee of a horse when entered in a class where only the merits of the horse or horse/rider combination are to be considered. In Equitation Classes, Exhibitor refers to the rider.

GR122 Falls

1. A rider is considered to have fallen when he is separated from his horse, that has not fallen, in such a way as to

necessitate remounting or vaulting into the saddle.

2. A horse is considered to have fallen when the shoulder and haunch on the same side have touched the ground or an obstacle and the ground. Exception: see EV142.4, EV150.9 and RN103.5.I.

GR123 Family

For competition purposes the term family includes husband, wife, parent, step-parent, child, brother, step-child, sister, half brother and sister, aunt, uncle, niece, nephew, grandmother, grandfather, grandchildren, and in-laws of the same relation as stated above.

GR124 Gender

Whenever in these rules the words he, him, or his are used, unless the context requires otherwise, they shall include she, her, or hers.

GR125 Hand

1. The height of all animals is stated in hands. A hand is 4".
2. Horses must be over 14.2 hands. Exceptions:
   a. Registered Arabians, Half or Anglo Arabians, Connemaras, English Pleasure entries, Morgans, Paso Finos, and Welsh Cobs.
   b. Dressage.
3. Ponies are 14.2 hands and under. Exceptions:
   a. Dressage;
   b. Combined Driving, see DC930.

GR126 Horse

1. The term "horse" as used in these rules denotes either a horse or pony.
2. In all levels of all Federation licensed Driving and Endurance Competitions and in the case of any other Federation Rule as it relates to the Driving or Endurance disciplines as the context permits it, the term "horse" shall also include a mule. See DC Annex 9, EN102.1.

Mules are also eligible to compete in dressage classes with the exception of:

1. USEF Championships, USEF qualifying and selection trials, and observation classes,
2. any other classes designated as qualifying or selection classes for international or international high performance competition, and
3. championships where such participation is prohibited in the championship selection procedures. See DR119.1.
3. When the term "Horse" or "Pony" is used or intended in prize lists and catalogues of Licensed Competitions where height is one of the qualifications of the class, the word Horse denotes animals over 14.2 hands.
   a. Exceptions: Registered Arabians, Half or Anglo Arabians, Connemaras, English Pleasure entries, Friesian, Morgans, Paso Finos, Welsh Cobs and Dressage.
   b. In the Dressage Division, a Horse is an animal over 148 cm without shoes, and 149 cm with shoes.
   c. For Combined Driving, see DC930.

GR127 Junior

1. An individual who has not reached his 18th birthday as of December 1st of the current competition year.
2. The age of an individual on December 1st will be maintained throughout the entire competition year.
3. Persons born on December 1st assume the greater age on that date.
4. If a competition is in progress on any November 30th, junior status at the start of the competition will be maintained throughout that competition.

5. Exceptions: Eventing, Dressage, Reining, Arabian and Paso Fino Competitions, see EV104.2, RN104.c, PF106.1-3, DR119.3 and AR110.

GR128 Ladies' Classes

1. Ladies' classes may be restricted to riders, drivers or handlers who are no longer eligible to compete as a junior exhibitor.

2. Stallions are not permitted unless division rules allow their use for ladies.

GR129 Lessee

See GR1108.

GR130 License Rights

Granting of a license by the Federation does not give the Licensee property rights or perpetual rights but constitutes merely revocable licenses which are venue specific and which are governed by the terms and conditions of the license agreement and the rules, policies and procedures of USEF as the same may change from time to time. Approval of all competitions at all times remains a prerogative and property interest of the Federation, and licenses may not be relocated, transferred, sold, assigned, revised, perpetuated, limited, expanded, or otherwise affected without the Federation's advance knowledge and written consent. By applying for and accepting the license agreement, all applicants and their agents, licensees, employees, officers, representatives, and successors in interest are deemed to agree to and be bound by the foregoing, and agree to hold the Federation harmless in all respects.

GR131 Licensed Competition

A competition subject to a license agreement for a fixed term. The parties to the agreement will be USEF and the licensee.

GR132 Licensee

A Licensee is a person or legal entity who has obtained legal permission from the Federation to conduct a licensed competition.

GR133 Local Classes

1. Entry is restricted by management as to a territory of reasonable size and character and which is so described in the prize list and catalogue.

2. Local classes are not considered in reckoning Competition Championships awarded on points nor do they count toward Horse of the Year Awards.

3. Classes restricted to members of a club are considered Local unless membership is open to and easily obtainable by all exhibitors.

4. In classes which restrict entries by state such as Kentucky Bred, the word bred is defined as foaled in the state (not necessarily mated).

   a. For competition purposes bred means foaled.

   b. NOTE: American Bred classes are limited to horses foaled within the borders of the United States. These classes are not considered Local.

5. For Dressage Sport Horse Breeding (DSHB), see DR203.12.

GR134 Longeur

For purposes of these rules, a longeur is the individual responsible for the control of the horse within the vaulting arena during a vaulting competition.

GR135 Maiden, Novice, and Limit Classes

1. Maiden, Novice and Limit classes are open to horses which have not won one/ three/six first place ribbons respectively, at Regular Competitions of the Federation or Equine Canada in the particular performance division or level in which they are shown. See DR137 for all rules related to Maiden, Novice and Limit classes in Dressage Competitions.

2. The Maiden, Novice or Limit status of both riders and drivers is affected by winnings at Regular and Local Competitions. (Exception: Arabian)

3. Ribbons won in one-horse classes do not count in reckoning the maiden, novice or limit status of either horse and/ or rider/driver in any division.

4. The status of Maiden, Novice or Limit entries is as of the closing date of entries for any particular Licensed Competition.

5. A Maiden, Novice or Limit Pair is one which has not won more than the specified number of ribbons as a pair.

6. Winnings in Four-In-Hands, Tandems, Teams, Unicorns and Pairs; and winnings in Combination, Local, Model, Breeding and Futurity classes are not considered in reckoning the status of Maiden, Novice or Limit horses.

7. Ponies or horses which lose their Maiden, Novice, Limit or other classification in any division or section will not regain those classifications when shown in the Hunter Pony division or Junior Hunter division. Ponies or horses shown in the Hunter Pony division or Junior Hunter division which lose their classification will not regain them when shown in any other divisions or sections, unless specific regulations are set forth (e.g. Jumper division).

8. In the Andalusian, Arabian, Friesian, Morgan, American Saddlebred, Roadster, and Western divisions, ribbons won within one section do not count in the reckoning of Maiden, Novice or Limit status if the animal competes in a different section (e.g., Arabian Park to Arabian Western Pleasure, Fine Harness to Five-Gaited, Five-Gaited Show Pleasure to Three-Gaited Show Pleasure, Saddle Horse English Country Pleasure to Saddle Horse Hunter Country Pleasure, Western Pleasure to Trail, or Morgan English [Park or Pleasure] to Morgan Western or Morgan Harness [Park or Pleasure] and vice versa).

9. In the Hackney division, ribbons won within those sections (i.e. Hackney Harness, Hackney Pleasure) do not count in the reckoning of Maiden, Novice, or Limit status if the pony competes in another section of the Hackney division. However, ribbons won in the Roadster Pony section of the Roadster Division will count towards the maiden/ novice/ limit status of Hackney Roadster ponies.

10. In all other divisions, ribbons won within one section or division do count in the reckoning of Maiden, Novice, or Limit status if horses and ponies compete in a different section or division.

11. In a change of status from horse to pony, or vice versa, ribbons won in one height classification do not count in reckoning the Maiden, Novice or Limit status of an entry.

GR136 Not in Good Standing

1. Any person referenced in GR701 who has been expelled or suspended by the Federation.

2. Any licensee suspended pursuant to GR703 or GR707 or who is indebted to the Federation pursuant to GR309.

GR137 Open Classes

1. An Open class is open to all horses and ponies of any age, size or sex, regardless of previous awards received, in accordance with division rules.

2. There is no qualification for the rider, driver or handler except as specified in division rules for the particular category or level of classes.

GR138 Opportunity Classes

1. Unrated, grass roots level classes held at breed restricted, multi-breed, Carriage Pleasure Driving, Western competitions, Western Dressage or Hunter and/or Hunter Jumper competitions with no FEI recognized classes.

Opportunity Classes cannot be held at FEI discipline competitions (exception: Dressage Competition Levels 1-3, per GR821). At any USEF licensed competition, Opportunity Classes may not be restricted to Friesians.

2. For further information, reference GR821, GR407.1 and GR901.9.

GR139 Owned by Him or Her

1. For purposes of applying suspension only, the phrase "owned by him or her" with regard to a horse shall include any individual who is one of the following: an owner, a partial owner, a lessor (pursuant to GR703.1c, a lessee may apply for the release from suspension of a leased horse), a lessee, a holder of a partnership interest in a horse, or an owner of shares in a corporation, limited liability company, syndicate or any similar entity which owns or leases a horse either directly or indirectly, in whole or in part, and spouses or domestic partners of such persons. See GR703.1c, GR1301.4a, GR1302.2c, GR1308.2b, and GR913.1.

2. This rule is not applicable in determining ownership for any other purposes in the rules.

GR140 Owner

See GR1105 and GR1106.

GR141 Owner's Classes

1. Every competitor must be an amateur and the owner, or an amateur member of the owner's family, unless the prize list states otherwise. Exception: Paso Fino Division.

2. Owners' classes may be restricted to riders, drivers or handlers who are no longer eligible to compete as a junior exhibitor.

3. Combined ownership is not permitted in Owner's or Amateur Owner's classes unless all owners are members of the same family. Leased horses are not eligible. Exception: Paso Fino Division.

GR142 Para-Equestrian

Para-Equestrian (PE) is a competition, division or section that provides equestrian competition opportunities for eligible individuals with a diagnosed permanent, physical disability as determined by the USEF Para-Equestrian Classification System. (See GR1311.)

GR143 Pony

1. Ponies are animals that do not exceed 14.2 hands.
   a. Exceptions: for Combined Driving, see DC930;
   b. In the Dressage Division, a Pony is an animal that does not exceed 148 cm without shoes, and 149 cm with shoes.

GR144 Professional

See GR1306.

GR145 Protests, Charges and Grievances

1. For a description of a protest, see Chapter 6 in general, and specifically GR603.

2. For a description of a charge, see Chapter 6 in general, and specifically GR604.

3. For a description of a grievance, see Chapter 6 in general, and specifically GR605.

GR146 Shown and Judged

1. To be shown and judged in any class in which horses compete together, an animal must perform at all required gaits both ways of the ring in the original workout and must remain in the ring until excused by the judge. Exceptions:
   a. Roadster Division, see RD104.

b. Paso Fino Division, see PF102.5.

GR147 Trainer

1. Any adult, or adults who has the responsibility for the care, training, custody or performance of a horse.

2. Said person must sign the entry blank of any Licensed Competition whether said person be an owner, rider, agent and/or coach as well as trainer.

3. Where a minor exhibitor has no trainer, a parent or guardian must sign and assume responsibility of trainer.

4. The name of the trainer must be designated as such on the entry blank. See also GR404.

GR148 Veterinarian

A graduate of an accredited veterinary school.

GR149 Young Rider

In the International Disciplines individuals are eligible as Young Riders or Young Drivers from the beginning of the calendar year in which they reach the age of 16 until the end of the calendar year in which they reach the age of 21.

SUBCHAPTER 1-B ADOPTION AND AMENDMENT OF FEDERATION RULES

GR150 Rules

1. In the event a division or section rule makes a clear exception to a general rule, or clearly departs from a general rule, the division or section rule shall govern; in all other instances, General Rules Chapters 1-13 shall take precedence.

2. The rules of the Federation take precedence over the rules of any other Association. (Exception: See GR915.2.) All divisions and sections for which rules are provided herein must be conducted accordingly and cannot be held under rules that are not in agreement.

   a. FEI rules take precedence as to international classes and events over Federation rules at all FEI Sanctioned Competitions.

   b. Federation rules take precedence as to national classes and events which are not FEI Sanctioned at FEI Sanctioned Competitions.

   c. In connection with Endurance Riding Events, The Federation shall nationally enforce the prohibition of the gastric ulcer medications ranitidine and omeprazole, in accordance with GR409.1

   d. At FEI Sanctioned Competitions which include no national classes, a licensee is not required to have a Federation steward or technical delegate. (Exception: FEI Sanctioned Jumper competitions licensed by the Federation must have a Federation steward.)

3. Any question not covered by the rules of the Federation shall be decided by the Directors of the competition at which it arises. Such decisions by a Show Committee may be reviewable by the Federation. Show Committees are cautioned not to make use of the authority here granted unless completely certain that the Book does not cover the points in question.

4. Standard rule changes become effective December 1st of the year approved, unless otherwise specified, and supersede prior rules. All competitions are governed by the rules in effect on the first day of the competition.

5. Every Licensed Competition and every person participating at the competition including exhibitor, owner, lessee, manager, agent, rider, driver, handler, judge, steward or technical delegate, competition official or employee is subject to the Bylaws and Rules of the Federation and to the local rules of the competition.

GR151 Rule Change Procedures

These rules may be added to, altered or amended at any meeting of the Board of Directors by a majority vote of those present as provided herein below. The USEF Legislative Committee is responsible for review, analysis, and oversight of the Federation's rule change process, subject to review and approval by the Board of Directors. (See Bylaw 502, Section 11.) Rule Change Categories: Standard, Clarification, Extraordinary, and FEI.

1. Standard Rule Changes. Individual Federation members, Federation Staff, Federation Committees, and Recognized Affiliate Associations (Recognized Associations and International Discipline Associations) may propose standard rule changes. See Bylaw 221 and 222.

   a. Standard rule changes must be submitted to the Federation in writing on the USEF official form within the following deadlines in order to be considered within the current rule change year.

      1. Individual Federation members June 1

      2. Federation Senior Staff June 1

      3. Federation Committees September 1

      4. Affiliated Entities (Bylaw 221) September 1

      5. Recognized Affiliate Associations (Bylaw 222) September 1

   b. The proponent's name must be clearly listed on the official rule change form. When the proponent is other than an individual, such submissions shall be accompanied by minutes or certification signed by the Committee Chair or Recognized Affiliate Association's President that document the review and action taken at a meeting.

   c. The Legislative Committee may reject a proposal for:

      1. failure to comply with the requirements of the official form;

      2. lateness;

      3. incompleteness;

      4. inexact or confusing language;

      5. a proposal that was disapproved the prior year;

      6. attempts to amend a rule or rules in effect for less than a year;

      7. proposing to change a rule that is solely within the Federation's purview

      8. any other specified reason in the Committee's discretion.

   d. In the event the Legislative Committee rejects a proposal, the proponent must be notified in writing. Proponents of a rejected proposal may revise and resubmit a proposal. Any decision to reject a proposal made by the Legislative Committee shall prevail subject to review by the Board of Directors.

   e. The Legislative Committee will designate review of the proposed rule change by any and all standing Federation Committees and each assigned entity deemed appropriate.

2. Rule Clarifications:

   a. Contradictory language, missing or incorrect phrasing, and other wording or punctuation errors that cause inconsistent interpretations of the intent of a rule, may be clarified via a Federation Official Rule Clarification form. This form will be submitted to the Rule Change Coordinator, who will obtain comments from relevant Federation Departments and Committees.

   b. The General Counsel, with the approval of the Legislative Committee, may approve clarifications and post them on the USEF website and include them in the next available Federation Rule Book. The General Counsel may immediately correct misspelled words, minor punctuation errors, missing or incorrect references and other similar clarifications deemed minor.

3. Extraordinary Rule Changes.

   a. An Extraordinary rule change is defined as: (i) one that, unless expedited, would create or continue a severe hardship or a gross unfairness to the Federation, its members or their horses, its Licensed Competitions, or its Recognized Affiliate Associations; or (ii) one that is certified by a Recognized Affiliate Association Board or Executive Committee by a formal vote that without passage would disadvantage the membership of the Recognized Affiliate Association. The rule change proposal form MUST contain a statement describing clearly how the proposed change meets the above criteria. The Rule Change Coordinator must then get certification that the proposed extraordinary rule change in fact, does meet the necessary criteria to bypass the normal rule change process. Such certification will come from the Legislative Committee in conjunction with the General Counsel, or at least two USEF Officers.

 b. Once the proposal is certified, and with a required minimum five business days notice, the Board of Directors at any meeting may entertain and take immediate action on such an Extraordinary Rule Change. However, the five-day notice requirement may be waived upon the affirmative vote of a majority of the Board present with the reasons for the waiver stated in their meeting minutes.

 c. Extraordinary Rule Changes shall be effective as specified by the Board and if not specified, shall be effective immediately upon passage.

 d. Following adoption of any Extraordinary Rule Change, prompt written notice must be given via the Federation's web site.

4. FEI Rule Changes. In order to comply in a timely manner with changes in FEI rules which may be published by the FEI outside the Federation's normal rule change schedule, certification is waived and the Board of Directors may consider and act to conform to any FEI rule change as deemed necessary.

GR152 Presidential Modifications

1. Modifications may be made in the application of the Federation Rules under special circumstances (see Bylaw 332.1f). Requests should be submitted to the office of the President and will be forwarded to appropriate committee chairmen for their recommendations before being submitted to the President for consideration.

 a. Senior Active Members of the Federation may submit a request for Presidential Modification to the Rules with supporting documentation and a non-refundable $50 processing fee.

 b. The President has the authority to waive the processing fee.

 c. When a horse has a chronic condition and has previously been granted at least one annual Presidential Modification to Dressage or Eventing rules related to the condition, an application can be submitted for approval of a special three-year Presidential Modification related to the same condition. The application must be accompanied by sufficient supporting documentation that the condition is unlikely to improve during the three-year period.

CHAPTER 2 MEMBERSHIP CATEGORIES AND REQUIREMENTS

SUBCHAPTER 2-A MEMBERSHIPS

SUBCHAPTER 2-B AFFILIATED ASSOCIATIONS

SUBCHAPTER 2-C NON-MEMBERS

SUBCHAPTER 2-D FEDERATION FEES AND DUES

SPONSORED BY HAGYARD EQUINE MEDICAL INSTITUTE || © USEF 2016

CHAPTER 2 MEMBERSHIP CATEGORIES AND REQUIREMENTS

SUBCHAPTER 2-A MEMBERSHIPS

GR201 Membership Categories

1. Competing Membership(s)

Competing members are those individuals who desire to participate in Federation Licensed Competitions. Competing members are eligible to participate as a licensed official, rider, driver, handler, vaulter, longeur, owner, lessee, agent, trainer, coach, competition manager, or competition secretary. The competing membership options are:

    a. Life Member. Life Members are Senior Active or Junior Active Members who attain Life Membership upon a single payment of $2,500. Life Members shall have all rights and privileges of Members and be subject to all liabilities and penalties which may be imposed upon Members. They shall be exempt from annual dues.

    b. Senior Active Member. Senior Active Members are those Members who are at least 18 years of age. Their annual dues are $55. Senior Active Members shall be sent notice of and shall be entitled to attend the Annual Meeting of the Federation.

    c. Junior Active Member. Junior Active Members are those Members who have not reached their 18th birthday as provided for in GR127. Their annual dues are $55.

2. Non-competing Membership(s)

Non-competing members are those individuals who do not desire to participate in Federation Licensed Competitions. Non-competing members are not eligible to participate as a licensed official, rider, driver, handler, vaulter, longeur, owner, lessee, agent, trainer, coach, competition manager, or competition secretary. The non-competing membership options are described on the membership application form.

GR202 Membership Requirements

1. To be eligible to participate as a rider, driver, handler, vaulter, longeur, owner, lessee, agent, coach or trainer at Regular Competitions, Eventing Competitions at the Preliminary Level or above, Dressage Competitions, Combined Driving Competitions at the Advanced Level, Endurance Rides, Reining Competitions, ParaEquestrian Competitions, and Vaulting Competitions, persons must be Members of the Federation as provided in Bylaw 201. No organization, other than the USEF and its Recognized Breed and Discipline Affiliates, may require mandatory membership or a non-member fee as a condition of participation in a USEF Licensed Competition. (See GR1210.13 for further information regarding the collection of mandatory participation fees at USEF licensed competitions).

2. All Life, Senior Active and Junior Active Members of the Federation must designate a primary breed/discipline affiliation upon joining or must do so annually upon renewing. A member will be deemed to continue his or her primary designation unless prior to the record date (November 30 of each year) such Life Member notifies the Federation in writing of change. This shall be considered the member's affiliation for the purpose of allocating Voting Director seats as provided in Bylaw 211.

3. Lessees are considered owners in connection with this membership requirement. If a horse(s) is owned by multiple individuals, only one owner need be a Member or pay a Show Pass fee.

4. If a horse(s) is owned by a farm or any other entity, only one principal owner of the farm or entity needs to be a member or pay a Show Pass fee. (To be eligible for Horse of the Year Awards, a farm or any other entity that owns a horse(s) must also obtain an exhibitor registration pursuant to GR1106.)

5. Non-members must pay a Show Pass fee of $30.

6. The competitions will be responsible for forwarding Show Pass forms with the names of individuals who pay Show Pass fees at the competition to the Federation with the post competition report. Payment of Show Pass fees for purposes of competing does not entitle the individual to any other privileges of USEF membership.

GR203 Effective Date of Membership

1. Effective Date of Memberships
    a. Membership is effective the date the correct application and fees are received in the Federation office, with the following exceptions:
        1. For applications submitted at licensed Dressage Competitions, reference Bylaw 223, Section 1, applications are considered effective on the date the application and dues are received by the Competition Secretary provided the application is signed and dated by the Competition Secretary on that same day.
        2. Applications completed online at any Dressage competition are effective the date the application is submitted.
        3. For applications submitted at all Competitions other than Dressage Competitions, reference Bylaw 223, Section 1, applications are considered effective on the start date of said Competition provided the application and dues are received by the Competition Secretary and the application is signed and dated by the Competition Secretary during the period of the Competition.
        4. Applications completed online at any competition other than Dressage are effective, for points and eligibility to compete only, the start date of the Competition.

SUBCHAPTER 2-B AFFILIATED ASSOCIATIONS

GR204 Affiliated Associations and Associated Youth Organizations

1. Recognized Affiliate Associations
Recognized Affiliate Associations consist of corporations, organizations, and associations in good standing that have been approved by the Board of Directors of the Federation. Recognized Affiliate Associations shall comply with and be bound by these bylaws and the Rules of the Federation and decisions of the Federation including those of the Hearing Committee, and must pay annual fees and/or dues as determined by the Federation. Recognized Affiliate categories shall include:
    a. International Discipline Associations where the discipline is recognized through the Federation to the FEI or the USOC. The Federation may only recognize one International Discipline Association for each discipline recognized by the FEI. International Discipline Associations are sometimes referred to as the "FEI Affiliates"; or
    b. National Associations where the national breed or discipline has competition rules which have been approved by the Board of Directors of the Federation for inclusion in the Federation's Rule Book. The Federation may only recognize one national breed/discipline association for each breed or discipline with competition rules in the Rule Book. If a Recognized National Affiliate Association ceases to affiliate with the Federation, the Board of Directors may in its discretion replace the organization that has seceded or been removed for cause with another association involving the same breed or discipline or the Board of Directors may replace the organization with an appropriate Federation Breed or Discipline Committee. Such Committee shall be deemed a Recognized National Affiliate Association for purposes of Bylaw 303. Recognized National Affiliate Association requirements are established by the Board of Directors from time to time. Appeals involving the recognition of any association or committee must be made in writing to the National Office within 30 days of the announcement. Appeals will be heard by the Hearing Committee in the same manner as date disputes. The decision of the Hearing Committee shall be final and shall be deemed to have the force and effect of a ruling in arbitration. Recognized National Affiliate Associations are sometimes referred to as "National Affiliates."
2. Alliance Partners consist of corporations, associations, educational institutions offering equine related programs, or other organizations approved by the Federation. Alliance Partners must pay annual fees and/or dues as determined by the Federation.
3. Any Alliance Partner that is also a member of a Federation Recognized Affiliate may utilize only the applicable Breed/Discipline rules contained in the Federation Rule Book as a guideline for conducting non-Federation

competitions. Such use does not include access to the Federation regulatory process. The use of any other Federation rules is prohibited unless written permission is granted by the Federation.

4. Any non-Federation competitions using the applicable Breed/Discipline rules as described in .3 above must give notice to exhibitors in the prize list that Federation rules do not apply.

SUBCHAPTER 2-C NON-MEMBERS

GR205 Participation

A non-member, who wishes to participate as a rider, driver, handler, vaulter, longeur, owner, lessee, agent, coach or trainer at Regular Competitions, Eventing Competitions at the Preliminary Level or above, Dressage Competitions, Endurance Rides, Reining Competitions, Vaulting Competitions, and Combined Driving Competitions at the Advanced Level, must pay a Show Pass fee for each competition in which competing. Lessees are considered owners in connection with this membership requirement. In the event of an entry under multiple ownership, only one owner need be a Member or pay a Show Pass fee. The competition is responsible for listing either the active member or the owner that paid the Show Pass fee in the results. The competitions will be responsible for forwarding copies of all Show Pass forms completed at the competition to the Federation with the post competition report. Payment of Show Pass fees for purposes of competing does not entitle the individual to any other privileges of USEF membership.

SUBCHAPTER 2-D FEDERATION FEES AND DUES

GR206 Show Pass Fee

1. Federation Show Pass fee. The amount of the Show Pass fee will be established annually by the Federation. Unless otherwise established, the fee will be $30 and must be collected by all appropriate competitions and remitted to the Federation (for exceptions see GR901.9). Non-US citizens who are members in good standing of their National Federations are exempt from payment of the Federation Show Pass fee.

2. Recognized Affiliate Association non-member fee. A Federation Recognized Affiliate Association as defined under Bylaw 222, Section 1 (1) and 1 (2) may establish a non-member fee for their respective breed or discipline. If established, the amount of the non-member fee will be determined annually by the applicable Recognized Affiliate Association. This fee must be collected by all appropriate licensed competitions and remitted to the Recognized Affiliate Association (for exceptions see GR901.9).

GR207 High Performance Fees

1. International High Performance

    a. In order for an individual to be eligible to compete as a rider, driver, vaulter, or longeur, in competitions as defined herein, said individual must be a member of the Federation and must pay an International High Performance (IHP) Fee as noted below: (Exception: GR207.1k)

    b. The IHP fee is $35 per entry at defined competitions in the United States as noted below for each discipline. The fee is capped at $420 per competition year. Please refer to the USEF website for policy and instructions on requesting reimbursement for payments over $420 in the same competition year.

        1. For purposes of this rule, an entry is defined as each horse, horse/vaulter combination, vaulting team, or driving single, pair or team.

        2. Competition secretaries are responsible for collecting the fees and sending them to USEF with the post-competition report.

    c. Dressage

        1. FEI Recognized Events [CDIO/CDI's, including the North American Junior and Young Rider Championships (NAJYRC)].

   d. Eventing

      1. FEI Recognized Events [CCIO/CCI's and CIC's, including the North American Junior and Young Rider Championships (NAJYRC)].

   e. Jumping

      1. FEI Recognized Events [CSIO/CSI's, including for Children, Young Riders, Seniors, and the North American Junior and Young Rider Championships (NAJYRC)].

      2. USEF recognized Grand Prixes included on the USEF Show Jumping Ranking List (Maximum one fee per horse per competition).

   f. Driving

      1. FEI Recognized Events (CAIO/CAI's).

   g. Endurance

      1. FEI Recognized Events (CEIO/CEI's).

   h. Para-Equestrian

      1. FEI Recognized events (CPEDIO/CPEDI's) at the 3* level or above.

   i. Reining

      1. FEI Recognized Events [CRIO/CRI's, including the North American Junior and Young Rider Championships (NAJYRC)].

   j. Vaulting

      1. FEI Recognized Events(CVIO/CVI's)

   k. In order to compete in competitions in the US as defined above, foreign competitors must be a member in good standing of their National Federation and are required to pay the $35 IHP per entry fee as listed above.

2. All Senior Active Members who receive funding from USEF for High Performance training or competitions, if called upon by the USEF President, shall personally donate at least two days of service for each calendar year in which they have received funding. However, such service is not required to be given during the same calendar year in which funding is received. Such service may be, at the President's discretion, given to either the Federation and/or the members' respective affiliate. In person participation at Board and Committee meetings shall be credited toward fulfilling this service requirement. Such requested service shall not affect a member's amateur status. A member's competition schedules and prior commitments shall be taken into serious consideration by the USEF President when calling upon members to fulfill this requirement. An administrative penalty may be levied by the President for non-compliance at the recommendation of the Director for Sport Programs, and after consultation with the Regulation Director.

GR208 Competition Fees

1. For every horse participating in any competition licensed by the Federation, a $16 Federation fee will be collected ($8 shall be an Equine Drugs and Medication fee to provide for research, inspection, and enforcement of rules regarding use of medications and drugs; see GR407.1, .2 and .3). Exception: Horses entered in classes exempted from the Equine Drugs and Medication fee are also exempt from the balance of the Federation fee.

2. The following fees may be paid by competitors when applying for membership at a competition: any fees as provided in GR206, GR207, GR208.1, and GR1307.3.

CHAPTER 3 COMPETITION LICENSING

CHAPTER 3 COMPETITION LICENSING

SubChapter 3-A COMPETITION CLASSIFICATIONS AND PRIVILEGES

GR301 Classification

1. Licensed Competitions may be classified as Regular Competitions, Local Competitions, Eventing Competitions, Dressage Competitions, Driving Competitions, Endurance Competitions, Reining Competitions, Vaulting Competitions and Honorary Competitions. An Honorary Competition is a show held in another country which has been elected to this classification by the Federation but does not enjoy any of the privileges of Licensed Competitions. (See Bylaw 223).

2. Special Competitions. A Special Competition is an event, which may not fully meet the requirements for obtaining Federation licensing; however, it has been deemed in the best interest of the breed and/or discipline and/or sport, and the Federation that the event be sanctioned by the Federation. After written application to the Federation at least six months prior to an event, a competition may be approved for Special Competition classification upon approval of the Board of Directors. The Federation must provide the applicable Recognized Affiliate, Council, and discipline or breed committee with all information pertaining to the request, including mileage and any other conflicts, for the purpose of making a recommendation as to approving or disapproving the request. A non-refundable processing fee must be submitted with the application. Special Competition classification may include, but is not limited to, the following: Olympic Games or Trials; Pan Am Games or Trials; World Equestrian Games or Trials; World Cup Finals or Qualifiers; FEI CSI 5* events held as a standalone event and not in conjunction with any other competition; Nations Cup Finals; Nations Cup CSIO's; Federation National Finals; Federation National Championships; Recognized Affiliate championships; and any other events deemed by the Board of Directors as fitting in this classification. Competitions classified as Special Competitions are exempt from the mileage rules for the classes and divisions approved by the Board of Directors.

3. Divisions and sections of Regular Competitions are classified as follows for the purpose of reckoning points toward the Federation Annual Horse of the Year Awards. (Exception: Jumper Division, see GR1114.)
    a. A, B, or C; or
    b. To include any of the following individually or combined:
        1. Andalusian/Lusitano;
        2. Arabian;
        3. Friesian;
        4. Hackney;
        5. National Show Horse;
        6. Morgan;
        7. Roadster;
        8. American Saddlebred;
        9. Shetland;
        10. Western Dressage

4. Divisions and sections of Local, Dressage, Driving Competitions, Endurance Competitions, Reining Competitions, Vaulting Competitions and Eventing Competitions are not rated. However, Dressage Competitions are categorized by levels.

5. Federation Endorsed Competitions, Divisions, or Levels. Those events receiving approval pursuant to the Federation Bylaws.

6. Honorary Designations
    a. Honorary designations are reserved for those competitions within the sport of Equestrian that have been

established for a long period of time and have made a substantial contribution toward development and promotion of the sport of equestrian, both within the sport and as well as within the broader community, by achieving, maintaining and promoting the equestrian ideals of sportsmanship and competition.

b. Approval for all Honorary Designations requires:

1. Recommendation by USEF/CEO
2. Approval by USEF Affiliate primarily represented by the competition.
3. Approval of the USEF Board of Directors at the Annual or Mid Year meeting.

c. Benefits of Honorary Competition designations

1. May apply for an extended Competition License for comparable dates; 5 years for Heritage designation, 7 years for Foundation designation.

    a. If an extended license is approved, it may also be revoked by the USEF Board of Directors with a 2/3 vote
2. Included in the USEF promotional program for Competitions with Honorary Designations.
3. Entitled to use of the applicable Honorary designation on Prize list and promotional material.
4. Listing of competitions with Honorary designations in the USEF rule book and online on a special section of the USEF website.
5. Foundation competitions will receive one complimentary full page advertisement annually in equestrian magazine.

d. An Honorary designation may be removed from a competition with or without cause by 2/3rds vote of the USEF Board of Directors.

e. Eligibility for Heritage Designation requires:

1. Minimum of 25 consecutive years of operation excluding any Act of God interruption
2. Application by the Competition Licensee
3. The Competition must be in good standing with both USEF and the representing affiliate.
4. Significant involvement and support from the community where the competition is held
5. Significant contribution to promotion of the sport of equestrian.
6. Widely recognized within the sport of equestrian as being a Regional, National or International level of competition, or possessing other characteristics that make it unique within the sport of equestrian.

f. Eligibility for Foundation Designation is reserved for the highest level of event in the sport of equestrian and requires:

1. Current designation as a Heritage Competition
2. Minimum of 50 consecutive years of operation, excluding any Act of God interruption.
3. Must award a minimum amount of prize money from the time of application. A minimum of $100,000 for all hunter/jumper competitions and $25,000 for all other competitions.
4. Nomination by the USEF Affiliate primarily represented by the competition. The Affiliate must take this responsibility very seriously and only put forward to USEF their most important competitions.
5. Nominations for Foundation Competitions will only be accepted every three years, beginning in 2012. Nominations will be voted on by the USEF Board of Directors at their Mid-Year meeting and awarded at the USEF Annual Meeting Pegasus Dinner.

GR302 Privileges

1. Licensed Competitions enjoy privileges not available to other competitions including:

a. a position on the Federation schedule of competition dates;

b. assistance of Federation Committees, including Division and Hearing Committees and the facilities and assistance of the Federation office, staff and records;

c. the privilege of holding International Competition;

d. the opportunity to purchase insurance protection made available to most Federation competitions;

e. subscription to equestrian, the official publication of the Federation.

f. assurance of the highest national standards in the sport, and the ability to advertise that a competition is nationally recognized;

g. a commitment to fair competition and the welfare of the horse which can only be provided by the Equestrian Federation of the United States through its rules and their firm enforcement, based on decades of legal precedent;

h. through those rules, the Federation's Drugs and Medications Program, bringing the world's highest standard of research and testing to the sport;

i. attraction to an event of horses and riders properly registered with the Federation to compete for Zone and National awards, as well as other competitions supervised by the Federation, such as its Medal classes;

j. assistance of the Federation to set high standards of competition through access to licensed and experienced officials, and in assuring financial responsibility of entrants;

k. reduced rates for advertising in equestrian magazine, the official magazine of American Equestrian sport since 1937;

l. provide non-exclusive licenses to the Federation's licensed and endorsed competitions and events to perform, present or cause the live and recorded performance of all non-dramatic renditions of the separate musical compositions in the ASCAP and BMI repertories.

GR303 National Championships

United States Equestrian Federation, Inc. (the Federation) shall have the exclusive right to designate national championships in the disciplines for which the Federation is designated as the National Governing Body by the United States Olympic Committee and in the disciplines for which the Federation is designated as the National Federation by the Federation Equestre Internationale (Dressage, Driving, Endurance, Reining, Show Jumping, Three-Day Eventing and Vaulting). The allocation of national championships in the foregoing disciplines, including issuance of date approvals, licensing of officials, approval of name and all copyright, trademark, trade name, television, video and other broadcast rights and all sponsorship matters shall be solely reserved to the Federation Board of Directors acting upon the advice and recommendation of the relevant Federation committee(s), Budget and Finance Committee and the USEF Officers. All persons or organizations, including affiliate organizations, organizing committees and/or competitions managements, wishing to receive Federation approval to hold a national championship in the foregoing divisions must apply to the Federation in writing on appropriate form(s) provided by the Federation and to be received by the Federation's office no later than the deadlines applicable to the respective disciplines outlined in GR306.8. The Board of Directors shall be entitled to condition the Federation's designation and granting of approval for a national championship in any manner which in its discretion it deems appropriate.

SubChapter 3-B COMPETITION LICENSES

GR304 General

1. License Application - Applications for a competition license agreement must be made on the form provided by the Federation. The forms must be signed by the Licensee requesting the date and shall contain the following statement: In applying for the above dates the licensee agrees to abide by the rules of the Federation and understands that failure to do so constitutes a breach of the license agreement and may constitute a violation of the rules which may subject the licensee to penalty under the provisions of GR707.

2. Any changes to the License agreement including location, dates, rating, level, or prize money, will require a license modification request with payment of a fee. USEF may or may not approve the requested changes. Competitions that are not conducted in accordance with the terms of the license agreement will have breached the terms of the

license agreement, and such breach may result in cancellation or nonrenewal of the license agreement, or the licensee may be ineligible for a license in the future, or other penalties under the provisions of GR707.

    a. Holding a competition on a date(s) other than that approved shall constitute a violation of the rules unless a request to change the date(s) is received in the Federation's office at least 30 days prior to the competition (exception: Eventing) and permission is duly given. For Eventing competitions, requests for change of competition date(s) must be received 10 days prior to the first day of the competition.

    b. Holding a competition at a location other than as stated on the date application shall constitute a violation of the rules unless a request to change the location is received in the Federation's office at least 60 days prior to the competition date and permission is duly given.

    c. Failure to obtain the permission of the Federation at least 30 days prior to the competition (exception: Eventing) to add a division, not offer an approved division, or change the rating of an approved division, may constitute a violation of the rules. For Eventing competitions, requests to add or cancel a division must be received 10 days prior to the first day of the competition.

3. License Applications for competitions that USEF is unable to approve for any reason, including mileage conflicts will be sent written notification by the Competitions Department and the application will be held for a period of 30 days from the date of that notification to allow the competition in question to submit the information required, seek alternative dates, submit written permission from the competition in conflict, or make other amendments, as applicable. At the end of the 30-day period the application will be considered to have been withdrawn and the fees will be refunded, unless an extension has been granted by the Competitions Department or the matter is being handled pursuant to GR307. Except as provided herein, there will be no holding of applications or fees.

GR305 Agreement

1. All applications for a Federation license are accepted with the explicit agreement of competition officials that all classes (rated or unrated) to be held on a Federation licensed date must be recognized by the Federation and are governed by all applicable Federation rules, and that no unrecognized classes will be held on any date for which Federation recognition is requested, except that:

    a. Horse Trials at Eventing Competitions below the Preliminary Level,

    b. Eventing Tests at all levels

    c. Combined Driving below the Advanced Level

    d. Classes at Regular or Local Competitions restricted to breeds or disciplines whose rules are not included in the USEF Rulebook

    e. Non-affiliated National Breed or discipline association classes

    f. Vaulting levels/classes below A-Team, Gold, Silver and Pas de Deux

    g. Academy classes

    h. Qualifying classes for Youth Reining classes or Reining classes at USA Reining and NRHA approved competitions.

    i. Exhibitions for which there are no breed or discipline division rules

    j. Hunter/Jumper competitions designated "Outreach" competitions by USHJA and limited to one competition day or one competition ring.

    k. These above named classes/levels can be held as unrecognized only provided a separate entry blank is used and the prize list and/or Omnibus clearly states that the classes are not recognized by the Federation.

    l. Exception: FEI rules take precedence as to international classes and events over Federation rules at all FEI Sanctioned Competitions. Federation rules take precedence as to national classes and events which are not FEI Sanctioned at FEI Sanctioned Competitions. In connection with Endurance Riding Events, the Federation shall nationally enforce the prohibition of the gastric ulcer medications ranitidine and meprazole, in accordance with

GR306 License Procedures

1. All processing of new and renewal license applications will be performed by the USEF Competitions Department. The Competitions Department will be responsible for the administration of the process and for the approval of licenses in accordance with established procedures.

2. Any required inspection of a competition venue will be conducted at the applicant's expense.

3. All USEF license applications will be considered confidential as to content. The identity of applicant(s) or licensee(s) will not be confidential. USEF may request additional information from an applicant, however, USEF is under no obligation to do so. Applicants are expected to supply all relevant information with their application. The license will define the obligations of both USEF and the licensee and are subject to nonrenewal or termination by either party.

4. Existing licensed dates and locations will be posted on the USEF Web site. When a date that has been licensed becomes available (New Open Date) it will be posted on the USEF Web site until the end of the month following the month in which the date becomes available. A date may become available as a result of:

   a. A timely renewal license application not being received by the USEF. See GR306.6

   b. Failure of the existing competition to achieve a satisfactory Competition Evaluation.

   c. Licensee not meeting the "good standing" requirement for License.

5. Complete License Applications must be accompanied by the appropriate fees and either sent certified mail, postmarked, overnight with tracking, or by receipted fax. Applications must be received by the date specified by 6. below. Applications for FEI Competitions cannot be submitted to the FEI until the national competition has been licensed by the Federation. Applications for competitions which are not made in accordance with the above will be returned and not considered.

6. Applications for competitions unable to be approved for any reason, excluding mileage conflicts, will be sent written notification by the Competitions Department and held for a period of 30 days from the date of that notification to allow the competition in question to submit the information required, seek alternative dates, or make other amendments, as applicable. At the end of the 30-day period, if the application has not been completed or the 30-day period extended by the Competitions Department, the application will be considered to have been withdrawn and the dues will be refunded. Except as provided herein, there will be no holding of applications or dues, and applicants must reapply from year to year. Applications that seek approval for a License to conduct a competition on a date that has been open for more than the web posting period will be accepted at any time. All applications for dates that have been open for more than the new open date web posting period will be considered on a first received basis.

7. Renewal License Applications are due as follows:

   a. For multi-year licenses, renewals must be received within sixty days of the last day of the next to last competition under an existing license.

   b. For single year licenses, renewals must be received within sixty days of the last day of the licensed competition.

   c. License renewal applications received more than sixty days after the last day of the applicable competition under an existing license will be considered as a new application subject to all new application policies and procedures including posting period for open dates.

   d. Applications for new licensed competitions will be accepted beginning December 1 each year for the subsequent competition year.

8. A complete application accompanied by appropriate fees to hold a Regular Competition, Reining Competition, or Dressage Competition must be received in the Federation's office at least sixty days prior to the date(s) requested. A complete application accompanied by appropriate fees for a Local Competition or Driving Event must be received thirty days prior to the date(s) requested. A complete application accompanied by appropriate fees for an Eventing

Competition must be received ninety days prior to the date(s) requested. A complete application accompanied by appropriate fees to hold an Endurance Event or Vaulting Competition must be received 45 days prior to the date(s) requested. A complete application accompanied by appropriate fees for a Hunter Breeding competition must be received ninety days prior to the date(s) requested.

9. Competition Permission. Competitions that have previously been operating with a competition permission may seek renewal of the permission pursuant to GR307.

10. License Duration. The duration of the License agreements will normally be three (3) years. During this period, Licensed Competitions will be subject to Competition Evaluation. Licenses for a shorter period may be requested. On or after December 1, 2007, licenses with a longer term may be offered. However, terms in excess of seven (7) years would require Board of Directors approval. License agreements for periods greater than three (3) years will occur only after consideration of licensee experience, the time/investment required to develop corporate sponsors, media support, and the capital investment in the venue, all in conjunction with what is in the best interest of equestrian sport. Such licenses may provide for successor clauses during the term of the license as deemed necessary.

11. Competition Fees. Application and/or competition fees will be payable annually in April for the following competition year under an existing license agreement. License fees may be modified during the period of a license.

12. Cancellation. A licensee may cancel without charge an existing licensed competition by notifying USEF of the cancellation and returning the license to USEF not less than ten (10) months prior to next competition date under the license. When a cancellation is received more than three (3) months but less than ten (10) months prior to the first day of the next competition date under the license, 75 percent of competition dues will be refunded, subject to a minimum processing fee. If written notice of a cancellation is received less than three (3) months prior to the first day of the competition, the licensee will forfeit the application fee and will also be assessed a penalty fee equal to that of the minimum competition dues, unless the cancellation is due to an act of God.

13. Ineligible License Applicant. A License application or renewal from a Licensee may not be accepted if it has been determined by USEF that the licensee has outstanding issues which may relate to financial matters, safety matters, failure to comply with USEF rules, breach of a prior license agreement, or any other issues that may be prejudicial to the best interest of the sport. When possible USEF will inform the licensee of any outstanding issues in order that, when possible, the Licensee may have the opportunity to address the matter.

14. Grandfathered Competitions.

a. If the mileage rule in effect on December 1, 2005 creates a conflict of dates between Recognized Grandfathered Competitions existing prior to December 1, 2005, each competition so affected may be provided with a license without regard to application of the current mileage rule. Grandfathered competition License agreements are subject in all respects to future changes in rules including mileage and Competition Evaluation in accordance with the license agreement process.

b. If the mileage rule in effect on December 1, 2011 creates a conflict of dates between Recognized Grandfathered Arabian, National Show Horse, American Saddlebred, Hackney, and Roadster Competitions existing prior to December 1, 2011, each competition so affected may be provided with a license without regard to application of the current mileage rule. Grandfathered competition License agreements are subject in all respects to future changes in rules including mileage and Competition Evaluation in accordance with the license agreement process.

GR307 Competition Mileage Exemption and Competition Permission.

1. Federation Objective. One objective of the Federation is to provide a competition environment that is in the best interest of the sport of Equestrian and to provide for viable competitions and a balanced competition calendar to meet the needs of the sport at all levels within a geographic area. The Federation utilizes mileage as a method of managing the calendar and to assist in achieving an adequate base of competitors, thus enabling a competition to better meet the rules, requirements, and standards for a given rating or level. The licensing authority, licensing

decisions, and calendar management rest solely with the Federation.

2. Mileage Exemption. When a competition license application is denied by the Federation due to a mileage conflict, the Applicant may seek a mileage exemption to allow the applying competition to occur. The Federation will send a Mileage Exemption Request Form along with the notification of denial to the Applicant.

3. The Federation may consider different circumstances in determining whether a mileage exemption is warranted. These include, but are not limited to, the following:

   a. Competition Standards: Priority Date Holder's adherence to competition standards.

     1. Whether the Applicant competition may alleviate concerns about the safety and welfare of horses, competitors, and/or spectators for a given rating and/or level at a Priority Date Holder's competition;

     2. Whether the Applicant competition may enable a Priority Date Holder to better achieve the competition standards for a given rating and/or level;

     3. Whether the Applicant competition may alleviate overcrowding of horses and/or competitors in a given geographic area at a given venue.

   b. Competition and Calendar Factors:

     1. Whether the Applicant competition provides access to competitors that may need a choice based on a Priority Date Holder's costs to competitors or offered ratings and/or levels;

     2. Whether the Applicant competition serves a need that the Priority Date Holder does not serve as to the schedule of classes, sections, and divisions, which may be too limited;

     3. Whether the Applicant competition should be given an opportunity to enter the marketplace where a Priority Date Holder seemingly dominates the calendar in a given geographical area, which may create unilateral competition effects;

     4. Whether the Applicant competition alleviates the negative impact on competitors that may occur when the number of consecutive competitions of the same rating and/or level in a given geographic area at a given venue creates unilateral competition effects.

   c. Sport Growth and Visibility:

     1. Whether the Applicant competition may create growth and visibility of the sport in one of the following ways, which is not exclusive:

     2. The Applicant competition is warranted due to community support and/or involvement;

     3. The Applicant competition may broaden access to competitors at all levels of the sport;

     4. The Applicant competition is unique and provides exceptional promotional benefits to the sport.

In addition, the Federation will consider the following factors in determining whether a mileage exemption should be granted:

   a. Geographic location and time of year with regard to concentration and migration of competitors;

   b. Experience and expertise of competition management;

   c. Competitions outside of boundary mileage of Priority Date Holder and Applicant Competition, which may affect density and competitive level of competitors;

   d. Density and competitive level of competitors in a given geographic area at a given time of year.

4. Mileage Exemption Procedure

   a. An Applicant must first contact the Priority Date Holder(s) and seek cooperation in running the proposed event.

     1. If the Priority Date Holder(s) agree to the exemption request, then the terms and conditions of any agreement must be fully disclosed to the Federation in writing along with submission of the Mileage Exemption Response. Submission of these materials indicates that the parties agree that the Federation is not responsible for the enforcement or performance of the terms and conditions of the agreement between the competition organizer and those parties expressly waive any claim against the Federation for failure to perform.

     2. If the Priority Date Holder(s) does not agree to the exemption request, then the Applicant shall submit the

Mileage Exemption Request Form to the Federation in accordance with these rules.

b. Beginning with competitions conducted in the 2017 competition year, the Applicant shall submit the Mileage Exemption Request Form, fully completed, to the Federation no earlier than three hundred sixty (360) calendar days and no later than two hundred forty (240) calendar days before the start date of the proposed competition. The fully completed Mileage Exemption Request Form must be accompanied with the non-refundable application fee of $500.00. A mileage exemption request is not accepted as submitted unless the Mileage Exemption Request Form is fully completed and the application fee is paid in full.

c. Within twenty-one (21) days of acceptance of a properly submitted request and application fee, the Federation will notify the Priority Date Holder(s) and provide the submitted Mileage Exemption Request Form. An Applicant is not permitted to advertise or promote the proposed competition until the competition has received final approval. Non-compliance with this requirement will disqualify the applicant and will result in disapproval of the application.

d. The Priority Date Holder(s) has twenty-one (21) calendar days from the date of the Notification letter and the Mileage Exemption Request Form to submit to the Federation a fully completed Mileage Exemption Response Form. The Priority Date Holder(s) must provide written comments justifying the denial of the mileage exemption request given the considerations in paragraph 3 above.

e. Within fifteen (15) calendar days of receipt of a completed Mileage Exemption Response Form and the terms and conditions of an agreement, if such agreement was reached between the affected parties, the request will be reviewed by the Federation Internal Review Panel, which shall determine whether it is in the best interest of the sport to either deny or grant the approval and under what terms and conditions such approval shall be given. The Federation Internal Review Panel consists of the Federation Chief Executive Officer or his designee; the Director of Competitions; and a staff member from the relevant breed or discipline chosen by the Sport Director.

f. Within fifteen (15) calendar days of receipt of a completed Mileage Exemption Response Form from Priority Date Holder(s) objecting to the request, or the expiration of the twenty-one (21) day response period if no completed Mileage Exemption Response Form is submitted, the Federation will notify the applicable Recognized Breed/ Discipline Affiliate and provide all documentation received in the process from any party. The applicable Recognized Breed/Discipline Affiliate has thirty (30) calendar days from notification from the Federation to submit to the Federation Competitions Department, a recommendation to approve or disapprove the exemption request accompanied by a detailed explanation based on the considerations enumerated in paragraph 3 above.

g. Within fifteen (15) calendar days of receipt of written comments from the Recognized Affiliate, a Federation Internal Review Panel consisting of the Federation Chief Executive Officer or his designee; the Director of Competitions; and a staff member from the relevant breed or discipline chosen by the Sport Director shall convene to review the recommendation of the Affiliate in light of all materials submitted and the considerations enumerated in paragraph 3 above. If this Panel agrees with the Recognized Affiliate's recommendation, then a decision letter will be issued to the affected parties accordingly. If this Panel disagrees with the Recognized Affiliate recommendation, or identifies further consideration that should be given, the Federation President has thirty (30) days to appoint a Mileage Exemption Panel to review the request. If for any reason the President is unable to appoint this Panel, the Vice-President, if available, or the Secretary/Treasurer, if the Vice-President if unable, shall appoint the Panel.

h. The Federation Mileage Exemption Panel consists of the Federation Chief Executive Officer or his designee; a Senior Active Member with competition management experience; and a Senior Active Member who participated in the determination of the Affiliate. Together this Panel shall consider all materials received from all parties related to the request, the recommendation of the Recognized Affiliate, the comments of the Internal Review Panel, and the considerations in paragraph 3 above. Upon completion of its review, the Federation Mileage Exemption Panel shall determine whether it is in the best interest of the sport to either deny or grant the approval and under what terms and conditions such approval shall be given.

    i. The identity of the Federation Mileage Exemption Panel members must be provided to the Applicant and Priority Date Holder(s). These parties have five (5) days to submit a written objection to any Panel member. Objections must specifically articulate the basis of the objection and how the appointee cannot render a fair and unbiased decision. Objections will be evaluated and a determination will be made whether a replacement is warranted. Failure to timely object is deemed acceptance of the appointed panelists. At no time may the Applicant or the Priority Date Holder(s) contact any Panel member, directly or indirectly, concerning the request. Contacting a Panel member in any way may result in the imposition of penalties and/or an adverse decision of the request.

    j. The Federation, through the Federation Internal Review and Federation Mileage Exemption Panels, shall have final decision-making authority on all exemption requests and will not delegate this responsibility. The Panel's decision will be provided to the Applicant, Priority Date Holder(s), and the Recognized Affiliate. The Panel's decision is provisional until such time that any dispute process under these rules has been exhausted. An Applicant shall not advertise or promote the proposed competition unless and until the competition has received final approval. Non-compliance with this requirement may result in withdrawal of the application.

    k. Modifications or amendments to an approved exemption is not permitted. If a modification is necessary, the Applicant must initiate a new request for mileage exemption.

    l. Mileage Exemptions are granted for one year only. Approval in one year does not guarantee future approval of a mileage exemption request.

    m. All Licensed Competitions operating under an approved mileage exemption shall have the applicable mileage protection against new competitions. This does not preclude the Federation from granting additional mileage exemption requests for new competitions to be held within any mileage boundary.

5. Special Competitions. After written application to the Federation at least six months prior to an event, a competition may be approved for Special classification upon approval of the Board of Directors. All information pertaining to the request including mileage and any other conflicts, if any, must be provided by the Federation to the applicable Recognized Affiliate; Council; and discipline or breed committee making a recommendation as to approval or disapproval of the request. A non-refundable processing fee must be submitted with the application. A Special Competition is an event, which may not fully meet the requirements for obtaining Federation licensing, however, it has been deemed in the best interest of the breed and/or discipline and/or sport, and the Federation that the event be sanctioned by the Federation. Special Competition classification may include, but is not limited to, the following: Olympic Games or Trials; Pan Am Games or Trials; World Equestrian Games or Trials; World Cup Finals or Qualifiers; FEI CSI 5* events held as a stand-alone event and not in conjunction with any other competition; Nations Cup Finals; Nations Cup CSIO's; Federation National Finals; Federation National Championships; Recognized Affiliate championships; and any other events deemed by the Board of Directors as fitting in this classification.

Competitions classified as Special Competitions are exempt from the mileage rules for the classes and divisions approved by the Board of Directors. All other Federation rules must be complied with unless the Federation grants an express exemption in the approval. *BOD 6/30/15 Effective 12/1/15*

GR308 Mileage - General

1. Mileage application provisions

    a. To determine a mile radius, the distance shall be measured using mapping software, to measure the distance between the locations where the competitions are being conducted. (i.e. address of the facility where each of the competitions will be held or the longitude and latitude if an exact address does not exist.) (except between Long Island and the mainland). Application of this process will not adversely affect the license rights of competitions already licensed.

    b. In any instance where the shortest road mileage distance between the competition facility locations is greater than one and one half (1 1/2) times the radial mileage between the competition facility locations, the required mile distances between competitions shall be based upon the shortest road mileage distance rather than radial mileage.

c. Mileage between competitions with different mileage requirements will be subjected to the lower of the mileage requirements.

d. Long Island, N.Y. The distances between competitions held on Long Island, NY, and competitions held on the mainland shall be determined by measuring a straight line distance from the point at which Interstate Highway 278 (across the Triborough Bridge) intersects the shore of Long Island, to the location where the Long Island competition is being conducted. (i.e. address of the facility where each of the competitions will be held or the longitude and latitude if an exact address does not exist) and by measuring the mile radius from the bridge to the location where the other competition is being conducted. (i.e. address of the facility where each of the competitions will be held or the longitude and latitude if an exact address does not exist) Application of this process will not adversely affect the license rights of competitions already licensed.

e. If the mileage between competitions is less than the applicable distance specified by this rule, conflicting dates may be approved by USEF in accordance with GR307, and providing all other requirements for recognition are met.

f. New competitions offering Level 4 or 5 (A or AA) rated hunter or jumper divisions or sections will not be licensed on dates conflicting with those of any other Licensed Competition within the applicable distance specified by this rule which offers Level 4 or 5 (A or AA) rated hunter or jumper divisions or sections, regardless of class scheduling. In the case of a multi-breed or multi-discipline competition, a question of conflict shall be determined with reference only to those dates, inclusive, during which hunter or jumper divisions or sections are to be held. The mileage restrictions will not prevent two Hunter/Jumper competitions from being approved if the two competitions have different competition managements and the competition with priority gives written permission, to be renewed annually, and the mileage distance between competitions is at least 10 miles.

g. The foregoing distance rules do not apply to events comprised exclusively of classes recognized by the FEI and the USOC. The National Championships for Dressage, and Dressage Competitions offering USEF High Performance qualifying or selection trials, or observation classes and National classes held in conjunction with a CDI are exempted from the mileage rule. When a CDI is approved on one or more days where another competition has date priority, national classes can only be held on the day of the FEI Jog and on days where at least one CDI class is held or is not held due to no entries. When CDI classes are not held on all approved CDI dates (except due to no entries) the competition might not be granted approval for those dates in subsequent years. Certain competitions held in conjunction with events also holding FEI competitions and/or selection trials for international competitions, at the discretion of the Board of Directors, may be exempted from the mileage rule.

h. Existing competition is a licensed competition not requiring permission that may or may not be within the mileage indicated of the new license applicant.

i. Proposals to change mileage rule or rules may be submitted for consideration by the USEF Board of Directors. Any such mileage rule change will have an effective date of December 1 of the following calendar year. In no event will changes to mileage become effective in less than 12 months from the date of the rule change approval. Proposals for mileage rule changes submitted by Affiliates may only be considered after they have been considered at the annual meeting of the appropriate recognized National Affiliate.

2. Mileage Charts. Mileage consideration may be applicable to more than one mileage chart.

   a. The below divisions will be conducted under the following mileage:

      1. Andalusian/Lusitano: 250 miles;

      2. Arabian: 250 miles;

      3. Friesian: 250 miles;

      4. Hackney: 100 miles;

      5. Morgan: 100 miles;

      6. National Show Horse: 50 miles;

      7. Roadster: 100 miles;

      8. Shetland: 100 miles;

      9. American Saddlebred: 100 miles;

     10. Western Dressage: 100 miles.

Local Regular: Any breed competition restricted to one breed or multi-breed competition including any of the above listed breeds (1-9), regardless of number of classes offered: 50 miles.

   b. Mileage Charts USEF Licensed Competitions in USHJA Zones 1 & 2. Hunter and/or Jumper competitions are categorized by Rating and/or Level. Additional criteria required for each Rating and/or Level in the Hunter and

     Jumper Mileage Charts can be found on the USEF website at www.usef.org under Competitions.

     1. The distances between Licensed Competitions held in USHJA Zones 1 & 2 (ME, NH, VT, MA, CT, RI, NJ, NY, and PA) offering hunter or jumper divisions or sections shall be in accordance with the mileage tables (H1 & J1) shown below effective 12-01-08. Hunter mileage shall be independent of the Jumper mileage and applied separately to each division/section of a competition.

     2. Hunter Division/Sections.

Hunter Mileage Chart - H1 USHJA Zones 1&2					
	New Competitions w/ Same Rated Sections				
Priority Date Holders		Premier (AA)	National (A)	Regional I (B)	Regional II (C)	Local
	Premier (AA)	125	125	90	50	40
	National (A)	125	125	90	50	40
	Regional I (B)	90	90	75	50	40
	Regional II (C)	50	50	50	50	40
	Local	40	40	40	40	40

3. Jumper Division/Sections

Jumper Mileage Chart - J1 USHJA Zones 1&2					
New Competitions w/ Same Rated Sections					
	Level 5 & 6	Level 4	Level 3	Level 2	Level 1
Level 5 & 6	125	125	90	0	0
Level 4	125	125	90	0	0
Level 3	90	90	75	0	0
Level 2	0	0	0	0	0
Level 1	0	0	0	0	0

(left axis label: **Priority Date Holders**)

4. Jumper Levels are based on the prize money offered see JP104.

c. Mileage Charts USEF Licensed Competitions in USHJA Zones 3 thru 12. Hunter and/or Jumper competitions are categorized by Rating and/or Level. Additional criteria required for each Rating and/or Level in the Hunter and Jumper Mileage Charts can be found on the USEF website at www.usef.org under Competitions.

1. The distances between Licensed Competitions held in USHJA Zones 3 thru 10 and Canada [with the exception of Florida in the first trimester - December through March - see GR308.2d] offering hunter or jumper divisions or sections shall be in accordance with the mileage tables (H2 & J2) shown below effective 12-01-08. Hunter mileage shall be independent of the Jumper mileage and applied separately to each division/section of a competition.

2. Hunter Division/Sections

Hunter Mileage Chart - H2					
USHJA Zones 3 thru 12 and Canada (excluding FL in 1st trimester)					
New Competitions w/ Same Rated Sections					
	Premier (AA)	National (A)	Regional I (B)	Regional II (C)	Local
Premier (AA)	250	250	100	75	50
National (A)	250	250	100	75	50
Regional I (B)	200	200	100	100	75
Regional II (C)	75	75	100	100	75
Local	50	50	50	50	50

(left axis label: **Priority Date Holders**)

    3. Jumper Division/Sections

Jumper Mileage Chart - J2 USHJA Zones 3 thru 12 and Canada (excluding FL in 1st trimester)					
New Competitions w/ Same Rated Sections					
	Level 5 & 6	Level 4	Level 3	Level 2	Level 1
Level 5 & 6	250	250	100	0	0
Level 4	250	250	100	0	0
Level 3	200	200	100	0	0
Level 2	0	0	0	0	0
Level 1	0	0	0	0	0

(Priority Date Holders)

    4. Jumper Levels are based on the prize money offered: see JP104.

d. Mileage Charts USEF Licensed Hunter/Jumper Competitions held in Florida in the first trimester (December through March). Hunter and/or Jumper competitions are categorized by Rating and/or Level. Additional criteria required for each Rating and/or Level in the Hunter and Jumper Mileage Charts can be found on the USEF website at www.usef.org under Competitions.

    1. The distances between Licensed Competitions offering hunter or jumper divisions or sections held in the state of Florida during the first trimester of each competition year shall be in accordance with the mileage tables (H3 & J3) shown below effective 12-01-08. Hunter mileage shall be independent of the Jumper mileage and applied separately to each division of a competition which offer hunter or jumper divisions or sections shall be in accordance with the mileage tables. The remainder of the competition year mileage shall be in accordance with mileage tables H2 and J2. (GR308.2d.2 and .3)

    2. Hunter Division/Sections (1st Trimester Florida - December through March)

Hunter Mileage Chart - H3 (1st Trimester Florida)					
	New Competitions w/ Same Rated Sections				
Priority Date Holders		Premier (AA)	National (A)	Regional I (B)	Regional II (C)	Local
	Premier (AA)	225	200	100	75	50
	National (A)	200	200	100	75	50
	Regional I (B)	200	200	100	100	75
	Regional II (C)	75	75	100	100	75
	Local	50	50	50	50	50

3. Jumper Division/Sections (1st Trimester Florida - December through March)

Jumper Mileage Chart - J3 (1st Trimester Florida)					
	New Competitions w/ Same Rated Sections				
Priority Date Holders		Level 5 & 6	Level 4	Level 3	Level 2	Level 1
	Level 5 & 6	225	200	100	0	0
	Level 4	200	200	100	0	0
	Level 3	200	200	100	0	0
	Level 2	0	0	0	0	0
	Level 1	0	0	0	0	0

e. Dressage Mileage Charts USEF Licensed Competitions with Open Dressage Divisions/classes.

   1. In the case of a Regular or Local Competition holding "open" Dressage Division classes, the question of conflict shall be determined with reference only to those dates, inclusive, during which "open" dressage classes are to be held. See DR127.15 for a map of USDF regions.

   2. In the case of Dressage Competitions, or Regular or Local Competitions holding "open" Dressage Division classes, a 75 mile radius will apply to competitions held in contiguous USDF regions for which different distances are specified.

      a. 50-mile radius for all other Dressage Competitions in USDF Regions 1, 2, 6, & 8 (excluding competitions restricted to one breed)

      b. 100-mile radius for Dressage Competitions in USDF Regions 3, 4, 5, 7 and 9 (excluding competitions restricted to one breed).

   3. Two or more Dressage Competitions may never be held at the same or adjacent locations on the same days.

Exception: Dressage Competitions that are limited to Dressage Sport Horse Breeding classes may be held at the same or adjacent location as another Dressage Competition that does not offer Dressage Sport Horse Breeding classes.

4. All dressage competitions are categorized by Level. Criteria for each level in the charts below can be found on the USEF website.

Dressage Mileage Chart - Contiguous USDF Regions - D1 USEF Dressage Competitions or Regular or Local Competitions with Open Dressage Classes					
Priority Date Holders	**New Competitions**				
		Level 5	Level 4	Level 3	Level 2	Level 1
	Level 5	75	75	75	75	75
	Level 4	75	75	75	75	75
	Level 3	75	75	75	75	75
	Level 2	75	75	75	75	75
	Level 1	75	75	75	75	75

Dressage Mileage Chart USDF Regions 1, 2, 6 & 8 - D2 USEF Dressage Competitions or Regular or Local Competitions with Open Dressage Classes (excluding competitions restricted to one breed)					
Priority Date Holders	**New Competitions**				
		Level 5	Level 4	Level 3	Level 2	Level 1
	Level 5	50	50	50	50	50
	Level 4	50	50	50	50	50
	Level 3	50	50	50	50	50
	Level 2	50	50	50	50	50
	Level 1	50	50	50	50	50

SPONSORED BY HAGYARD EQUINE MEDICAL INSTITUTE || © USEF 2016

Dressage Mileage Chart USDF Regions 3, 4, 5, 7 & 9 - D3 USEF Dressage Competitions or Regular or Local Competitionswith Open Dressage Classes (excluding competitions restricted to one breed)						
Priority Date Holders		New Competitions				
		Level 5	Level 4	Level 3	Level 2	Level 1
	Level 5	100	100	100	100	100
	Level 4	100	100	100	100	100
	Level 3	100	100	100	100	100
	Level 2	100	100	100	100	100
	Level 1	100	100	100	100	100

f. Mileage Chart USEF Licensed Eventing Competitions.
   1. Eventing competitions are not subject to the mileage charts

GR309 Dues, Fees and Insurance

1. No competition dates will be assigned to a Licensee which has not paid dues, fees or fines owing to the Federation with respect to any past Licensed Competitions.
2. Any licensee who fails to pay sums owed to the Federation, or who makes payment for fees to the Federation which is not negotiable, will be notified by the Federation of its indebtedness and warned that unless settlement is made within two weeks of the Federation's notice, said licensee will automatically be fined the sum of $250 to be paid to the Federation; and, further, that said licensee and any horses owned by licensee will automatically be barred from taking any part whatsoever in Licensed Competitions until payment or settlement is made of the total indebtedness to the Federation. Notice of suspension will be published on the Federation's web site.
   a. If any licensee affected by GR309.2 disputes that the amounts in question are owed or unpaid, said licensee may request to have the matter reviewed by the Hearing Committee, provided his or her written statement specifying the grounds for such review is received at the Federation's office within said two week period accompanied by a fee of $100, which will be refunded if the dispute is settled in favor of said licensee.
   b. In the event a licensee makes non-negotiable payment for fees to the Federation on three or more occasions, said licensee is subject to further disciplinary action. In addition, any future payments made to the Federation, must be submitted in the form of a certified check, cashier's check, money order, or valid credit card.
3. The annual dues for each licensed competition are as follows:
   a. License application fee
      1. $100 for competitions with 299 or fewer horses in prior year
      2. $250 for competitions with 300 or more horses in prior year
   b. Per horse fee
      $1.50 per horse paid on post competition report
4. The annual dues for each Local Competition are $50.
5. A fee of $75 will be charged to any competition which applies for a change of location.
6. A fee of $50 will be charged to any Licensed Competition which applies for a change in its name. This fee is waived when a competition changes its name to include the title of a regional or national championship or when the name

reverts back to its original name.

7. A fee of $75 will be charged to any Licensed Competition which applies for a change of date. The fee may be waived by the CEO.

8. A penalty fee of $500 will be charged to any competition that states in the prize list that the competition is licensed before the competition has been granted licensing by the Federation.

9. A fee of $50 will be retained from the minimum competition dues submitted with any competition application that is unable to be approved and its application is subsequently withdrawn.

10. A Licensee may request an account audit from the Federation. The request must be submitted in writing and a fee of $100 will be charged for each competition audited. An audit is a lengthy investigation into a Licensee's financial dealings with the Federation, encompassing multiple transactions, competitions, and possibly years. The fee must accompany the request. If staff error, fee will be refunded.

11. A Licensee may request an inquiry into the history of a competition date. The request must be submitted in writing and a fee of $100 will be charged per each request. The fee must accompany the request. If staff error, fee will be refunded.

12. A certificate of insurance for each competition must be received by the Federation office at least fourteen calendar days prior to the competition by mail with proof of delivery or submitted electronically via e-mail, or via fax. Competitions faxing their certificate of insurance to the Federation must retain a copy of the fax confirmation. If the certificate is not received fourteen days prior to the competition, insurance coverage will be acquired through Equisure and the competition invoiced as outlined in GR309.13. Each certificate must name the Federation as additional insured for each day of the competition, including set-up and take-down days, with minimum limits of $1,000,000 third party general liability insurance and $50,000 on equipment and property. Competitions failing to provide proof of such coverage (or such coverage to the extent permitted by local law) will automatically be enrolled in the Equisure policy for competitions and will then be invoiced the then prevailing premium for such insurance. Competitions outside the United States must provide evidence of equivalent coverage of such insurance and will not be enrolled in the Equisure group policy. Competitions must notify the Federation in writing of cancellation of their insurance policies by their insurance provider.

13. An automatic fine of $200 will be imposed on any competition for which evidence of adequate insurance is not received at least two weeks prior to the competition. The fine is in addition to the amount of the invoice for the automatic enrollment in the Equisure policy. A competition disputing that the invoice and/or the fine is properly owing may appeal in writing to the Federation within 30 days of management's receipt of the Federation's notice of billing and/or fine, specifying the grounds for the appeal. The Federation's CEO or his designee, a special committee appointed by the president or the Hearing Committee will consider the appeal and may waive part or all of the billing and/or fine upon a finding of good cause why the evidence of insurance was not timely filed and/or a finding that extreme hardship results from the automatic penalty.

14. Western Division competitions may retain Local Competition status regardless of the amount of prize money offered.

GR310 Cancellation of Competitions (See also GR110)

1. A Licensee may cancel without charge an existing Licensed competition by notifying USEF of the cancellation and returning the License to USEF not less than 10 months prior to next competition date under the License. When a Cancellation is received more than 3 months but less than 10 months prior to the first day of the next competition date under the License 75% of competition dues will be refunded, subject to a minimum processing fee. Written notice of cancellation less than 3 months prior to the first day of the competition will be assessed a penalty fee equal to that of the minimum competition dues, unless the cancellation is due to an Act of God.

2. If a licensed competition is cancelled for two consecutive years for a reason other than an act of God, loss of

facility, or due to extenuating circumstances approved by the CEO, the applicable license will be revoked.

3. Cancellation of 50% or more of "open" dressage classes as listed in the prize list by any Recognized competition for two consecutive years for other than acts of God, including failure to hold classes or sections whether for lack of entries or other reasons, shall constitute relinquishment of prior comparable dates for the third and subsequent consecutive years. In all such instances of cancellation for two consecutive years of 50% or more of dressage classes, approvals for that competition to hold "open" dressage classes for the third and any subsequent year shall not be accorded priority.

4. Competitions declaring cancellation due to an Act of God must provide written documentation, such as newspaper articles or photographs of the extenuating circumstances; absent severe and unusual circumstances, such as hurricane winds, floods, tornadoes, or blizzards, weather conditions shall not be considered Acts of God; whether or not a cancellation is due to an Act of God shall be decided by the CEO or his designee in the first instance subject to review and approval by the Board of Directors upon written demand.

5. Any Licensee that cancels three or more competitions in a competition year shall not have priority for comparable dates for the cancelled competitions for the following competition year; provided, however, that this provision shall not be applicable to a competition cancelled due to an Act of God, loss of a facility or due to extenuating circumstances, based upon a review by the CEO or his designee.

SUBCHAPTER 3-C LICENSED COMPETITION STANDARDS

GR311 Restrictions on Local Competitions

1. The total cash prizes shall not exceed $500. Except Open Western Division(see ratings chart GR313), 100% sweepstakes and Reining Competitions; not including value of trophies offered.
2. The designation Local Competition must be stated on the cover of the prize list.
3. The Federation and applicable Federation Recognized Affiliate Association non-member/Show Pass fee will not apply.
4. Local Competitions benefit from all the general rules of the Federation and must abide by applicable division rules unless class specifications are printed otherwise in the prize list.

GR312 General

1. For the purpose of equalizing competitions for the National Horse of the Year Awards, divisions and sections of Regular Competitions fall into one of three classifications: "A", "B" or "C" rated.

2. In the Hunter division, the Increment System will determine points for ribbons won in any rated section. The point value for ribbons won in "A", "B" or "C" rated hunter sections is determined according to the Increment System utilizing a combination of the base points for each placing at each level of section rating and adding one point for each entry shown in the first performance class. Exception: In addition in the First and Second Year Green Hunter, High Performance Hunter, Performance Working Hunter 3'3" and 3'6", Green Conformation Hunter and Regular Conformation Hunter, standings for all National Horse of the Year Awards based on money won will be determined by dollars won in the horses respective sections. See GR1131.

GR313 Determining Ratings

1. A division or section rating or classification is determined from the number of classes, amount of cash premiums offered in these classes and the holding of required classes in certain divisions. A competition may not offer the minimum requirements for a rating higher than the rating approved by the Federation. See Ratings Charts.

2. A competition may qualify for several different ratings. Some competitions will earn an "A" or "B" rating in all divisions and sections; others, perhaps due to local conditions and more interest in certain breeds, may find themselves with a combination of ratings. If more than the minimum number of classes are offered prize money should

be increased proportionately.

3. The Paso Fino Division is rated "C" regardless of the number of classes or amount of prize money offered. A competition may apply for an "A" rating if offering a minimum of $2,000 and prior year competition had more than 250 horses. The PFHA National show shall be an "A" rated Federation Licensed Competition as per PF155.1i. Exception: the Paso Fino Division may be offered at Local Competitions.

4. In Stake classes in "A" and "B" divisions or sections competitions must guarantee amount offered as prize money except where the monies offered in other classes are sufficient to meet the Horse of the Year Award minimum requirements. In such cases Stake classes may run as sweepstakes.

5. The Connemara and Half-bred Connemara is "C" rated, regardless of the number of classes or amount of prize money offered. Exception: the Connemara and Half-bred Connemara Division may be offered at local competitions.

6. The following are rated "C" regardless of the number of classes or amount of prize money offered: Small Hunter, Hunter Breeding, Ladies Side Saddle Hunter, Adult Amateur, Children's Hunter, Pre-Green Hunters and Thoroughbred Hunter.

HUNTER SECTIONS	"A" Required Classes	"A" Min Money	"B" and "C" Required Classes	"B" Min. Money
Amateur Owner 3'6"	4-6*	500	3-4	100
Amateur Owner 3'3"	4-5	500	3-4	100
Green Conformation	4-6*	500	3-4	50
Reg. Conformation	4-6*	500	3-4	50
Green Working	4-6*	500	3-4	100
High Performance Working	3-5	750**	3-4	200
Hunter Pony	4-5*	400	3-4	100
Green Hunter Pony	4-5*	250	3-4	50
Junior Hunter	4-5*	500	3-4	100
Junior Hunter 3'3"	4-5*	500	3-4	100
Performance Hunters 3'3"	3-5	400	3-4	50
Performance Hunters 3'6"	3-5	500	3-4	100

(*See HU158.3 regarding Model Classes).

(**At Premier competitions, minimum prize money for High Performance Working must be $1500)

7. All classes offered in a licensed Open Western Division shall be conducted in accordance with GR818, unless the competition has applied for and received a rating. (See ratings chart GR313.)

8. Any breed-restricted division, or combination of breed-restricted divisions, may be offered at Local Regular Competitions, in accordance with GR311.

9. IMPORTANT: See Chapter HU. There are special conditions and requirements for determining the ratings of Hunter

SPONSORED BY HAGYARD EQUINE MEDICAL INSTITUTE || © USEF 2016

sections. Management's attention is directed to these conditions in particular, HU116 and HU164-HU167.

Division or Section	"A" Rating Requirements		"B" Rating Requirements	
	minimum number classes	minimum prize money	minimum number classes	minimum prize money
English Pleasure				
Saddle Seat	2	0	1	0
Hunter Seat	2	0	1	0
Driving	2	0	1	0

Division or Section	"A" Rating Requirements		"B" Rating Requirements	
	minimum number classes	minimum prize money	minimum number classes	minimum prize money
Welsh				
Welsh Pleasure Sections A & B (12.2h & under/junior to ride)	3	$100	3	$50
Welsh Pleasure Section B (over 12.2h-14.2h/junior to ride)	3	$100	3	$50
Welsh Pleasure Sections C & D (junior and adult to ride)	3	$100	3	$50
Adult Welsh Pleasure Sections A & B (14.2h & under/adult to ride)	3	$100	3	$50
Half/Part-Bred Welsh Pleasure (junior and adult to ride)	3	$100	3	$50
Welsh Pleasure Driving Sections A & B (junior and adult to drive)	3	$100	3	$50
Welsh Hunter Sections A & B (12.2h & under/junior to ride)	3	$100	3	$50
Welsh Hunter Section B (over 12.2h-14.2h/junior to ride)	3	$100	3	$50
Welsh Hunter Sections C & D (junior and adult to ride)	3	$100	3	$50
Adult Welsh Hunter Sections A & B (14.2h & under/adult to ride)	3	$100	3	$50
Half/Part-Bred Welsh Hunter (junior and adult to ride)	3	$100	3	$50

Division or Section	"A" Rating Requirements		"B" Rating Requirements	
	minimum number classes	minimum prize money	minimum number classes	minimum prize money
Western **				
Reining				
Trail	2	$100	1	$50
Pleasure	2	$100	1	$50
	2	$100	1	$50

Any class or section not meeting the requirements shown in this chart will be rated "C".

*Western Division competitions may retain Local Competition status regardless of the amount of prize money offered.

GR314 Special Conditions

1. The following classes do not count toward the minimum number of classes nor toward the minimum prize money required for any division or section rating; these following classes do not count toward HOTY awards unless included in the specific division award rules:

   a. Breeding;

   b. Classes restricted as to area;

   c. Classes which restrict the number of ribbons won by any rider, handler or driver, e.g., Maiden, Novice, Limit and other such rider restricted classes.

   d. Owners, except in Amateur Owner sections and Paso Fino Division;

   e. Classes that do not count toward a Hunter or Jumper Championship;

   f. Bareback, Grooms, Consolation, Races, Parades, Command, Cutting classes, and except in the Paso Fino Divisions, Costume classes; Exhibitions.

   g. Classes restricted to one breed (except in one breed divisions), type or color;

   h. Classes restricted to horse or rider, i.e., age or sex, unless complementary classes are offered for other entries. Ladies classes will count toward the rating requirement even if complementary classes for Gentlemen are not offered.

   i. Any class in which the judging specifications are not in accordance with the Federation.

   j. Opportunity classes

   k. Academy classes

2. Monies offered to classes restricted to established futurity/maturity programs, local restricted jackpots, sweepstakes, or other breed specific programs offered by a recognized breed affiliate or by the National Reining Horse Association will not be included in tabulation of competition dues or in determining division ratings.

SUBCHAPTER 3-D REVIEW AND RENEWAL OF COMPETITION LICENSES

GR315 Inactive Competitions

1. Any Licensed Competition held the previous year which notifies the Federation by 120 days prior to its competition date that it will not hold a competition that year, may retain Inactive Membership by the additional payment of $100.

2. An Inactive Competition will be listed as "Inactive" on the USEF website and other USEF competition lists, and will retain its date priority for the following year, provided it meets the applicable date and competition requirements of the

Federation.

3. If an Inactive Competition cancels the following year, that cancellation will constitute a second cancellation in a row per GR310.2, and the applicable license will be revoked. However, this provision shall not be applicable to a competition cancelled due to an Act of God, loss of a facility, or due to extenuating circumstances approved by the CEO.

GR316 Competition Evaluation

To the extent appropriate, additional information of the Competition Evaluation process and procedures will be contained in the License agreement.

1. Schedule. USEF licensed competitions will be subject to a Competition Evaluation which will enable USEF to determine if renewal of a license and the use of the USEF dates are in the best interest of the sport of equestrian. A Competition Evaluation in accordance with the USEF competition evaluation procedure will be commenced no later than 10 months before the expiration of the license agreement. For licenses with a term of 3 years, a Competition Evaluation will be conducted following the second anniversary of the license. Licenses with a term longer than 3 years are subject at least every third year thereafter to an interim Competition Evaluation for the purpose of identifying possible improvements to the competition.

2. Competition Evaluation Considerations:

   a. Has the Licensee complied with the terms of the License agreement? (License agreement terms must be definable, measurable and enforceable.)

   b. Have reports filed on the conduct of the competition indicated that the competition has been properly conducted? Primary sources of reports would be USEF competition officials, USEF affiliates and exhibitors.

   c. Has the Licensee made application for renewal and met financial obligations in a timely fashion? Financial obligations to USEF which have not been met are grounds for cancellation or nonrenewal of license.

   d. Has the competition, as structured, received adequate competitor support?

   e. Any renewal evaluation will consider entries, dates, classes actually held and prize money paid in determining the renewal level of each competition.

   f. Does it appear, following consultation with affected Affiliates, if any, that continued use of the dates by this competition is in the best interest of the sport of equestrian?

   g. Has the competition been successful in achieving the applicable standards (attendance/sponsorship/media/facilities, etc.) relating to that specific level of competition?

   h. Do Competition Reports received from the licensee reflect a realistic view of issues that should be addressed by the licensee; and, if so, did the licensee adequately address the issues?

   i. Does the conduct on the part of the Licensee reflect favorably on the sport of equestrian and USEF?

   j. Is the Licensee in good standing?

   k. Has this Competition demonstrated to the satisfaction of USEF based upon a factual analysis that use of the dates by this competition is in the best interest of the sport of Equestrian?

3. License Renewal Evaluation Results. Any competition license renewal will be subject to the mileage rule and other rules and conditions in existence at the time of renewal. (See GR306.13 Grandfathered Competitions regarding application of mileage that was in effect on December 1, 2005.) Under certain circumstances, therefore, license renewal may not be available. Subject to the above reservation, when a Licensee is determined to have complied with all the terms and conditions of the USEF License Agreement, to have satisfactorily achieved the required Standards applicable to the Competition, and to have achieved a satisfactory result under the Competition Evaluation process, then said

licensee will be offered an opportunity to continue as a licensee for the same dates and location.

The Competition Evaluation will result in one of the following:

1. Renewal of the license agreement for those competition dates for another License period.

2. Nonrenewal based on an unsatisfactory Competition Evaluation.

3. Renewal with a change in license terms and/or Rating Level.

4. Probation. In lieu of termination, USEF, at its sole discretion, may place the licensed competition on probationary status for one year, during which time the competition must correct the License failures reported by USEF or have the License terminated. USEF will appoint the Steward(s)/TD(s) for a competition on probation; cost of steward(s)/TD(s) shall be paid by the competition.

5. When a nonrenewal determination is made after the unsatisfactory Competition Evaluation at the end of the web posting of the "Open date", USEF may award the dates to another competition.

6. When there is a rule modification that results in date conflicts between existing license holders, USEF may modify the existing license agreements to a common expiration date and conduct a Competition Evaluation of the affected competitions. The competition determined by USEF, based upon objective criteria, to have the best Competition Evaluation will be offered a license and the other license(s) will not be renewed.

GR317 Sale or Transfer of License

The Sale or Transfer of a License is subject to the approval of the Federation, following consultation with the applicable Recognized National or FEI Affiliate. The final decision to approve or deny the sale or transfer of a license is at the sole discretion of the Federation. Approval of a license sale or transfer shall not be unreasonably withheld. Competition licenses may be sold or transferred during the term of the License to another Licensee acceptable to USEF, subject to the following conditions:

1. The Licensee that acquires the License must comply with rules, requirements and Standards which are in effect or established for the Competition Rating and/or Level at the time the acquisition occurs, even if the rule requirements and standards were different or did not exist when the license was initially granted to the original licensee.

2. Both the Seller and the Purchaser of the License must disclose all relevant terms of the transfer of License and must obtain USEF approval before the transaction can be completed. Prior to any such approval or denial by USEF, the Recognized National or FEI Affiliate, if any, shall be consulted in regard to the request for sale or transfer. The Recognized National or FEI Affiliate will be provided, on request, with all terms and conditions relating to the proposed transaction. USEF shall advise the Recognized National or FEI Affiliate of any terms or conditions relevant to the terms of the transfer, and any special conditions or other considerations that USEF feels may be appropriate. Such approval or denial by USEF shall not subject USEF to any liability or obligate it to any third party. Both Seller and Purchaser of the License must agree to indemnity and hold harmless both USEF and the Recognized National or FEI Affiliate from any liability or legal expense arising from approval or denial of the agreement. Failure to completely disclose terms and conditions of a License transfer may result in termination of the License by USEF and any sanctions, penalties or other remedies available to USEF.

3. The Selling Licensee shall remain financially responsible until the following conditions are met.

    a. USEF issues written approval of the Sale/Transfer

    b. Payment of the applicable USEF Sale/Transfer fee

    c. Seller has met all other financial obligations to USEF

4. Only the remaining years in the term of an existing License may be sold or transferred. Purchasing licensee will have the same rights to apply for approval of comparable dates as the Selling licensee.

5. USEF may consider concentration of dates in the control of a single License holder or group of related Licensees

when determining the appropriateness of a sale or transfer of a License.

SUBCHAPTER 3-E DISPUTES AND RESOLUTION

GR 318 License Application Disputes and Resolution

1. Any competition license applicant may dispute the denial of a license application or renewal. In addition, a Mileage Exemption Request applicant and Priority Date Holder(s) may dispute a mileage exemption request decision. The initiation of a license dispute must be made in writing and received by the Federation within ten (10) calendar days of the date on the Federation notice of the approval or denial and must be accompanied by a fee of $1,000.00. If the petitioner prevails, $500.00 will be refunded.

2. License disputes will be decided by the Federation Hearing Committee in accordance with the Federation rules and procedures. The Hearing Committee shall only determine if the mileage exemption process was conducted in accordance with the rules. The Hearing Committee shall provide the parties with the opportunity to be heard pursuant to written submissions and shall issue a written decision within thirty (30) calendar days following receipt of the initiation of dispute and response(s) from affected parties. If the Hearing Committee finds a procedural defect, the exemption request will go back through the process beginning at the point where the defect occurred.

3. The Hearing Committee's decision is final and not appealable.

SPONSORED BY HAGYARD EQUINE MEDICAL INSTITUTE || © USEF 2016

CHAPTER 4 DRUGS AND MEDICATIONS

CHAPTER 4 DRUGS AND MEDICATIONS

GR401-408. Equine Drugs and Medications Provisions Applicable to All Breeds and/or Disciplines

GR401 Determining the Equine Drugs and Medications Designation for Each Breed or Discipline

1. The Board of Directors shall designate every Breed, Discipline, and/or Group competing under Federation Rules as either a Prohibited Substance Group or a Therapeutic Substance Group, as outlined herein below.

2. At each Annual Meeting, each Division Committee shall determine by a majority vote and shall indicate to the Chief Administrator of the Equine Drugs and Medications Program its preference for its Breed or Discipline to be designated as (or to be part of) either a Prohibited Substance Group or a Therapeutic Substance Group. In any instance where more than one Division Committee is responsible for a Breed and/or Discipline Group, after each committee has determined its preference by a majority vote, unanimity between and/or among the Division Committees of the Group shall be required to invoke a recommendation to be designated a Prohibited Substance Group. Absent such concurrence, the joint recommendation of the Division Committees of the Group shall be construed as a recommendation in favor of designation as a Therapeutic Substance Group.

3. Each Division Committee shall have responsibility to recommend for its division.

4. At its meeting at the Federation's Annual Meeting, the Equine Drugs and Medications Committee shall take into consideration these recommendations and the written recommendations of the respective Affiliate Associations in this regard, and it shall enact the designation for each Breed, Discipline, and/or Group. The effective dates of these designations shall coincide with the effective dates of the newly published Rule Book.

5. These designations shall be reviewed by each Division Committee at the subsequent Rule Change Convention.

6. Every horse and/or pony competing at Federation competitions and/or events shall be subject to either the Prohibited Substance Provisions (GR409) or the Therapeutic Substance Provisions (GR410-412), depending upon its Breed's, Discipline's, and/or Group's designation, and it shall be required to compete in compliance therewith, whether competing in unrated or rated classes and/or divisions.

7. Any horse and/or pony that competes in more than one Breed, Discipline, and/or Group at a competition, one of which is a Prohibited Substance Group, shall be required to be in compliance with the Prohibited Substance Provisions at all times while competing in any and/or all classes and/or divisions at that competition.

GR402 Testing

1. Horses and/or ponies competing at a Licensed Competition are subject to examination by a licensed veterinarian who must be appointed by the Administrator of the Equine Drugs and Medications Program. Said appointed veterinarian, with the approval of the Administrator, may appoint a technician to perform certain duties under this Rule. The examination may include physical, urine, blood tests and/or any other test or procedure at the discretion of said veterinarian necessary to effectuate the purposes of this rule. Said veterinarian may examine any or all horses and/or ponies in a class or all classes in a competition or any horses and/or ponies entered in any class, whether in competition or not, if on the competition grounds, or any horse and/or pony withdrawn by any exhibitor within 24 hours prior to a class for which it has been entered.

2. Whether a horse and/or pony is in competition or not, refusal to submit the horse and/or pony for examination or to cooperate with the veterinarian or his agents constitutes a violation and subjects the responsible person to penalties under GR406.

3. Trainers who are not able to accompany Federation drug testing personnel and the horse and/or pony to the location where sample collection is to take place, to act as witness to the collection and sealing of blood and urine

samples, and to sign the drug collection documents in the appropriate places as witness, must appoint an agent to do so. The absence of such a witness shall constitute a waiver of any objection to the identification of the horse and/or pony tested and the manner of collection and sealing of the samples.

4. Upon the collection of a sufficient number of tubes of blood from the horse or pony, the tubes shall be divided into two groups. One group shall be labeled and identified as Blood Sample A and the other as Blood Sample B, and they shall be sealed accordingly. Upon the collection of a sufficient volume of urine from the horse or pony, a portion of the sample shall be poured into a second urine sample container. One container shall be labeled and identified as Urine Sample A and the other as Urine Sample B, and they shall be sealed accordingly. These procedures shall be performed whether or not the trainer or his/her appointed witness is present as provided for in Section 3 above.

5. In the event reasonable attempts at sample collections from the horse or pony do not provide a sufficient number of tubes of blood or a sufficient volume of urine to be divided, labeled, and identified as Samples A and B, as determined by the testing veterinarian and/or technician, the sample(s) obtained (if obtained) shall be labeled and identified as Sample(s) A only, and it shall be recorded in the records of the Equine Drugs and Medications Program that the corresponding Sample(s) B does (do) not exist, in which event the obtained Sample(s) shall be subject to testing.

6. A blood sample may be retested under these Rules at any time exclusively at the direction of the Federation. The retesting of a sample may lead to a violation only if the sample was retested within three (3) years from the sample collection date. In order to constitute a violation under these rules, the substance detected in the retested sample must (i) have been forbidden at the time of sample collection; and (ii) not a therapeutic substance, which for purposes of this rule includes only the Controlled Medications on the FEI Prohibited Substances List (available at http://www.fei.org/fei/cleansport) in effect on the sample collection date.

7. In the event that the retested sample proves positive, and the retest was conducted more than one (1) year since the date of collection, no prizes or awards will be required to be returned.

GR403 Cooperation

1. Cooperation with the veterinarian and/or his agent(s) includes:
   a. Taking the horse and/or pony and the veterinarian and/or his agent(s) immediately to the location selected by said veterinarian and/or agent(s) for testing the horse and/or pony and presenting it for testing.
   b. Assisting the veterinarian and/or his agent(s) in procuring the sample promptly, including but not limited to removing equipment from the horse and/or pony, leaving it quietly in the stall and avoiding any distractions to it. Schooling, lengthy cooling out, bandaging and other delays of this type shall be construed as noncooperation.
   c. Polite attitude and actions toward the veterinarian and/or his agent(s).

GR404 Accountability of Trainers and Other Persons Responsible

1. Trainers and other Persons Responsible, in the absence of substantial evidence to the contrary, are responsible and accountable under the penalty provisions of these rules. The trainer and other Persons Responsible are not relieved from such responsibility as a result of the lack or insufficiency of stable security.

2. The Persons Responsible may include the individual who rides, vaults, or drives the horse and/or pony during a competition; the Owner; and/or Support Personnel.

3. Support Personnel is defined to include but is not limited to grooms, handlers, longeurs, and veterinarians may be regarded as additional Persons Responsible if they are present at the competition or have made a relevant decision about the horse and/or pony.

4. A trainer is defined as any adult or adults who has or shares the responsibility for the care, training, custody, condition, or performance of a horse and/or pony. Said person must sign the entry blank of any Licensed Competition

whether said person be a trainer, owner, rider, agent and/or coach. Where a minor exhibitor has no trainer, then a parent, guardian or agent or representative thereof must sign the entry blank and assume responsibility as trainer. The name of the trainer must be designated as such on the entry blank. It is the responsibility of trainers as well as competition management to see that entry blanks contain all of the required information. The responsibilities of a trainer include, but are not limited to the following:

    a. for the condition of a horse or pony at a Licensed Competition (whether or not they have signed an entry blank),

    b. to guard each horse and/or pony at, and sufficiently prior to, a Licensed Competition such as to prevent the administration by anyone of, or its exposure to, any forbidden substance, and

    c. to know all of the provisions of this Chapter 4 (including any advisories or interpretations published in equestrian) and all other rules and regulations of the Federation and the penalty provisions of said rules. For purposes of this rule, substantial evidence means affirmative evidence of such a clear and definite nature as to establish that said trainer, or any employee or agent of the trainer, was, in fact, not responsible or accountable for the condition of the horse and/or pony. If any trainer is prevented from performing his or her duties, including responsibility for the condition of the horses and/or ponies in his or her care, by illness or other cause, or is absent from any Licensed Competition where horses and/or ponies under his or her care are entered and stabled, he or she must immediately notify the competition secretary and, at the same time, a substitute must be appointed by the trainer and such substitute must place his or her name on the entry blank forthwith. Such substitution does not relieve the regular trainer of his/her responsibility and accountability under this rule; however, the substitute trainer is equally responsible and accountable for the condition of such horses and/or ponies.

5. The trainer and owner acknowledge that the trainer represents the owner regarding horses and/or ponies being trained or managed, entries, scratches for any reason and any act performed on any horse and/or pony under the care and custody of the trainer.

6. In the case of a horse and/or pony competing under the Therapeutic Substance Provisions, any trainer and/or Persons Responsible subject to these rules who actually administers, attempts to administer, instructs, aids, conspires with another to administer or employs anyone who administers or attempts to administer a forbidden substance to a horse and/or pony which might affect the performance of said horse and/or pony at a competition licensed by the Federation without complying with GR411, is subject to the penalties provided in GR406.

7. Any trainer and/or Persons Responsible subject to these rules who administers, attempts to administer, instructs, aids, conspires with another to administer or employs anyone who administers or attempts to administer any substance to a horse and/or pony by injection or by any other route of administration, whether the substance is forbidden or permitted, in the competition ring of a competition licensed by the Federation during a scheduled class, is subject to the penalties provided in GR406. *BOD 6/30/15 Effective 12/1/15.*

GR405 Equine Drugs and Medications Testing in Connection with an Appeal Measurement

1. Each animal submitted for an appeal measurement is subject to the Drugs and Medications Chapter at the time of said measurement and/or concurrent examinations, and said animal must be in compliance therewith.

2. Each animal submitted for an appeal measurement must have drug testing samples collected at the time of said measurement and/or concurrent examinations. No sample is a drug testing sample unless it is collected by and/or under the direct supervision of Federation drug testing personnel, who must be appointed by the Administrator of the Equine Drugs and Medications Program to collect samples from the animal in question in connection with said measurement.

3. Each animal submitted for an appeal measurement must have both a urine sample and a blood sample collected at the time of said measurement and/or concurrent examinations. Both the urine sample and the blood sample must be of sufficient volume for drug testing purposes, as determined by the Administrator of the Equine Drugs and

Medications Program. Said sample collections shall be conducted in accordance with procedures which are the sole prerogative of the Federation drug testing personnel. As deemed necessary by the Federation testing veteri-narian, the animal shall be administered furosemide to cause it to produce a urine sample in a timely manner.

4. Every blood sample and/or urine sample collected in connection with an appeal measurement and all portions thereof are the sole property of the Federation. Said samples and all portions thereof must remain in the sole custody of the Federation drug testing personnel at all times during said measurement and/or concurrent examina-tions, and subsequently they must be submitted to the Federation's laboratory for testing in accordance with the instructions of the Administrator of the Equine Drugs and Medications Program.

5. The entire cost of sample collections and testing conducted in connection with an appeal measurement, including the fees and expenses of Federation drug testing personnel, shipping costs for equipment and samples, laboratory charges, etc., as determined by the Administrator of the Equine Drugs and Medications Program, must be paid in full by the appellant within 30 days of the submission of an invoice, regardless of the outcome of said measure-ment, and regardless of the laboratory results. A deposit in cash or certified check equal to the costs of sampling and testing, as estimated by the Administrator of the Equine Drugs and Medications Program, may be required prior to the measurement.

6. No appeal measurement is valid absent written affirmation of the CEO or his designee confirming the receipt of negative drug testing results from the Federation's laboratory, indicating that both the urine and blood sample collected from the animal in question in connection with said measurement and/or concurrent examinations were found to contain no forbidden substance, said results having been issued to the Administrator of the Equine Drugs and Medications Program. Any instance involving a finding of forbidden substance shall additionally result in the issuance of a charge of violation of Chapter 4 for adjudication by the Hearing Committee in accordance with the provisions of Chapters 6 and 7.

GR406 Results, Confirmatory Analysis, and Retest

1. Blood and urine samples labeled and identified as Samples A shall be subjected to chemical analysis by the Feder-ation Drug Testing Laboratory or by a laboratory with which the Federation has contracted for its services. Blood and urine samples labeled and identified as Samples B shall be stored securely, unopened, at the Federation Drug Testing Laboratory, to be used in the event of a confirmatory analysis, or in the event of a future analysis.

2. In the event the chemical analysis of Blood or Urine Sample A is negative, i.e., no forbidden substance or any metabolite or analogue thereof is found to be present in the sample, the corresponding Blood or Urine Sample B may be frozen and maintained, at the Federation Equine Drug Testing and Research Laboratory, for possible future chemical analysis.

3. In the event the chemical analysis of Blood or Urine Sample A is positive, i.e., a forbidden substance or any metab-olite or analogue thereof is found to be present in the sample, this shall be prima facie evidence that the forbidden substance was administered in some manner to said horse or pony, whether intentionally or unintentionally, or otherwise was caused to be present in the tissues, body fluids or excreta of the horse or pony at the competition, whether intentionally or unintentionally, such that the trainer(s) deemed responsible and accountable for its condi-tion is (are) liable under the provisions of GR404.

4. In the event the chemical analysis of Blood or Urine Sample A is positive, and upon the issuance of Notices of Charge to persons deemed responsible and accountable under the rules, a person charged who requests a con-firmatory analysis of the corresponding Blood or Urine Sample B must make the request in writing to Counsel of the Equine Drugs and Medications Committee, and it must be received within 15 days of the date of the Notice of Charge.

5. The confirmatory analysis of the corresponding Blood or Urine Sample B shall be performed by a drug testing laboratory that must be mutually agreed upon by the person charged who requests the confirmatory analysis and

Counsel of the Equine Drugs and Medications Committee, which laboratory must have demonstrated proficiency in performing the necessary confirmatory analysis, provided the corresponding Blood or Urine Sample B exists and is of sufficient volume to permit a confirmatory analysis. In the event the drug testing laboratory that analyzed Sample A is the only laboratory that has demonstrated proficiency in performing the necessary confirmatory analysis, as determined by Counsel of the Equine Drugs and Medications Committee, this laboratory shall be the only laboratory to which Counsel of the Equine Drugs and Medications Committee shall agree to perform the confirmatory analysis of the corresponding Sample B. Upon the completion of the confirmatory analysis, the laboratory performing the confirmatory analysis shall forward its findings and supporting data to all parties.

6. In the event no agreement is reached as to a laboratory as required in section 5 above, and the person charged who requests the confirmatory analysis does not revoke his/her request, the confirmatory analysis of the corresponding Blood or Urine Sample B shall be performed by the Federation Drug Testing Laboratory, or by a laboratory with which The Federation has contracted for its services, as determined by Counsel of the Equine Drugs and Medications Committee, which laboratory shall forward its findings and supporting data to all parties. Both the results of the analysis of Sample A (and supporting data) and the results of the confirmatory analysis of the corresponding Sample B, if any (and supporting data, if any), shall be admissible as evidence in any hearing or proceeding pertaining to this matter.

7. In the event the corresponding Blood or Urine Sample B does not exist, or is of insufficient volume to permit a confirmatory analysis, as determined by Counsel of the Equine Drugs and Medications Committee, and there exists a remaining aliquot of Blood or Urine Sample A which is of sufficient volume to permit a retest, as determined by Counsel of the Equine Drugs and Medications Committee, a person charged who requests the retest of Blood or Urine Sample A must make the request in writing to Counsel of the Equine Drugs and Medications Committee, and it must be received within 7 days of the determination that the corresponding Blood or Urine Sample B does not exist or is of insufficient volume to permit a confirmatory analysis.

8. Any requested re-test of the remaining aliquot of Blood or Urine Sample A, provided it is of sufficient volume to permit a retest, shall be performed by the Federation Drug Testing Laboratory, or by a laboratory with which The Federation has contracted for its services, as determined by Counsel of the Equine Drugs and Medications Committee.

9. The retest of the remaining aliquot of Blood or Urine Sample A may be witnessed by a Witnessing Analyst appointed by the person charged who requests such analysis at the same time as the retest is requested. The Witnessing Analyst must be a qualified analytical chemist employed by an equine drug testing laboratory. If no Witnessing Analyst is appointed by the person requesting the retest, or if the Witnessing Analyst is unavailable within a reasonable time, the requested retest of the remaining aliquot of Blood or Urine Sample A shall proceed without the Witnessing Analyst.

10. In the event the Witnessing Analyst appointed by the person requesting the retest of the remaining aliquot of Blood or Urine Sample A is satisfied that the positive result is correct, Counsel of the Equine Drugs and Medications Committee must be informed immediately by fax with confirmation by letter.

11. In the event the Witnessing Analyst is not satisfied that the result of the retest of the remaining aliquot of Blood or Urine Sample A is correct, Counsel of the Equine Drugs and Medications Committee must be informed immediately by fax followed by a written report setting forth the basis for the Witnessing Analyst's opinion. Copies of the original and subsequent results and supporting analytical data must be submitted to the Federation Hearing Committee as part of the hearing record in the case, for resolution by it of any and all issues regarding the original analysis of Blood or Urine Sample A and the retest of the remaining aliquot of Blood or Urine Sample A.

12. By requesting the confirmatory analysis of the corresponding Blood or Urine Sample B, or the retest of the remaining aliquot of Blood or Urine Sample A, or by requesting that the retest be witnessed by a Witnessing Analyst, the person charged who makes such request(s) agrees to and must pay any and all fees, costs and expenses relating to the confirmatory analysis or the retest, whether it is performed by a mutually agreed upon laboratory, by the

Federation Drug Testing Laboratory, or by a laboratory with which The Federation has contracted for its services, upon the presentation an invoice by Counsel of the Equine Drugs and Medications Committee, and any and all fees, costs, and expenses relating to the Witnessing Analyst.

13. In the case of a horse and/or pony competing under the Therapeutic Substance Provisions, if the chemical analysis of the sample taken from such horse and/or pony indicates the presence of a forbidden substance or any metabolite or analogue thereof and all the requirements of GR411 have been fully complied with, the information contained in said Equine Drugs and Medications Report Form and any other relevant evidence will be considered by the Federation in determining whether a rule violation was committed by any person(s) responsible or account-able for the condition of the horse and/or pony under the provisions of this rule.

14. When a positive report is received from the chemist identifying a forbidden substance, or any metabolite or analogue thereof, a hearing will be held in accordance with Chapter 6, except as may otherwise be provided by GR412. No trainer, responsible or accountable for the condition of said horse and/or pony, will be suspended, or a horse and/or pony barred from competition, until after an administrative penalty has been assessed or after the conclusion of a hearing and a written ruling thereon has been made.

15. The owner or owners of a horse and/or pony found to contain a forbidden substance or any metabolite or ana-logue thereof may be required to forfeit all prize money, sweepstakes, added money and any trophies, ribbons and "points" won at said competition by said horse and/or pony and the same will be redistributed accordingly. The owner must pay a fee of $300 to said competition. Points accumulated toward Horse of the Year Awards prior to said competition may be nullified and redistributed at the discretion of the Hearing Committee. If, prior to or at a hearing, the Federation as the charging party, determines that one or more persons, not previously charged as a trainer should also be charged as a trainer, then, upon application by the Federation, the Hearing Committee may, in its discretion, continue or adjourn the hearing, in whole or in part, to permit a new or amended charge to be issued (unless the person(s) to be charged waive notice).

16. A trainer of a horse and/or pony found to contain such forbidden substance or any metabolite or analogue thereof is subject to whatever penalty is assessed by the Hearing Committee, except for administrative penalties issued by the Chairman of the Equine Drugs and Medications Committee and accepted, as provided by GR412. Said trainer may be fined and may be suspended from all participation in Licensed Competitions for a period of one year for the first offense, and for a longer period for a second or later offense, said suspension to be served at any time at the discretion of the Hearing Committee.

The horse and/or pony may be suspended for any period of time specified by the Hearing Committee. In deter-mining an appropriate penalty under these rules, the Hearing Committee may take into account such factors and circumstances as it may deem relevant, including but not limited to

a. the pharmacology of the forbidden substance,

b. the credibility and good faith of the person charged or of other witnesses,

c. penalties determined in similar cases, and

d. past violations of any Federation rules (or the lack thereof).

e. reliance upon the professional ability or advice of a veterinarian who is a licensed graduate of an accredited veterinary school and who is in good standing in the state in which he/she primarily practices.

17. If the Hearing Committee determines that any violation or attempted violation of this Rule was willful and/or inten-tional, there shall not be any limit to the period of a suspension, and the Hearing Committee may impose other and significantly greater penalties than it would have in the absence of such a determination.

18. A blood sample may be retested under these Rules at any time exclusively at the direction of the Federation. The retesting of a sample may lead to a violation only if the sample was retested within three (3) years from the sample collection date. In order to constitute a violation under these rules, the substance detected in the retested sam-ple must (i) have been forbidden at the time of sample collection; and (ii) not a therapeutic substance, which for

purposes of this rule includes only the Controlled Medications on the FEI Prohibited Substances List (available at http://www.fei.org/fei/cleansport) in effect on the sample collection date.

19. In the event that the retested sample proves positive, and the retest was conducted more than one (1) year since the date of collection, no prizes or awards will be required to be returned.

GR407 Management Procedures

1. To provide funds for research, inspection and enforcement of rules regarding use of medications and drugs, each Licensed Competition, except where prohibited by law, must assess the exhibitors a fee of $8 for each horse and/or pony entered in the competition, except the fee shall be $20 for each horse entered in an FEI sanctioned competition or a USEF High Cap Computer List Class. Participants in the following classes are exempted from payment:

   a. leadline

   b. exhibitions

   c. games and races,

   d. classes for 4-H members,

   e. Academy classes (Academy classes are classes limited to horses used regularly in a lesson program)

   f. Opportunity classes

   g. Classes at Regular or Local Competitions restricted to breeds or disciplines whose rules are not included in the USEF rulebook.

   h. However, these classes are not exempt from the Drugs and Medications Chapter itself. Within 10 days after a competition, competition management must forward to the Federation a sum representing the above fee times the number of horses and/or ponies entered in the nonexempt classes of the competition plus the number of horses and/or ponies scratched where the fee is not refunded, such sum to be held by the Federation in a separate fund for use to accomplish the purpose set forth above.

2. It is a violation for a Licensee to assess and/or collect a drug enforcement fee in excess of or in addition to that specified and required by GR407.1 of these rules, unless said assessment is approved in writing by the Federation in advance, and then only under the terms and conditions set forth.

3. It is a violation for a Licensee to withhold from the Federation any or all of the drug fees collected in accordance with GR407.1, for any purpose, including to defray the expenses incurred providing stalls, passes, and other items to the Federation drug testing personnel, as required by GR407.4 and .5.

4. Each Licensed Competition shall, at its own cost and expense, set aside and make available to The Federation testing personnel upon request suitable facilities conveniently located for the veterinarian appointed by the Federation and his or her technicians to collect equine blood and urine samples. Suitable facilities means one or more stalls if available, as requested, that are well lit, clean, dry, freshly bedded, and having a door or gate that can be secured.

5. Each Licensed Competition, upon request, must furnish the veterinarian appointed by The Federation and/or the Administrator of the Equine Drugs and Medications Program by mail forthwith, with the requested number of official passes and parking passes for the veterinarians and technicians to have immediate and free access to all areas at said Licensed Competition.

6. Competition management must cooperate with and exhibit polite attitude and actions toward the veterinarian and/or his agents.

GR408 Interpretations of the Federation Equine Drugs and Medications Chapter and its Application to Particular Substances

Any questions regarding the interpretation of this Chapter, including the application of this Chapter to particular substances, should be directed to the office of the Federation Equine Drugs and Medications Program, 956 King Avenue,

Columbus, Ohio 43212-2655. (800) 633-2472, (614) 299-7707, FAX (614) 299-7706. Trainers and/or owners who seek advice concerning the interpretation and application of this rule should not rely solely upon interpretations or advice by private or competition veterinarians, competition officials, competition personnel, or other persons, but should also obtain verification of any such interpretations or advice from the Federation Equine Drugs and Medications Program office. Any trainer or owner who is uncertain about whether this rule applies in any given situation would be well advised to withdraw the affected horse and/or pony from competition until such time as the Federation Equine Drugs and Medications Program office has been consulted.

GR409 Equine Drugs and Medications, Prohibited Substance Provisions

1. This paragraph applies only to FEI Banned Substances and Methods.

For all Federation Equestre Internationale (FEI) recognized disciplines, Articles 2 (what constitutes a violation), 3 [proof of violations (except 3.1 and 3.2.3)], 4 (banned substances and methods), and 8.2 (principles of fair hearing) of the FEI Equine Anti-Doping rules govern. Those Articles are incorporated by reference as if fully set out herein and can be found at www.fei.org or the Drugs & Medications tab at www.usef.org. For purposes of this rule, the designation of "Person Responsible" in the incorporated provisions of the FEI Equine Anti-Doping rules shall refer to the individual(s) found to be the trainer of the horse as defined by GR404.

2. No horse and/or pony competing in a Breed or Discipline designated as (or part of) a No Prohibited Substance Group is to be shown in any class at a competition licensed by the Federation if it has been administered in any manner or otherwise contained in its tissues, body fluids or excreta a prohibited substance as defined in the FEI Equine Anti-Doping and Controlled Medication Regulations, which can be found at www.fei.org.

3. EXHIBITORS, OWNERS, TRAINERS, AND VETERINARIANS ARE CAUTIONED AGAINST THE USE OF MEDICINAL PREPARATIONS, TONICS, PASTES, AND PRODUCTS OF ANY KIND, THE INGREDIENTS AND QUANTITATIVE ANALYSIS OF WHICH ARE NOT SPECIFICALLY KNOWN, AS MANY OF THEM NO DOUBT CONTAIN ONE OR MORE FORBIDDEN SUBSTANCES.

GR410 Equine Drugs and Medications, The Therapeutic Substance Provisions

1. No horse and/or pony competing in a Breed or Discipline designated as (or part of) a Therapeutic Substance Group is to be shown in any class at a competition licensed by the Federation (see also GR402.1, last sentence) if it has been administered in any manner or otherwise contains in its tissues, body fluids or excreta a forbidden substance except as provided in GR411. Any horse and/or pony that competes in more than one Breed, Discipline, and/or Group at a competition, one of which is a Prohibited Substance Group, shall be required to be in compliance with the Prohibited Substance Provisions at all times while competing in any and/or all classes and/or divisions at that competition. For purposes of this rule, a forbidden substance is:

   a. Any stimulant, depressant, tranquilizer, local anesthetic, psychotropic (mood and/or behavior altering) substance, or drug which might affect the performance of a horse and/or pony (stimulants and/or depressants are defined as substances which stimulate or depress the cardiovascular, respiratory or central nervous systems), or any metabolite and/or analogue of any such substance or drug, except as expressly permitted by this rule.

   b. Any corticosteroid present in the plasma of the horse/pony other than dexamethasone (see GR410.5b).

   c. Any nonsteroidal anti-inflammatory drug in excess of one present in the plasma or urine of the horse/pony (GR411 does not apply); exception: salicylic acid.

   d. Any substance (or metabolite and/or analogue thereof) permitted by this rule in excess of the maximum limit or other restrictions prescribed herein.

   e. Any substance (or metabolite and/or analogue thereof), regardless of how harmless or innocuous it might be, which might interfere with the detection of any of the substances defined in (a), (b), (c) or (e) or quantification of substances permitted by this rule.

    f. Any anabolic steroid (GR411 below does not apply).

2. EXHIBITORS, OWNERS, TRAINERS, AND VETERINARIANS ARE CAUTIONED AGAINST THE USE OF MEDIC-INAL PREPARATIONS, TONICS, PASTES, AND PRODUCTS OF ANY KIND, THE INGREDIENTS AND QUAN-TITATIVE ANALYSIS OF WHICH ARE NOT SPECIFICALLY KNOWN, AS MANY OF THEM MAY CONTAIN A FORBIDDEN SUBSTANCE.

3. The full use of modern therapeutic measures for the improvement and protection of the health of the horse and/or pony is permitted unless:

    a. The substance administered is a stimulant, depressant, tranquilizer, local anesthetic, drug or drug metabolite which might affect the performance of a horse and/or pony or might interfere with the detection of forbidden substances or quantification of permitted substances; or

    b. More than one nonsteroidal anti-inflammatory drugs are present in the plasma or urine of the horse/pony (GR411 does not apply); exception: salicylic acid; or

    c. The presence of such substance in the blood or urine sample exceeds the maximum limit or other restrictions prescribed herein below.

4. Restrictions concerning the nonsteroidal anti-inflammatory drugs are as follows:

    a. The maximum permitted plasma concentration of diclofenac is 0.005 micrograms per milliliter.

    b. The maximum permitted plasma concentration of phenylbutazone is 15.0 micrograms per milliliter.

    c. The maximum permitted plasma concentration of flunixin is 1.0 micrograms per milliliter.

    d. The maximum permitted plasma concentration of ketoprofen is 40.0 nanograms per milliliter.

    e. The maximum permitted plasma concentration of meclofenamic acid is 2.5 micrograms per milliliter.

    f. The maximum permitted plasma concentration of naproxen is 40.0 micrograms per milliliter.

    g. Not more than one of the substances listed in (a) through (g) are permitted to be present in the same plasma or urine sample (GR411 does not apply).

    h. The maximum permitted plasma concentration of firocoxib is 0.240 micrograms per milliliter.

    i. Any nonsteroidal anti-inflammatory drug not listed in (a) through (g) above is forbidden to be present in the plasma or urine sample (GR411 does not apply); exception: salicylic acid.

    j. Any nonsteroidal anti-inflammatory drug that becomes approved for use in horses can be added to the list of those permitted, after the completion, review and approval of the needed research.

5. Restrictions concerning other therapeutic substances are as follows:

    a. The maximum permissible plasma concentration of methocarbamol is 0.5 micrograms per milliliter.

    b. The maximum permitted plasma concentration of dexamethasone is 0.5 nanograms per milliliter.

6. Thresholds for substances of possible dietary origin are as follows:

    a. The maximum permissible urine concentration of theobromine is 2.0 micrograms per milliliter.

7. Additional restrictions concerning particular classes and/or divisions (GR411 does not apply):

    a. In the breeding/in-hand classes for three-year-olds and under in the Arabian, Half Arabian, and Anglo Arabian Division, any anabolic steroid is forbidden. (See HOW LONG DRUGS REMAIN DETECTABLE in the current Drugs and Medications Rules Pamphlet for guidelines).

GR411 Conditions For Therapeutic Administrations of Forbidden Substances

1. A horse and/or pony exhibiting at a Licensed Competition pursuant to the Therapeutic Substance Provisions that receives any medication which contains a forbidden substance is not eligible for competition unless all of the following requirements have been met and the facts are furnished in writing on a timely-submitted official Equine Drugs and Medications Report Form:

    a. The medication must be therapeutic and necessary for the diagnosis or treatment of an existing illness or injury.

Administration of a forbidden substance for non-therapeutic or optional purposes (such as, by way of example only, shipping, clipping, training, turning out, routine floating or cleaning of teeth, non-diagnostic nerve blocking, uncasting, mane pulling or non-emergency shoeing) is not considered to be therapeutic. Any trainer who is uncertain about whether a particular purpose is considered to be therapeutic would be well advised to consult the Federation Equine Drugs and Medications Program office.

b. The horse and/or pony must be withdrawn from competition for a period of not less than 24 hours after the medication is administered.

c. The medication must be administered by a licensed veterinarian, or, if a veterinarian is unavailable, only by the trainer pursuant to the advice and direction of a veterinarian.

d. Identification of medication—the amount, strength and mode of administration.

e. Date and time of administration.

f. Identification of horse and/or pony, its name, age, sex, color and entry number.

g. Diagnosis and reason for administration.

h. Statement signed by person administering medication.

i. Equine Drugs and Medications Report Form filed with the Steward/Technical Delegate or Designated Competition Office Representative within one hour after administration or one hour after the Steward/Technical Delegate or Designated Competition Office Representative returns to duty if administration is at a time other than during competition hours.

j. The Steward, Technical Delegate, or Designated Competition Office Representative must sign and record the time of receipt on the Equine Drugs and Medications Report Form.

k. At selection trials for World Championships, and/or Olympic and/or Pan American Games, the requirement of subsection (b) above, that the horse or pony must be withdrawn from competition for a period of not less than 24 hours after the medication is administered will not apply, provided that:

1. the competition is conducted pursuant to the written selection procedures as approved by the Federation Board of Directors;

2. the written selection procedures specifically allow for therapeutic administrations of medications by a USEF-appointed veterinary panel within 24 hours preceding competition, and the written selection procedures are in no case less stringent in this regard than the FEI Veterinary Regulations (Articles 1006.7 and 1006.8) and guidelines pursuant thereto;

3. all requirements of the written selection procedures regarding therapeutic administrations of medications have been met;

4. all requirements of this Rule have been met except subsection GR411.1(b); and all persons competing in the competition are eligible and competing for selection.

2. Where all the requirements of GR411 have been fully complied with, the information contained in said Equine Drugs and Medications Report Form and any other relevant evidence will be considered by the Federation in determining whether a rule violation was committed by any person(s) responsible or accountable for the condition of the horse and/or pony under the provisions of this rule.

NOTE: The official Equine Drugs and Medications Report Form is available from the officiating Steward/Technical Delegate and/or Competition Secretary. All required information must be included when filing a report. Failure to satisfy and follow all the requirements of this Rule and to supply all of the information required by such Equine Drugs and Medications Report Form is a violation of the rules. The Steward/Technical Delegate must report any known violations of this Rule to the Federation for such further action as may be deemed appropriate.

3. Flunixin, in addition to one other substance listed in GR410 (a) through (g), may be found in the same plasma and/or urine sample of a horse under the following conditions and for the treatment of colic or an ophthalmic emergency only: (i) must comply with GR411.1; (ii) the flunixin must have been administered by a veterinarian; (iii) the required

medication report form must be signed by the administering veterinarian; and (iv) the horse must be withdrawn from competition for 24 hours following the administration.

GR412 Administrative Penalties

1. The provisions for administrative penalties shall apply to any potential or alleged violation of the Equine Drugs and Medications Rule. The Federation shall hold in abeyance the issuance of charges of rule violation pending further determination by the Chairman of the Equine Drugs and Medications Committee, who shall take into consideration all pertinent information available, including the seriousness of the alleged violation(s), precedents in similar Federation drug cases, and any prior rule violation(s) by the individual(s). At all times while consideration is given as to a determination by the Chairman of the Equine Drugs and Medications Committee, the identity of the horse, rider, trainer, coach, and owner must not be known or disclosed to him.

2. The Chairman of the Equine Drugs and Medications Committee shall, upon consultation with staff, and within 60 days of receipt of laboratory results, make a determination in his or her discretion whether to recommend the issuance of charges by the Federation, whether to recommend a plea agreement, whether to impose administrative penalties, or whether to take no further action in the matter, and shall communicate that decision in writing to the Federation's CEO or his designee.

3. In the event the Chairman of the Equine Drugs and Medications Committee determines to impose administrative penalties in accordance with GR412.2, in lieu of a recommendation to issue charges, he or she shall be authorized to impose any or all of the penalties enumerated in Chapter 7, GR703, setting forth the terms and conditions for compliance. The trainer(s) and owner(s) shall after receiving written notice of the right to a hearing, after their written waiver of same, and written acceptance of an administrative penalty, be subject to any and all administrative penalties imposed by the Chairman of the Equine Drugs and Medications Committee.

4. The Federation shall give written notification to trainer(s) and owner(s) of administrative penalties determined pursuant to GR412.3 above, the terms and conditions of which shall not be subject to negotiation. An administrative penalty must be approved by the Hearing Committee Co-Chairs before it is offered to the Respondent(s). Once accepted by all parties and by the Hearing Committee, an administrative penalty shall have the same force and effect as would a finding of rule violation by the Hearing Committee following a hearing pursuant to Chapters 6 and 7, and will be published on the Federation's web site.

5. Any trainer(s), or owner(s), or both, who have received notice of an administrative penalty under GR412.4 and who have not accepted same in writing shall receive a hearing before the Hearing Committee, in accordance with Chapters 6 and 7. Administrative penalties accepted in accordance with this Rule shall be effective immediately, shall be final, and shall not be subject to further review under any circumstance(s).

6. In the event an administrative penalty is not accepted in writing, the Federation shall issue a written charge or charges pursuant to Chapter 6, and the Hearing Committee shall conduct a hearing pursuant to Chapters 6 and 7 upon said charge(s). In the event of a finding of a violation, the Hearing Committee shall not be limited in choice of penalties to those that might have been imposed in accordance with GR412.2 and .3, nor in any such instance shall the Hearing Committee be limited in any other way in exercising all of its prerogatives as set forth in the Bylaws and Rules.

7. A blood sample may be retested under these Rules at any time exclusively at the direction of the Federation. The retesting of a sample may lead to a violation only if the sample was retested within three (3) years from the sample collection date. In order to constitute a violation under these rules, the substance detected in the retested sample must (i) have been forbidden at the time of sample collection; and (ii) not a therapeutic substance, which for purposes of this rule includes only the Controlled Medications on the FEI Prohibited Substances List (available at http://www.fei.org/fei/cleansport) in effect on the sample collection date.

8. In the event that the retested sample proves positive, and the retest was conducted more than one (1) year since

the date of collection, no prizes or awards will be required to be returned.

GR413 Human Drug Testing

1. In accordance with the rules of the FEI and of the World Anti-Doping Agency (WADA), any Federation member shall comply with in-competition, no advance notice (NAN), and other out-of-competition drug testing conducted by the FEI, WADA, US Anti-Doping Agency (USADA) or by a WADA-authorized organization or USADA-authorized organization at any time without advanced notice. Failure to cooperate with such in-competition, NAN or other out-of-competition drug testing shall be a violation of Federation rules.

2. In conjunction with the above-described NAN or other out-of-competition drug testing, the Federation is required to submit the names, current addresses, telephone numbers, training times and training and competition locations for individuals and teams as requested by the FEI, WADA, or USADA to enable FEI, WADA, or USADA to conduct NAN or other out-of-competition drug testing. Notwithstanding the foregoing, compliance with anti-doping regulations rests with the individual subject to testing.

3. A finding of violation of human drug rules by USADA or WADA shall be deemed a violation of Federation rules, and the reciprocity provisions of GR615.2 shall be applied.

GR 414 Prohibited Practices

1. No injectable substances may be administered to any horse or pony within 12 hours prior to competing, with the following three exceptions subject to paragraph 2 below:

   a. Therapeutic fluids, which amount must consist of a minimum of 1L of polyionic fluids per 100lb of body weight; and which must be used in accordance with the manufacturer's recommendations and guidelines. The fluids must not be supplemented with concentrated electrolytes, such as magnesium.

   b. Antibiotics. Procaine penicillin G is prohibited under this exception.

   c. Dexamethasone. This is permitted only for the treatment of acute urticaria –(hives). The dose must not exceed 0.5 mg per 100 lb (5.0 mg for 1000 lb horse) if administered more than 6 hours and less than 12 hours prior to entering the competition ring, and must not exceed 1.0 mg per 100 lb (10.0 mg for 1000lb horse) within any 24 hour period.

2. The above exceptions are permitted only when (i) the substance is administered by a licensed veterinarian and no less than 6 hours prior to competing; and (ii) the "Trainer" as defined under General Rule 404 properly files, or causes to be properly filed, an Equine Drugs and Medications Report Form with the Steward/Technical Delegate or competition office representative within one hour after the administration of the substance or one hour after the Steward/Technical Delegate or competition office representative returns to duty if the administration occurs at a time outside competition hours. The Steward/Technical Delegate or competition office representative shall sign and record the time of receipt on the Equine Drugs and Medications Report Form.

3. No horse may be injected with any substance, forbidden or permitted, into an intra-synovial space (joint, tendon sheath, or bursa) within the 4 days preceding competition. No horse less than two years of age may be treated with intrasynovial injections within the 30 days preceding competition.

4. Shockwave Therapy may only be administered by or on the order of a licensed veterinarian. If sedation is required for Shockwave Therapy, only sedation performed by a licensed veterinarian and administered at the same time as the Shockwave Therapy will be considered therapeutic and GR411 will apply. No sedation associated with Shockwave Therapy will be considered therapeutic if administered within 24 hours prior to competition. No horse may be treated with Shockwave Therapy within the 3 days preceding competition with the following exception:

   a. Shockwave Therapy may be administered by a licensed veterinarian within the 3 day prohibited period, but no closer than 12 hours prior to competing, and is limited to application to the back and dorsal pelvis areas. No Shockwave Therapy is permitted within the 12 hours prior to competing. This exception is permitted only when the "Trainer" as defined under GR404 properly files, or causes to be properly filed, an Equine Drugs and Medications Report Form with the Steward/Technical Delegate or competition office representative within one hour after the administration of Shockwave Therapy or one hour after the Steward/Technical Delegate or competition office representative returns to duty if the administration occurs at a time outside competition hours. The Steward/Technical Delegate or competition office representative shall sign and record the time of receipt on the Equine Drugs and Medications Report Form.

SPONSORED BY HAGYARD EQUINE MEDICAL INSTITUTE || © USEF 2016

CHAPTER 5 MEASUREMENT OF ENTRIES

SubChapter 5-A CONDITIONS

Subchapter 5-B PROCEDURES

Subchapter 5-C MEASURING

Subchapter 5-D QUESTIONING AND PROTESTING

Subchapter 5-E MEASUREMENT APPEAL

Subchapter 5-F OFFICIAL MEASUREMENT

CHAPTER 5 MEASUREMENT OF ENTRIES

SubChapter 5-A CONDITIONS

GR501 Other Measurement Rules

The rules in Chapter 5 do not apply to measurement of entries in Hunter, Jumper and Welsh Pony Divisions: refer to rules HU168-179. For all other measurements, see GR502-517. For Combined Driving, see DC930 Appendix A. For Dressage, see DR135.

GR502 General

1. Management shall not permit an animal to be shown in a performance class at a Federation Member competition in any division or section that requires a measurement card unless; a) the owner is in possession of a measurement card issued by the Federation or Equine Canada bearing the date of 1982 or later; or b) he possesses a copy of a valid measurement form; or c) or management confirms measurement electronically with the Federation Office; or d) For Shetlands the owner is in possession of a measurement card issued by ASPC. At Regular Competitions, management may not give out an exhibitor's number for an animal showing in a division or section that requires a measurement card before the above requirements have been complied with. (See GR1302.2b)

2. A Show Committee may require the measurement of all animals in any division in which height is a qualifying factor.

3. Animals in competition in any division or section that requires a measurement card are subject to measurement by a licensed veterinarian and Registered steward appointed by Federation. The Federation CEO or his designee may require the measurement of any animal competing at a Federation Licensed Competition in any division in which height is a qualifying factor.

4. Measurements must take place at a Licensed Competition in which the animal is entered to compete. The Federation Approved Measuring Stick must be used. The animal must be measured by an officiating steward and any one of the following officials officiating in the competition: a veterinarian, a judge or another steward. Heel and toe measurements, where applicable, must be done by an officiating steward.

5. The officials appointed to measure animals at a competition are responsible for their true measurement and must check the measurement devices for accuracy. The names of the measuring officials will be printed on the measurement card and they and other measuring officials will be subject to penalty under the provisions of Chapters 6 and 7 if it is determined that a measurement is incorrect.

6. Measurements are solely for the internal use of the Federation, its Licensed Competitions and its licensed officials in connection with competing for prizes, and do not constitute any representation or warranty regarding measurement information; accordingly, the Federation, its Licensed Competitions and its licensed officials make no representation and shall have no liability whatsoever for measurement errors.

7. Once a foal year has been submitted to the Federation office, the original date cannot be changed without a copy of the animal's breed registration papers or a signed statement from a veterinarian certifying the animal's age.

8. Prior to presenting the pony for measurement it is the responsibility of the owner, and in his interest, to ensure that the pony is handled properly, accustomed to the application of a measuring stick, and correctly prepared for measurement.

GR503 Required Measurements and Re-measurements

1. An animal must be measured each competition year until it reaches the age of six. Animals five years and under will be issued a card designating the year measured. Animals six years and older will be issued a measurement card which does not have to be renewed. Those animals which are measured (and for which a valid measurement form is received by the Federation office) in the month of December immediately preceding the calendar year in which they turn six years of age will be issued a measurement card that does not have to be renewed. With the exception

of animals under six years old, once an animal is issued a measurement card, a new card will not be issued unless the measurement is questioned or protested, an appeal is made or after an official measurement is performed.

2. All animals that have been assigned a card prior to March 1, 1982 must be re-measured. If the owner, either member or non-member, is in possession of a measurement card issued prior to the aforementioned date, there will be no fee for re-measurement.

3. In the event an animal has been officially measured after December 1, 1982 and the owner does not have the measurement card or valid measurement form in his immediate possession, the animal must be re-measured for the purposes of competing in that particular competition only. Measurement forms are sent to the Federation office, but not given to the owner. If an owner fails to present a valid measurement card at a competition, the owner must have the animal re-measured at said competition. If an owner fails to present measurement card at more than one (1) competition he will be fined for each subsequent re-measurement necessary.

4. If the shoeing status of an animal changes from that which is indicated on its measurement card (due to an injury causing corrective shoeing or the sale of animal, etc.) a new card reflecting the new shoeing status may be issued provided the animal is re-measured in accordance with GR504 and the original measurement card is surrendered to the Federation office.

5. All Hackney Roadster and Roadster Ponies must be re-measured and issued new measurement cards prior to competing in licensed competitions for the year 2004 and beyond.

6. Exception: GR503 does not apply to the Dressage Division. For Dressage and Dressage Sport Horse Breeding, see DR135.

Subchapter 5-B PROCEDURES

GR504 Membership Requirements

Before any animal is measured the person presenting the animal must have in his possession the owner's membership number, a signed statement signifying that membership has been applied for, or proof of Equine Canada membership.

GR505 Completing the Measurement Form

1. The measurement form must be filled out completely in duplicate and the number of the stick must be on the form. Measurement cards will not be issued if the form is not completely filled out and legible. Exhibitors are cautioned to make sure their measurement forms are filled out accurately and completely.

2. The form must include:

   a. The name and date of the competition, the height of the animal, height of heel (except for Dressage and Dressage Sport Horse Breeding), name, color and markings, sex, year foaled which must be verified at time of measurement and designate whether the animal is shod or unshod. (American Saddlebred measurements must be entered on left measurement box of form)

   b. The name and address of owner and Federation membership number must be given.

   c. The form must be signed by the person furnishing the above information immediately before the animal is measured and then signed by the competition officials appointed to measure.

   d. The person providing the information that appears on the measurement form must be 18 years or older and is responsible for the accuracy of such information and care should be taken that all is in order before signing. When this individual signs the form he/she is certifying that all information is complete and correct. If a measurement form is signed by a person under the age of 18 and submitted to the Federation office, the measurement will be invalid.

   e. No changes can be made to such information once the form is signed. Any alterations, scratch outs, or rewrites to any part of the height, height of fore heels, or thickness of shoe/pad must be clearly indicated and initialed by the measuring officials. Care should be taken that all information is in order before signing.

3. The white copy of the measurement form is given to the owner or trainer, the blue copy is returned to the Federation office and the pink copy should be retained by the steward.

4. The owner will retain the white copy which, when properly signed by the two measuring officials, is valid for 45 days from the time the animal is measured, regardless of age. Exception: Hackney, Roadster, and American Saddlebred ponies: the white copy which owners retain will remain valid for the remainder of the current competition year.

Subchapter 5-C MEASURING

GR506 Measurement Devices

Only the Federation Approved Measuring Stick may be used. The Federation Approved Measuring Stick is a straight, stiff, unbendable stick that is equipped with a plumb bob or spirit level to make sure that the stick is perpendicular to the ground and that the crosspiece or arm is parallel with the ground surface, and must be shod with metal. All Federation approved measuring sticks will be numbered, carry the Federation logo and the legend Federation Approved. A Federation Approved Measuring Stick with a metric scale must be used for Dressage, Dressage Sport Horse Breeding, and Driving measurements. See DR135 for specific requirements regarding Measurement Devices at Dressage Competitions.

GR507 Measurement Surface

1. The measurement surface must be level and under no circumstances should animals be measured on dirt or gravel. A concrete slab or other paved surface is most desirable but, when not available, a sheet of heavy plywood can be used. Exception: plywood may not be used for Dressage or Dressage Sport Horse Breeding measurements.

2. If a suitable surface is not available at a competition, animals without a measurement card issued after December 1, 1982 or a valid measurement form must be measured to compete in that competition, but no measurement form shall be given to the owner. See GR1210.2 and GR1210.3.

GR508 Position of Animal

1. The animal must stand squarely on all four feet in such a position that the front legs are vertical to the ground and the back of the hocks are in a vertical line with the point of the animal's quarters. The head must be held low enough to reveal the highest point of the withers and no lower. The animal must be free of all appliances. Handlers must not interfere with the animal in any way that will prevent it from standing in this position; blinkers may be allowed.

2. For the Hackney Division: The animal should be standing with his front legs perpendicular to the ground. Ideally his head should be lower than his withers. This easily locates the highest part of the withers where the measurement should take place. Handlers must not interfere with the animal in any way that will prevent it from standing in the correct position; blinkers may be allowed.

GR509 Method of Measurement

With the animal in the aforementioned position, measure the vertical distance from the highest point of the withers to the ground. The cross-piece, arm or bar of the measuring device must be placed over the highest point of the withers and no measurement taken at any other part of the animal's body will count. Additional pressure must not be applied to the cross-piece, arm or bar.

GR510 Method of Measuring Toe and Heel

Using a six (6) inch metal ruler, the length of the toe is determined by measuring the front of the hoof, in the center, from the skin line on the lower side of the coronary band to the ground. The skin line on the lower side of the coronary band is to be defined by palpation. The thumb should be used to press on the horny hoof wall proceeding from the ground toward the hairline. The first compressible soft tissue palpated is the lower side of the coronary band. The hairline does not necessarily coincide with the lower side of the coronary band. The height of heel is determined by measuring from the skin line on the lower side of the coronary band to the ground, with the ruler perpendicular to the ground (See illustration).

METHOD OF MEASURING TOE AND HEEL

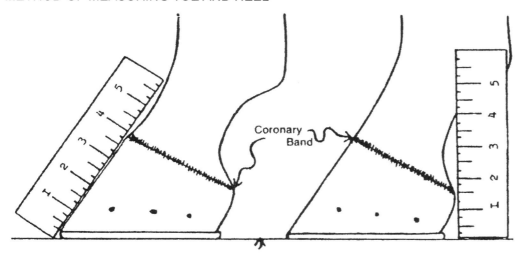

Smooth Flat Surface

GR511 Exceptions for Breed Measurements

1. American Saddlebred-

    a. Ponies five years of age and under are eligible to compete in classes restricted to American Saddlebred-type ponies. Ponies must be presented annually for measurement unshod (note: for purposes of protection a 1/4" pad or plate may be nailed to the foot and then deducted from the official measurement).

    b. In order to obtain a permanent USEF measurement card American Saddlebred-type ponies, six years of age and over must be presented for measurement unshod (note: for purposes of protection a 1/4" pad or plate may be nailed to the foot and then deducted from the official measurement).

    c. If an American Saddlebred-type pony (regardless of age) measures up to 1 inch over 14.2 hands the pony will be issued a measurement card reflecting its height and permitted to compete in American Saddlebred-type pony classes restricted to ponies 14.2 hands and under.

2. Shetland- The animal may be presented with or without shoes regardless of how shown.

Subchapter 5-D QUESTIONING AND PROTESTING

GR512 Height

1. An owner or trainer may protest the height of only one animal competing in a class in which he is also competing. (See GR603) If a protest is filed the animal's heel must be measured by the officiating steward immediately upon exiting the arena so that no change can be made by re-shoeing or the animal must be accompanied by an official until the measurement procedure is completed. The heel measurement will be taken from the skin line to the ground (see GR510), recorded by the competition Steward and signed by the exhibitor. The animal must be measured for height within one hour of the conclusion of the session, at an officially designated measurement location for that competition. If it is determined that the animal's shoeing has been changed between the time of the measurement of the heel and the official measurement of the animal, the protest will be upheld and the owner will forfeit entry fees and winnings for the entire competition and the animal is barred from competing for the balance of the

competition year. All points accumulated for Horse of the Year Awards are nullified.

2. Animals Five Years of Age or Under

    a. If it is determined that an animal five years of age or under is being shown with the same heel measurement as indicated on its measurement card or valid measurement form, or a lower heel measurement than as indicated on the measurement card or valid measurement form, said animal may continue to show at the height indicated and its height cannot be protested.

    b. If it is determined that the animal is being shown with a greater heel measurement than as indicated on its measurement card or valid measurement form, the animal must be measured in accordance with GR512.1

GR513 Toe Length

1. An owner or trainer may protest the length of toe of any animal competing in a class in which he is competing.

2. If the length of toe of any animal is protested, the Show Committee must have the official veterinarian and a judge or steward officiating in the competition measure the toe immediately so that no change can be made by reshoeing.

3. If the limit for length of toe is exceeded, the animal must be disqualified for the balance of the competition and the owner of the animal forfeits entry fees and winnings for the entire competition.

GR514 Results of Questioning or Protesting

1. The measurement card or valid measurement form of any animal that is required to transfer into another division or section must be surrendered to the competition steward who must forward it to the Federation office with his report.

2. The name of any animal barred from showing due to its height exceeding the limit for the animal's section by more than one half inch (1/2") is listed in equestrian.

The decision of competition measuring(s) officials is final for the competition where the protesting occurred. An appeal may be filed with the Federation to cover future and prior competitions.

Subchapter 5-E MEASUREMENT APPEAL

GR515 Conditions

An owner or trainer of an animal declared ineligible for a division or section on account of height may appeal a measurement. The animal is barred from competing in the particular height division or section for which he was declared ineligible until the measurement is performed.

GR516 Procedures

1. The appeal must be made to the Federation office in writing within seven (7) days of the measurement and must be accompanied by the required deposit.

2. All expenses including veterinary fees must be paid by the appellant who must make a deposit with the Federation as an advance on anticipated costs prior to the measurement.

3. The Federation will select a location and time for the appeal measurement as convenient as possible. The owner or trainer must deliver the animal to the location at his own expense within 45 days of filing the appeal.

4. The measurement must be performed by at least two persons appointed by the Federation which shall include one veterinarian who is a member of the American Association of Equine Practitioners and one Registered steward or Technical Delegate, as permitted by division rules. The officials whose measurement is being appealed cannot be part of the team conducting the measurement appeal.

5. Any animal submitted for an appeal measurement must show no evidence of lameness. If found to be lame by the examining veterinarian, the animal cannot be measured or remeasured for thirty (30) days and the appellant forfeits his deposit and any veterinary expenses incurred. Each animal submitted for an appeal measurement must be tested for drugs and medications in accordance with General Rules, Chapter 4, GR405. (Exception: Hackney,

Roadster, and American Saddlebred.)

6. If the appeal is not upheld or the appellant fails to submit the animal within 45 days, the animal is barred from showing for the balance of the competition year. The deposit is forfeited and all points accumulated for Horse of the Year Awards are nullified.

7. The measurement made under the terms of an Appeal is final.

Subchapter 5-F OFFICIAL MEASUREMENT

GR517 Conditions

An owner or trainer may request an official measurement for an animal six (6) years or over provided: a) the animal has never been shown in a Licensed Competition; or b) has never been declared ineligible for a division on account of height; or c) was declared ineligible for a division on account of height prior to December 1, 1982; or d) has had a bona fide transfer of ownership; e) except for those applied for prior to December 1, 1987.

GR518 Procedures

1. The request for an official measurement must be made to the Federation in writing and accompanied by a deposit which is not refundable.

2. All expenses including veterinary fees must be paid by the person requesting the measurement who shall make a deposit with the Federation, as an advance on anticipated costs, prior to the measurement. Both the owner and trainer are required to sign a waiver and consent on a form prepared by and acceptable to the Federation agreeing to the arrangements for the official measurement, agreeing to the administration of Lasix to the animal to aid in the collection of a urine sample for laboratory tests for Federation forbidden substances. (Exception: Hackney, Roadster, and American Saddlebred.)

3. The Federation will select a location and time for the official measurement as convenient as possible. The owner or trainer must deliver the animal to the location at his own expense.

4. The measurement must be performed by at least two persons appointed by the Federation which shall include a veterinarian who is a member of the American Association of Equine Practitioners and one Registered steward. The officials whose measurement is being appealed cannot be part of the team conducting the measurement appeal.

5. Any animal submitted for an official measurement must show no evidence of lameness.

6. An official measurement is final.

CHAPTER 6 PROTESTS, CHARGES, ATHLETE GRIEVANCES, HEARINGS, ADMINISTRATIVE PENALTIES AND PLEA AGREEMENTS

SPONSORED BY HAGYARD EQUINE MEDICAL INSTITUTE || © USEF 2016

CHAPTER 6 PROTESTS, CHARGES, ATHLETE GRIEVANCES, HEARINGS, ADMINISTRATIVE PENALTIES AND PLEA AGREEMENTS

GR601 General

1. Fair notice and an opportunity for a hearing shall be accorded to any amateur athlete, coach, trainer, manager, administrator, or official before the Federation may declare such individual ineligible to participate in any amateur athletic competition. Exception: When a determination of violation has been made by WADA or USADA and the Federation is required to implement and enforce any FEI penalties imposed by WADA or USADA, further Federation proceedings are not required. (See GR615.2) Any hearing conducted hereunder shall be conducted in accordance with the provisions of Chapter 6.

2. Neither the Federation nor any member of the Federation may deny or threaten to deny any member athlete, coach, trainer, manager, administrator or other official the opportunity to compete in the Olympic or Pan American Games, World Championship competitions or such other "protected competition" as defined in the USOC BYLAWS; nor may the Federation, or any member of the Federation, subsequent to such competition, censure or otherwise penalize any such athlete who participates in any such competition.

3. Any individual identified in Section 1 above who alleges that he or she has been denied by the Federation or a member of the Federation a right established by Section 2 of this Rule shall immediately inform the president of the Federation and the USOC's AAC representative for equestrian who shall cause an investigation to be made and steps to be taken to settle the controversy. Notwithstanding any efforts taken by the Federation to settle the controversy informally or through the Federation's grievance procedures set forth in Bylaws 701-704 and GR605 of Chapter 6, the individual may refer the matter to the USOC for action, as appropriate, under Section 9 of the USOC Bylaws, which can be found at the USOC web site: www.teamusa.org, under the section entitled "Legal".

4. The construction and application of Federation rules are governed by the laws of the State of New York. It shall be the duty of the Federation Hearing Committee to hear protests and charges in connection with alleged violations of the rules, to hear appeals from the Licensed Officials Committee's non-renewal or revocation of a licensed official's license, and to hear athlete and other grievances pursuant to GR602.8 and GR605.

5. For the rules and procedures which govern hearings of grievances by athletes and others, see Bylaws 701-704, and Chapter 6, GR601-602 and GR605-615.

Subchapter 6-A FILING AND CONTENTS OF PROTESTS, CHARGES AND ATHLETE GRIEVANCES

GR602 Contents, etc

1. A protest, charge or grievance must state the full name and address (if known) of the accused, must list each Rule number alleged to have been violated and must contain a complete statement of the acts which constitute the alleged violation. The maker of the protest, charge or grievance must be prepared to substantiate the protest, charge or grievance by his or her own personal testimony at a hearing or by the testimony of at least one other witness with personal knowledge who is subject to cross-examination, and by additional evidence including but not limited to sworn statements, other witnesses. The Hearing Committee, at the request of a party or on its own motion may excuse the requirement of personal testimony in the hearing of a protest, charge or grievance as it deems appropriate, if the parties to the protest, charge or grievance stipulate to the relevant facts (with the exception of any charge, protest, or grievance which may possibly affect the opportunity of any individual identified in GR601 to participate in or attempt to qualify for selection to participate in "protected competition.") unless the respondent advises the Hearing Committee at least ten (10) days prior to the hearing that he or she will be present, in person or by representative, and that he or she wants the requirement of the maker's personal testimony not to

be excused. In that case, the Hearing Committee may not excuse the requirement of personal testimony by either the maker as eyewitness or one (1) other eyewitness. The notice of hearing of any such charge or protest shall advise the respondent of this provision.

2. A protest or charge against a Licensed Competition must be referred to the Federation by the steward, technical delegate, Show Committee, competition manager or competition secretary.

3. Protests or charges that a steward or technical delegate has failed to attend the competition, perform his duties, or has otherwise violated the Rules; or that a judge has failed to conduct a class in accordance with the specifications or has otherwise violated the Rules are made in accordance with GR603-605. Such protests or charges must be referred to the Federation. In the event the accused is found guilty, he or she may be subject to any of the penalties under GR703 and notification of any penalty imposed will be published on the Federation's web site.

4. The Federation may investigate any protest, charge or alleged violation, may intervene in any protest, charge or grievance and present evidence at a hearing concerning any protest, charge or alleged violation at its discretion. The Federation may also attempt to arrange a plea agreement or dismissal of a protest or charge in lieu of a hearing by reviewing all evidence and/or conducting interviews with the maker(s) and the respondent(s) to the protest or charge (see GR617).

5. The Chair(s) of the Hearing Committee, or if unavailable the Vice Chair(s), may designate one or more members of the Hearing Committee or any other individual to investigate any protest, charge or alleged violation, to conduct any necessary fact finding, to hear evidence, to review memoranda submitted by interested parties, and to make proposed factual findings to the Hearing Committee, provided, however, that this provision shall not apply to any matters heard pursuant to Chapter 6, Subchapter 6-C, GR611.2(i) or (ii).

6. Non-protestable Decisions.

   a. The soundness of a horse, when determined by an official veterinarian of the competition or by a judge, is not protestable.

   b. A judge's decision, representing his/her individual preference or opinion, is not protestable unless it is alleged to be in violation of Federation rules.

   c. A protest questioning the height of a horse or the length of a horse's foot may only be made to the Show Committee. See GR512-514 and HU177.

7. Withdrawal of a Protest or Charge. If, prior to a hearing being held, the maker of a protest or charge wishes to withdraw it, he or she must make written application to the Hearing Committee, setting forth the reasons for the request. Following review of said application, the Hearing Committee will determine whether to allow the protest or charge to be withdrawn or whether to schedule the matter for hearing at a later date.

8. Any member of the Federation may file a protest or charge or grievance with the Hearing Committee pertaining to any matter within the cognizance of the Federation and alleging a violation of any provision of the Federation's Bylaws or Rules, the Amateur Sports Act of 1978, or the USOC's Constitution or By-Laws.

GR603 Protests

1. Any rider, driver, handler, vaulter, longeur, exhibitor, owner, agent, trainer or the parent of a junior exhibitor, or any Life, Senior, or Junior member present at the competition may file a protest with the Show Committee of a Licensed Competition or The Federation Hearing Committee alleging violation of any Federation rule(s). The protest must contain all information as specified in GR602.1 and must be:

   a. in writing,

   b. signed by the protester,

   c. addressed to the Show Committee of the competition at which the alleged violation occurred, or to the Hearing Committee,

   d. accompanied by a deposit of $200 if made by a Federation member or the parent of a junior exhibitor member or $300 if made by a non-member (if check, payable to the competition or to the Federation); said deposit will be refunded in the event the protest is upheld, and

e. received by the steward, technical delegate, a member of the Show Committee, the competition manager or the competition secretary within 48 hours of the alleged violation. If made directly to the Hearing Committee, the protest must be received at the Federation office by the tenth business day following the last recognized day of the competition, or by the tenth business day following the date on which the alleged violation occurred if it occurred other than at a Licensed Competition.

GR604 Charges

1. Any official of a USEF Licensed Competition, any Steward or Technical Delegate assigned to a USEF licensed competition, any National Officer of the Federation or the CEO of the Federation or his designee may file a charge with the Show Committee or the USEF Hearing Committee alleging a violation of any Federation rule(s).

2. A charge must be:

   a. in writing,

   b. signed by the person making the charge,

   c. addressed to the secretary of the competition at which the alleged violation occurred, or to the Hearing Committee and

   d. if made to a Show Committee it must be received by the steward, technical delegate or a member of the Show Committee within 48 hours of the alleged violation. If made to the Hearing Committee it must be received by the Federation within a reasonable time.

GR605 Grievances

1. A grievance may be filed by any amateur athlete, or other eligible athlete, coach, trainer, manager, administrator or official regarding his/her opportunity to participate in, or to attempt to qualify for selection to participate in any equestrian event of the Pan American Games, Paralympic Games, the Olympic Games, World Championship competitions or any other protected competitions as that term is defined in Section 1.3 (w) of the USOC Bylaws, including any domestic amateur athletic competition or event organized and conducted as part of the selection procedure directly qualifying each successful competitor therein as an athlete representing the U.S. in such equestrian international competitions. Any grievance must be made in writing over the signatures of the person or persons presenting the same, and must state the full name(s) and address(es) of the athlete, coach, trainer, manager, administrator, official, the Federation, another organization which is an Affiliate Member of the Federation, a committee of the Federation or a committee of an Affiliate Member of the Federation against whom the grievance is made, and must include with specificity a complete statement of the acts which constitute such grievance, including the requested relief sought. The maker(s) must be prepared to substantiate the grievance at a hearing by a preponderance of the evidence by personal testimony of a witness or witnesses with personal knowledge subject to cross-examination and by sworn statements, other witnesses and by other competent evidence. The requirement of personal testimony may be excused by the Hearing Committee if the parties to the protest, charge or grievance stipulate to the relevant facts. The accused shall have the right to be assisted in the presentation of his/her case at the hearing, including the assistance of legal counsel, if desired; the right to call witnesses and present oral and written evidence and argument; the right to confront and cross-examine adverse witnesses; and the right to have a record made of the hearing if desired.

2. The grievance should be addressed to the Hearing Committee and should be transmitted to the attention of the Federation CEO or his designee at the Federation office by hand delivery or by certified mail or by facsimile as soon as practicable following the events which are the subject of the grievance.

As soon as practicable after the receipt of such grievance, the CEO or his designee shall promptly communicate informally with the parties and the president of the Federation and the USOC's AAC representative for equestrian, or, in the event there is a conflict of interest, the AAC alternate representative and they shall make every effort to resolve the grievance to their and the parties' mutual satisfaction, and if unsuccessful, the CEO or his designee shall, without prejudice to the right of the complainant to pursue remedies available pursuant to the Amateur Sports Act of 1978 and the USOC Constitution, arrange for a prompt hearing of the grievance by the Hearing Committee.

3. Any person, committee, association or organization, including the Federation or any affiliate, member or member organization, against whom a grievance has been filed pursuant to either GR602 or GR605 of the Rules is entitled to a hearing. Such hearing shall be after advance written notice of the specific charges or alleged violations, and of the time, place and opportunity to participate in person and/or by counsel or other representative given to the person(s) presenting the grievance, the accused and all other possibly affected parties. Notices of hearing must be accompanied by a copy of the written grievance and shall set forth the possible consequences if the charges are found to be true.

4. The Hearing Committee shall review the record of any grievance hearing and promptly issue its written findings and determination based on the evidence in record in accordance with Chapter 6, which shall be final and binding upon the parties, except where otherwise provided in the Bylaws of the USOC.

5. The hearing shall take place no earlier than 20 days after receipt of notice by the person charged and not later than 60 days from such receipt so as to ensure that the person charged has sufficient time to prepare a defense.

6. The pre- and post-hearing procedures set forth in Subchapter 6-B and Subchapter 6-D and the hearing procedures set forth in Subchapter 6-C, GR611, shall apply with the exception that hearings pursuant to GR602, GR605.1 and GR611.2 may not be heard by a Hearing Officer and that temporary suspensions pursuant to GR609 may not be imposed prior to a hearing by the Hearing Committee.

Subchapter 6-B PRE-HEARING PROCEDURES

GR606 Notice

1. Any person, group of persons or competition against whom a protest or charge is filed are entitled to a hearing. Such hearing shall be after at least twenty (20) days' written notice to the accused except that a Show Committee may hold a hearing during or within 48 hours of a competition after 24 hours' written notice to the accused unless this notice requirement is waived in writing by the accused. Notice of hearing must contain a brief statement of the facts constituting the alleged violation, the Federation rules allegedly violated and must specify the time and place at which the hearing is to be held.

2. Initial written notice of a protest or charge must be sent to the accused within sixty (60) days from the date the protest or charge is received in the Federation office or from the date a charge is issued by the CEO, his designee or National Officer of the Federation. This initial notice may either specify a time and place at which the hearing is to be held or state that the hearing will be held at a date to be determined. If the initial notice does not specify a date and place, a subsequent notice of hearing specifying the date and place of the hearing will be sent at least twenty (20) days prior to the hearing date.

3. Any notice sent to the last known address on file with the Federation shall be deemed sufficient notice.

GR607 Continuances & Emergency Postponements

1. A respondent, protester or charging party may request a continuance of a scheduled hearing. A motion for continuance must be made in writing prior to the hearing and received by the Federation at the address designated in the Notice of Hearing as soon as the need for a continuance is known, but in any event at least 21 days prior to the time set for the hearing. A first continuance motion must be accompanied by a $750 fee which will be refunded if the continuance is not granted. Any second or subsequent application for continuance will only be considered upon receipt of a written continuance motion and $1500 fee which will be refunded if the continuance is not granted.

Motions for continuance will only be granted at the discretion of the Hearing Committee upon good cause shown. Prior engagements of counsel may or may not be considered good cause. A second request or repeated requests by defense counsel for continuances due to counsel's unavailability on a scheduled hearing date or dates may in the discretion of the committee's co-chairs be grounds for the denial of a continuance request. In that event, the respondent must promptly arrange to proceed with or without substitute counsel. (Note: When the Federation, as charging party or its representative(s) requests a continuance, there will be no fee.)

2. An emergency postponement of a scheduled hearing will be granted to a respondent, protester or charging party in case of severe illness, natural catastrophe or other emergency circumstances that would prevent the individual's attendance at the hearing. Such a motion must be in writing, setting forth the reasons and providing proof, if available, and must be received by the Federation at the address designated in the Notice of Hearing as soon as the need for continuance is known. A first motion for an emergency postponement must be accompanied by a fee of $250 and any second or subsequent motion for an emergency postponement must be accompanied by a fee of $1,000. These fees may be waived or refunded at the discretion of the Hearing Committee

3. Motions for a continuance or emergency postponement received prior to a scheduled hearing will be ruled upon by the Co-Chairs, or at least a quorum, of the Hearing Committee.

GR608 Evidence

1. Accused persons may attend their hearing at their option, with or without counsel, and may bring witnesses, submit sworn statements or other evidence on their behalf.

2. The proponent of a protest, charge or grievance has the burden of proof by a preponderance of the evidence.

3. Upon the written request of an accused or accuser or of a representative of the Federation when it is a party to the proceeding, there shall be furnished to the requesting party reasonably in advance of the hearing copies of any evidence proposed to be introduced into evidence at the hearing, the names of witnesses and the substance of their testimony and the notice of hearing shall so advise. When the Federation is not a party to the matter, such exchange must take place between the parties to the matter.

4. The parties are required to copy one another on all documents and evidence sent to the Federation.

5. In connection with charges brought by a steward, TD or competition official when they are not themselves eyewitnesses to the matters addressed in the charge, they may participate at the hearing by teleconference call unless the Hearing Committee determines otherwise in its discretion.

GR609 Temporary Suspension

In connection with any protest, charge, or any other matter which may properly fall within the jurisdiction of the Hearing Committee, and upon a finding that considerations involving the health, safety or welfare of Federation members and/or their horses, or the best interests of horse showing generally, warrant prompt action pending consideration of the matter by the Hearing Committee, the CEO or his designee may, by giving written notice of such action, temporarily suspend any person from participating in any manner in the affairs of the Federation or participating in or attending all Licensed Competitions until the Hearing Committee can hear the protest, charge or other matter and take such further temporary or other disciplinary action as it deems appropriate under these Rules, including temporarily suspending any person from participating in any manner in the affairs of the Federation or participating in or attending all Licensed Competitions, until the Hearing Committee can hear or determine the protest, charge or other matter, provided, however, that in instances involving GR605 and GR611.2(i) or (ii) where the USOC Bylaws apply, a hearing by the Hearing Committee shall be held on notice before any suspension is imposed.

GR610 Proceedings Before a Show Committee

1. Receipt of Protest (GR603) or Charge (GR604):
   a. The Show Committee shall receive the protest or charge within 48 hours of the alleged violation;
   b. Protests shall comply with the requirements of GR 603;
   c. Charges shall comply with the requirements of GR 604;
   d. Unless the protest or charge involves a time sensitive issue that must be resolved at the competition the protest or charge must be forwarded to the USEF Hearing Committee;
   e. If the Show Committee holds a hearing, it shall give the accused and person bringing the protest or charge 24 hours written notice of the hearing pursuant to GR 606 unless the accused waives the 24 hour requirement in writing;
   f. The hearing must be held prior to the end of the competition.

2. Procedure:
   a. The pre-hearing procedures of Subchapter 6-B, GR 602, 603, 604 and 606 shall apply;
   b. Before the hearing, based on the content of the protest or charge as required by GR 602.1, the Show Committee shall obtain all relevant evidence and information from the documents (such as entry blanks) and witnesses (such as Competition Officials) under its control.
   c. The proponent of the protest or charge has the burden of proof by a preponderance of the evidence.
   d. If the accused attends the hearing, the accused may bring counsel, witnesses, and submit sworn statements and other evidence on the accused's behalf.
   e. The show Committee shall then decide the issues impartially.

3. Determination:
   a. If a protest is sustained, the deposit shall be returned to the protester; if not sustained, the deposit shall be forfeited to the competition.
   b. A Show Committee may disqualify a person and/or his or her entries at that competition after holding a hearing and finding proof of the protest or charge by a preponderance of the evidence.
   c. If a Show Committee cannot reach a decision in regard to a protest or charge, it shall be referred to the Hearing Committee. If it is a protest, it shall be accompanied by the protest deposit. If the protest is sustained by the Hearing Committee, the deposit shall be returned to the protester; if it is not sustained by the Hearing Committee, the deposit will accrue to the Federation.
   d. At the close of the hearing the Show Committee shall report its findings of fact and conclusions setting out whether a rule(s) violation occurred, the specific rule(s) involved and any penalty imposed.
   e. The Show Committee shall make a written report of its findings and conclusions within 24 hours of the close of the hearing.
   f. A party to a protest or charge desiring to appeal a decision of the Show Committee to the Hearing Committee shall file an appeal in writing with the Hearing Committee at the Federation's office within thirty (30) days of the initial decision. The Hearing Committee will not review findings of fact; but will determine whether the rules were properly interpreted and applied.

GR611 Proceedings Before Hearing Committee

1. The Hearing Committee will hear grievances as provided in Bylaws 701-704, and will hear protests and charges in connection with alleged violations of Federation rules, in accordance with the powers and duties referred to below.
2. The Hearing Committee shall provide fair notice and an opportunity to expeditiously hear grievances regarding the opportunity of any amateur athlete, rider, driver, handler, vaulter, longeur, owner, lessee, agent or trainer, riding

coach or driving coach, coach, trainer, manager, administrator or official to participate in, or to attempt to qualify for selection to participate in, the Pan American Games, Paralympic Games, the Olympic Games, World Championship competitions or any other "protected competitions" as that term is defined in Section 1.3 (w) of the USOC Bylaws whether such grievances be against a competition, athlete, coach, trainer, manager, administrator or official of The Federation, another organization which is an affiliate member of The Federation, a committee of The Federation, or a committee of an affiliate association or a committee of The Federation. In (i) hearing grievances and (ii) hearing any protest or charge within the jurisdiction of the Hearing Committee arising out of a "protected competition," affecting the opportunity or ability of any amateur athlete, rider, driver, handler, vaulter, longeur, owner, lessee, agent or trainer, riding coach or driving coach, coach, trainer, manager, administrator or official to compete or participate, five members of the Hearing Committee shall be appointed by the co-chairs of the Hearing Committee, after consultation with the President, to constitute the hearing panel, of whom at least two shall be Athlete members of the Committee, who are not competing in the discipline which is involved in the dispute. The Hearing Committee shall promptly issue its findings in accordance with the Federation's Bylaws and Chapter 6, which findings shall be final, except where otherwise provided in the Constitution and Bylaws of the USOC.

3. The functions of any member of the Hearing Committee or any other presiding person participating in any decision shall be conducted in an impartial manner, subject to the published Rules of the Federation and within its powers. The Hearing Committee and other persons presiding on pre-hearing motions and at hearings shall give all parties a fair hearing and act as authorized by Federation rules. All members of a hearing panel must be present during the entire hearing to hear and consider all the evidence, as well as to deliberate and decide the outcome of the matter, except as may be otherwise agreed by all parties to the proceedings.

4. Any member of the Hearing Committee or any presiding or participating person may at any time disqualify himself or herself. Upon request of a party or in matters heard pursuant to GR611.2(i) or (ii) the identity of the persons who will preside and participate at a hearing shall be disclosed reasonably in advance of the hearing. On the submission in good faith, of a timely and sufficient affidavit of personal bias or other grounds for disqualification of a presiding or participating person, the presiding person, persons or Hearing Committee will consider and decide the matters raised as a part of the record and decision in the case.

5. The Hearing Committee or any person or persons presiding at any pre-hearing proceedings, the reception of evidence and any review or appeal of a decision shall prepare a written record of the proceedings which shall include the evidence considered in the proceeding, each finding of fact based on the evidence, the conclusions and decisions regarding alleged rule violations and a statement of penalties, if any, imposed and of other relief granted or denied. This written record constitutes the official record and decision of the Hearing Committee, or any presiding person or persons, and all decisions, including initial recommended and final decisions are a part of the official record. In order to expedite the issuance of a written ruling or rulings the written record may be issued in abbreviated form in the discretion of the presiding person(s), but in such event the presiding person(s) shall retain the option of replacing the abbreviated ruling with a complete written record at any time, and shall do so if requested in writing by a party to the matter or by the Federation Board of Directors. The written record shall be issued within 10 business days of the hearing of a grievance or other matter heard pursuant to GR611.2(i) or (ii) and may be issued in abbreviated form.

6. Opening and closing statements may be made by the parties to the protest, charge or grievance or their representative, but the Hearing Committee reserves the right to limit the length of such statements.

7. The Federation will not require a verbatim stenographic transcript of the hearing to be made, but parties to the hearing may arrange for one through the Federation in advance of the hearing and one will be ordered for them and the Federation at the expense of the party or parties requesting the transcript. If a transcript is ordered, it becomes part of the official record of the proceeding, cannot be canceled after the hearing is held, and must be paid for by the requesting party or parties. If the Federation itself requests and arranges for the transcript, copies will be provided

to the respondent(s) by the Federation only upon payment by the respondent(s) to the Federation of one-half (1/2) the cost to the Federation of the transcript. If another party requests the transcript, a copy will be provided to Federation upon payment by Federation of one-half (1/2) the cost to the party of the transcript.

8. Upon the consent of the parties to a protest, charge or grievance, the co-Chairs of the Hearing Committee may direct that the matter be summarily heard and decided on an expedited basis upon such notice acceptable to the parties as time and circumstances allow for justice to be done. Even absent the consent of the parties, the co-Chairs of the Hearing Committee may in their discretion direct that a hearing of any grievance heard pursuant to either GR602.8 or GR605 of the Rules shall be expedited whenever in their opinion by majority vote it is necessary to expedite the matter in order to resolve it and produce a sufficiently early decision to do justice to the affected parties. Upon the request of an athlete or other party that it is necessary to expedite such hearing in order to resolve a matter relating to a competition which is so scheduled that compliance with regular procedures would not be likely to produce a sufficiently early decision to do justice to the affected parties, the hearing shall be so expedited to be concluded prior to the competition. The hearing may be conducted at the site of athletic competition or by telephone conference if necessary. The notice of hearing may be oral, or in writing, and shall in every instance contain the following: the party filing the charge, protest or grievance; any other party involved; identification of the person or persons subject to the charge, protest or grievance; the Federation bylaw or rule allegedly violated or about to be violated; a concise statement of facts surrounding the alleged violation; and the action that the party filing the charge, protest or grievance wants taken. The decision of the hearing panel may be rendered orally, shall be final and may be made effective immediately, but shall be reduced to writing at the earliest possible time, shall include findings of fact and conclusions based upon such findings, and shall be promptly provided to all of the parties involved.

9. Whether or not the same are specifically provided for elsewhere in the Rules, in all hearings conducted pursuant to GR611.2(i) or (ii), above, the parties shall be accorded:

   a. Notice of the specific charges or alleged violations in writing, and possible consequences if the charges are found to be true;

   b. Reasonable time between receipt of the notice of charges and the hearing within which to prepare a defense;

   c. The right to have the hearing conducted at such a time so as to make it practicable for the person charged to attend;

   d. A hearing before a disinterested and impartial body of fact finders wherein the proponent of the charge must substantiate the charge by a preponderance of the evidence;

   e. The right to be assisted in the presentation of one's case at the hearing, including the assistance of legal counsel, if desired;

   f. The right to call witnesses and present oral and written evidence and argument; The right to confront and cross-examine adverse witnesses, including the right to be provided the identity of witnesses in advance of the hearing;

   g. The right to have a record made of the hearing if desired;

   h. A written decision, with reasons therefor, based solely on the evidence of record, handed down in a timely fashion;

   i. Written notice of appeal or review pursuant to GR612 procedures, where applicable, if the decision is adverse to the person charged, and prompt and fair adjudication of the appeal or review.

Subchapter 6-D POST HEARING PROCEDURES

GR612 Review of Decisions

1. By the Hearing Committee
   a. A respondent, protester or charging party who wishes to request a review of the Hearing Committee's original decision must make such request in writing, setting forth the reasons why a review is sought. Said request must be accompanied by a fee of $500, which fee is not refundable except in the discretion of the Hearing Committee. Said request and fee must be received within 30 days from the issuance of the ruling being reviewed.
2. Appeal of decisions made by other than the Hearing Committee
   a. When the presiding person, persons or Show Committee other than the Hearing Committee makes an initial decision, that decision then becomes the decision of the Federation without further proceedings, unless there is a written appeal to the Hearing Committee for review by a party to the proceeding or by the Federation, which must be received within thirty (30) days from the issuance of the ruling being reviewed. On appeal from the initial decision, the Hearing Committee will not review findings of fact; but will determine whether the rules were properly interpreted and applied.

GR613 Rehearing

Upon the discovery of new facts not discoverable by due diligence prior to a hearing, a party may request a hearing before the Hearing Committee. Such request must be in writing and must contain a statement of the new facts upon which it is based and must be accompanied by a fee of $250, which fee is not refundable except in the discretion of the Hearing Committee. Said request and fee must be received by the Federation within 30 days from the issuance of the ruling which is being contested. Rehearings will not be granted as a matter of right but are at the discretion of the Hearing Committee.

GR614 Notification

1. When a decision has been reached regarding a charge or protest heard by the Hearing Committee the Federation shall send out the findings within 60 days of the decision, including references to GR704, as applicable. Where findings cannot be issued within 60 days of the decision, the Federation shall send written notification to all concerned parties that the findings are not yet available and when the findings are expected to be released.
2. The Federation will publish on the Federation's web site a notice of every penalty assessed against any person, horse or Licensed Competition and the period of any suspension. Any Licensed Competition which allows a suspended or expelled person or horse to participate is itself liable to penalty, including suspension or expulsion.
3. The Federation may report disciplinary action taken by the Federation to another association if in its opinion reporting is advisable for the protection of mutual interests.

GR615 Reciprocity

1. On receipt of notice that disciplinary action has been taken by an administrative agency, arbitration or other tribunal body, humane society or court of law, whether civil, criminal, arbitral or administrative, against a person, a National Officer of the Federation or the CEO of the Federation or his designee may make a charge against the person under the provisions of Chapter 6 and following a hearing, the Hearing Committee may impose any penalty provided for in Chapter 7.
2. On receipt of notice that USADA or WADA has taken disciplinary action and has applied penalties in accordance with FEI General Regulations against a person subject to Federation rules, with notice to the affected parties but without further proceedings, the Federation shall impose any sanction resulting from the adjudication process in accordance with USADA or WADA protocols, as applicable.
3. Upon receipt of notice that a court of law has entered a judgment or final order against a person, corporation,

partnership or other entity for monies owing to a Federation Senior Active or Life Member related to equestrian activities (e.g. training fees, coaching fees, stabling fees, horse board, horse transport, veterinary fees) and in connection with Licensed Competition, which order or judgment is final and not subject to further appeal, a National Officer or the CEO of the Federation or his designee may make a charge against such person or entity under the provisions of Chapter 6, and following a hearing, the Hearing Committee may suspend such person or entity pursuant to Chapter 7, GR703.1.b and .c and/or Chapter 7, GR707.1b but any such suspension shall not extend beyond the time that such judgment or order is satisfied of record in said court of law and may be for shorter period of time in the discretion of the Hearing Committee.

4. On receipt of notice that the Federation Equestrian Internationale (FEI) has imposed penalties in accordance with FEI General Regulations against a person subject to Federation rules, with notice to the affected parties but without further proceedings, the Federation shall recognize and enforce the sanction.

5. Following a hearing, The Federation's Hearing Committee may deny or suspend the privilege to participate in or go upon the grounds of Licensed Competitions, and/or deny, expel or suspend the privileges or membership in the Federation to any person, whether or not a member of the Federation, whom an indictment, information or charge has asserted, or whom any civil, criminal or administrative court or arbitration or other tribunal has found, to have committed or participated in any plan or conspiracy to commit any act of cruelty or abuse to a horse, whether or not any such alleged or actual act, plan, or conspiracy occurred on the grounds of a Licensed Competition, or was in conjunction with, or was an element of some other offense, actual or alleged. For purposes of this subsection, cruelty and abuse shall include, but shall not be limited to, any of the acts enumerated in GR839.4, and, in addition, killing, crippling, abandoning, mistreating, neglecting, or any other form of abuse of a horse.

Subchapter 6-E ADMINISTRATIVE PENALTIES AND PLEA AGREEMENTS

GR616 Administrative Penalties

1. Administrative Penalties for violations of Chapter 4 (Drugs and Medications) will be handled pursuant to Chapter 4, GR412. For violations of any other rules, the procedures outlined below will be utilized.

2. In the event of an apparent rule violation, other than one involving Chapter 4, which is brought to the attention of the Federation and where no protest or charge has been filed, the Federation may hold in abeyance the issuance of charges of rule violation pending further determination by the Federation CEO or his designee.

3. After investigating the situation, the CEO or his designee shall make a determination in his or her discretion whether to issue charges of rule violation, impose administrative penalties, issue a warning or take no further action in the matter.

4. In the event the CEO or his designee determines to impose administrative penalties in lieu of the issuance of charges of rule violation, he or she shall be authorized to impose any or all of the penalties enumerated in Chapter 7, GR703 and/or Chapter 7, GR707, setting forth the terms and conditions for compliance. The parties offered the administrative penalty shall, after written notice, be subject to any and all administrative penalties imposed by the CEO or his designee, unless a timely written request for a hearing is made pursuant to the provisions of GR616.6.

5. The Federation shall give written notification to the accused of administrative penalties determined pursuant to GR616.4, the terms and conditions of which shall not be subject to negotiation. An administrative penalty must be approved by the Hearing Committee Co-Chairs before it is offered to the Respondent(s). Once accepted by all parties and by the Hearing Committee, an administrative penalty shall have the same force and effect as would a finding of rule violation by the Hearing Committee following a hearing and will be published on the Federation's web site. In the event that the Hearing Committee does not approve an accepted administrative penalty, written notification of same will be sent to the accused and shall constitute a timely written request for a hearing pursuant to GR616.6.

6. Any accused person who receives notice of an administrative penalty under GR616.5 may request a hearing before the Hearing Committee. A written request for a hearing must be actually received in the Federation office within 30 days of the date of receipt by the accused of the notice of administrative penalty(ies), after which time the right to a hearing shall be deemed to have been permanently waived. Once accepted by the accused and approved by the Hearing Committee, administrative penalties shall be effective immediately, shall be final, and shall not be subject to further review under any circumstance(s).

7. In the event a timely written request for a hearing is received in accordance with GR616.6, the Federation shall issue written charges pursuant to GR602 and GR604 and the Hearing Committee shall conduct a hearing upon said charge(s). In the event of a finding of a violation, the Hearing Committee shall not be limited in choice of penalties to those that might have been imposed in accordance with GR616.4, nor in any such instance shall the Hearing Committee be limited in any other way in exercising all of its prerogatives as set forth in the Bylaws and Rules.

8. An offer of an administrative penalty will not preclude the filing of charges by a party other than the CEO or his designee pursuant to GR602 and GR604. Such a charge, however, must be received by the Federation before the administrative penalty is approved by the Hearing Committee. In the event such a charge is filed and in the event the CEO or his designee is subsequently unable to adjust the matter pursuant to GR617 to the satisfaction of the charging party and the accused, then the offer of administrative penalty shall be nullified and the matter shall proceed to hearing.

GR617 Plea Agreements

1. The provisions of this Rule will apply to violations of Chapter 4 (Drugs and Medications) as well as violations of any other rules.

2. The Federation CEO or his designee may investigate any pending protest or charge and attempt to settle the matter in lieu of having it proceed to hearing.

3. After investigating the situation, the CEO or his designee shall make a determination in his or her discretion whether to offer a plea agreement, direct that the matter proceed to hearing, or recommend dismissal of the protest or charge.

4. In the event the CEO or his designee determines to offer a plea agreement, he or she shall be authorized to offer any or all of the penalties enumerated in Chapter 7, GR703, setting forth the terms and conditions for compliance. The parties offered the plea agreement shall, after written notice, be subject to any and all penalties imposed by the CEO or his designee, unless a timely written request for a hearing is made pursuant to the provisions of GR617.6 or unless the maker of the protest or charge challenges the plea agreement pursuant to GR617.8.

5. The Federation shall give written notification to the accused and to the maker of the protest or charge of an offer of a plea agreement determined pursuant to GR617.4, the terms and conditions of which shall not be subject to negotiation. Plea agreements accepted by both the accused and the maker of the protest or charge in accordance with this Rule are subject to approval by the Hearing Committee and in the case of an allegation of a violation of Chapter 4, to approval by the Chairman of the Federation Equine Drugs and Medications Committee. Once accepted by all parties and by the Hearing Committee, a plea agreement shall have the same force and effect as would a finding of rule violation by the Hearing Committee following a hearing and will be published on the Federation's web site. In the event that the Hearing Committee does not approve an accepted plea agreement, written notification of same will be sent to the accused and to the maker of the protest or charge and shall constitute a timely written request for a hearing pursuant to GR617.6.

6. Any accused person or maker of a protest or charge who receives notice of a proposed plea agreement under GR616.5 may request a hearing before the Hearing Committee. A written request for a hearing must be actually received in the Federation office within 30 days of the date of receipt by the parties of the notice of the offer of a plea agreement, after which time the right to a hearing shall be deemed to have been permanently waived. Once

accepted by the parties and approved by the Hearing Committee, plea agreements shall be effective immediately, shall be final, and shall not be subject to further review under any circumstance(s).

7. In the event a timely written request for a hearing is received from the accused in accordance with GR617.6, the Federation shall schedule the matter for hearing and the Hearing Committee shall conduct a hearing upon said protest or charge. In the event of a finding of a violation, the Hearing Committee shall not be limited in choice of penalties to those that might have been imposed in accordance with GR617.4, nor in any such instance shall the Hearing Committee be limited in any other way in exercising all of its prerogatives as set forth in the Bylaws and Rules.

8. If the accused accepts the offer of the plea agreement and the maker of the protest or charge does not, said person(s) can request a hearing before the Hearing Committee upon submission of a written request, and in the case of a protest, upon payment of a $250 fee (which is not refundable), and the matter shall proceed to hearing.

9. If after investigation of a protest or charge, it is the recommendation of the CEO or his designee that the matter should be dismissed, he or she will notify the maker of the protest or charge and the accused. If the maker of the protest or charge does not agree, said person(s) can request a hearing before the Hearing Committee upon submission of a written request and in the case of a protest, upon payment of a $500 fee (which will be refunded in the event the protest or charge is upheld) and the matter shall proceed to hearing.

CHAPTER 7 VIOLATIONS AND PENALTIES

SUBCHAPTER 7-A INDIVIDUALS

SUBCHAPTER 7-B LICENSED COMPETITIONS

CHAPTER 7 VIOLATIONS AND PENALTIES

SUBCHAPTER 7-A INDIVIDUALS

GR701 General

The provisions of this rule apply in connection with any Licensed Competition to the following persons: owner, exhibitor, agent, trainer, manager, rider, driver, handler, competition official, competition staff (see GR112 and GR113), a veterinarian who, while on the competition grounds, prescribes, dispenses, or administers a forbidden substance to a horse and member of the family of the above, a member of the Federation or any person who acts in a manner in violation of the rules of the Federation or deemed prejudicial to the best interests of the sport and the Federation. Any act in connection with a Licensed Competition in violation of the Rules by a member of the family of a person participating in the competition who is described in the previous sentence, may be deemed to have been committed by such person and subject him or her to penalties.

GR702 Violations

1. A violation is any act prejudicial to the best interests of the Federation, including but not limited to the following:
   a. Violation of the rules of the Federation.
   b. Disqualification by a Licensed Competition.
   c. Penalization by an administrative agency, humane society or court of law for violation of Federation rules.
   d. Acting or inciting or permitting any other to act in a manner contrary to the rules of the Federation, or in a manner deemed improper, unethical, dishonest, unsportsmanlike or intemperate, or prejudicial to the best interests of the sport and the Federation.
   e. Any act committed or remark made in connection with the competition considered offensive and/or made with the intent to influence or cast aspersions on the character or integrity of the licensed officials, approaching a judge before or after a decision without first obtaining permission from the show committee or steward/technical delegate, inspecting a judge's card without the judge's permission, or public verbal abuse of competition officials.
   f. Physical assault upon a person and/or cruelty to a horse as defined in GR839.
   g. Failure to obey any penalty imposed by the Federation.
   h. Exhibiting any horse while in the care, training or custody of a suspended trainer.
   i. Riding, exhibiting, coaching or training for the benefit, credit, reputation or satisfaction of a suspended person.
   j. Failure to pay indebtedness to the Federation or indebtedness for hearing transcripts or other hearing expenses arranged through the Federation.
   k. Participating in any manner at a licensed competition while not in good standing or competing horses not in good standing at a licensed competition. (See GR136)
   l. Prescribing, dispensing, or administering a drug by a veterinarian which results in a finding of a forbidden substance. In the event a positive report is received by the Federation for a horse or pony to which a forbidden substance has been administered in any manner and the veterinarian is identified in any manner as the source of said forbidden substance, said violation will be addressed pursuant to GR412.
   m. Any action which is subject to Reciprocity by the Federation under GR615.
   n. Violation of any of the policies included in the Safe Sport Policy Handbook found at safesport.usef.org.

GR703 Penalties

1. If found guilty, the accused will be subject to such penalty as the Hearing Committee, or other individuals with authority to assess penalties may determine, including but not limited to the following. The penalties set forth below will be published on the Federation's web site.
   a. CENSURE. A vote of Censure will be listed under the defendant's name in the Secretary's Record of Penalties.

If found guilty of a further violation the defendant will be subject to a heavier penalty than for a first offense.

b. SUSPENSION of such person for any period from showing or having others show, exhibit or train for him or her.

1. A suspended person is forbidden for the time specified in the decision from the privilege of taking any part whatsoever in any Competition licensed or endorsed by the Federation and is excluded from all competition grounds during Competitions licensed or endorsed by the Federation, as an exhibitor, participant or spectator.

2. In addition, a suspended person is forbidden from participating in all Federation affairs and activities, to hold or exercise office in the Federation or in any Competition licensed or endorsed by the Federation, to attend, observe or participate in any event, forum, meeting, program, clinic, task force, or committee of the Federation, sponsored by or conducted by the Federation, or held in connection with the Federation and any of its activities.

   a. Not withstanding the above, a Director may be removed from the Board of Directors only in accordance with the applicable provisions of the Bylaws.

   b. If the Hearing Committee deems it appropriate, it may send its findings concerning a Director to the Board for its consideration.

3. Where practical and appropriate in the opinion of the Hearing Committee, suspension may include the comparable dates during which the violation occurred.

c. SUSPENSION for any period of the horse or horses, owned by him or her, or shown in any name or for his, her, or their credit or reputation, whether such interest was held at the time of the alleged violation or acquired thereafter. The Board of Directors or the Hearing Committee may at a later date remove the suspension of said horse or horses if it is demonstrated to their satisfaction that a sale or transfer thereof was made by such person, partnership, or corporation in such as to be a bona fide transaction and not with the intention of relieving the suspended owner of penalty. See GR139.

d. SUSPENSION for any period of any volunteer or any employed person who rides or exhibits for the benefit, credit, reputation or satisfaction of another suspended person.

e. EXPULSION from all Licensed Competitions.

f. EXPULSION or SUSPENSION from membership in the Federation.

g. FORFEITURE of trophies, ribbons, prize money, and/or sweepstakes won in connection with the offense committed, which will be redistributed accordingly and payment of a fee of $300 to the competition in question. Federation points may be nullified and redistributed at the discretion of the Hearing Committee.

h. SUSPENSION from office as steward, technical delegate, judge, course designer or competition official.

i. REVOCATION of judge's, steward's, technical delegate's or course designer's license.

j. FINE.

2. Federation Affiliated Associations must honor all Federation penalties. See GR204.

GR704 Regulations as to Suspended Persons

1. The purpose of this Rule shall be to prevent the avoidance by suspended exhibitors, trainers, coaches and other persons of the terms and conditions of their suspensions, or the penalties intended by the Hearing Committee as appurtenant to such suspensions. This Rule shall apply to the spouse of a suspended person as well as to any other persons or entities, including, without limitation, companions, family members, employers, employees, agents, partnerships, partners, corporations or other entities, whose relationship, whether financial or otherwise, with a suspended person would give the appearance that such other persons are riding, exhibiting, coaching or training for the benefit, credit, reputation or satisfaction of the suspended person.

2. No suspended person's spouse or companion shall assume any of the suspended person's responsibilities whatsoever at Federation competitions during the term of said suspension. Companion shall be defined as any person who co-habits with, or otherwise shares living accommodations with, a suspended person.

3. No suspended person's spouse or companion may fill out any entry blanks for any of the suspended person's customers for Federation competitions during the term of the suspended person's suspension, or pay or advance entry fees on behalf of customers for Federation competitions during said period.

4. Any person who assumes the responsibility for the care, custody or control of an unsuspended horse completely or in part owned, leased, trained by or coached by a suspended person, must not:

   a. Be paid a salary directly or indirectly by or on behalf of the suspended person; or

   b. Receive a bonus or any other form of compensation in cash, property or other remuneration or consideration such as to make up for any such lost salary; or

   c. Make any payments of any kind, or give any remuneration or other compensation or consideration, to the suspended person, his/her spouse or companion, any corporation, partnership or other entity owned or controlled by said suspended person or to any other person for transfer to any of said individuals or entities for the right to ride, exhibit, coach or train for the suspended person or any of the suspended person's customers during Federation Licensed Competitions; or

   d. Use the farm or individual name of the suspended person.

5. An individual who takes over the horses of a suspended trainer or coach must:

   a. Bill customers directly on his/her own bill forms for any services rendered at or in connection with any Federation Licensed Competitions;

   b. Maintain a personal checking account totally separate from and independent of that of the suspended person for purposes of paying all expenses of and depositing all income from customers;

   c. Pay all his/her employees working at Federation competitions, none of whom may be employees, directly or indirectly, of the suspended person;

   d. Keep checks, books, employee records and make withholding of taxes and other regular deductions from his/her employees' paychecks;

   e. Pay all feed bills, motel, van bills, travel expenses, etc. from his/her separate and independent checking account and preserve, for six months after the date that said suspension is terminated, invoices for said bills;

   f. If such individual makes use of any equipment of a suspended trainer, the use of said equipment must be enumerated in detail in a written lease, the form and substance of which must be satisfactory to counsel for the Federation and shall be at the fair rental value for said equipment and said price must be included in said agreement;

   g. File such federal and state tax returns as will reflect as his or her income the income from said training or coaching responsibilities at Federation Licensed Competitions;

   h. Not borrow funds from a suspended trainer or coach, his/her spouse or companion, their families, corporations, partnerships or any other entities owned or controlled by said suspended trainer or to any other person for the purpose of going into business for himself or herself at Federation Licensed Competitions during the period of said suspension, nor will he/she allow any of the above-named parties or entities to sign or guarantee any notes or any type of loans to enable him or her to go into business as described above.

6. Suspended trainers and coaches, and individuals taking over the horses or customers of a suspended trainer or coach may be requested to make their books, canceled checks, invoices, tax returns and other evidence available to Federation representatives to verify and affirm the details of any relationship between them and suspended trainer or coach.

7. This Rule is intended to provide guidance for suspended persons and anyone contemplating taking over the responsibility for the riding, exhibiting, coaching, or training, of an unsuspended horse from a suspended person. It is not intended to anticipate every potential circumstance in which the intent of a suspension may be frustrated, and the Hearing Committee shall have the power to determine whether the facts and circumstances peculiar to any particular case compel a finding that there was or is a violation of the rules prohibiting exhibiting any horse while in

the care, training or custody of a suspended trainer, or riding, exhibiting, coaching or training for the benefit, credit, reputation or satisfaction of a suspended person (see GR702.1h and .i).

SUBCHAPTER 7-B LICENSED COMPETITIONS

GR705 General

The provisions of this Chapter apply to all Regular Competitions, Local Competitions, Eventing Competitions, Dressage, Driving, Endurance and Vaulting Competitions.

GR706 Violations

1. Any competition licensed or endorsed by the Federation is subject to penalty by the Hearing Committee or other individuals with authority to assess penalties for violation of the rules. Violations include, but are not limited to, the following. All penalties will be published on the Federation's web site.

    a. Failure to conduct a competition in accordance with the Federation rules.

    b. Failure to pay its indebtedness to the Federation.

    c. Failure to pay premiums and other indebtedness within 30 days.

    d. Failure to report the disqualification of a person at the competition.

    e. Failure to honor written contracts with judges, stewards or other competition officials and employees.

    f. Failure to furnish the Federation with entry blanks, judge's cards, class sheets or any other documents it may request in connection with the competition.

    g. The use of judges not licensed in those divisions covered by Federation rules if due notice has been received from the Federation.

    h. The use of judges in divisions in which they have not been enrolled without obtaining in advance the required Special or Guest judge's card.

    i. The use of stewards, technical delegates, or where required, course designers who are not Federation licensed if due notice has been received from the Federation.

    j. The listing of a judge, steward, technical delegate or course designer in the prize list or catalogue before the invitation to serve has been accepted in writing by such licensed official.

    k. Permitting individuals, entities or horses that were placed on suspension at least seven days prior to the competition start date to be on the grounds and/or to participate in any manner.

    l. Permitting acts which are improper, intemperate, dishonest, unsportsmanlike or contrary to the rules of the Federation, or prejudicial to the best interests of the sport and the Federation.

    m. Acting in a manner prejudicial to the best interests of the sport and the Federation.

    n. Assessing and/or collecting a drug enforcement fee in excess of, or in addition to, that specified and required by GR407.1 of these rules, unless said assessment is approved in writing by the Federation in advance, and then only under the terms and conditions set forth.

    o. Withholding from the Federation any or all of the drug fees collected in accordance with GR407.1, for any purpose, including to defray the expenses incurred providing stalls, passes, and other items to the Federation drug testing personnel, as required by GR407.4 and .5.

    p. Using the name or title of a championship that has not been assigned to that Licensed Competition during the same competition year.

GR707 Penalties

1. A Licensed Competition found guilty of a violation will be subject to penalty including but not limited to the following:

    a. CENSURE. A vote of Censure will be listed under the defendant's name in the Secretary's Record of Penalties. If found guilty of a further violation, the defendant will be liable to a heavier penalty than for a first offense.

    b. SUSPENSION for any period from the list of Licensed Competitions.

    c. EXPULSION from membership in the Federation.

    d. FINE.

CHAPTER 8 CONDUCT OF LICENSED COMPETITIONS

SUBCHAPTER 8-A ATTIRE AND EQUIPMENT

SUBCHAPTER 8-B COMPETITION AWARDS, HONORS, AND PRIZES

SUBCHAPTER 8-C COMPETITION AND CLASS CONDITIONS AND ELIGIBILITY

SUBCHAPTER 8-D SCHEDULING DURING COMPETITION

SUBCHAPTER 8-E SCHOOLING

GR834 General

GR835 Designated Areas

GR836 Trail

GR837 Hunter

GR838 Jumper (See also JP103 and Appendix A)

SUBCHAPTER 8-F WELFARE OF THE HORSE

GR839 Cruelty to and Abuse of a Horse

GR840 Attention Getting Devices

GR841 Soundness

GR842 Falls

GR843 Mandatory Reporting and Cooperation of Horse/Pony Collapse

GR844 Poling

GR845 Equine Vaccination Rule

CHAPTER 8 CONDUCT OF LICENSED COMPETITIONS

SUBCHAPTER 8-A ATTIRE AND EQUIPMENT

GR801 Dress

1. It is the tradition of the competition ring that riders and drivers be correctly attired for the class in question, that attendants be neatly dressed and horses be properly presented.

2. It is compulsory for all persons at Federation licensed hunter, jumper or hunter/jumper competitions when mounted anywhere on the competition grounds, to wear properly fastened protective headgear which meets or exceeds ASTM (American Society for Testing and Materials)/SEI (Safety Equipment Institute) standards for equestrian use and carries the SEI tag. It must be properly fitted with harness secured. Exception: In Hunter or Jumper classes, adults may be allowed to remove their headgear while accepting prizes and during the playing of the National Anthem only; they must refasten their headgear prior to the lap of honor. It is compulsory for riders in Paso Fino classes, both open and breed restricted including Hunter Hack, where jumping is required and when jumping anywhere on the competition grounds to wear properly fastened protective headgear which meets or exceeds ASTM (American Society for Testing and Materials)/SEI (Safety Equipment Institute) standards for equestrian use and carries the SEI tag. It must be properly fitted with harness secured. A Show Committee must bar riders without protective headgear from entering the ring for classes in which protective headgear is required and may bar any entry or person from entering the ring if not suitably presented to appear before an audience.

3. Except as may otherwise be mandated by local law, all sub-junior exhibitors in the Paso Fino division, while riding or driving or while in the driving cart anywhere on the competition grounds, must wear properly fitting protective headgear which meets or exceeds ASTM (American Society for Testing and Materials)/SEI (Safety Equipment Institute) standards for equestrian use and carries the SEI tag. Harness must be secured and properly fitted. Any rider violating this rule at any time must immediately be prohibited from further riding until such headgear is properly in place. For all exhibitors competing in the hunter, jumper, or hunter seat equitation section, if a rider's chin strap becomes unfastened, the rider may stop, re-fasten the chin strap and continue his/her round without penalty or elimination. A judge may, but is not required to stop a rider and ask them to refasten a chin strap which has become unfastened, again without penalty to the rider. Members of the Armed Services or the Police may wear the Service Dress Uniform.

4. Any exhibitor may wear protective headgear (ASTM/SEI) and/or a protective vest either body protecting or inflatable, specifically designed for use in equestrian sport in any division or class without penalty from the judge. The Federation recommends that the vest pass or surpass the current ASTM standard F1937 or be certified by the Safety Equipment Institute. For Eventing, inflatable vests are permitted only when worn over a body protecting vest.

5. See DC928 for protective headgear requirement in Combined Driving.

6. See DR120 for protective headgear requirement in Dressage.

7. Except as may otherwise be mandated by local law, the Federation strongly encourages all riders, while riding anywhere on the competition grounds, to wear protective headgear with harness secured which passes or surpasses ASTM (American Society for Testing and Materials)/SEI (Safety Equipment Institute) standards for equestrian use and carries the SEI tag. (Exception hunter, jumper, or hunter/jumper competitions refer to GR801.2) It is the responsibility of the rider, or the parent or guardian or trainer of the junior exhibitor to see to it that the headgear worn complies with appropriate safety standards for protective headgear intended for equestrian use, and is properly fitted and in good condition, and the Federation, Show Committee, and Licensed Officials are not responsible for checking headgear worn for such compliance.

8. The Federation makes no representation or warranty, express or implied, about any protective headgear, and cautions riders that death or serious injury may result despite wearing such headgear as all equestrian sports involve

inherent dangerous risk and as no helmet can protect against all foreseeable injuries.

9. Boots/shoes worn while riding anywhere on the competition grounds must have a distinguishable heel. (Exception: Arabian, Hackney Pony, Morgan, National Show Horse, Parade, Roadster, American Saddlebred, and Saddle Seat Equitation).

10. Competitors must display the correct number which must be clearly visible while performing in any class unless otherwise stated in the prize list. Competitors may be penalized at the discretion of the judge. Numbers to be supplied by management in compliance with GR1213.11. Refer to DR121.11 (Dressage) and DR207.8 (Dressage Sport Horse Breeding).

11. Refer to EQ105.1& 2 and HU125.

GR802 Artificial Markings and Appliances

1. Any change of color or markings other than mane, tail or hoof is prohibited. (Exception: Arabian and Half/Anglo Arabian halter, see AR106; Reining Division; Friesian Division; Paso Fino, see PF101.5-.6). Only clear grooming materials are allowed on the hide and hair. Materials may be used to remove stains.

2. All artificial appliances other than those permitted in division rules are prohibited (Exception: Reining and Jumper Divisions). Bandages, tailsets, chains or other training devices are prohibited in the ring in Breeding/Halter classes.

GR803 Use of Whips

No item may be used inside or outside the ring while showing a horse except one whip per handler. If whips are allowed, they must be no longer than 6' including the snapper or lash. No appendages of any kind are permitted. One lungeing whip is permitted only when lungeing. Some breed and/or disciplines may have use of whip division rules that depart from this rule and as such, the division rule governs. (GR150.1)

GR804 Shoeing Regulations

1. In some parts of the country, it is common practice to show unshod horses in certain classes. A horse cannot be barred from the ring because of being unshod but, in classes in which it is common practice for all horses to be shod, a barefoot horse may be penalized at the judge's discretion.

2. Competitions offering classes in a division that designates a maximum weight for shoes (Morgan, Paso Fino, Welsh) must provide accurate scales for weighing. If any horse casts a shoe in any of these classes, the shoe, including pad if used, but not including nails must be immediately weighed by the judge. In these classes, a competitor may not be excused from the ring until the judge is satisfied that the horse has not cast a shoe. Refer to GR109.2.

3. If the weight of a shoe and pad is protested, the owner may either withdraw the entry and forfeit all entry fees and winnings of the protested entry for the entire competition, in which event the protest must be withdrawn and the fee refunded or, have the shoe and pad removed in the presence of the competition veterinarian and steward so it can be weighed immediately.

4. Whether cast or removed, if the shoe including pad exceeds the weight limit, the entry must be disqualified for the balance of the competition and all entry fees and winnings of the entry for the entire competition will be forfeited. Removal and replacement of any protested shoe and pad is the sole responsibility of the owner of the entry; however, if the protest is not upheld, the protestor must pay $15 to defray the cost of removal and replacement of the shoe.

5. See AR106 for Arabian shoeing regulations.

SUBCHAPTER 8-B COMPETITION AWARDS, HONORS, AND PRIZES

GR805 Challenge Trophies

1. A Challenge Trophy is a trophy donated to or offered by a competition which must be won a specified number of

times under specified conditions. When originally placed in competition, it becomes the property of the Show Committee and cannot be withdrawn by the donor.

2. The conditions of the Challenge Trophy may not be changed without the consent of the trophy donor or his legal representative and of all who have qualified as potential winners of the trophy, except in the event that the conditions stipulated are in conflict with the current rules of the Federation. In such an event, the Show Committee must confer with the Federation as to procedure.

3. The winner of a leg on a Challenge Trophy in competition is entitled to possession of such trophy for a period of 10 months from date of winning unless a competition stipulates that the trophy will remain in its possession. The winner is responsible for protection and care of the trophy while in his possession. At the expiration of 10 months, or two months prior to the next annual competition, the competition may demand return of trophy if it has not been won outright. Failure of an exhibitor to return the trophy constitutes a violation under Chapter 7 and renders the exhibitor subject to penalty.

4. If a Challenge Trophy is competed for at more than one competition per year, the committee may elect to keep the trophy in its possession.

5. If a Challenge Trophy is destroyed, stolen or lost and therefore cannot be returned, the exhibitor who had possession of the trophy must pay to the competition the cost of replacing it with a trophy equally suitable and satisfactory to the Show Committee. The exhibitor will be exempt from penalty if the trophy is replaced before the next competition.

6. Should a competition or class be discontinued or not held for any period of time, any unretired Challenge Trophies offered at such competition must be returned at the expiration date of ten months to the last active Show Committee. This committee will determine the disposition of such trophies but they may not be placed in competition at any competition unless the provisions of paragraph 2 are met.

7. In the event of the death of an exhibitor who has won one or more legs on a Challenge Trophy, a member of that exhibitor's family may include such previous winnings in any further competitions for such Challenge Trophy in which they may engage.

8. If a Challenge Trophy is competed for and won under a farm name and the farm is later sold to another person who retains the farm name, legs won on the trophy by the first owner will not be counted by the subsequent owner of the farm in his competition.

GR806 Perpetual Trophies

A Perpetual Trophy is a trophy donated to or offered by a competition which is never awarded permanently to an exhibitor but remains the property of and in the possession of a competition. The Show Committee may present a replica or souvenir trophy to the annual winner. The conditions of a Perpetual Trophy are identical with those of a Challenge Trophy. Exception: previous winners need not be consulted when and if specifications are changed.

GR807 Prize Ribbons

1. At all Licensed Competitions, the prize ribbons are to be the following colors:

Grand Champion	Blue, Red, Yellow and White
Reserve to Grand Champion	Red, Yellow, White and Pink
Champion	Blue, Red and Yellow
Reserve Champion	Red, Yellow and White
First Prize Blue	Sixth Prize Green
Second Prize Red	Seventh Prize Purple
Third Prize Yellow	Eighth Prize Brown
Fourth Prize White	Ninth Prize Gray
Fifth Prize Pink	Tenth Prize Light Blue

2. It is recommended that competitions offer one ribbon for every six entries. (Exception: It is required that competitions offer at least the number of ribbons to match the minimum USEF Horse of the Year Awards point placings for the American Saddlebred, Roadster and Hackney divisions).

3. A Licensed Competition located outside the United States may conform to the practice of the country in which it is situated with respect to the color of the ribbons used.

GR808 Awarding Championships

1. Championship classes for a specific height or sex may be offered in any division as set forth in the respective division rules. Judging specifications must follow those of the Open Championship class.

2. In the Hunter divisions, Championships must be awarded on points. In the Morgan and Welsh Pony divisions, Championships may be awarded on points or held as performance classes. (See JP110.2 for Jumper Championships)

3. When Championships are awarded on points, all competitors must be given an equal opportunity to obtain points. In all other divisions, Championships must be awarded in a Championship Performance class and all entries must be given an opportunity to qualify.

4. Only the first four ribbons in each class are counted regardless of the number offered. Ribbons have the same point value even if less than the specified four places are awarded due to lack of entries, etc. Exception: See JP110.2 for Jumper Championships.

5. Point Value:

Blue ribbon	5 points	Yellow ribbon	2 points
Red ribbon	3 points	White ribbon	1 points

6. In Hunter sections only the first six ribbons in each class are counted regardless of the number offered. Ribbons have the same value even if less than the specified six places are awarded due to lack of entries. First Place...10 points, Second Place...6 points, Third Place...4 points, Fourth Place...2 points, Fifth Place...1 point, Sixth Place...1/2 point.

GR809 Performance Championships

1. A Show Committee must designate all qualifying classes and can require any or all winners in a qualifying class at that competition to compete in a Performance Championship class provided this is stated in the prize list and the gaits required are the same as in the qualifying class. Any exhibitor failing to comply must forfeit all prize money in the qualifying class. If an exhibitor or trainer qualifies more than one horse for a Championship class he can elect to show only one. (This does not apply to Regional and National Breed Affiliate approved Competitions.)

2. To be eligible to show in a Performance Championship class a horse must have been properly entered, shown and judged in one qualifying class at that competition in the same division or section. (This does not apply to Regional and National Breed Affiliate approved Competitions.)

3. An entry which while performing in a qualifying class fails to qualify by reasons of equipment repair, shoeing time, illness (certified by the official veterinarian) or failure of a class to fill shall be permitted to pay double fee and make a post entry in another qualifying class in the section or if no subsequent qualifying class is available for such post entry, the horse shall be considered qualified for the Performance Championship class, provided the horse has previously been entered in the Championship or Stake. Exception: Dressage. (See also GR117.3)

4. To avoid divided Performance Championship classes, eligibility for a Championship class may be limited to ribbon winners in qualifying classes.

GR810 Breeding or In Hand Championships

1. Junior Breeding or In-Hand Championships may be offered for two-year-olds and under; Senior Breeding or In-Hand Championships for three-year-olds and over. In the event a competition offers a Junior Championship and

a Senior Championship, as well as a Show Championship, only the first and second place ribbon winners are eligible to compete for the Show Championship unless division rules prohibit foals and yearlings.

2. Entry in a Breeding class does not qualify a horse for a Performance Championship class. Exceptions: in the Hackney Pony, Morgan, Roadster and American Saddlebred Horse divisions any performance class, including futurities and/or classics, qualifies for a Performance Championship class at that competition.

3. In a Breeding section of the Welsh division, the Championship will be awarded to one of the horses which has placed first in a qualifying class. After the Championship has been awarded the horse which has placed second in the qualifying class to the horse awarded the Championship shall compete with the remaining first place winners for the Reserve Championship.

4. In a Breeding section of the Hackney, Morgan, American Saddlebred, or Shetland divisions, the Championship and Reserve Championship will be awarded to horses that have placed first or second in their qualifying classes.

5. In a Breeding section of the Arabian division, the Junior, Senior or Show (Grand) Championship will be awarded to one of the horses which has placed first in a qualifying class. Qualifying classes for championships must be designated in the prize list. After the Championship has been awarded, the horse which has placed second in the qualifying class to the horse awarded the Championship shall compete with the remaining first place winners for the Reserve Championship. If a Show (Grand) Championship class is held, the Senior Champion and the Reserve Senior Champion as well as the top two ranking two-year-olds will be eligible to compete. (Exception: AR118.1).

6. In any case, should any first or second place winners in a qualifying class not compete for the Championship or be disqualified for being unsound, being unruly or not performing the class routine in the Championship class, the horse receiving the next highest ribbon in the qualifying class shall have the option of moving up for the Championship and Reserve only.

7. None of the above applies to Dressage/Sport Horse Breeding.

8. None of the above applies to the Andalusian/Lusitano Division. For Breeding and In Hand Championships see AL106.

9. None of the above applies to the Friesian Division. For Breeding and In Hand Championships see FR118.

GR811 Sweepstakes

When a Sweepstake class is offered, providing for a division of entry fees, either with or without monies added by the Show Committee, the total to be distributed must include the entry fees of all entries listed in the catalogue, whether or not the horses are shown, plus all fees covering other entries legally in the class, unless a competition stipulates in its prize list that portion of the entry fees which will be withheld.

GR812 Retirement Ceremony

1. If a retirement ceremony is allowed at the request of the owner of a horse, that horse may not be permitted to compete at the competition. Any horse officially retired at a Licensed Competition is barred for life from further competition at Licensed Competitions except by special permission of the Board of Directors; however, they can continue to be shown in Academy classes, Leadline classes, Get of Sire and Produce of Dam classes.

2. The Federation will give necessary publicity to all official retirement ceremonies and will notify all Licensed Competitions. See GR1214.7.

3. Any ceremony announcing an exhibitor's retirement from competition is prohibited.

SUBCHAPTER 8-C COMPETITION AND CLASS CONDITIONS AND ELIGIBILITY

GR813 Classes for Horse and Rider

In a class where the performances of both horse and rider are considered, the horse and rider together constitute an entry and neither can appear in a different combination except in Eventing, Dressage classes or Western Dressage.

GR814 Amateur

Amateur classes may be offered in any division using the specifications set forth in the respective division rules. If Amateur classes are offered leading to a Championship, judging specifications will be those of amateur classes or amateur Championships unless the prize list specifically states that open judging specifications will be used.

GR815 Breeding or In-Hand

1. Breeding or In-Hand classes may be offered in any section in which they are indicated in the respective division rules. The prize list must specify as to each class the age, sex and manner of showing.
2. All Futurity classes are considered part of the respective Breeding sections.

GR816 Junior Exhibitor

Classes, sections or competitions may be limited to junior exhibitors if so desired. Where special rules and class specifications are given for classes so limited, they should be used throughout the junior exhibitor classes offered and shall take precedence over such class specifications as those for Championship classes. A Show Committee should bear in mind that a horse suitable for a junior exhibitor should have good manners and it is suggested that the specifications for a Ladies' or Amateur class be followed throughout.

GR817 Ladies

Ladies' classes may be offered in any division using the specifications set forth in the respective division rules. If Ladies' classes are offered leading to a Ladies' Championship, judging specifications should follow those of the Ladies' class rather than those of the Championship class.

GR818 Local

Any competition may offer Local classes or complete Local divisions provided the meaning of the local designation is fully and clearly defined. Class specifications must follow those listed in the respective division rules as closely as possible.

GR819 Maiden, Novice and Limit

A competition may offer Maiden, Novice or Limit classes or complete sections in any division using the specifications set forth in the respective division rules. If a Championship class is held, it must be judged in accordance with the Maiden, Novice or Limit class specifications rather than those of the Championship class as listed unless otherwise specified.

GR820 Model Classes

1. Model classes may be offered in any section in which they are indicated in the respective division rules. They may be divided as to age, sex or height and may be held prior to a Breeding section to provide a standard for judging.
2. Model classes may be included in the number of classes required for a division or section rating. Exception: Hunter Division and Welsh Pony Division.
3. Entry in a Model class does not qualify a horse for a Performance Championship class.

GR821 Opportunity Classes

1. Opportunity Classes:
   a. may be held at breed restricted or Hunter and/or Hunter Jumper competitions with no FEI recognized classes, Western Dressage competitions, Western Regular or Local Competitions. Classes must be open to all breeds unless it is a breed restricted competition. In a breed restricted competition it must be stated in the prize list if the classes will be restricted or open. Exception: At any USEF licensed competition, opportunity classes may not be restricted to Friesians.

    b. are limited to 10% of the total number of the competition's classes, with a maximum of 20 Opportunity Classes per competition, whichever is less.

    c. may be held in addition to Exhibition Classes.

2. Opportunity Classes:

    a. do not count towards Horse of the Year Awards and the results from Opportunity Classes may not be used by any entity for a national awards program. Only with permission of the respective recognized affiliate organization may results from Opportunity Classes be used for regional awards.

    b. cannot be used as a qualifying class for any championship class held at the competition except an Opportunity Class championship at the competition.

    c. cannot be considered in reckoning Competition Championships awarded on points except an Opportunity Class championship at the competition.

    d. do not count towards the minimum number of classes nor amount of prize money offered when determining the rating of the competition.

    e. Dressage classes can be offered as Opportunity classes at Dressage Competitions or Regular/Local Competitions with "Open" Dressage classes as described below:

        1. Classes are limited to the following competition levels and dressage tests:

            a. Level 1 competitions may offer two tests and only two classes per level per day at Introductory - Second Level one of which can be the Riders Test at Training - Second levels.

            b. Level 2 competitions may offer two tests and only two classes per level per day at Introductory - First Level one of which can be the Riders Test at Training and First levels.

            c. Level 3 competitions may offer two tests and only two classes per level per day at Introductory - Training Level one of which can be the Training Level Riders Test.

            d. Level 4 and Level 5 competitions may not offer Opportunity classes.

        2. Opportunity Classes are for entry level riders.

        3. Freestyles may not be offered as Opportunity classes. Opportunity classes cannot be offered as "Test of Choice" classes.

        4. If opportunity classes at Dressage Competitions or Regular/Local Competitions with "Open" Dressage classes are restricted to amateurs, riders are required to have an amateur status with USEF.

        5. All rules and regulations in GR821 must be followed, except for GR821.6.

        6. Horses, riders, owners, trainers, and coaches participating only in Opportunity classes are exempt from Federation and affiliate organization membership and Horse Identification (HID) requirements and non-member/Show Pass fees, but are required to list the Federation membership number if the participant is a member.

    f. Breed restricted Dressage classes can be offered as opportunity classes at Regular/Local breed restricted competitions.

    g. Opportunity Classes for Hunter/Jumper/Equitation Divisions

        1. Opportunity Classes are for entry level riders.

        2. May be held at USEF regular or local rated competitions.

        3. All Opportunity classes and divisions must have fences 2'6" or below.

        4. Any rider that has shown in a Zone pointed division, such as a children's hunter division is not eligible.

        5. Any rider that has shown in a regular division (such as regular ponies) is not eligible.

        6. All rules and regulations in section GR821 should be followed, except GR821.7 (no crossing over into rated divisions).

3. Horses entered only in these classes are still subject to and must comply with the Drugs and Medication rules and are subject to drug testing.

4. Horses entered only in these classes:

a. are exempt from the Federation fee, including the Equine Drugs and Medication fee.

b. are not required to have a Horse Identification (HID) or Recording Number but are to list the HID or Recording number if the horse has been assigned this number.

5. Riders/drivers/handlers entered only in these classes are exempt from the Federation membership requirements and are not required to pay a Show Pass fee but are required to list the Federation membership number if the participant is a member.

6. The prize list must state whether or not horses and/or riders/drivers/handlers entered in Opportunity Classes can cross enter into the rated/recognized classes at the same competition. If cross entry is allowed, all applicable fees and membership requirements apply.

7. The list of Opportunity Classes offered must include "Opportunity" in the class name. The classes may include but are not limited to the following categories:

a. Opportunity Pleasure (Saddleseat, Hunter, and/or Western)

b. Opportunity Equitation (Saddleseat, Hunter, and/or Western)

c. Opportunity Costume (Historic and/or Contemporary)

d. Opportunity Trail (English and/or Western)

e. Opportunity Driving (Show Pleasure Driving and/or Carriage Pleasure Driving)

f. Opportunity Walk-Trot (Pleasure and/or Equitation)

g. Opportunity Gaited (Three-gaited, Five-gaited, and/or Paso Fino)

h. Opportunity Reining

i. Opportunity In-hand classes (Amateur and/or Junior Handler)

j. Opportunity Fun Classes

k. Opportunity classes for Hunter/Jumper/Equitation Divisions 2'6" and under

l. Opportunity classes for Dressage

m. Opportunity classes for Western Dressage.

8. Unless the competition is using existing USEF class specifications, the prize list must list the class specifications for each Opportunity Class, to include but not be limited to:

a. Gaits required

b. Judging criteria

c. Attire, tack and equipment allowed

9. Opportunity Classes may be judged by any judge officiating at the competition. Conflict of interest rules in GR1304 apply.

10. The competition must submit full results of all Opportunity Classes as required in GR1214. Horses with HID or Recording members and participants with USEF membership numbers are to have these numbers listed in the results.

GR822 Owners' Classes

Owners' classes may be offered in any division using the specifications as set forth in the respective division rules. If Owners' classes are offered leading to an Owners' Championship judging specifications should follow those of the Owners' class rather than those of the Championship class.

GR823 Dividing Classes

1. Classes can be divided by sex into three groups (stallions, mares and geldings) or a Show Committee may prefer to require mares and geldings, or stallions and geldings to show together.

2. If a Show Committee wishes to divide junior exhibitor classes, it may offer separate classes for boys and girls or offer several age limits. The following three age limits are suggested but may vary according to local conditions:

a. Juniors who have not reached their 11th birthday,

b. Juniors who have reached their 11th but not their 14th birthday

c. Juniors who have reached their 14th but not their 18th birthday.

3. When divided as above horses cannot be entered in more than one age section of the same class. Exceptions: Arabian, Morgan, Equitation and American Saddlebred divisions.

A Show Committee may offer classes divided by age of adult exhibitor.

GR824 Stallions

Stallions are barred from any Ladies' or Junior Exhibitors' classes except as provided for in division rules. Unless competition rules state otherwise, stallions may be shown by anyone in other classes in every division.

GR825 Ponies.

1. Ponies may be ridden only by junior exhibitors. Exceptions: Adults may ride ponies in the Eventing, Connemara, Dressage (other than (1) USEF High Performance Championships, USEF qualifying and selection trials, and observation classes (2) FEI Pony, Junior and Young Rider tests), Hunter, Jumper, American Saddlebred and Welsh Pony divisions.

2. If an animal 14.2 hands or under is eligible to compete as a horse in the Arabian, Half or Anglo Arabian, Connemara, Morgan, Paso Fino, National Show Horse or American Saddlebred Divisions, it may also compete as a horse in other appropriate classes (except for Dressage; see DR119.1). It cannot, however, compete as a horse in one class and a pony in another class at the same competition.

3. Once an animal is shown in a class restricted to horses, except in the aforementioned divisions and as provided for in SB204.4, it cannot be shown as a pony the same year.

GR826 Combined Ownership

Combined ownership is permitted in classes when more than one horse constitutes an entry unless the prize list states otherwise.

GR827 Hors de Concours

Entering a class Hors de Concours (without being judged) is prohibited except as provided for below. If a horse competes Hors de Concours, the horse cannot compete in a subsequent class for prize money in the same ring on the same day. However, the rider of an Hors de Concours horse may compete in subsequent classes.

a. For Dressage Competitions (out of competition); see DR119.5 and DR119.7

b. For Eventing Competitions: see EV106.6

c. For Driving Competitions, see DC915

d. For Jumpers - at management's discretion.

GR828 Permission to Compete in Foreign Competitions

1. International (FEI) Competitions: In accordance with Article 102.3 of the FEI General Regulations which states: "All competitors invited or nominated for an international event must be entered by their NFs", individuals wishing to compete in foreign International (FEI recognized) Competitions must apply to the Federation for each international competition they wish to enter, (this includes competitions in Canada and Mexico). He/she must complete an application providing information such as: the name and date of the particular competition(s) requested; the name(s) and details of the horse(s) to be ridden. A non-refundable application fee per competition must be enclosed. (Competitors may also opt to pay a non-refundable annual prepaid application fee in the amount of ten times the per competition fee (in lieu of paying a non-refundable per competition application fee). In the event of an oversubscription in dressage, driving, eventing, or reining, the discipline's Credentials Committee will rank the applicants,

providing that they have submitted a timely application as defined in the discipline criteria. The rankings will be based upon the indvidual's experience in competing in the U.S. and abroad, his/her recent results and ranking (if applicable) and other discipline specific criteria (if applicable). If the competition in question is on borrowed horses, the Credentials Committee will consider the experience the applicant has had in riding and competing on various horses. For endurance, jumping and vaulting, please refer to each discpline's criteria for procedures in selecting riders in the event of an oversubscription. Individuals wishing to compete in foreign international competitions who have not met the established criteria to compete in foreign FEI competitions may apply for a waiver, for which there is a fee. Copies of application and criteria for each discipline are available from the Federation website or Federation office.

2. National Competitions: Individuals wishing to compete in FEI recognized disciplines in National Competitions in foreign countries must receive permission from the Federation. An application for permission to compete must be completed and returned to the Federation. Copies of the application on the Federation website or from the Federation office. The competitor will be asked to provide the following information:

    a. whether or not the individual is a United States citizen and a current member of the Federation;

    b. whether he/she wishes to compete as an amateur or professional;

    c. whether he/she wishes to compete in National or International Competitions;

    d. the disciplines in which he/she wishes to compete (i.e., Jumping, Dressage, Eventing, Driving, Vaulting, Reining, or Endurance Riding);

    e. the length of stay in each country;

    f. whether he/she has been charged, offered an Administrative Penalty, protested or found in violation of FEI or Federation rules or the rules of any other National Federation or Federation affiliated association; and

    g. whether he/she has been indicted, named in an information, convicted or disciplined by an administrative agency, arbitration or other tribunal, body, humane society or court of law, whether civil, criminal, arbitral or administrative, for an act which would be a violation of Federation rules if committed during a Recognized Competition.

3. Permission to compete must be applied for each year.

4. Foreign Competitors: Riders, drivers, vaulters and longeurs who are not citizens of the United States, regardless of Federation membership status and country of origin.

    a. Foreign Competitors who desire to compete in non-breed restricted, National Competitions in the FEI recognized disciplines in the United States must have proof, in English, of membership in good standing from their National Federation or must be members in good standing of the United States Equestrian Federation.

    b. Competition management must request proof, in English, of current membership in good standing from their respective National Federation, or proof of current USEF membership.

5. Denial of Permission. Any application for permission to compete abroad answering affirmatively as to GR828.2f or .g shall be referred to a Committee of the Federation Board of Directors consisting of the Officers and two active athlete directors appointed by the President; the President shall serve as Chairman of the Committee and at any meeting the presence of at least four officers and one active athlete director shall constitute a quorum; the Committee shall by majority vote determine whether any such application shall be granted or denied, taking into account whether in the opinion of a majority of the Committee members any affirmative information regarding GR828.2f or .g causes other applicants to be considered more appropriate to serve as representatives of the sport and country in competing in foreign countries. Any such ruling by a majority vote of the Committee denying the privilege of a license to compete in foreign countries is final and not subject to appeal or review except where otherwise provided in the Constitution and By-Laws of the USOC, or where a review is granted in the discretion of the Committee, which upon further application may give further consideration to any applicant, may direct a hearing upon the application by the Committee or by the Hearing Committee, or may make any other ruling regarding the application considered by the Committee appropriate under the circumstances.

SUBCHAPTER 8-D SCHEDULING DURING COMPETITION

GR829 Length of Competition

1. A competition may not hold classes more than 16 hours out of any 24-hour period from the start of the first class to the finish of the last class, including intermissions. There must be a recess of at least 8 hours between the finish of the last class of an evening performance and the first class of a morning performance the following day. A fine in the amount of $250 per hour or part thereof will be imposed for exceeding the 16-hour time limit or not allowing an 8-hour recess. Exception: Competitions offering only Hunter, Jumper and Hunter Seat Equitation classes may not run more than 14 hours of actual performance time. Warm-up sessions, judged or unjudged, are included except sessions held at the beginning of the day where no fee is charged.

    a. If management disputes that the time limits were not exceeded and the above fine is not properly owing, it may request a hearing of these issues before a special committee appointed by the President provided a written statement specifying the grounds for the hearing is received at the Federation's office within 30 days of management's receipt of Federation's notice of fine. The special committee shall hear the matter and determine whether the fine is properly owing. The special committee may waive a part or all of the automatic penalty upon a finding of good cause why the time limits were exceeded and a finding that extreme hardship results from the automatic penalty.

2. All classes in any section for junior exhibitors in any one day must be held within a twelve-hour period, excluding intermissions.

3. No classes may be started after midnight.

GR830 Time Schedule

1. The announced order or time for classes may not be changed unless at least 12 hours notice of such change be given to each exhibitor and judge affected or each exhibitor affected consents in writing.

2. Provided the order of events is not changed, the Show Committee may call any class up to 30 minutes ahead of its scheduled time. Exception: Vaulting exhibitors must be given one hour's notice.

3. Once the first horse in a Reining class has been entered, shown and judged, the class must be run in entirety before commencing with the next scheduled class.

4. None of the above applies to Eventing (see EV107).

5. None of the above applies to Dressage. For Dressage Competitions, the following conditions apply: (1) Rides may be rescheduled up to one hour earlier or later than announced in the official schedule if each competitor is individually notified at least two hours prior to his/her rescheduled ride time. Rides within a class may be rescheduled in a different order. (2) Ride times or classes may not be changed more than one hour from the time announced in the official schedule unless 12 hours notice of such change is given to each exhibitor and judge affected or each exhibitor affected consents in writing to the change. Public address announcements, schedule changes posted on the show grounds or internet, and statements published in the prize list or entry documents do not meet the notification requirements of this rule.

6. None of the above applies to Western Dressage classes/competitions. For Western Dressage, follow the same conditions as listed in GR830.5.

GR831 Delay of Classes

1. When the start of any class requiring horses to be shown individually is delayed by horses not ready to perform, the competition may be closed at the order of the judges or Show Committee, provided a warning is issued and exhibitors are given three (3) minutes to appear at the in-gate ready to participate. (Exception: in hunter, hunter seat equitation and jumper classes with a specified jumping order, see HU156, JP112, JP135.14a & JP136.2.) In classes where horses compete collectively, a warning is issued and the in-gate must be closed two minutes after

the first horse enters the ring. (Paso Fino, see PF102.7) Judging must not commence until the gate is closed or at the end of the two-minute call. An official timer must be appointed to enforce this rule.

2. It is recommended that a starting enforce order be established in all classes in which horses compete individually and to allow one minute for an entry to enter the ring. At competitions using only one ring, a starting order must be established. If a jump order is used, it must be posted at least 30 minutes prior to the start of the class.

GR832 Interruption of Procedure

1. If weather appears to be imminently affecting the safety and welfare of horses and/or exhibitors, it shall be the responsibility of competition management (Exception: Eventing see EV110) to stop the competition until it is safe to recommence. If a competition in progress must be stopped due to a storm, accident, or other emergency, the Show Committee will decide whether to re-commence. Any interrupted classes may be re-commenced within the session in which they were originally scheduled or at a succeeding session of the competition. (Exception: Dressage GR832.7, Driving, Eventing EV110, Reining GR832.9.) If a Licensed Competition's Prize List does not advise exhibitors that refunds of entry fees will not be given in the event a class or classes, or all or part of the competition is cancelled due to a storm, accident or other emergency, the Licensee is required to refund entry fees for the cancelled class or classes upon written request by an exhibitor within 30 days of the cancellation.

2. The Show Committee will also decide whether awards for classes not held is warranted and called for. No Championship, awarded on points, can be awarded in any division, however, unless more than 50% of the scheduled classes in that division have been held. Any action thus taken by the Show Committee will not be referred to the Federation in as much as the matter is one of discretion and not regulation.

3. If a class is in operation at the time a competition is stopped, no placements involving Horse of the Year Awards will be made. If a tie for a Championship exists in the Hunter or Jumper division at the time the competition is stopped, points toward Horse of the Year Awards will be divided between the tied horses.

4. If classes are postponed to a day not included in the original competition dates, exhibitors are entitled to a refund of entry fees in the class postponed and are relieved of any obligation to show back in postponed classes.

5. If a class in which horses compete either collectively or individually is in progress and must be stopped due to a storm, accident, or other emergency, the following procedure shall govern (Exception: Dressage, Driving, Reining, Eventing, Jumper, Western Dressage):

   a. If a class is continued during the same session or a succeeding session of the competition, the judge along with the steward(s) and management will decide:

      1. to hold the class over in its entirety in which case no scores credited in the first session will count, or

      2. to recommence the class where it was interrupted.

      3. In the case of a hunter classic, or a two round class and one round is complete; it may be decided to pin the class with the first round scores.

6. Jumper:

   a. A Jumper Class that Management decides to postpone due to storm, accident or emergency per GR832.1 may be combined with a subsequent class in the same section with the prize money of the postponed class added to the prize money of the subsequent class. Management must make this decision prior to the first horse competing in the postponed class. The start fee for the postponed class will be added to that of the subsequent class and must be refunded to those declared competitors of the postponed class who choose not to declare for the combined class.

   b. In a jumper class which has reached the jump-off stage when the class is stopped, only those competitors involved in the jump-off need compete in the succeeding session. Jumper classes scored under Table II, Sec. 2b or 2c, Table IV, Sec. 4b or 4c or Table V Sec. 2b or 2c must be held over in their entirety unless the competition is continued over the original course at a later session, in which case the class shall continue from the point where it was stopped and scores earned by horses which have already competed shall stand.

7. Dressage: If it becomes necessary to interrupt a dressage competition for any reason, the unfinished portion may be recommenced and rescheduled for the same or following day at the option of the Show Committee with the Ground Jury's consent. All scores recorded before the interruption will stand. When classes are re-commenced after a delay on the same day, competitors must be given at least 30 minutes' notice of the starting time. Exhibitors whose ride times are changed to or on a subsequent day as a result of an interrupted competition or inclement weather conditions, must be individually notified at least two hours prior to a rescheduled ride time.

8. Eventing: See EV110.1.

9. Reining: If it becomes necessary to interrupt a reining competition for any reason, the unfinished portion may be recommenced and rescheduled for the same or following days at the option of the Show Committee and the judge(s). All scores recorded before the interruption will stand.

10. Western Dressage: see GR832.7.

GR833 Time-Out

A suspension of judging which may be requested by a competitor or directed by the judge(s).

1. A competitor is entitled to request a time-out for a period not to exceed five minutes in aggregate in order to make obvious adjustments or to repair broken equipment or to rectify a similar condition, or to replace a shoe (See GR804). (Exception: Arabian Hunter, AR108 and HU129.6; Arabian Jumper, AR108 and JP133.6; Dressage, GR833.9 and DR122.7j; Jumper, JP133.6; Hunter Seat Equitation, EQ107.4; Reining, RN103.5g; Vaulting, VA111). Time-outs are not allowed in Western Dressage.

2. If division rules allow a competitor to call for a time-out, the competitor may call only one time-out per class (Exception: Paso Fino and Welsh where a competitor may request a time-out no more than two times.) The penalty for exceeding the allowed time out(s) is for the entry to be excused.

3. To request a time-out for any such emergency, the competitor must go to the center of the ring (if possible) and or be acknowledged by the judge. The announcer will declare that a request for time-out has been made and permission granted; time will be taken from the moment such announcement is made.

4. If a horse casts a shoe in a class, time starts (after weighing, measuring and/or gauging has concluded, if applicable) when the farrier or his assistant touches the shoe or the horse. No more than three minutes will be allotted to find a shoe; if the shoe is not found, the exhibitor may elect to continue or withdraw. If a horse is removed from the ring for the purposes of shoeing, the steward or judge shall accompany and remain with the horse until it is returned to the ring or excused from the class.

5. Two attendants are permitted in the ring to assist a competitor during his/her time-out. If at the expiration of five minutes the repair has not been made, the competitor may proceed as is or be eliminated.

6. The steward or judge is responsible for timing unless an official timer is present.

7. Competitors who are not involved in a time-out may make minor adjustments that can be performed with the assistance of one attendant and not be charged with a time-out. Minor adjustments do not include replacing shoes.

8. At any time the judge(s) considers it necessary he/she may call for a time-out. Said time-out may be charged to a competitor that, in the judge's opinion, is responsible for the suspension of judging as long as the competitor is so informed by the judge prior to calling the class back to order.

9. None of the above apply to the Eventing, Dressage or Driving divisions; see specific division rules. Time-outs are not permitted in the Dressage or Western Dressage division.

SUBCHAPTER 8-E SCHOOLING

GR834 General

1. A Licensed Competition must provide a sufficient area for schooling horses. A separate schooling area must be

provided for each ring.

2. Adequate lighting must be provided in schooling areas used after dark.

3. In addition to the official schooling area, competitions should designate an exercise area.

4. Competitions offering A rated sections other than hunter and jumper must provide an exercise area at least 80' by 200' or its equivalent. If, due to space limitations, a competition does not have an adequate schooling area or a competition offering an A rated section cannot provide the required exercise area, one ring must be open for a minimum of 5 hours within each 24-hour period. Adequate lighting must be provided.

GR835 Designated Areas

Schooling over obstacles in the ring or over any part of an outside course is permitted only at the time designated by the Show Committee. All other schooling over obstacles is permitted only within clearly identified areas and only at times designated by the Show Committee. Schooling over obstacles in any other area of the competition ground or at any other time is prohibited.

GR836 Trail

A schooling area must be provided prior to and during trail classes with enough elements to adequately school a trail horse.

GR837 Hunter

1. Schooling areas for hunters must contain adequate hunter-type fences. A trotting fence, a vertical and an oxer are required. See also HU154.

2. It is recommended that separate schooling areas be provided for hunters. A separate schooling area and jumps should also be provided for ponies.

3. A supervisor of schooling must be appointed for the schooling area designated for hunters if the area is less than 20,000 sq. ft. in size or more than 500 horses are entered in the competition.

4. A Steward/schooling supervisor must be present in the schooling area during any Hunter class offering $10,000 or more in prize money.

5. The Steward/schooling supervisor's decision regarding schooling fences, or tack and equipment in the warm-up area is final.

GR838 Jumper (See also JP103 and Appendix A)

SUBCHAPTER 8-F WELFARE OF THE HORSE

GR839 Cruelty to and Abuse of a Horse

1. Cruelty to or the abuse of a horse by any person at a Licensed Competition is forbidden, constitutes a violation under Chapter 7, and renders the offender subject to penalty. The Show Committee must bar violators from further participation for the remainder of the competition. It is the duty of the competition officials and any properly constituted humane organization to report to the Federation any person who indulges in this practice for such further action as may be deemed appropriate.

2. The Federation or the Judge, Steward, or TD may appoint a veterinarian to inspect any animal in competition. Refusal to submit an animal for examination by an authorized veterinarian after due notification shall constitute a violation.

3. Show Committees are encouraged to contact the American Humane Association, 1400 16th Street NW, Suite 360, Washington DC 20036, which will provide experienced humane inspectors to work with them in eliminating cruel practices.

4. The following acts are included under the words Cruelty and Abuse but are not limited thereto:

a. Excessive use of a whip on any horse in a stall, runway, schooling area, competition ring or elsewhere on the competition grounds, before or during a competition, by any person. Except in emergency situations, any striking of the horse's head (on the poll and forward of the poll) with the whip shall be deemed excessive.

b. Rapping the legs of a horse with the butt end of a riding crop or other implement.

c. Use of any substance to induce temporary heat.

d. Manual poling with any object other than a bamboo pole.

e. Use of a wire or chain in conjunction with any schooling jump.

f. Use of electric device in schooling or showing.

g. Use of shackles, hock hobbles and similar devices (not to be construed as rubber or elastic exercising devices).

h. Showing a horse with raw or bleeding sores around the coronets, pasterns or legs.

i. Use of any explosive (e.g., fire crackers, torpedoes, fire extinguishers except in case of fire, etc.) or laser beam devices anywhere on the competition grounds, except in an exhibition or if required in class specifications.

j. Withholding of feed and water for prolonged periods.

k. Letting blood from a horse for other than diagnostic purposes.

l. Inhumane treatment of a horse in a stall, runway, schooling area, competition ring or elsewhere on the competition grounds, by any person.

m. Use of any object that prevents the horse's ability to close his mouth. (Exception: use of an oral speculum by a veterinarian or equine dentist to provide legitimate dental/oral medical care.)

n. Soreing and/or the use of an action device on any limb of a Tennessee Walking Horse, Racking Horse, or Spotted Saddle Horse (each a breed not recognized by the Federation) in any class at a Federation Licensed Competition is prohibited. An action device is defined by the USDA as any boot, collar, chain, roller, or other device that encircles or is placed upon the lower extremity of the leg of a horse in such a manner that it can rotate around the leg or slide up and down the leg so as to cause friction or strike the hoof, coronet band, fetlock joint or pastern of the horse. (Protective bell boots or heel boots are specifically excluded from this definition). The use of a weighted shoe, pad, wedge, in conjunction with a hoof band or other device or material (commonly referred to as a performance package) placed on, inserted in, or attached to any limb of a Tennessee Walking Horse, a Racking Horse, or Spotted Saddle Horse (each a breed not recognized by the Federation) constructed to artificially alter the gait of such a horse, and which are not protective or therapeutic in nature, in classes at a Federation Licensed Competition is prohibited.

5. Any action(s) against a horse by a competitor or an exhibitor, which are deemed excessive by a judge, Federation steward, technical delegate or competition veterinarian, in the competition ring or anywhere on the competition grounds may be punished by official warning, elimination, or other sanctions which may be deemed appropriate by the Show Committee. Such action(s) could include, but are not limited to excessive use of the whip, spurs, or bamboo poles. Competitors and exhibitors have the right to contest any action taken pursuant to GR839.5 by filing a protest or grievance pursuant to Chapter 6 of the Rules for hearing and determination by the Hearing Committee.

GR840 Attention Getting Devices

Attention getting devices &/or other noisemakers (including but not limited to tape measures, blow horns, altered bamboo poles, explosives, etc.) are not allowed in and around the make up/schooling/warm-up and competition rings during scheduled competition sessions. (Except for the National Show Horse division.) Use of explosives and fire extinguishers by or for exhibitors/competitors (except in the case of fire) is not allowed on competition grounds at any time. (See also GR839.4i)

GR841 Soundness

Unless specific division rules state otherwise, all animals except stallions and mares in Breeding classes must be serviceably sound for competition purposes i.e., such animal must not show evidence of lameness or broken wind. Animals with complete loss of sight in either eye may be found serviceably sound at the Judge's discretion, except in a class over fences where a Judge may ask a rider to change horses.

GR842 Falls

The fall of horse and/or rider does not disqualify the competitor unless due to bad manners of the horse. Exception: Andalusian (see AL101.14), Dressage, Driving, Eventing, Equitation, Hunter, Jumper, Reining, Vaulting and Western classes, in which specific rules prevail.

GR843 Mandatory Reporting and Cooperation of Horse/Pony Collapse

This rule applies to collapses of horses/ponies. For purposes of this rule, a "collapse" is defined as a fall to the ground with no apparent cause at any time from when entries arrive at the venue until departure from the venue. Other falls are not considered to be a collapse and are defined in GR122 and specified division rules. Refer to GR1034.4 for reporting requirements for all other falls and accidents.

1. The trainer as defined in GR 404, or the owner if the trainer is unavailable, or the rider if the trainer and owner are both unavailable, shall notify the Steward/Technical Delegate as soon as possible but no later than three hours after such occurrence of any collapse of a horse or pony. When a collapse occurs outside of competition hours or before the competition begins, notification must occur as soon as possible but no later than three hours after the Steward/TD reports to the show or returns to duty.

2. The Steward/TD shall report to Competition Management and the Federation within one hour of notification of a collapse.

3. In addition to the duties set forth in GR 1034.4, the Steward/TD shall file an Accident/Injury/Equine Collapse Report Form or Equine Fatality Report Form with the Federation within 24 hours of notification, except in exceptional circumstances such as no internet access at the venue.

4. The Federation, at its expense, may appoint a veterinarian to inspect the horse or pony that has collapsed and provide a full report to the Federation. Refusal to submit an animal for examination by an authorized veterinarian after due notification shall constitute a violation of this rule.

5. Any horse or pony that collapses at a licensed or endorsed competition is subject to drug and medication testing in accordance with Chapter 4 of these rules. In the absence of a Federation testing veterinarian, a veterinarian appointed under paragraph 4 (above) or the official competition veterinarian is authorized to collect and submit fluid samples in accordance with these rules.

6. The rider, owner, and trainer as defined in GR 404 shall cooperate with the Federation as to any investigation it undertakes with respect to a collapse or death of a horse/pony. This includes providing information requested by the Federation within 10 days of the request.

GR844 Poling

1. If a Licensed Competition allows manual poling and the relevant state laws do not prohibit such practices, it must be done in the designated schooling areas. Manual poling is prohibited for all horses competing in Jumper classes at Regular Competitions. Horses found to be in violation of these rules by the Competition Steward or other Federation official shall be eliminated/disqualified from competing within the upcoming 24-hour period and shall forfeit all entry fees for such competition. In addition after consultation between Competition Management, the Steward, or other official involved, and a senior judge in the Jumper division additional penalties including disqualification from the balance of the competition may be imposed. Exception: Eventing Division (see EV111.2); Jumpers (see JP103.1).

2. Single poles of bamboo only (not rattan or any other material) must be used, and may not be filled with sand or any other foreign substance. They may be taped to prevent splitting but they may not be wired, contain tacks or have

a diameter of over 2" at the large end. Pole must be held by one person only, using either one or two hands. Pole shall not be supported by any other means (i.e., standard, cup, or ring fence). There shall be no ropes, lunge reins or any other devices attached to said poles. Exhibitors must furnish their own poles and no other object may be manually employed.

3. Manual poling is permitted at a vertical fence only but a bamboo pole may be used as an off-set bar at either a vertical or spread fence. An off-set bamboo pole is one which is placed at any height behind or in front of the elements of the obstacle itself instead of being placed in the same vertical plane or planes. The length of the "off-set" bamboo pole may not exceed the length of the obstacle's rails. No other form of off-set or false ground line (ground line cannot be behind the vertical plane of the face of the fence or more than 3 feet in front, any trotting rail or placement pole may not be less than 8' to fence) is permitted. The spread fence must be jumped in the right direction.

4. Violators will be automatically penalized by elimination of the horse involved from the class in which it is participating and the next succeeding class in which it is entered. If the violation occurs after the horse has completed its performance in a class or between classes, it will be eliminated from the next two succeeding classes in which it is entered. All such violations must be recorded in the Steward's Report and, if cruelty or abusive behavior is evident, it will be reviewed by the Hearing Committee for such action as may be deemed appropriate to the particular circumstances.

GR845 Equine Vaccination Rule

1. At Federation licensed competitions, horses entering the grounds must be accompanied by documentation of Equine Influenza Virus and Equine Herpes Virus (Rhinopneumonitis) vaccinations within six months prior to entering the stables. Horses not in compliance with this rule may be required to leave the competition grounds upon request by Competition Management. Documentation should consist of one of the following methods mentioned below. The frequency of vaccine administration should be per the vaccine manufacturers' or veterinarian's recommendations. It is recommended that vaccines are administered by or under the direction of a veterinarian.

2. In the case of vaccines administered by a veterinarian, the exhibitor, upon request by Competition Management, must provide documentation from the veterinarian on documenting that the horse in question received the vaccinations; name of the vaccines and date of vaccine administration.

3. In the case of vaccines administered by a person other than a veterinarian, the exhibitor, upon request by Competition Management, must provide a receipt of the vaccine purchase which is signed by the owner, or agent with care, custody, and control of the horse; name, serial number and expiration date of the vaccine; and date of vaccine administration.

4. In the case of a horse that is unable to receive either of the vaccinations due to a history of adverse reactions, the exhibitor, upon request by Competition Management, must provide a letter from the veterinarian on official letterhead stating that the horse in question cannot be vaccinated due to medical concerns and a log of temperatures taken twice daily for the seven days prior to entering the competition grounds. These horses must also have their temperature taken and logged twice daily while on the competition grounds. The log of temperatures should be provided to the Competition Management, steward, or technical delegate when requested.

5. Competition Management may not amend or enhance vaccination requirements without prior approval of the Veterinary Committee. *BOD 1/17/15 Effective 12/1/15.*

CHAPTER 9 COMPETITION PRIZE LISTS AND ENTRIES

SUBCHAPTER 9-A PRIZE LISTS

GR901 Requirements

GR902 Class Specifications

GR903 Preliminary Correction Service

GR904 Changes in Prize List

GR905 Entry fees

SUBCHAPTER 9-B ENTRY BLANKS

GR906 Requirements

SUBCHAPTER 9-C SUBMISSION, ACCEPTANCE, AND REFUSAL OF ENTRIES

GR907 Requirements

GR908 Agreement

GR909 General

GR910 Post Entries

GR911 Substitutions

GR912 Cancellation and Withdrawal of Entries

GR913 Unpaid Entries

GR914 Refusal of Entries

GR915 Limiting Entries

GR916 General Conditions

CHAPTER 9 COMPETITION PRIZE LISTS AND ENTRIES

SUBCHAPTER 9-A PRIZE LISTS

GR901 Requirements

See GR1212 for procedures regarding submitting prize lists to the Federation office. The prize list of every Licensed Competition must contain the following:

1. Federation Page. This must be printed in its entirety and placed in a conspicuous position in the prize list of each Licensed Competition in typeface large enough to be easily legible. If a Licensed Competition prints a catalogue, the Federation page must be included and the competition is urged to instruct its announcer to invite the attention of spectators to this page at each session.

2. Classification of competition and level or ratings of divisions or sections on the Federation Page.

3. Entry blank, which must contain the rule to be signed by each exhibitor, rider, driver, handler, coach and trainer(s), or his/her agent(s). (See GR908).

4. Names of the officiating judges with the division(s) in which they will adjudicate and the names of the Federation stewards or technical delegates, provided they have accepted to serve. (See GR706.1j) Both division and sections to be adjudicated must be listed for breed division judges, provided they have accepted to serve. (See GR 706.1j)

5. List of competition officials. (See GR113).

6. The name of the Licensee (see GR132 and GR304.2) and the name of the Chief Executive Officer or the person with the largest ownership interest.

7. The name of the Hunter and Jumper and/or Trail course designer or responsible person. Exception: Arabian, American Saddlebred, Morgan and Andalusian/Lusitano divisions.

8. The name of the veterinarian and, if on call, the phone number where he can be reached during the competition. If not known, the prize list must state where the information will be posted during the competition.

9. The following statement must be published in BOLD TYPE for all Regular Competitions; Eventing Competitions at the Preliminary Level or above, Combined Driving Competitions at the Advanced Level, Dressage Competitions, Endurance Rides and Vaulting Competitions:

(See GR828.4 of the Federation rules).

Life, senior active and junior active members shall be eligible to participate in all classes at Regular Competitions, Eventing Competitions at the Preliminary Level or above and Combined Driving Competitions at the Advanced Level, Dressage, Reining and Vaulting Competitions and Endurance Rides. A non-member may participate as a handler, rider, driver, owner, lessee, agent, coach or trainer at Regular Competitions, Eventing Competitions, Dressage Competitions, Reining Competitions and Combined Driving Competitions upon payment of a $30 Show Pass fee. Participants in the following classes are exempted from the Requirements of this rule: 1) leadline; 2) exhibitions; 3) games and races; 4) classes for 4-H members; 5) walk trot and academy classes (academy classes are classes limited to horses used regularly in a lesson program); 6) USDF introductory level tests, pas de deux and quadrille classes; 7) NRHA Endorsed Reining Competitions. 8) Opportunity classes, 9) citizens of other nations who have proof, in English, of current membership in good standing of their own National Federation, 10) USEA beginner novice division; and 11) assistant handlers in Dressage Sport Horse Breeding classes.

10. Complete class description and judging specifications for all classes offered that are not included in this Rule Book must either be included in the Prize List or referred in the Prize List to a conspicuous place on the competition's web site.

11. Statement as to entry fees, prizes offered in each class and Show Pass fees pursuant to GR206 which the Federation is assessing certain participants who are not current members of the Federation. If a licensed competition's prize list does not state whether or not the competition will refund entry fees in the event of cancellation of classes

due to severe weather or other emergency, refunds of entry fees must be made upon written request by the exhibitor within 30 days of the cancellation. See GR832.

12. Statement as to Federation fee (see GR208.1).

13. Statement as to when and how prize money will be paid.

14. Statement concerning post entries.

15. A tentative schedule of classes, by sessions.

16. Statement as to which of the Federation Medal Classes, Federation Equitation Classes and USEF/USDF Qualifying Classes are to be offered.

17. Statement concerning a particular system of judging to be used. In the American Saddlebred Horse Division, the particular three-judge system to be used must be specified.

18. The exact date and location of competition.

19. A map and/or directions to the competition grounds.

20. For Local Competitions, the designation Local Competition must be on the cover.

21. Stabling.

    a. Statement as to type of stabling and whether stall doors will be provided.

    b. The prize list for competitions offering "A" rated Hunter sections must state that stabling will be offered and the cost must be included on the entry blank.

22. Statement as to method for establishing a jumping order for jumper classes.

23. Statement as to method for breaking ties for other than first place in jumper classes.

24. The prize list for competitions offering A rated sections and/or Jumper sections of $10,000 or more, must be printed and available to exhibitors at least 21 days prior to the closing date of entries. For competitions offering a Jumper Class of $25,000 or more, the prize list must be printed and available to exhibitors at least 30 days prior to the closing date of entries. Upon request, a copy of the competition's prize list must be provided by mail at no cost to the exhibitor.

25. All competitions must state the type of footing available in warm-up areas and competition arenas. The dimensions of the competition arenas must also be stated.

26. Competitions offering Dressage or Western Dressage classes must state the type of footing available in Dressage or Western Dressage warm-up arenas and Dressage or Western Dressage competition arenas.

27. If Jumper sections are offered which are not covered within the definitions contained in Chapter JP, full specifications (including eligibility requirements) must be contained in the prize list.

28. If Championships are offered in the Jumper Division, the prize list must state the method of determining those Championships (see JP110). If the Jumper Division offers Stake Classes, or other classes for which horses must qualify during the competition, the means of determining qualification must be stated in the prize list.

29. GR1301.7 must be published in the prize list in its entirety.

30. If local laws are more restrictive than the requirements of GR801 relating to protective headgear, the Licensee is required to publish the more restrictive local law (which shall control) in the prize list.

31. At competitions where the official veterinarian is on call, the prize list must include the time period when the veterinarian will be available to conduct measurements. If the veterinarian is required to measure at any time other than as stated in the prize list, the owner is responsible for paying veterinarian fees. See DR135.4-5 for more information on measurements at Dressage Competitions.

32. The Federation Prize List must direct competitors to the FEI Definite Schedule for information on FEI classes or include the FEI Definite Schedule in the Prize List. The Federation Prize List may identify the FEI Event Category (ies), Level (i.e. CSI2*, CDI-W, etc.), and include the FEI classes in the tentative time schedule but for all other FEI technical information, competitors must be directed to the FEI Definite Schedule. Individual discipline omnibus' are exempt from this rule provided they direct competitors to the FEI Definite Schedule. *BOD 1/17/15 Effective 12/1/15*

GR902 Class Specifications

1. All classes offered at Licensed Competitions for which specifications appear in the Rule Book must be governed by current specifications, to the end that uniformity will prevail in the competition and in the adjudication. To cover any omission it is recommended that the prize list contain the following statement in a prominent position: "EVERY CLASS OFFERED HEREIN WHICH IS COVERED BY THE RULES AND SPECIFICATIONS OF THE CURRENT FEDERATION RULE BOOK WILL BE CONDUCTED AND JUDGED IN ACCORDANCE THEREWITH."

2. A Licensed Competition is not limited to classes listed in the Rule Book. If a special class is offered which is not included in the Rule Book, the prize list or competition web site must furnish detailed specifications.

3. All classes (rated or unrated) to be held on a Federation licensed date are governed by all applicable Federation rules. No unrecognized classes can be held on any Federation licensed date, except

    a. Horse Trials at Eventing Competitions below the Preliminary Level,

    b. Eventing Tests at all levels

    c. Combined Driving below the Advanced Level

    d. Classes at Regular or Local Competitions restricted to breeds or disciplines whose rules are not included in the USEF rulebook

    e. Non-affiliated National Breed or discipline association classes

    f. Vaulting levels/classes below A-Team, Gold, Silver and Pas de Deux

    g. Academy classes

    h. Qualifying classes for Youth Reining classes or Reining classes at USA Reining and NRHA approved competitions.

    i. Exhibitions for which there are no breed or division rules

    j. These above named classes/levels can be held as unrecognized only provided a separate entry blank is used and the prize list and/or Omnibus clearly states that the classes are not recognized by the Federation. See GR305.

    k. Exception: FEI rules take precedence as to international classes and events over Federation rules at all FEI Sanctioned Competitions. Federation rules take precedence as to national classes and events which are not FEI Sanctioned at FEI Sanctioned Competitions. In connection with Endurance Riding Events, the Federation shall nationally enforce the prohibition of the gastric ulcer medications ranitidine and meprazole, in accordance with GR410. See GR305.

GR903 Preliminary Correction Service

A draft of a prize list may be sent to the Federation for advance corrections and suggestions, provided two copies are submitted and at least two weeks are allowed to make a thorough analysis. There is no fee for this service for competitions in their first two years of membership; but thereafter a fee of $10 for each competition day or $50 maximum will be charged. The fee must accompany the two drafts.

GR904 Changes in Prize List

If the prize list must be changed after it has been distributed to potential exhibitors the following procedures must be followed. Notification of specific changes to a prize list must be made to the Federation and exhibitors via email or mail as well as being posted on a competition's website. This will serve as notification for the requirements of this rule. In the cases where electronic communication is not available, then notification must be made as specified under this rule.

1. If errors are discovered or changes made up to 10 days prior to the closing of entries, notify potential exhibitors in writing of the specific changes.

2. If errors are discovered or changes made after that date, notify exhibitors on receipt of entries, and in writing when they arrive at the competition of the specific changes.

3. If classes are omitted or premiums decreased, notify only affected exhibitors 5 days prior to the competition in writing, by e-mail or by wire, thereafter these classes cannot be reinstated. In this instance, entry fee refunds must be given in all cases. (For Jumper Division, see JP108.2)

4. If classes are added or premiums increased, unless required under division rules, notify potential exhibitors in writing, by e-mail or by wire at least 5 days prior to the competition. Post entries must be accepted in such classes without a post entry penalty fee.

5. If the change in (3) or (4) adds a new division or section or alters a division's or section's rating, permission therefore must be obtained from the Federation at least 30 days prior to adoption.

6. Competitions are allowed to add additional classes from the following divisions as competition management deems necessary: Andalusian/Lusitano, Arabian, Connemara, Friesian, Hackney, Morgan, National Show Horse Roadster, Saddle Seat Equitation, American Saddlebred and Shetland. Unrated Hunter classes may be added as competition management deems necessary. If classes are added less than 5 days prior to the competition (See GR904.4), competition management must advise exhibitors of the additions upon check in, post notices in the competition office, and make the appropriate announcements during the competition.

GR905 Entry fees

An established entry fee figure must be clearly stated in the prize list for all Hunter classes. Once that figure has been printed it may not be changed regardless of the number of entries shown.

SUBCHAPTER 9-B ENTRY BLANKS

GR906 Requirements

1. The entry blank of each Licensed Competition must contain the name, age (if nine years or over, the term aged may be used), sex, color and in case of all horses four years old or over, the height of each horse entered in any class. This information is not required for Four-in-Hand, Team, Collection, Championship and other classes in which the conditions state that the entry need not be named.

2. For disciplines recognized by the FEI at non-breed-restricted events, the entry blank of each Recognized competition must contain the citizenship of the riders, drivers and vaulters.

3. The entry blank must contain a space for an emergency contact phone number.

4. The entry blank or prize list of each licensed competition must contain the following statement ("Federation Entry Agreement"), printed as below; failure of a Licensed competition to print this rule on every entry blank or prize list and to require that the entry blank be signed constitutes a violation of the rules and the competition is liable to penalty under GR707. If the Federation Entry Agreement is printed only in the prize list, the entry blank must contain the following abbreviated statement in lieu of the entire rule:

Federation Entry Agreement

I have read the United States Equestrian Federation, Inc. (the "Federation") Entry Agreement (GR906.4) as printed in the Prize List for [insert name here] ("Competition") and agree to all of its provisions. I understand and agree that by entering this Competition, I am subject to Federation Rules, the Prize List, and local rules of the competition. I agree to waive the right to the use of my photos from the competition, and agree that any actions against the Federation must be brought in New York State.

The complete statement is as follows:

FEDERATION ENTRY AGREEMENT

By entering a Federation-licensed Competition and signing this entry blank as the Owner, Lessee, Trainer, Manager, Agent, Coach, Driver, Rider, Handler, Vaulter or Longeur and on behalf of myself and my principals, representatives, employees and agents, I agree that I am subject to the Bylaws and Rules of The United States Equestrian Federation, Inc. (the "Federation") and the local rules of the competition.

I agree to be bound by the Bylaws and Rules of the Federation and of the competition. I will accept as final the decision of the Hearing Committee on any question arising under the Rules, and agree to release and hold harmless the competition, the Federation, their officials, directors and employees for any action taken under the Rules.

I represent that I am eligible to enter and/or participate under the Rules, and every horse I am entering is eligible as entered.

I also agree that as a condition of and in consideration of acceptance of entry, the Federation and/or the Competition may use or assign photographs, videos, audios, cablecasts, broadcasts, internet, film, new media or other likenesses of me and my horse taken during the course of the competition for the promotion, coverage or benefit of the competition, sport, or the Federation. Those likenesses shall not be used to advertise a product and they may not be used in such a way as to jeopardize amateur status. I hereby expressly and irrevocably waive and release any rights in connection with such use, including any claim to compensation, invasion of privacy, right of publicity, or to misappropriation.

The construction and application of Federation rules are governed by the laws of the State of New York, and any action instituted against the Federation must be filed in New York State. See GR908.4.

SUBCHAPTER 9-C SUBMISSION, ACCEPTANCE, AND REFUSAL OF ENTRIES

GR907 Requirements

1. When Entries are based strictly on a first-come, first-served basis: if the prize list restricts entries to mailed entries it must specify that entries may only be received by mail postmarked on or after a specified date which must be at least two weeks subsequent to the issuance of the prize list; if entries are to be made by other means (e.g. by hand, by fax, email or other electronic submission) that must be clearly specified in the prize list together with the earliest date for receipt which must be at least two weeks subsequent to the issuance of the prize list; competition management must maintain and make available for examination accurate records regarding proof of receipt of entries (e.g. postmarks, fax, email and other electronic transmittal records, hand delivery receipts); the prize list must further specify that entries will be accepted based solely on the priority of receipt of entries, and that ties regarding entries received at any time on the same day will be broken by lot on a date, time and location specified in the prize list with the right of any potential entrant to be present in person or by representative at the drawing of lots.

2. In Breeding classes (except Dressage/Sport Horse Breeding), provided a stud book exists for the horse in question, each horse must be registered in the recognized stud book of the breed and its registered number, sire and dam must be given on the entry blank. Horses competing in Dressage Sport Horse Breeding (DSHB) classes are not required to be registered with any stud book, but if a horse is registered with any breed, the name of the breed, sire, dam, dam sire and breeder must be given on the entry blank. For unregistered horses competing in DSHB classes, the above information is strongly recommended, if available.

3. Horses over two years of age must be named and the same name must be listed in all classes except those that permit nominations after the close of entries. If a horse has been recorded it must be entered under its original recorded name unless the name has been officially changed under the provisions of GR1101. It must also be entered under the name of the owner or lessee of record, or of the registered exhibitor name, which must appear in the catalogue. When entered by an agent, the owner's name or lessee's name must also be given.

4. Misrepresentation of a horse's identity, name, height, age, eligibility for the class, registered or recorded number or other information on an entry blank for the class in question results in the exhibitor's forfeiture of any ribbon, trophy, cash prize or other award won by such misrepresented or substituted animal. For Dressage Competitions, any

documentation such as negative EIA certification that is required for entry to a competition must list the same horse name and description as is listed on the entry blank and on the USEF horse identification or recording documents. The exhibitor is liable for further penalty as described in GR703.

5. Misrepresentation of the identity of the trainer responsible for the training, custody or performance of a horse by any person shall constitute a violation of the rules (see also GR147).

GR908 Agreement

1. Every entry at a Licensed Competition constitutes an agreement that the person making it, owner, lessee, trainer, manager, agent, coach, driver, rider, handler, vaulter, longeur, and the horse are subject to the Bylaws and the rules of the Federation and the local rules of the competition. Exhibitors are cautioned to abide by restrictions concerning exhibiting horses before judges as provided for in GR1304. Participants utilizing an online entry system for a Licensed Competition do so with the agreement that they have read the Official Prize List and agree to follow all the class specifications, requirements and conditions in the Official Prize List.

2. Every exhibitor, rider, driver, handler, vaulter, longeur, coach and trainer or his/her agent(s) must sign an entry blank. In the case of a rider, driver, handler, vaulter or longeur under the age of 18, his/her parent or guardian, or if not available, the trainer, must sign an entry blank on the minor's behalf. Unless specifically provided otherwise by law, any of the above persons may alternatively sign an entry blank in electronic form which shall have the same validity, force and effect as a signature affixed by hand. If any of the above persons fails to do so, his/her first entrance into the ring as an exhibitor, rider, driver, handler, vaulter or longeur shall be construed as his/her acceptance of the rules of the competition involved and of the Federation and shall ipso facto render him/her subject to said rules. Upon the failure of an owner, trainer, rider, driver, handler, vaulter, longeur, coach or agent(s), or parent or guardian or trainer of a minor rider, driver, handler, vaulter or longeur, to sign an entry blank as required, and upon confirmation of any such violation(s) by the steward or secretary of the competition, such person(s) shall be subject to an automatic fine of $250 imposed for each such violation.

3. Violation of the rules in connection with entries may be cause for disqualification of the exhibitor, rider, driver, handler, vaulter, longeur, coach and trainer by the Directors of the Licensed Competition (see GR1218.4) and for report to the Federation.

4. The Federation, incorporated in 2003, is a New York Not-For-Profit corporation. Pursuant to Chapter 6, the construction and application of Federation rules are subject to the laws of the State of New York. It is expressly agreed by and between the Federation and its members and any other persons in any way participating or in any way seeking to participate in a Licensed Competition or otherwise utilizing or seeking to utilize the privileges or services of the Federation, that any lawsuit (except for an arbitration pursuant to Bylaw 705 of the Federation) brought against the Federation by or on behalf of any such member (whether or not still a member at the time such suit is brought), or by or on behalf of any such person, shall be commenced and adjudicated only in the United States District Court for the Southern District of New York or in the Supreme Court of the State of New York, County of New York, to the exclusion of the courts of any other jurisdiction or venue.

5. The entry blank of each Licensed competition must contain the following USEF RELEASE as printed below, in an easily visible location, separated from any other language on the entry blank, and appearing immediately above or next to the required signatures as specified in GR908.2. No other material may come between this RELEASE and the required signatures.

6. All USEF fees appearing on the entry blank must be grouped together in one section of the page, preferably in a box separating them from other fees.

SPONSORED BY HAGYARD EQUINE MEDICAL INSTITUTE || © USEF 2016

Release, Assumption of Risk, Waiver and Indemnification

This document waives important legal rights. Read it carefully before signing.

I AGREE in consideration for my participation in this Competition to the following:

I AGREE that "the Federation" and "Competition" as used herein includes the Licensee and Competition Management, as well as all of their officials, officers, directors, employees, agents, personnel, volunteers and Federation affiliates.

I AGREE that I choose to participate voluntarily in the Competition with my horse, as a rider, driver, handler, vaulter, longeur, lessee, owner, agent, coach, trainer, or as parent or guardian of a junior exhibitor. I am fully aware and acknowledge that horse sports and the Competition involve inherent dangerous risks of accident, loss, and serious bodily injury including broken bones, head injuries, trauma, pain, suffering, or death. ("Harm").

I AGREE to hold harmless and release the Federation and the Competition from all claims for money damages or otherwise for any Harm to me or my horse and for any Harm of any nature caused by me or my horse to others, even if the Harm arises or results, directly or indirectly, from the negligence of the Federation or the Competition.

I AGREE to expressly assume all risks of Harm to me or my horse, including Harm resulting from the negligence of the Federation or the Competition.

I AGREE to indemnify (that is, to pay any losses, damages, or costs incurred by) the Federation and the Competition and to hold them harmless with respect to claims for Harm to me or my horse, and for claims made by others for any Harm caused by me or my horse while at the Competition.

I have read the Federation Rules about protective equipment, including GR801 and, if applicable, EV114, and I understand that I am entitled to wear protective equipment without penalty, and I acknowledge that the Federation strongly encourages me to do so while WARNING that no protective equipment can guard against all injuries.

If I am a parent or guardian of a junior exhibitor, I consent to the child's participation and AGREE to all of the above provisions and AGREE to assume all of the obligations of this Release on the child's behalf.

I represent that I have the requisite training, coaching and abilities to safely compete in this competition.

I AGREE that if I am injured at this competition, the medical personnel treating my injuries may provide information on my injury and treatment to the Federation on the official USEF accident/injury report form.

BY SIGNING BELOW, I AGREE to be bound by all applicable Federation Rules and all terms and provisions of this entry blank and all terms and provisions of this Prize List. If I am signing and submitting this Agreement electronically, I acknowledge that my electronic signature shall have the same validity, force and effect as if I affixed my signature by my own hand.

SEE PRO FORMA AT END OF THIS RULE

GR909 General

1. Entries must be made in writing and signed by the (1) exhibitor (2) the rider, driver, handler, vaulter or longeur, (3) the trainer, and (4) the coach, if applicable, or by the agent(s) of such person(s) and must be accompanied by funds to cover entry fees, stall fees and Federation fee (see GR208.1). In the case of a rider, driver, handler, vaulter or longeur under 18, his/her parent or guardian, or if not available, the trainer, must sign an entry blank on the minor's behalf. Or: by transmitting the required entry data to a designated collection agent via the internet, accompanied by a valid credit card payment to cover entry fees, stall fees, Federation fee (see GR208.1) and applicable processing fees, and including the name(s) of the (1) exhibitor, (2) rider, driver, handler, vaulter or longeur, (3) the trainer, and (4) the coach, if applicable. The secretary of the competition will accept such an entry as complete (see 1.1 below).

    a. In the case of on-line entries, no competition number will be issued until the Competition Secretary has received an entry form, the signatures of the (1) exhibitor, (2) the rider, driver, handler, vaulter or longeur, (3) the trainer, and (4) the coach, if applicable, or of the agent(s) of such person(s). In the case of a rider, driver, handler, vaulter or longeur under 18, his/her parent or guardian, or if not available, the trainer must sign an entry blank on the minor's behalf.

b. Submission of on-line entry accompanied by a valid credit card or other type of electronic payment shall be construed to be acceptance by the person(s) named in the entry of the provisions of GR906-GR908 and GR911-GR914.

c. Electronic signatures on an entry form and in online entry systems must be submitted and accepted in compliance with applicable laws in the location where the competition is held.

2. In the event that a catalogue contains a statement as to an entry not in accordance with the exhibitor's original entry blank, it is the duty of the Show Committee to take all steps necessary, including public announcement, to correct the error, giving precedence to the exhibitor's entry blank and not the catalogue in error, as authority.

3. In the Dressage or Western Dressage Division and for open dressage or western dressage classes at Regular and Local Competitions, all entries received by the closing date of entries shall be acknowledged by the competition secretary. (Note: This would include DSHB, but not breed-restricted dressage classes.)

GR910 Post Entries

1. Post entries are any entries made after the advertised closing date.

2. Post entries should not be encouraged in classes listed in the prize list since this practice often results in unfair competition, confusion during the competition, inability to collect the proper fees, extreme difficulty in recording winnings of horses not listed in the catalogue and disruption of the time schedule. Furthermore, the exhibitor and his horses are worthy of having their names in the program. In the interest of good sport, a Show Committee is strongly urged to require that entries be made in advance and printed in the catalogue. This does not apply, however, to classes in which the prize list states that post entries will be accepted, such as pairs of saddle horses, hunt teams, etc.

3. When a Licensed Competition does not accept post entries it must be stated in the prize list and no exceptions can be made.

4. When a Licensed Competition does accept post entries it must be stated in the prize list and post entries can only be accepted prior to the starting of the class and upon signature of exhibitor or his agent and trainer.

GR911 Substitutions

1. Substitution of a horse may not be made after the announced date of the closing of entries, except in classes where more than one horse represents an entry (i.e., Pairs, Teams, Tandems). In such cases substitution of one horse may be made provided a veterinarian's certificate of disability is submitted. (Exception: Friesian) (Local Competitions exempt).

2. If a horse is sold or injured after the closing of entries, Competition Management may allow an exhibitor to post enter another horse in the same class but the new entry must be given another number.

3. Substitution of a rider or driver or longeur may be made during a class only under the following conditions:

a. in case of injury to or illness of the original rider or driver or longeur;

b. in a Combination class unless the prize list states that the same rider or driver is required for the entire class;

c. in a Reining division when one rider may show several horses in the individual workout. See RN101.5.

4. Substitution of rider is not allowed in Equitation classes.

GR912 Cancellation and Withdrawal of Entries

1. A Licensed Competition may adopt its own policy covering the refunding of fees to an exhibitor who cancels his entries after the official closing date and prior to the competition's beginning. If a Licensed Competition does not specify its refund policy in the prize list, refunds are required to be made for entries cancelled before the

competition begins, upon written request by the exhibitor within 30 days of the competition.

2. A Licensed Competition can set the penalty governing an exhibitor who is permitted to cancel his entries or withdraw from the competition. Such penalty applies only at the competition in question. See GR1305.

3. Competition management must refund any entry fees, (stabling and processing fees exempted) paid in advance by an exhibitor for any horse(s) which is subsequently named to an official US team, participation on which will prevent him/her from competing in that competition.

4. After the competition starts, if a rider is unable to compete due to illness or injury, class fees will be refunded upon presentation of a doctor's certificate unless otherwise stated in prize list. Stall fees and office fees need not be refunded.

GR913 Unpaid Entries

1. Any Competition Licensed or endorsed by the Federation which accepts entries without the payment of the required fees, does so at its own risk and the Federation will not be responsible for the collection of fees (See also GR1213.10). However, if a person makes payment for fees which is not negotiable, the Licensed Competition, after first contacting the individual at least once in writing (with delivery confirmation), may report the name and address of the person in writing to the Federation within 150 days of notification of denied payment, (See GR1213.1) giving the names of the horses and the names and complete addresses of the owners for which the non-negotiable funds were to cover, a copy of the entry blank, a copy of the front and back of the check or receipt with credit card information and signature, and a copy of the delivery confirmation showing the competition's attempt to notify the individual of the non-negotiable payment. The amount of all fees for each horse must be itemized. On receipt of such notice, the Federation will notify said person, of his or her indebtedness to the competition as well as the imposition of a processing fee in the amount of $50 payable to the Federation. If the person fails to make settlement with the competition and/or the Federation within 30 days from the date of the notice from the Federation, he or she will be fined the additional sum of $250 payable to the Federation and he or she and any horses owned by him or her and any horses and/or persons for which the non-negotiable sums have been paid will automatically be barred from taking any part whatsoever in any competition Licensed or endorsed by the Federation until settlement is made both of indebtedness to the competition and to the Federation. If the indebtedness to the competition is paid within thirty days of the notice from the Federation and only the $50 processing fee is not paid to the Federation within that timeframe, the Federation will assess a $250 fine and the suspensions as referenced above will remain until the debt to the Federation is paid in full. Publication of the suspension will be published on the Federation's website. Exception: Persons who are engaged to compete on horses owned by individuals with whom they have no current business relationship regarding the ongoing training, care, custody, or control of the horse are not responsible for indebtedness under this rule provided that said persons have not tendered the non-negotiable payment.

2. If the person disputes that the amounts in question are owing or unpaid, he or she may request a review of these issues before the Hearing Committee provided a written statement specifying the grounds for a review, accompanied by a fee of $100 (which will be refunded if the dispute is settled in favor of said person) is received at the Federation's office within said 30 day period. The Hearing Committee is the only entity that can waive the fines assessed as the result of this rule.

3. In the event a person is reported three or more times for making unnegotiable payment for entry fees, etc., to any competition Licensed or endorsed by the Federation, he is, after a hearing, subject to further disciplinary action.

GR914 Refusal of Entries

1. In addition to entries of persons suspended or expelled from the Federation, a Licensed Competition may refuse any entry of an exhibitor or the participation of any agent, trainer, rider, driver or handler who has shown an objectionable attitude or behavior at a Licensed Competition or towards its management, which management is able

to substantiate, or previous unsportsmanlike behavior at a Licensed Competition which management is able to substantiate.

2. A competition licensed by the Federation and an affiliate association may refuse the entries of horses and riders in Maiden, Novice, Limit and Green classes if they are ineligible under the rules of the Affiliate Association, except for:

   a. A class open to horses in a specified area (Examples: State Championship, New England Championship, and Kentucky-bred horses).

   b. A class where the winnings form part of a total score in a competition for a trophy,

   c. Classes in which the identical award may also be competed for at another Licensed Competition.

   d. Classes counting for USEF Horse of the Year Awards.

GR915 Limiting Entries

1. Management can limit the number of horses entered by an owner and the number of horses ridden by a rider.

2. Any competition that sets restrictive criteria for accepting entries and/or offers classes or events which are part of a league, series or other ranking or award system must do so by meeting the applicable requirements described below:

   a. Based strictly on a First-Come, First-Served basis (See GR907.1) under this method the prize list must be distributed at least two weeks prior to close of entries to any person requesting a prize list as well as at least three times the number of potential entrants as there will be entries accepted.

   b. Qualification based only on winnings: (i.e., ribbons and/or prize money or dressage scores during a specified time period, of at least eight (8) consecutive weeks' duration, established by Competition Management and published in the prize list or otherwise prior to the end of the specified period. (See applicable breed/discipline rules for further requirements under this rule).

   c. By Council Approval: Any other competition wishing to set restrictive criteria for accepting entries other than as specified above must make written application to the applicable Council, accompanied by a nonrefundable fee of $50, at least 120 days prior to the event detailing the criteria being requested. The Federation office may refer the application to the appropriate discipline or other committee for its recommendation regarding the application prior to the application and any recommendation being considered by the Council. The Council will consider such recommendations and may approve any such applications in its discretion and may condition any such approval in its discretion, and must require, if approved, that there be publication in the prize list or otherwise of such restrictive criteria sufficiently in advance of the closing date of entries, where appropriate, for all interested to have a fair opportunity to enter. The foregoing provisions do not apply to national championships, qualifying events for national championships, and any other events with selection criteria approved by the Board of Directors.

3. Leagues, Series, and Finals:

   a. Definitions:

      1. "Finals" means any championship, trophy or other award final, league final or other final class or final event with entries based upon the outcomes of earlier contests.

      2. "System" means classes or events which are part of a league, series, ranking/tracking lists or championship, final trophy or other award system, whether or not generated or tracked by a computer program or otherwise.

   b. All of the following requirements must also be met:

      1. The league or series must be run under the auspices of either a Recognized Affiliate or an Alliance Partner of the Federation.

      2. All the qualifying classes must be held at licensed competitions or at competitions recognized by a Recognized Affiliate or an Alliance Partner of the Federation.

      3. The league or series must award the qualifying classes to licensed competitions on an equal basis. If a

licensed competition meets the requirements to hold a qualifying class and wishes to do so, it must be given the opportunity.

4. The organization or individuals financially responsible for the system must be USEF Members, Federation Recognized Affiliates, or Federation Alliance Partners and must agree to be bound by and comply with all applicable Federation rules in the conduct of the system and its application in the league or series.

5. If there is an award category for classes in the league or series and the above requirements are met, HOTY points will be awarded for the qualifying classes and for the finals held at licensed competitions.

6. If the finals of a league, series or other ranking system are not held at a licensed competition, HOTY points for the finals will not be awarded.

GR916 General Conditions

Except as permitted by the FEI for FEI recognized classes, all entries at a Licensed Competition must be on the same basis. A competition cannot give free or reduced entries, free or reduced transportation or other expenses to one exhibitor unless the same privileges are extended to all exhibitors in the same section or subset of competitors. The requirements to obtain these privileges must be advertised to all potential exhibitors. No fees may be imposed that are not listed in the prize list.

UNITED STATES EQUESTRIAN FEDERATION, INC. ENTRY AGREEMENT

I have read the United States Equestrian Federation, Inc. (the "Federation") Entry Agreement (GR906.4) as printed in the Prize List for this Competition and agree to all of its provisions. I understand and agree that by entering this Competition, I am subject to Federation Rules, the Prize List, and local rules of the competition. I agree to waive the right to the use of my photos at the competition, and agree that any actions against the Federation must be brought in New York State.

RELEASE, ASSUMPTION OF RISK, WAIVER AND INDEMNIFICATION

This document waives important legal rights. Read it carefully before signing.

I **AGREE** in consideration for my participation in this Competition to the following:

I **AGREE** that the "Federation" and "Competition" as used above includes all of their officials, officers, directors, employees, agents, personnel, volunteers and affiliated organizations.

I **AGREE** that I choose to participate voluntarily in the Competition with my horse, as a rider, driver, handler, vaulter, longeur, lessee, owner, agent, coach, trainer, or as parent or guardian of a junior exhibitor. I am fully aware and acknowledge that horse sports and the Competition involve inherent dangerous risks of accident, loss, and serious bodily injury including broken bones, head injuries, trauma, pain, suffering, or death ("Harm").

I **AGREE** to hold harmless and release the Federation and the Competition from all claims for money damages or otherwise for any Harm to me or my horse and for any Harm of any nature caused by me or my horse to others, even if the Harm arises or results, directly or indirectly, from the negligence of the Federation or the Competition.

I **AGREE** to expressly assume all risks of Harm to me or my horse, including Harm resulting from the negligence of the Federation or the Competition.

I **AGREE** to indemnify (that is, to pay any losses, damages, or costs incurred by) the Federation and the Competition and to hold them harmless with respect to claims for Harm to me or my horse, and for claims made by others for any Harm caused by me or my horse while at the Competition.

I have read the Federation Rules about protective equipment, including GR801 and, if applicable, EV114 and I understand that I am entitled to wear protective equipment without penalty, and I acknowledge that the Federation strongly encourages me to do so while WARNING that no protective equipment can guard against all injuries.

If I am a parent or guardian of a junior exhibitor, I consent to the child's participation and **AGREE** to all of the above provisions and **AGREE** to assume all of the obligations of this Release on the child's behalf.

I represent that I have the requisite training, coaching and abilities to safely compete in this competition.

I **AGREE** that if I am injured at this competition, the medical personnel treating my injuries may provide information on

my injury and treatment to the Federation on the official USEF accident/injury report form.

BY SIGNING BELOW, I AGREE to be bound by all applicable Federation Rules and all terms and provisions of this entry blank and all terms and provisions of this Prize List. If I am signing and submitting this Agreement electronically, I acknowledge that my electronic signature shall have the same validity, force and effect as if I affixed my signature by my own hand.

Rider/Driver/Handler/Vaulter/Longeur (mandatory)

Signature: _____

Print Name: _____

Parent/Guardian Signature: _____

      (Required if Rider/Driver/Handler/Vaulter/Longeur is a minor)

Print Parent/ Guardian Name: _____

Emergency Contact Phone No. _____

Is Rider/Driver/Vaulter a U.S. Citizen: ____ Yes ____ No

Owner/Agent (mandatory)

Signature: _____

Print Name: _____

Trainer (mandatory)

Signature: _____

Print Name: _____

Coach (if applicable)

Signature: _____

Print Name: _____

CHAPTER 10 LICENSED OFFICIALS

SUBCHAPTER 10-A LICENSED OFFICIALS COMMITTEE
GR1001 Duties

GR1002 Applications

GR1003 Review

SUBCHAPTER 10-B GENERAL RULES AND FEES
GR1004 General

GR1005 Fees

SUBCHAPTER 10-C CLASSIFICATIONS - JUDGES
GR1006 General

GR1007 Senior Judge

GR1008 Registered Judge

GR1009 Recorded Judge

GR1010 Special Judge

GR1011 Guest Judge

GR1012 Learner Judge

SUBCHAPTER 10-D CLASSIFICATIONS - STEWARDS
GR1013 General

GR1014 Registered Steward

GR1015 Recorded Steward

GR1016 Special Steward

SUBCHAPTER 10-E CLASSIFICATIONS - TECHNICAL DELEGATES
GR1017 General

GR1018 Registered Technical Delegates - Eventing and Dressage

GR1019 Recorded Technical Delegates - Eventing and Dressage

GR1020 Driving Technical Delegates

GR1021 Vaulting Technical Delegates

SUBCHAPTER 10-F CLASSIFICATIONS - COURSE DESIGNERS
GR1022 General

GR1023 Jumper Course Designers

GR1024 Hunter, Hunter/Jumping Seat Equitation Course Designers

GR1025 Special Hunter Course Designer

GR1026 Special Jumper Course Designer

GR1027 Eventing Course Designers

GR1028 Combined Driving Course Designer

GR1029 Guest Combined Driving Course Designer

SUBCHAPTER 10-G CLASSIFICATIONS - OTHER
GR1030 Course Advisor

GR1031 Assigned Steward or Technical Delegate

SUBCHAPTER 10-H REGULATIONS GOVERNING OFFICIALS

GR1032 General

GR1033 Judges

GR1034 Stewards and Technical Delegates

GR1035 Special Duties of a Technical Delegate

GR1036 Warning Card - Stewards and Technical Delegates

GR1037 Conflicts of Interest and Restrictions - Judges (See also GR107 and GR1303.)

GR1038 Conflicts of Interest and Restrictions - Stewards and Technical Delegates (See also GR107 and GR1304)

GR1039 Conflicts of Interest and Restrictions - Licensed Officials

SUBCHAPTER 10-I LICENSE APPLICATIONS, ENROLLMENT,

PROMOTION, AND MAINTENANCE

GR1040 General

GR1041 Clinic and Officiating Requirements

GR1042 Andalusian/Lusitano Judges

GR1043 Arabian Judges

GR1044 Carriage Pleasure Driving Judges

GR1045 Combined Driving Judges

GR1046 Combined Driving Course Designer

GR1047 Combined Driving and Carriage Pleasure Driving Technical Delegate

GR1048 Connemara Judges

GR1049 Dressage Judges

GR1050 Dressage Sport Horse Breeding Judges

GR1051 Dressage Technical Delegates

GR1052 Eventing Judges

GR1053 Eventing Technical Delegates

GR1054 Eventing Course Designers.

GR1055 Friesian Judges

GR1056 Hackney Judges

GR1057 Hunter Judges

GR1058 Hunter Breeding Judges

GR1059 Hunter/Jumping Seat Equitation Judges

GR1060 Hunter, Hunter/Jumping Seat Equitation Course Designers.

GR1061 Jumper Judges

GR1062 Jumper Course Designer

GR1063 Certified Jumper Schooling Supervisor.

GR1064 Morgan Judges

GR1065 National Show Horse Judges

GR1066 Paso Fino Judges

GR1067 Reining Judges

GR1068 Roadster Judges

GR1069 American Saddlebred Judges

GR1070 Saddle Seat Equitation Judges

GR1071 Shetland Pony Judges

GR1072 Stewards - Category 1 and Category 2

GR1073 Vaulting Judges

GR1074 Vaulting Technical Delegates

GR1075 Welsh Pony Judges

GR1076 Western Judges

GR1077 Western Dressage Judges

CHAPTER 10 LICENSED OFFICIALS

SUBCHAPTER 10-A LICENSED OFFICIALS COMMITTEE

GR1001 Duties

The Licensed Officials Committee will act upon every completed application for enrollment, annual renewal, promotion, recommendation to the FEI, and change of status of judges, course designers, stewards and technical delegates. The Committee will issue an official's card to each approved applicant. Cards are valid for the current competition year only.

GR1002 Applications

1. The Committee will carefully review all applications, solicit confidential evaluations from the appropriate Breed/Discipline Committee members and others as it may elect as provided in GR1041.4, including names furnished by the applicant, and consider returned questionnaires, competition reports, any letters received regarding the applicant and other relevant information submitted to the Committee. For all applicants, the Committee will request and give due consideration to recommendations received from Recognized National and FEI Affiliates before granting a new license or promotion. All such submissions shall be strictly confidential, shall not be subject to examination by the applicant, and shall be made available only to Committee members and staff. All applicants specifically waive their rights to examine such submissions.

2. The Committee may in its discretion revoke a current license, place a license on probationary status, reduce a license by one level, temporarily suspend, or refuse to renew an official's license at its expiration following a hearing on at least ten days written notice to the official in question who shall have the right to appear, to be represented, and to bring witnesses. The Committee shall issue its written ruling specifying the substance of the Committee's reasons for said decision without breaching the confidentiality of any of the foregoing submissions.

3. The Committee at its discretion may reinstate an official who has allowed his/her license to lapse for one year or may require him/her to reapply.

4. All applications whether for initial enrollment, renewal, promotion, or for change of status or recommendation to the FEI shall contain a statement to be signed by the applicant, indicating that the applicant waives his/her right to review confidential submissions and the file, and has read and understands the rules governing the application process, and agrees to be bound thereby.

GR1003 Review

1. Any person whose application for enrollment, renewal, promotion or change of status or for recommendation to the FEI has been denied or whose license has been revoked, placed on probationary status, reduced by one level or temporarily suspended may request a review by the Licensed Officials Committee to reconsider the decision. The request must be in writing and mailed to the Licensed Officials Committee within 30 days from receipt of the written ruling of the Committee sought to be reconsidered and accompanied by a check for $300 payable to The Federation, which is non-refundable.

2. The review shall be after ten (10) days written notice to all parties concerned. The notice shall contain a brief statement of the facts supporting the position of the Licensed Officials Committee and shall specify the time and place at which the review is to be held. The person requesting the review may attend and may bring witnesses, sworn statements or other evidence on his/her behalf. Upon the written request of a representative of the Licensed Officials Committee or the person requesting the review, there shall be furnished before the Committee any evidence to be introduced, the names of witnesses and the substances of their testimony; however, all confidential submissions received by the Committee shall be maintained as confidential and shall not be provided to the applicant.

3. Following an adverse decision by the Licensed Officials Committee with regard to a non-renewal or revocation only,

an applicant may request the Hearing Committee to review the decision or to consider a hearing de novo, provided such application is made in writing within 20 days of receipt of the Licensed Officials Committee decision, and provided a nonrefundable fee of $500 payable to The Federation accompanies the application. The Hearing Committee may review the decision, or in its discretion, hold a new hearing. In either case, both the applicant and the Licensed Officials Committee shall be parties to the proceeding and shall have the right to make written submissions, be represented by counsel, and in the event of a hearing, to appear in person and present or cross-examine witnesses.

SUBCHAPTER 10-B GENERAL RULES AND FEES

GR1004 General

1. Only licensed officials in good standing may officiate at Licensed Competitions in those divisions covered by the rules and specifications of the current Rule Book.

    a. Unless stated otherwise, judges in the following classes are not required to be licensed by USEF nor is the competition required to obtain a guest card for the judge:

        1. Exhibition classes for Breed, hunter, jumper or Western.

        2. Opportunity Classes, with the exception of Dressage which must be judged by licensed Dressage judges.

        3. Opportunity classes in the Western Dressage Divison which must be judged by either licensed Dressage judges with the exception of Western Dressage Suitability, Western Dressage Hack and Western Dressage Seat Equitation or licensed Western Dressage judges including Western Dressage Suitability, Western Dressage Hack, and Western Dressage Seat Equitation. Breed licensed judges are also eligible to officiate Western Dressage Suitability, Western Dressage Hack and Western Dressage Seat Equitation classes.

        4. Academy Classes, with the exception of Dressage which must be judged by licensed Dressage judges.

2. All national level and Federation FEI officials must be Senior Active Members, 21 years of age or over. (Exception: Learner judges must be 21 years of age or over. Federation C1 Stewards and judges in the Paso Fino Division must be at least 25 years of age.)

3. Any USEF member who is a U.S. citizen holding a FEI license for which there is a comparable national level license must maintain the national level license with the Federation (Exception: Jumper judges). If the national license is not properly maintained, this in itself shall be deemed sufficient basis for the Federation to recommend to the FEI that the individual be removed from the FEI list of officials.

	FEI Judge	FEI Chief Steward	FEI Technical Delegate	FEI Course Designer	FEI Veterinarian
Dressage	"S" Dressage judge	"R" DTD	N/A	N/A	N/A
Driving	"R" Driving judge	N/A	"R" Driving TD	"R" Driving CD	N/A
Endurance	N/A	N/A	N/A	N/A	N/A
Eventing	"R" Eventing judge	N/A	"R" Eventing TD	"R" Eventing CD	N/A
Jumper	N/A	N/A	N/A	N/A	N/A
Reining	"R" Reining judge	N/A	N/A	N/A	N/A
Vaulting	"R" Vaulting judge	N/A	N/A	N/A	N/A

4. A judge licensed in a division restricted to one breed may judge all classes restricted to entries of that breed even though he may not be licensed in the divisions for all types of classes offered. Exceptions:

    a. A licensed Dressage judge must judge Dressage classes.

    b. Sport Horse classes in the Arabian, Half-Arabian and Anglo/Arabian Division are to be judged by Federation/Equine Canada judges licensed in Dressage Sport Horse Breeding, Hunter Breeding, Dressage, Hunter or Jumper divisions; no guest card will be required.

    c. For Carriage Pleasure Driving divisions, see CP201.

    d. Refer to GR1004.16 for Western Dressage.

5. Judges licensed in the Hackney Pony Division can judge Shetland Pony and Roadster Pony classes.

6. Registered Hunter judges can officiate in "A" rated Welsh Pony Hunter classes and "B" and "C" rated Welsh Pleasure classes. Registered Hunter judges may officiate a maximum of two times in "A" rated Welsh Pleasure classes.

7. Judges licensed by the FEI are eligible to officiate in Federation Licensed Competitions in the division in which they are Internationally licensed (except in Vaulting.) However, foreign FEI 2* Dressage Judges are eligible to judge only through the Prix St. Georges level.

8. In competitions restricted to entries of one breed, (i.e. Arabian, Morgan, Friesian), a judge licensed in a specific division (i.e. Hunter, Saddle Seat Equitation, Reining) may officiate the sections at that competition in which he/she is licensed. In this case a guest card is not required, nor is a Special Judges card required for recorded judges licensed in a specific division in order to judge these classes.

9. Judges licensed in the Western Division are eligible to officiate Reining classes in breed restricted competitions, provided the Reining Division is not USA Reining approved.

10. Judges licensed in the American Saddlebred division will officiate in the Parade division.

11. Judges licensed in the Hunter division or the Hunter Breeding Division are eligible to officiate in the Pony Hunter Breeding division.

12. Connemara classes shall be judged by a judge licensed in Connemara, Dressage Sport Horse Breeding or Hunter Breeding Divisions.

13. Judges licensed by the ADS in Pleasure Driving are eligible to officiate any level Carriage Pleasure Driving classes at Federation licensed competitions. A Guest Judge card is required. Restrictions of GR1001 must be met by any 'r' ADS judge obtaining a guest card.

14. Judges licensed in any breed that includes a Saddle Seat or English Pleasure section are eligible to officiate English Pleasure Saddle Seat classes. Judges licensed in Hunter or any breed that includes a Hunter Pleasure section are eligible to officiate English Pleasure Hunter Seat classes. Judges licensed in any breed that includes a Pleasure Driving section are eligible to officiate English Pleasure Driving classes.

15. Judges approved by USA Reining are eligible to officiate Reining classes at the following levels of Federation licensed competitions:

    a. 'R' Judges are those approved by USA Reining to officiate at any level of Reining competition and must be a current FEI, USEF or NRHA licensed judge;

    b. 'r' Judges are those approved by USA Reining to officiate Reining classes at breed restricted competitions that do not include a USEF or FEI Reining division;

    c. A Guest Judge card is required if the judge is not on the list of current USEF Reining judges.

16. A licensed Dressage or Western Dressage judge must judge Western Dressage classes.

    a. licensed Dressage judge may officiate all levels of Western Dressage classes (see also GR1007-1009 for exceptions);

    b. a licensed 'r' Western Dressage judge may officiate Introductory and Basic levels only and Western Dressage Suitability, Western Dressage Hack and Western Dressage Seat Equitation (see also GR1009);

    c. a licensed 'R' Western Dressage judge may officiate all levels of Western Dressage classes and Suitability,

Western Dressage Hack and Western Dressage Seat Equitation (see also GR1008)

   d. Breed licensed judges are eligible to officiate Western Dressage Suitability, Western Dressage Hack and Western Dressage Seat Equitation classes only.

17. U.S. Regional Shows, Pacific Slope Championships, East Coast Championships, East and West Canadian Breeders Championships and U. S. National Championship classes must be judged by a Registered ("R") Arabian Division USEF judge or Senior judge in EC who is on the AHA Recognized Judges List as an accredited National/Regional judge. Exception AHA "Specialty" classes: Working Hunter, Jumper, Cutting, Dressage, Hunter/Jumping Seat Equitation, Reining, Working Cow, Reined Cow Horse, Trail, Carriage Driving and Sport Horse. Detailed specifications for these sections can be found in the AHA Handbook.

18. A judge licensed in the Arabian and/or American Saddlebred Division may officiate in the National Show Horse Division.

GR1005 Fees

1. Judges, Stewards, Technical Delegates, and Course Designers:
   a. initial application or re-enrollment (one division): $125. Each additional division (limit of 3): $30.
   b. application for promotion, including promotion to FEI status: $50 per division.
   c. Hunter & Jumper Course Designer's Apprentice Program-$60

2. Annual renewal: $40 per national level licenses. FEI officials: $35 each person.

3. Officials' liability insurance: $15.

4. Special Judge, Steward, Jumper Course Designer, or Hunter Course Designer card: $55.

5. Guest cards for judges, Driving Technical Delegates or Combined Driving Course Designers: $55.

6. Learner judge's card: $40.

7. Learner Permit (HU, HE, HB, JP) application fee - $60.

8. All fees are non-refundable.

SUBCHAPTER 10-C CLASSIFICATIONS - JUDGES

GR1006 General

Licensed judges are classified as Senior, Registered, Recorded, Special, Guest and Learner. A judge will not be licensed in more than 12 divisions.

GR1007 Senior Judge

Senior judge classification (S) applies to Dressage. Senior Dressage judges may officiate in all national and FEI Level Dressage classes at Federation Licensed Competitions. Senior Eventing Judges may officiate at any level of Eventing (see also EV171.1b). A Senior Dressage judge may officiate all levels of Western Dressage with the exception of Western Dressage Suitability, Western Dressage Hack, and Western Dressage Seat Equitation.

GR1008 Registered Judge

1. A Registered judge (R) may officiate alone at any competition in the divisions in which he/she is Registered.

2. Registered Dressage judges may officiate in classes at Fourth Level and below except for FEI Dressage Tests for 5 and 6-year-old horses. Registered Dressage judges may officiate in FEI Junior Tests, FEI Pony Tests, FEI Childrens Tests, FEI Para-Equestrian Dressage Tests, FEI and USEF Dressage Tests for 4 year old horses, and USEF and FEI Eventing Dressage Tests at all levels. Registered Dressage judges may not officiate in any classes above Fourth Level.

3. Rated Hunter sections at Premier competitions must be judged by two Registered (R) judges.

4. A Registered Eventing judge may officiate the intermediate level and below (see also EV171.1c).

5. A Registered Dressage Judge may officiate at any level of Western Dressage with the exception of Western Dressage Suitability, Western Dressage Hack and Western Dressage Seat Equitation classes.

6. A Registered Western Dressage Judge may officiate at any level of Western Dressage including Western Dressage Suitability, Western Dressage Hack and Western Dressage Seat Equitation classes.

GR1009 Recorded Judge

1. A Recorded judge (r) may not officiate alone or independently in:

   a. an "A" or "B" division or section;

   b. a Jumper class offering more than $2,500;

   c. a Federation Hunter/Jumping Seat Medal Class at a National or Premier Rated Hunter competition; or

   d. a Saddle Seat Medal Championship/Finals. (See GR1009.5 for exceptions.)

2. A Recorded Dressage judge may officiate at Second Level and below and may not officiate at the Third Level and above. Recorded Dressage judges may not officiate in FEI or USEF Dressage Tests for 4 and 5 year-old horses or in FEI Pony Tests. Recorded Dressage judges may officiate in Eventing or FEI Para-Equestrian Dressage Tests equivalent to Second Level or below (Exception: Eventing Competitions).

3. A Recorded Eventing judge may officiate at the Preliminary level and below (see also EV171.1d).

4. Recorded hunter judges with Special judges' cards may not officiate alone at an "A" rated hunter section.

5. A Recorded judge may, however, officiate alone under the following circumstances:

   a. at a competition which is Local except in the Saddle Seat Medal Championship/Finals;

   b. in any "C" division or section or "B" rated Hunter section in which he/she is a Recorded judge;

   c. in any American Saddlebred Division;

   d. in any Arabian Division,

   e. in any Friesian Division;

   f. in any Morgan Division;

   g. in any division (except Dressage and Eventing) for which a competition has requested in writing that the Federation grant a Special judge's card to a Recorded judge for that particular competition and provided the Federation approves the issuance of such card;

   h. Recorded Hunter judges can officiate alone in "B" and "C" rated Welsh Pony Hunter classes;

   i. A recorded (r) Andalusian/Lusitano judge may officiate alone in any Andalusian/Lusitano class except for Regional or National Championship competitions.

   j. A Recorded (r) Carriage Pleasure Driving Judge may officiate alone in any Carriage Pleasure Driving competition that does not exceed one day or an aggregate of eight (8) hours judging time.

   k. A Recorded (r) Vaulting judge may officiate alone or be President of the Jury at any Federation licensed vaulting competition.

   l. A Recorded (r) Shetland judge may officiate alone at any Federation licensed Shetland competition.

   m. in any National Show Horse Division.

   n. in any Roadster Division.

   o. In the open Saddle Seat Equitation Division

6. A Recorded Dressage Judge may officiate at any level of Western Dressage with the exception of Western Dressage Suitability, Western Dressage Hack and Western Dressage Seat Equitation classes.

7. A Recorded Western Dressage judge may officiate Introductory and Basic Levels only and also Western Dressage Suitability, Western Dressage Hack and Western Dressage Seat Equitation classes.

GR1010 Special Judge

1. A Special judge is a Senior Active Member already enrolled as a Recorded judge to whom the Licensed Officials

Department may grant permission to officiate as a Registered judge in a division in which he is enrolled as a Recorded judge.

2. Such permission, which is not transferable, will be granted upon the request of a Licensed Competition for that competition only. The application must be made on the official form provided for that purpose and be accompanied by the required fee; the fee is non-refundable. The statement on the form that the competition holds itself responsible that the individual applied for is familiar with the Federation rules and is capable to adjudicate as requested must be signed by the competition manager.

3. Special cards are not issued for the Dressage or Eventing Divisions.

4. Special cards will not be issued to anyone whose application for re-enrollment, promotion or change of status has been denied by the Licensed Officials Committee for the respective license applied for.

5. Authority to act as a Special judge will not be granted to any person more than twice in a lifetime, in a particular division without the approval of the Licensed Officials Committee Chairmen or their designee, and any two members of the Licensed Officials Committee.

6. Application must be received in the Federation office at least 14 days prior to the start of the competition. In cases where special applications are received prior to the competition, but less than 14 days prior, the competition will be fined $50. If management disputes that the application was not timely filed or that the above fine is not properly owing, it may appeal in writing to the Federation within 30 days of management's receipt of the Federation's notice of fine, specifying the grounds for the appeal. The Federation's CEO or his designee, a special committee appointed by the President or the Hearing Committee will consider the appeal and may waive a part or all of the fine upon a finding of good cause why the application was not timely filed and/or a finding that extreme hardship results from the automatic penalty.

7. It is the responsibility of competition management to assure the eligibility of all judges.

GR1011 Guest Judge

1. A Guest official is a Senior Active Member 21 years of age or over, not enrolled as an official in a particular division, to whom the Licensed Officials department may grant permission to officiate in that division upon the request of a Licensed Competition and for that competition only. The fee is not refundable. The application must be made on the official form provided for that purpose and must be accompanied by the required fee. The statement on the form that the competition holds itself responsible that the individual applied for is familiar with the Federation rules and is capable to adjudicate as requested must be signed by the competition manager.

2. A full membership fee is not required for Guest Cards issued for classes in which the Federation does not have division rules or license judges and the applicant is not a Federation member, provided that a Show Pass fee of $30 for each such guest judge accompanies the application in addition to the guest judge fee.

3. The application for a Guest Card must be received in the Federation office at least 21 days prior to the start of the competition. In cases where the Guest Card application is received prior to the competition, but less than 21 days prior, the competition will be fined $50. If management disputes that the application was not timely filed or that the above fine is not properly owing, it may appeal in writing to the Federation within 30 days of management's receipt of the Federation's notice of fine, specifying the grounds for the appeal. The Federation's CEO or his designee, a special committee appointed by the President or the Hearing Committee will consider the appeal and may waive a part or all of the fine upon a finding of good cause why the application was not timely filed and/or a finding that extreme hardship results from the automatic penalty.

4. It is the responsibility of competition management to assure the eligibility of all officials.

5. Guest Cards will not be issued to anyone whose application for enrollment, re-enrollment, promotion, or change of status has been denied by the Licensed Officials Committee in the respective division in which the Guest Card is applied for.

6. Guest Cards are required for officials with foreign national licenses providing they have Senior status with their own federation and are officiating in the division for which they are licensed by their federation. Exceptions: Andalusian/Lusitano: Foreign experts who are licensed or approved to judge Andalusian/Lusitano horses in their respective countries.

7. Except in the circumstances below, Guest Cards will not be granted to any person more than twice in a lifetime in a particular division without the approval of the Board of Directors.

    a. There is no limit to the number of Guest Cards an official may receive in the following divisions:

        1. Arabian Speciality carded judges ie. Reining, Working Cow Horse, Trail.

        2. Judges for the USEF Show Jumping Talent Search Finals, US Hunter Seat Medal Finals, ASPCA Maclay Finals, and/or WIHS Finals.

        3. Carriage Pleasure Driving Judges approved by Foreign National Driving Societies.

        4. Saddle Seat Equitation: See GR1011.29.c.

        5. Foreign breeding experts officiating in Dressage/Sport Horse Breeding classes.

        6. Dressage: Retired foreign FEI Dressage judges at the Dressage level in which he/she had been eligible to officiate. However, retired foreign FEI 2* Dressage judges are eligible to judge only through the Prix St. Georges level.

        7. Foreign experts in the Andalusian/Lusitano, Arabian and Friesian divisions.

        8. Classes recognized by a national breed or discipline association and for which the Federation has no division rules and does not license judges.

    b. The following divisions have limits other than a maximum of twice in a lifetime:

        1. Hunter Breeding: See GR1011.20.b and .c.

        2. Friesian - Four Guest Cards may be granted in a lifetime (Exception: foreign experts).

        3. Roadster - Three Guest Cards may be granted in a lifetime.

8. Guest Cards are not required in the following circumstances:

    a. FEI officials providing they are officiating in the discipline for which they are licensed by the FEI. (For Dressage see GR1011.8.b and GR1011.12).

    b. Dressage- An FEI licensed Dressage Judge judging at any level at a Federation licensed competition. Foreign FEI 2* Dressage Judges are not required to have a Guest Card however, they are only eligible to judge through the Prix St. Georges level.

    c. Connemara - A Guest Card is not required for Dressage Sport Horse Breeding or Hunter Breeding Divisions if judged by a Federation licensed judge, see GR1004.12.

    d. Hunter- Senior Hunter Course Designers licensed by Equine Canada in the Hunter divisions at Federation competitions.

    e. Jumper – See GR1011.22.

    f. Saddle Seat Equitation – See GR1011.29.c.

    g. Vaulting – See GR1011.31.

9. Andalusian/Lusitano: Guest Judges are permitted at Andalusian/Lusitano competitions. See GR1011.6

10. Arabian

    a. Breeding/gelding in-hand - Guest cards will only be granted to foreign breeding experts. A list of foreign experts will be maintained by the Federation Licensed Officials Department.

    b. Pleasure Driving - An ADS Pleasure Driving judge may officiate alone in Arabian Carriage Pleasure Driving classes at an Arabian competition. A Guest Card is required.

    c. Reining – Judges licensed by the National Reining Horse Association (NRHA) and/or the National Reined Cow Horse Association (NRCHA) may officiate in Reining.

    d. Trail- Experienced National Reining Horse Association (NRHA), National Reined Cow Horse Association

(NRCHA) and/or judges licensed in another breed. (i.e. AQHA, APHA, ApHC, etc.) are allowed a Guest Card. Guest Cards are not required for Trail Course Designers (see AR219).

 e. Working/Reined Cow Horse Classes- Experienced National Reining Horse Association (NRHA), National Reined Cow Horse Association (NRCHA) and/or judges licensed in another breed (i.e. AQHA, APHA, ApHC, etc.) are allowed a Guest Card.

 f. A limit of two Guest Judges may serve on a multiple working western panel.

11. Connemara: Guest Judges must have **approved status from** the American Connemara Pony Society **to officiate in any class** in the Connemara **division at regular or local competitions with a Guest Card.**

12. Dressage: Guest Cards will only be issued to retired, foreign FEI Dressage judges or currently licensed judges with Senior Dressage status with another nation; they may officiate alone (See GR1011.8.a.&b.). Guest cards for Dressage Technical Delegates are not allowed.

13. Dressage Sport Horse Breeding: Guest Cards will only be issued to those persons who are currently licensed foreign FEI Dressage judges, and foreign breeding experts. A list of foreign breeding experts will be maintained by the Federation Licensed Officials Department. They may officiate alone.

14. Driving

 a. Carriage **Pleasure Driving:**

  1. Judges: must be a Federation licensed judge with experience in judging carriage driving

  2. The following may officiate as Guest Judges:

   a. American Driving Society (ADS) Pleasure Driving Judges, see CP201.

   b. Judges approved by foreign national driving societies; Guest Card limitations do not apply.

  3. Technical Delegates: must be chosen from American Driving Society (ADS) Combined Driving or Pleasure Driving Technical Delegates.

  4. Coaching: See CP301

  5. Driven Dressage: See CP524 and CP525

 b. Combined Driving

  1. Judges: from another country or American Driving Society (ADS) may be approved for a Guest Judge card, see DC987.

  2. Technical Delegate: must be chosen from a list of American Driving Society (ADS) technical delegates.

15. English Pleasure: allows guest judges to officiate alone at any competition.

16. Eventing: Issued only to those judges with Senior status with another nation.

17. Friesian: Guest judges are allowed to officiate alone at Friesian competitions.

18. Hackney: Guest Judges may officiate alone in the Hackney division provided the judge is USEF licensed in at least one other recognized breed division. In Hackney Pony classes, one Guest judge on a multiple judge panel is permitted.

19. Hunter: A guest judge may not officiate in any "AA", "A" or "B" rated divisions or sections.

20. Hunter Breeding: Guest Cards will only be permitted in the following circumstances:

 a. Judges currently holding an "R" or "r" Hunter license (In addition, see GR1011.7.b.ii).

 b. Registered (R) or recorded (r) Hunter judges may receive two Hunter Breeding Guest Cards per year.

 c. If a judge receives a Hunter Breeding Guest Card twice in one year, each Guest Card must be used in a different Zone.

 d. If a competition has 15 or more aggregate entries in the Hunter Breeding Section the previous year, they are ineligible to apply for a Guest Card and must have a judge(s) who holds a Hunter Breeding License.

21. Hunter/Jumping Seat Equitation:

 a. A Guest Judge may not officiate at any national or regional Hunter/Jumping Seat Equitation Finals. The following are exceptions:

1. USEF Show Jumping Talent Search Class/Finals, see EQ110.9.i

2. US Hunter Seat Medal Finals, see EQ110.5.d.5

3. WIHS Equitation Finals, see EQ110.10

4. ASPCA Maclay Finals, see EQ110.8.

   b. Guest judges may not officiate alone in any Federation Medal class.

22. Jumper: Guest Cards are not allowed in any division offering over $2,500

23. Morgan:

   a. Guest Judges may officiate alone in the Morgan division provided the judge is USEF licensed in at least one other recognized breed division. One Guest judge is allowed on a three-judge panel and may serve as a call judge provided he is licensed in at least one other division.

   b. Reining – Judges licensed by the National Reining Horse Association (NRHA)may officiate in Reining. A Guest Card is required.

24. National Show Horse: Guest Judges may officiate alone. Two Guest judges are allowed on a Three-judge panel, provided the judge is licensed in at least one other division. Either Guest Judge may serve as a call judge. Under this exception only, a judge may apply his/her Guest Card towards his/her learner judging requirements.

25. Paso Fino: Guest Judges may officiate with a Federation Licensed Paso Fino Registered "R" judge in any "B", "C", or Local rated competition. If competition is a multi-breed competition, a Guest Judge may officiate alone.

26. Reining: Guest Cards may be given to Judges approved by the USA Reining and who are not current USEF Reining, Western or FEI Reining judges. They may officiate in Reining classes at any Regular or Local competition.

27. Roadster: Guest Judges may officiate alone in the Roadster division; one Guest Judge is allowed on a multiple judge panel.

28. American Saddlebred: Guest Judges may officiate alone in the American Saddlebred division provided the judge is USEF licensed in at least one other recognized breed division. One Guest judge is allowed on a multiple judge panel.

29. Saddle Seat Equitation:

   a. A Guest Judge may not officiate at any national or regional Equitation Finals.

   b. A Guest Judge may not officiate alone in any Federation Medal Class.

   c. Any individual currently licensed by Equine Canada or the Riding Horse Judges Association of South Africa, as a Senior Saddle Seat Equitation judge shall automatically be eligible to officiate in the Saddle Seat division for the US Saddle Seat World Cup Trials, US Saddle Seat hosted Invitationals, and the Saddle Seat World Cup Competition hosted in US, without either an application or the fee required for a Guest Saddle Seat Equitation Judge's Card. There is no limit on the number of times that such an individual may officiate.

30. Shetland: Guest Judges may officiate alone.

31. Vaulting: Guest cards are not allowed.

32. Welsh: Guest Judges must have approved status from the Welsh Pony and Cob Society of America to officiate in any class in the Welsh division at regular or local competitions with a guest card.

33. Western Seat Equitation or Western:

   a. A Guest Judge may not officiate at any national or regional Equitation Finals.

   b. A Guest Judge may not officiate alone in any Federation Medal Class.

   c. Guest Cards may be issued to national breed association judges at Federation licensed Open Western Competitions (Maximum of two competitions in a lifetime). A maximum of two Guest Judges are permitted to officiate in an "A" rated competition. *BOD 1/17/15 Effective 12/1/15.*

GR1012 Learner Judge

1. A Learner judge is a Senior Active Member, 21 years of age or over, to whom the Federation may grant permission,

upon the request of a Licensed Competition and for that competition only, to accompany a licensed judge in the ring. Certain breeds/disciplines require learner judging to be with a Registered (R) judge. Exception: Hunter, Hunter Seat Equitation, Jumper and Hunter Breeding are not required to submit an application, pre-approval or payment. BOD 1/17/15 Effective 12/1/15.

   a. Permission will not be granted for more than one Learner judge to be in a ring at any one time. Dressage, Vaulting, Eventing and Western Dressage excepted. More than one Learner Judge may accompany a Registered judge in the Hunter, Hunter/Jumping Seat Equitation, Hunter Breeding, and/or Jumper divisions, with permission of competition management and the judge.

   b. The fee is not refundable.

   c. Learner Judging in Opportunity or Exhibition classes does not count toward licensing requirements.

   d. The application must be made on the official form provided for that purpose and must be accompanied by the required fee. After contacting the competition manager for permission, the individual wishing to officiate as a learner judge must obtain consent from that judge with whom he or she would be officiating.

      1. The statement on the form that the competition holds itself responsible that the individual applied for is familiar with the Federation rules and is capable to observe as requested, must be signed by the competition manager.

      2. The Licensed Competition may request additional specific information about an individual's experience before accepting him as a learner judge.

2. Completed Learner Judge Card Applications must be received in the Federation Office at least 14 days prior to the start of competition. Learner applications received prior to the show, but less than 14 days prior, will receive no credit.

3. There is no limit to the number of times a person may be granted a Learner judge's card. He should use a scorecard to evaluate the various entries, but a Learner judge has no authority as to the merits of the competitors.

4. Conflict of Interest

   a. An individual cannot learner judge in a licensed competition where a family member, cohabitant, companion, domestic partner, housemate, member of the learner judge's household, client, employer or employee is competing.

   b. An individual is allowed to learner judge with a family member, cohabitant, companion, domestic partner, housemate, member of the learner judge's household, client, employer or employee but that learner judge experience cannot be counted towards the minimum required experiences. It must be considered an extra learner judge experience.

SUBCHAPTER 10-D CLASSIFICATIONS - STEWARDS

GR1013 General

1. Licensed stewards are licensed by the Licensed Officials Committee as Registered, Recorded, and Special, in either one or both of the following Categories.

   a. Category 1 (C1) Steward is licensed to officiate the following specialized Divisions and Sections: Hunter, Hunter Breeding, Hunter/Jumping Seat Equitation, Jumper, Welsh, Connemara, and English Pleasure.

      1. Any steward officiating USEF Open (not restricted to a breed) hunter and/or jumper classes must be a Senior Active member in good standing of the United States Hunter Jumper Association, Inc.

   b. Category 2 (C2) Steward is licensed to officiate the following specialized Divisions and Sections: Andalusian/Lusitano, Arabian, Connemara, English Pleasure, Friesian, Hackney Harness, Morgan, National Show Horse, Parade, Paso Fino, Reining, Roadster, American Saddlebred, Saddle Seat Equitation, Shetland, Western/Reining Seat Equitation, Welsh, Western Dressage and Western.

2. A Category 1 or Category 2 steward is entitled to officiate in only the corresponding divisions and sections of the license category listed above.

GR1014 Registered Steward

1. A Registered (R) Category 1 or Category 2 steward is an individual so classified by the Licensed Officials Committee.

2. The Registered Category 1 or Category 2 steward is entitled to officiate alone unless the competition requires more than one steward.

GR1015 Recorded Steward

1. A Recorded (r) Category 1 or Category 2 steward is an individual so classified by the Licensed Officials Committee.

2. A Recorded Category 1 or Category 2 steward may not officiate alone in any "A" rated division or section or in a Jumper division at competitions offering over $2,500 in that division.

3. A Recorded Category 2 steward may officiate alone in any Arabian or National Show Horse division or section. Exception: Regional and National Arabian, Morgan, Andalusian/Lusitano and Friesian competitions and National Show Horse Finals must have Registered Stewards officiate their events.

4. A Recorded Category 2 steward may officiate alone in Hackney, Roadster, American Saddlebred, Western Dressage and Shetland divisions or sections without a Special Steward's card.

5. The Recorded Category 2, steward, may, however, officiate alone in an "A" rated division or section if the competition requests in writing that the Federation grant a Special Steward's card for that particular competition and provided the Federation approves the issuance of such card.

GR1016 Special Steward

1. A Special Category 1 or Category 2 steward is an individual already enrolled as a Recorded Category 1 or Category 2 steward, to whom the Licensed Officials Department shall grant permission to officiate as a Registered steward in an "A" rated division or section and/or Arabian, National Show Horse, Morgan, Andalusian/Lusitano and Friesian divisions or sections. Exception: Regional and National Arabian, Morgan, Andalusian/Lusitano and Friesian competitions and National Show Horse Finals cannot use Special Stewards.

   a. Such permission, which is not transferable, shall be granted upon request of a particular Licensed Competition for that competition only.

   b. The application must be made on the official form provided for that purpose and be accompanied by the required fee. The statement on the form that the competition holds itself responsible that the individual applied for is familiar with the Federation rules and is capable to officiate as requested, must be signed by the competition manager. Application must be received in the Federation office at least 21 days prior to the competition.

   c. Special cards will not be issued to anyone whose application for re-enrollment, promotion or change of status has been denied by the Licensed Officials Committee for the respective license applied for.

   d. Authority to act as a Special Steward will not be granted to any person more than twice in a lifetime, in a particular division without the approval of the Licensed Officials Committee Chairmen or their designee, and any two members of the Licensed Officials Committee.

   e. In cases where the special applications are received prior to the competition, but less than 21 days prior, the competition will be fined $50.

   f. If management disputes that the application was not timely filed or that the above fine is not properly owing, it may appeal in writing to the Federation within 30 days of management's receipt of the Federation's notice of fine, specifying the grounds for the appeal. The Federation's CEO or his designee, a special committee appointed by the president or the Hearing Committee will consider the appeal and may waive a part or all of the fine upon a finding of good cause why the application was not timely filed and/or a finding that extreme hardship results from the automatic penalty.

   g. It is the responsibility of competition management to assure the eligibility of all stewards.

2. Special cards for "A" rated competitions (divisions and sections) and/or Arabian or National Show Horse division or

sections will only be considered for Recorded Category 1 or Category 2 stewards of the same Category. Exception: Arabian Regional and National competitions cannot use Special Stewards.

SUBCHAPTER 10-E CLASSIFICATIONS - TECHNICAL DELEGATES

GR1017 General

1. Licensed technical delegates are licensed by the Licensed Officials Committee as Registered or recorded in Dressage, Eventing, Vaulting, Carriage Pleasure Driving, and Combined Driving.
2. Only licensed technical delegates in good standing may officiate at Licensed Eventing, Driving or Dressage Competitions.

GR1018 Registered Technical Delegates - Eventing and Dressage

1. A Senior (S) Eventing Technical Delegate is entitled to officiate alone in any division at any level of Eventing. A Registered (R) Eventing Technical Delegate is entitled to officiate alone at the Intermediate Level and below (see also EV173.1a).
2. A Registered Dressage Technical Delegate must officiate at Level 4 and Level 5 Dressage Competitions. A Registered Dressage Technical Delegate may officiate alone at USEF/USDF Championships, Federation Developing Program Championships, and USEF High Performance Championships, qualifying and selection trials and observation classes, at any Dressage Competition level or in the Dressage division or section at Regular or Local Competitions. (See GR1211.3a and .g).
3. A Registered (R) Dressage Technical Delegate must be a current member in good standing of the United States Dressage Federation (USDF). Only Dressage Technical Delegates who are current Participating Members of the United States Dressage Federation may officiate at USEF/USDF Regional and National Dressage Championships.

GR1019 Recorded Technical Delegates - Eventing and Dressage

1. A recorded ("r") Eventing technical delegate may not officiate alone at an Intermediate or Advanced Horse Trial or a Two or Three-Day Event but may officiate as the assistant to the technical delegate.
2. A Recorded Dressage Technical Delegate may officiate as the assistant to the Registered Technical Delegate(s) at Level 4 and Level 5 Dressage Competitions, and may officiate alone at Levels 1-3 Dressage Competitions. A Recorded Dressage Technical Delegate may not officiate alone at USEF/USDF Championships, Federation Developing Program Championships, and USEF High Performance Championships, qualifying and selection trials and observation classes, but may officiate as the assistant to the Registered Technical Delegate for these competitions or classes. A Recorded Dressage Technical Delegate may officiate alone in the Dressage division or section at Regular or Local Competitions. (See GR1211.3a and .g).
3. A Recorded (r) Dressage Technical Delegate must be a current member in good standing of the United States Dressage Federation (USDF). Only Dressage Technical Delegates who are current Participating Members of the United States Dressage Federation may officiate at USEF/USDF Regional and National Dressage Championships.

GR1020 Driving Technical Delegates

1. Combined Driving Technical Delegate - A Combined Driving Technical Delegate is an individual licensed by the Committee, and is entitled to officiate alone in Combined Driving Events. See DC988.2.3.3 and DC987.1.5.3 for information on Guest Cards for Combined Driving Technical Delegates.
2. Carriage Pleasure Driving Technical Delegate - A Carriage Pleasure Driving Technical Delegate is an individual so classified by the Committee, and is entitled to officiate alone in Carriage Pleasure Driving Competitions. See CP201.2 for information on Guest Cards for Carriage Pleasure Driving Technical Delegates.

GR1021 Vaulting Technical Delegates

A Vaulting Technical Delegate is an individual licensed by the Committee, who may officiate alone at any level of national Vaulting competition.

SUBCHAPTER 10-F CLASSIFICATIONS - COURSE DESIGNERS

GR1022 General

Course designers shall be licensed as Registered, recorded or Special in the Hunter/Hunter/Jumping Seat Equitation and Jumper Division; Registered or recorded in the Eventing and Carriage Pleasure Driving Divisions; Registered, Apprentice or Guest in the Combined Driving Division.

GR1023 Jumper Course Designers

1. A minimum of an 'r' license is required to officiate alone in any competition with a Jumper Rating 2 or higher.
2. An 'R' license is required to officiate alone for all classes offering $25,000 or more in prize money.
3. Any individual currently licensed by the FEI as a Level 2 or higher Course Designer for Show Jumping or by Equine Canada as a Senior Course Designer for Show Jumping shall automatically be eligible to officiate in the jumper division at Federation competitions without either an application or the fee required for a Special Jumper Course Designer Card. There is no limit on the number of times that such an individual may officiate.

GR1024 Hunter, Hunter/Jumping Seat Equitation Course Designers

1. A mininum of an "r" license is required to officiate alone at a National or Premier rated competition with a Hunter class offering up to $4,999 in prize money.
2. An "R" license is required to officiate alone in Hunter classes offering $5,000 or more in prize money.

GR1025 Special Hunter Course Designer

1. A Special Hunter Course Designer is a licensed "r" Hunter Course Designer to whom the Federation may grant permission to officiate a class or classes for which a "R" would otherwise be required, upon the request of a Licensed Competition and for that competition only.
2. Authority to act as a Special Hunter Course Designer shall not be granted more than twice to any one individual per lifetime. Special Hunter Course Designers shall be approved upon the recommendations of any two members of the USHJA Officials Committee.

GR1026 Special Jumper Course Designer

1. A Special Jumper Course Designer is a Senior Active Member 21 years of age or over, licensed as an "r" Jumper Course Designer to whom the Federation may grant permission to officiate a class or classes for which a "R" would otherwise be required, upon the request of a Licensed Competition and for that competition only.
2. Authority to act as a Special Jumper Course Designer shall not be granted more than twice to any one individual. Special Jumper Course Designers shall be approved upon the recommendation of the Chairman, or his designee, and any two members of the Jumper Committee. In principle, authorization to act as a Special Course Designer will be granted to those individuals who have completed all the requirements for a "R" Jumper Course Designer license but have not yet received their license.

GR1027 Eventing Course Designers

See Chapter EV - Eventing EV175.1 for officiating eligibility for 'S', 'R' and 'r' Eventing Course Designers.

GR1028 Combined Driving Course Designer

A "R" license is required to design courses at Federation licensed Combined Driving events.

 SPONSORED BY HAGYARD EQUINE MEDICAL INSTITUTE || © USEF 2016

GR1029 Guest Combined Driving Course Designer

1. A Guest Combined Driving Course Designer is a Senior Active Member 21 years of age or over, not enrolled as a course designer, to whom the President or Secretary may grant permission to officiate in that capacity upon the request of a Recognized Driving Competition and for that competition only.

2. Authority to act as a Guest Combined Driving Course Designer shall not be granted more than twice to any one official.

3. Any individual currently licensed by the FEI as an International Course Designer for Combined Driving shall automatically be eligible to officiate in the Combined Driving Division at Federation driving competitions without either an application or the fee required for a Guest Card. There is no limit on the number of times that such an individual may officiate.

SUBCHAPTER 10-G CLASSIFICATIONS - OTHER

GR1030 Course Advisor

1. An individual appointed as a Course Advisor pursuant to EV174 shall be a Licensed Official of the Federation. He/she shall be so designated by the Licensed Officials Committee upon notification by the President or CEO or his designee of his/her appointment.

2. There will be no annual fee for the license, and an official's card shall be issued to the Course Advisor, who is eligible for all benefits afforded to other Licensed Officials by the Federation.

GR1031 Assigned Steward or Technical Delegate

1. A Federation Assigned Steward or Technical Delegate is an individual who is currently a Steward or Technical Delegate and who meets the Federation's criteria for a Federation Assigned Steward or Technical Delegate and has been designated to serve as a Federation Assigned Steward or Technical Delegate as specified by the Federation.

2. There is no additional fee for the designation, and a Federation Assigned Steward or Technical Delegate is eligible for all benefits afforded to Licensed Officials by the Federation.

3. A Federation Assigned Steward or Technical Delegate may be sent by the Federation to randomly selected Licensed Competitions or, with the approval of the CEO or his designee, to particular Licensed Competitions, for cause, to oversee and report back to the Federation on his/her observations.

4. The Assigned Steward or Technical Delegate will have the full duties of their position.

SUBCHAPTER 10-H REGULATIONS GOVERNING OFFICIALS

GR1032 General

1. Failure of an official to attend a competition with which he has a signed agreement or failure to perform his duties in accordance with the rules, or to officiate in the classes to which he is assigned shall constitute cause for disciplinary action as provided for in Chapters 6 and 7, except in cases of extreme emergency.

2. Any official found guilty of cruelty to a horse or to have killed, abandoned, mistreated, neglected or otherwise abused a horse, by an administrative agency, body, humane society or court of law, whether such court or tribunal is civil, criminal or administrative may have his license(s) revoked.

3. No official is to be housed in a private home unless he has agreed before the competition.

4. In the event that an official officiates at a competition where he is ineligible, the official may be penalized as described in GR703.

GR1033 Judges

1. Good judging depends upon a correct observance of the fine points and the selection of best horses for the purpose described by conditions of the class. A judge serves three interests: his own conscience, exhibitors and

spectators. He should make it clear that the best horses win.

2. When judges are required to judge independently on a multiple judge panel, each judge must meet the requirements as outlined in Rules GR1004 through GR1011.

3. Except in the discharge of their official duty, the use of cellular phones or other similar communication devices, including computers, by judges while in the ring (including center ring), judges' box, judges' stand or on any part of a course during a competition is strictly prohibited.

4. A judge is obligated to adjudicate each division, section and class in conformity with the rules and specifications of that division, section and class as they appear in the Federation Rule Book. He is expected to be proficient in his division and to possess a thorough knowledge of the rules of the Federation.

5. The attention of judges is directed to the difference in requirements covering Maiden, Novice, Limit, Junior, Amateur and Ladies' classes versus Open classes. These differences must be observed in adjudicating classes.

6. The decisions of each judge constitute solely his individual preference and not as opinions of or decisions by the Federation. For decisions of a judge in regard to soundness, see GR1204.

7. Consulting with a Veterinarian

   a. Only the judge may call a veterinarian during a class but is encouraged to do so if his opinion necessitates the disqualification of an entry. The judge shall give the numbers of the horses in question and the veterinarian shall render his finding. If the veterinarian is not immediately available or not called upon, the judge's decision as to the serviceable soundness of a horse shall be accepted for the purpose of disqualifying a horse from showing in that class and shall be final. (Exception: The decision of the judge as to the serviceable soundness of a horse in Hunter classes is final, however the competition veterinarian may be consulted.)

   b. In regard to possible whip marks, or other matters other than soundness that are pertinent to the welfare of the horse, the judge may consult with a veterinarian during a class. The final decision rests with the judge.

   c. None of the above applies to Dressage, Driving, Eventing or Western Dressage. See DR122.6, EV134.8 and WD125.8.

8. When a judge is used as a referee and is called upon to break a tie, the other judges must give the ringmaster only the numbers of the two horses tied. The ringmaster will then take these to the referee who will indicate his preference by circling the number of his choice. The ringmaster will then return this written decision to the other judges who will proceed with the remaining placements, as the breakage of a tie for one placement by the referee does not automatically place the losing contender of the tie in the next position. This procedure is to be followed for each placement in turn, as ties occur. The referee shall turn in a judge's card only when called upon to break a tie, in which case only his tie breaking decision shall be indicated on the card.

9. All placements stated in the prize list/omnibus shall be awarded, beginning with first place and proceeding in order through all placements, unless there is an insufficient number of entries or an entry is eliminated, excused, or disqualified.

10. It shall be the prerogative of the Licensee to designate a particular system of judging and to post judges' cards and complete order of placement for public inspection. Judges accepting an invitation to officiate must recognize the Licensee's prerogative. Unless the Licensee designates a particular system of judging when an invitation is issued, a judge is not required to use a particular system of judging.

11. A judge must order from the ring any unruly horse or one whose actions threaten to endanger the rider, driver, handler, other exhibitors or their entries.

12. A judge must order from the ring any rider, driver or handler who exhibits inappropriate or dangerous behavior or whose actions would in any way threaten the safety of any exhibitor, their entries or the safety of class officials.

13. When over 40 horses or riders are entered in a performance class in which horses compete together, a judge must divide the class and work it in groups of less than 40. Unless individual tests are required in the class routine, he shall bring the top contestants from each group back into the ring for final adjudication. (Exception: See

AR107.7d and DR126.1a(4)).

14. In classes which have a maximum weight and/or measurement for shoes, the judge himself must immediately weigh and/or measure any shoe that is cast. In such classes the judge may not excuse an entry from the ring until satisfied that the entry has not cast a shoe.

15. In the Western and Western Seat Equitation division, when a single judge system is used, judge's cards shall be considered final and shall not be changed after the completion of the presentation of awards for that class.

16. Judges' cards and/or official score sheets are to be signed by the judge and retained (with the exception of score sheets returned to the exhibitor) as part of the competition's official records for a period of no less than three years. Electronic signatures through a PDA or similar device used to record scores will fulfill the signature requirement.

17. Judges must commence and complete classes in accordance with GR109.

GR1034 Stewards and Technical Delegates

1. Except in Hawaii and Alaska, no steward may officiate for more than three consecutive years at the same competition or at more than three consecutive competitions run by the same governing body, Board of Directors or Licensee. When three or more stewards are officiating, one steward will not be subject to these restrictions and will be eligible to serve as steward for a fourth consecutive competition run by the same governing body, Board of Directors or Licensee.

2. Except in Hawaii, no technical delegate may officiate for more than two consecutive years at the same competition or at more than two consecutive competitions run by the same governing body, Board of Directors or Licensee. In Alaska, no dressage technical delegate may officiate more than three consecutive years at the same competition, but are not otherwise restricted from officiating at consecutive competitions run by the same governing body, Board of Directors or Licensee. For the purposes of this rule, multiple, consecutive day Dressage Competitions held within a six-day period will be counted as one competition, if they are run by the same governing body, Board of Directors or Licensee.

3. A steward or technical delegate should clearly understand that he has no authority in connection with the management or the judging of a competition but should point out in a diplomatic manner any instance where Federation rules are not enforced. He should immediately report to the appropriate officials any violations of the rules which might invalidate a class; should keep himself available to judges, exhibitors and management at all times to clarify the application of Federation rules and investigate any situation where the rules are not upheld.

4. The other duties of a Licensed steward and technical delegate shall be but are not limited to, the following:

   a. To protect the interests of exhibitors, judges and Competition Management.

   b. To investigate and act upon any alleged rule violations without waiting for a protest.

   c. To report to the Show Committee any misrepresentation or substitution of entry without waiting for a protest.

   d. To ascertain that all judges either are licensed in divisions to which assigned or that the competition has a Guest or Special card for the judge for the divisions not covered by his license.

   e. To supervise and record time-out, if time-outs are permitted by division rules, in the event of a horse casting a shoe or breakage of equipment, if an official timer or judge is not available as provided for in GR833.

   f. To satisfy himself that the accommodations for horses, feeding, training areas, etc. are suitable in all respects. The steward or technical delegate must commence his duties early enough to deal with these matters.

   g. To measure all animals required to be measured as provided for in Chapter 5, Chapter DR (DR135) and Chapter HU, HU168-HU179, and if necessary return Measurement cards to the Federation.

      1. Registered (R) Dressage Technical Delegates must have attended a Federation Dressage/DSHB Pony Measurement Certification clinic where certification testing to measure ponies for dressage or DSHB is conducted. Recorded (r) Dressage Technical Delegates must attend a Federation Dressage/DSHB Pony Measurement Certification clinic prior to January 1, 2011 where certification testing to measure ponies for dressage or

DSHB is conducted. Refer to GR1052 and DR135 for additional measurement certification requirements.

2. Only a USEF-certified Dressage Technical Delegate, working with the Competition Veterinarian, is eligible to conduct Dressage/DSHB pony measurements.

3. In order for Registered (R) Combined Driving Technical Delegates to conduct measurement at a competition, they must have attended a Federation Combined Driving Pony Measurement Certification clinic where certification testing to measure ponies for Combined Driving is conducted. This certification must be completed by November 30, 2014 for current (R) Combined Driving Technical Delegates.

4. Only a USEF measurement certified Technical Delegate or Steward, working with the Competition Veterinarian is eligible to conduct Combined Driving pony measurements. (see Chapter 5 Appendix H).

h. Stewards and Technical Delegates are responsible for ensuring that measurements are conducted in accordance with the rules and that all required paperwork is completed in a legible manner. Offenders could be subject to a fine or administrative penalty at the discretion of the CEO or his designee.

i. To report to the Show Committee any offense or violation of the rules and prefer charges against violators if the violation is not properly handled by the Show Committee.

j. To furnish the Federation with a complete written report as to the conduct of the competition including any offenses or violations of the rules by the competition or any exhibitors, within fourteen (14) days after the last licensed day of the competition, on the form furnished by the Federation.

1. A written report is also required to be submitted for competitions comprised exclusively of FEI classes and at USEF competitions held in Canada.

2. If the Federation does not receive the completed report and/or attachments postmarked and/or electronically submitted within fourteen (14) days of the closing of the competition, the Steward/Technical Delegate will be fined a fee of $100. For the second offense and any offense thereafter in the same competition year, said official will be fined $250. A third offense and any offense thereafter will result in an automatic suspension from office as Steward or Technical Delegate for 90 days, in addition to the fines.

3. Failure to pay any fine within 30 days will result in a violation of rules and the Steward/Technical Delegate will be subject to an additional $100 late fee.

4. If the Steward/Technical Delegate disputes that the report was not timely filed, he/she may appeal in writing to the Federation within 30 days of receipt of the Federation's notice of the fine. The appeal must be accompanied by a check for $50., payable to the Federation, which will be refunded if the appeal is upheld. The CEO or his designee and three members of the Licensed Officials Committee will consider the appeal and may waive a part or all of the fine upon finding of good cause of why the report was not timely filed and/or a finding that extreme hardship results from the automatic penalty. Note: only the fine may be waived. The rule violation will remain on record for the official.

k. To collect all medication report forms filed, either with the Steward/Technical Delegate or Designated Competition Office Representative, and send them to the Federation's Office of Equine Drugs and Medications, 956 King Avenue, Columbus, OH 43212-2655.

l. To observe and report or charge in accordance with Chapter 6:

1. To see that each entry blank has been signed by a trainer;

2. To see that every rider, driver, handler, vaulter, longeur, owner, lessee, agent and trainer participating in any Regular Competitions, Eventing Competitions at the Preliminary Level or above, Combined Driving Competitions at the Advanced Level or above, Dressage Competitions, and Vaulting Competitions is a member of the Federation as required by the provisions of Bylaw 203;

3. To see that each Federation membership number appears on the entry blank or that a Show Pass fee has been paid; and

4. To see that every rider, driver and vaulter in a non-breed-restricted event in an FEI recognized discipline has

complied with GR828.4.

m. Observe and report that Competition Management has required each exhibitor, rider, driver, handler and trainer or his/her agent(s) to sign each entry blank, or charge in accordance with Chapter 6.

n. EXCEPTION: At Regular and Local Competitions, 4l and 4m above, are the responsibility of the Secretary not the C1 or C2 Steward.

o. To make routine inspections of the stable area and to ensure that the stalls are in compliance with GR1215.

p. To ensure that Federation Member Reports and Judge Evaluation Forms are publicly displayed and available for Federation members during the entire competition.

q. Notify exhibitors in classes where due to a violation, points will not count toward the Horse of the Year Awards (See GR1113).

r. To take all steps necessary for the enforcement of the Drugs and Medications Chapter (see GR411).

s. The Steward's and/or schooling supervisor's decision regarding schooling fences, tack and equipment in the warm-up area is final.

t. To report to the Federation details of injuries relating to both humans and equines on the official Accident/Injury Report form provided by the Federation. In the event of a fatality, the Federation or weekend on-call number must be notified as soon as possible but not later than 24 hours after the incident.

u. To submit to the Federation a copy of the competition's accident preparedness plan, along with his/her steward or technical delegate report as provided for in GR1211.5e.

5. No Steward or Technical Delegate may officiate at more than one competition at the same time. Exception: USEF Licensed Special Competitions excluding dressage. *BOD 1/17/15 Effective 12/1/15.*

6. Stewards and technical delegates must retain copies of steward/technical delegate report forms, and supporting documentation, for a period of three years.

GR1035 Special Duties of a Technical Delegate

1. In addition to the responsibilities of a steward listed in GR1035, the powers, duties and responsibilities of a technical delegate are as follows:

a. To inspect the courses and arenas to satisfy himself that the technical details are in accordance with the rules and regulations.

b. To satisfy himself, in addition, that the course is fair, at the standard of the level offered and that knowledge of local conditions does not play any part.

c. At Eventing Competitions, to assist the Ground Jury to supervise the technical and administrative conduct of the competition. Until he has indicated to the Ground Jury that he is satisfied with all the arrangements, the authority of the technical delegate shall be absolute. At Horse Trials at which the Ground Jury are occupied judging the Dressage Test and/or the Jumping Test, the technical delegate may supervise all arrangements made by the Organizing Committee for the judging and timekeeping of the Cross-Country Test and should be available at the Control Center to adjudicate, where possible, on unforeseen eventualities.

d. To protect the interests of competitors, judges and the event or competition organizers.

e. To report on the competition, including a record of all disputes and how adjudicated.

f. To instruct the Organizing Committee to make any alterations to the course or arena or to any technical detail associated with the conduct of the competition which he considers necessary.

g. To help the Ground Jury to supervise the technical conduct of the competition after he has indicated to the President of the Ground Jury that he is satisfied with the arrangements.

h. At Dressage Competitions, to observe and report that management and competitors are in compliance with all Dressage Division regulations regarding USEF/USDF Qualifying and Championship classes, Federation Junior Team Championships, and USEF Championships, qualifying and selection trials and observation classes.

    i. At Vaulting Competitions, to monitor the horse use rule (VA105) and make sure that horses are not used more than the maximum units allowed.

    j. Driving Technical Delegates: To ensure the Motorized Vehicle Notice is posted at the Event.

GR1036 Yellow Warning Card - Stewards and Technical Delegates

1. A Yellow Warning Card may be issued by a Steward, Technical Delegate, or Competition Official working in any of these capacities at the competition to any competitor, spectator or participant for improper conduct, or for non-compliance with the rules, provided the issuer considers the conduct not severe enough to cause the issuer to file formal Charges pursuant to GR604.

2. To issue a Yellow Warning Card, a Steward, Technical Delegate, or Competition Official must complete and sign the Yellow Warning Card.

3. A copy of the signed Yellow Warning Card must be provided to the alleged offender at the competition either in person or by any other suitable means. A copy of the Yellow Warning Card must then be sent to the Federation with the Steward's/Technical Delegate's Report Form and noted therein.

4. Upon receipt of the Yellow Warning Card, the Federation will send an acknowledgment of its receipt of the Yellow Warning Card to the alleged offender advising of the provisions of this Rule.

5. The issuance of a Yellow Warning Card is not meant to replace the filing of charges for a willful and serious violation of Federation rules, and in no case may a Yellow Warning Card be issued for abuse of a horse in any form. It is for lesser offenses only.

6. Immediately following receipt by the Federation of a third Yellow Warning Card indicating that a competitor, spectator, or participant has been issued three (3) Yellow Warning Cards within a sixteen (16) month period the CEO or his designee shall either levy a fine ranging from $500 to $1000 or issue a formal Charge pursuant to this Rule and GR604 alleging that the rules have been violated on all or any one of said three occasions pursuant to Chapter 6 of the Rules. If the alleged offender is found in violation of any or all of said violations they may be subject to the penalties set forth in Chapter 7 of the Rules.

GR1037 Conflicts of Interest and Restrictions - Judges (See also GR107 and GR1304)

1. A judge may not be an owner of any interest in a horse (including but not limited to syndicate and partnership shares), nor may he/she be an exhibitor, trainer, coach, lessor, lessee, rider, driver, halter handler, steward, technical delegate, or manager, nor may he/she be a family member of a competition licensee, steward, technical delegate or manager at any Federation Licensed Competition at which he/she is officiating, including unrated classes. Exceptions: In the Eventing division and in the Dressage division, except for Dressage Sport Horse Breeding classes, horses may be shown Hors de Concours in classes where the owner is not officiating See also GR1304.17-.20. In the Hunter and Hunter/Jumping Seat Equitation divisions a judge may not be an owner of any interest in a horse (including but not limited to syndicate and partnership shares) that competes before him/her at any Federation Licensed Competition at which he/she is officiating, including unrated classes.

2. A judge may not, during a competition at which he/she is judging, be the houseguest of a person who is exhibiting or competing at such competition or whose family is exhibiting or competing at such competition.

3. A judge may not discuss with an exhibitor the purchase, sale or lease of any horse during a competition at which he/she is officiating.

4. A judge may not officiate more than one time within 125 radial miles during any 20 day period in the following circumstances:

    a. In any one of the following classes: ASPCA Horsemanship, Washington International Horse Show Equitation, USEF Show Jumping Talent Search, or the US Hunter Seat Medal at Premier or National rated competitions

    b. In the same "A" rated division or section (Exception: Federation Licensed Special Competitions)

c. In the Andalusian/Lusitano, Arabian, Friesian, Hackney, Morgan, National Show Horse, Roadster, American Saddlebred, or Shetland division or section. *BOD 1/17/15 Effective 12/1/15*

Paso Fino Division: A judge may not officiate more than once within two hundred (200) road miles during any thirty (30) day period.

   a. This restriction does not apply to Guest Judges officiating classes recognized by a national breed or discipline association for which the Federation has no division rules and does not license judges.

5. Limitations for Andalusian/Lusitano Judges:

   a. A judge cannot officiate at two licensed competitions within the same IALHA Region (excluding the IALHA National Competition) within the same year unless the competitions are six (6) months apart and travel distance from one competition facility to the second facility is 200 miles or greater.

   b. A judge licensed in the Andalusian/Lusitano Division may not officiate at more than one Regional Championship competition in that Division during any one competition year.

   c. A judge that has officiated at an IALHA National Championship Competition is ineligible to officiate at another IALHA National Championship for the next three years.

GR1038 Conflicts of Interest and Restrictions - Stewards and Technical Delegates (See also GR107 and GR1304)

1. The following persons at a given competition are ineligible to serve as stewards and technical delegates: the president, chairman, other Show Committee officers, competition secretary, manager or other competition officials or employees, judges or exhibitors at that competition.

2. No steward or technical delegate may officiate in any competition in which any member of his family or any of his clients is judging.

3. No steward or technical delegate may officiate at a competition if he or any member of his family has any relationship with the competition which constitutes a conflict of interest with the steward's or technical delegate's duties under these rules. No member of the steward's or technical delegate's family (as defined in GR123) may serve as a Federation Licensed Official, Competition Licensee, Competition Manager or Competition Secretary at the competition where the steward or technical delegate is officiating.

4. No member of a steward's or technical delegate's family, nor any of the steward's or technical delegate's clients, may take part as a trainer, coach, lessor, lessee, exhibitor, rider, driver, handler or vaulter at a competition where the steward or technical delegate is officiating, including unrated classes.

5. In addition to the above restrictions, the following persons may not serve as the technical delegate at an Eventing Competition, Vaulting Competition or Dressage competition:

   a. A close relative of a competitor or owner of a horse entered in the competition.

   b. Chefs d'Equipe whose teams are entered in the competition.

   c. Instructors or trainers of competitors entered in the competition.

   d. A member of the Ground Jury, the course designer, a Dressage or Jumping judge at the event.

   e. The Director (Manager) of the competition or a member of the Director's family.

6. Stewards and technical delegates are not to be used as a ringmaster, announcer, timer or Judge, or in any other volunteer or paid position not related to their proper duties at Licensed Competitions where they are officiating with the following exception:

   a. At a competition where more than one steward or technical delegate is officiating, and after a Steward or Technical Delegate has entirely completed his/her duties at that Licensed Competition, he/she may serve in another capacity; including as a judge in the Jumper Division.

7. During the course of a competition, no steward or technical delegate may be the houseguest of a person who is exhibiting, or whose family is exhibiting, at the same competition.

8. A member of a manager's family may not officiate as a judge, steward, or technical delegate at said manager's competition.

9. A steward or technical delegate cannot own or operate any business (i.e. tack shop, braiding business, etc.) at the same competition where he/she is officiating.

10. No Steward or Technical Delegate who is presently receiving, or has received within the past 30 days, any form of compensation from a competition management firm for services other than as a USEF licensed official or schooling supervisor, may officiate at any of said management's competitions.

GR1039 Conflicts of Interest and Restrictions - Licensed Officials

1. Any individual serving as an official at a competition may not charge or receive direct financial benefit from tutoring a learner or apprentice at the same competition.

SUBCHAPTER 10-I LICENSE APPLICATIONS, ENROLLMENT, PROMOTION, AND MAINTENANCE

GR1040 General

1. Application must be made on the appropriate official enrollment or promotion form, signed by the applicant, and accompanied by the required fee which is not refundable.

2. Enrollment or promotion as a judge in more than four divisions at any one time will not be considered.

3. It is the responsibility of the licensed official to accomplish all necessary requirements for maintaining their license. The Federation is not required to provide notices of time periods within which requirements must be fulfilled.

4. Documented attendance of an FEI recognized course will count towards fulfilling the clinic requirement of the comparable national discipline judge, course designer, or technical delegate license (Exception: Jumper Judge and Dressage divisions. Dressage judge refer to GR1050.3b), providing it occurs during the same time frame required by the national license.

5. The Licensed Officials Committee, not the applicant, will send out evaluations concerning the applicant to such persons listed as references by the applicant and to such licensed officials, members of Division Committees and others as it may elect. No member of the Licensed Officials Committee may serve as a reference for an applicant for a judge's, steward's or technical delegate's license. All evaluations must be returned to the Committee.

6. In the case of those applicants whose applications are not reviewed by the Licensed Officials Committee because of an insufficient number of returned evaluation forms, the Committee will so advise the applicants and will hold those applications in a pending file for one more meeting of the Committee.

7. If an application is denied, the applicant is not eligible to reapply for the same division until 12 months after the Licensed Officials Committees decision. Denied refers to applicants that have been closed by the Licensed Officials Committee rather than those tabled and asked to complete additional requirements. *BOD 1/17/15 Effective 12/1/15*

8. Officials who do not pass the examination on their first attempt will have the opportunity to re-take the exam one additional time. If an official does not achieve a passing score on the make-up exam, they are ineligible to renew the license. They may take the comparable exam in the next competition year and if a passing score is achieved, submit a request for reinstatement of that license.

9. The Committee may require a person of any age to pass a physical examination before considering an application for enrollment, promotion or renewal. The Committee will not reject for physical reasons any application for enrollment, promotion or renewal before a physical examination has been conducted.

10. For the purposes of maintaining officiating requirements, the first full year after an official's approval will be considered as the start of their officiating record.

11. Unless stated otherwise, all persons when first approved as a judge in a division shall receive Recorded status regardless of age or experience unless the applicant holds Registered status with Equine Canada or status with the

FEI, or another National Federation.

12. All persons when first approved as stewards shall receive a Recorded Category 1, Category 2, or Combined Category status regardless of age or experience.

    a. If the applicant is licensed as a Senior or Senior National Steward by Equine Canada, the Licensed Officials Committee has the option to grant either Recorded or Registered status. The following conditions must be met by EC Stewards:

        1. USEF Steward's clinic must be attended within two years prior to application for USEF status.

        2. Upon receipt of the completed application, a written exam will be mailed to the applicant, with 30 days allowed for return; passing score 85%.

        3. Verification of Equine Canada status must be provided.

        4. USEF Clinic, exam, and officiating requirements to maintain the license apply.

13. All persons when first approved as Vaulting Technical Delegates shall receive Recorded ('r') status. (Exception: initial grandfather process which will allow either Recorded 'r' or Registered 'R' status at the discretion of the Licensed Officials Committee.)

14. Renewal, Reinstatement, Re-enrollment, and Re-application of Licenses

    a. An official who is eligible to renew (up to date on clinic, exam and officiating requirements) his/her license will have one full competition year after the lapse of their license(s) to renew by the standard procedure; i.e. hard copy renewal or the online renewal.

    b. If two competition years have passed since an official has renewed his/her license(s), they must request a reinstatement of licensing. A request for reinstatement must be submitted to the Licensed Officials Department for presentation to the Licensed Officials Committee.

    c. If three but less than five competition years have lapsed since an official has renewed his/her license(s) they must then apply for re-enrollment of those licenses, following the specific requirements outlined for each license.

    d. If five or more competition years have lapsed since an official has renewed his/her license(s) they must then re-apply for licensing, following the full license requirements specified for each license.

GR1041 Clinic and Officiating Requirements

1. Clinic and officiating requirements must be met by November 30 to be eligible to renew each license for the following competition year which begins December 1.

2. Any official who fails to fulfill clinic requirements or who fails to meet officiating requirements will not be eligible to have his/her license renewed and will have to apply for an extension. The Licensed Officials Committee has the option of allowing a one-year clinic extension with officiating restrictions or a one-year officiating extension. All requests must be received in writing via mail, email, or fax.

3. In the event that an official's clinic requirement falls due in a year in which a corresponding clinic is not offered, the deadline will automatically be extended to the following year with no restriction providing all other requirements of the license are met.

4. Documented adjudication of FEI recognized classes at foreign FEI sanctioned competitions will count towards maintaining the same national discipline judge or course designer license, providing it occurs during the same time frame required by the national license.

5. Verified judging of an Equine Canada competition will be considered a suitable substitute for a Federation competition for the purposes of maintaining a current license but not for enrollment or promotion learner/apprentice requirements. Written verification must be submitted to the Federation to substantiate EC officiating. Any requests for acceptance of officiating experience in countries other than Canada will be considered on an individual basis.

6. The LOC can require an official to complete additional educational experience.

GR1042 Andalusian/Lusitano Judges

1. No application will be considered until ten evaluation forms are returned from members of the Federation, one of which must be a recommendation from a member of the Federation Andalusian/Lusitano Committee.

2. Learner judge at a minimum of three different Federation Licensed Competitions, under three different Federation/Andalusian/Lusitano judges. These requirements must be fulfilled within a three-year period preceding application.

3. All persons applying for enrollment or re-enrollment must have attended a Federation/IALHA Clinic and receive a passing score of 85% or better on an examination administered by the Federation within three years preceding application.

4. The Committee will require Andalusian/Lusitano judges who do not officiate at one Licensed Competition within five years after obtaining a license or for any five year period thereafter, to re-apply for a license.

5. Judges must attend a Federation/IALHA Clinic every five years and receive a passing score of 85% or better on an examination administered by the Federation.

6. No applicant will be considered for promotion unless he has adjudicated Andalusian/Lusitano divisions in at least two Licensed Competitions during the past three years, verified by stewards' reports.

GR1043 Arabian Judges

1. No application will be considered unless and until 15 forms which actually evaluate the applicant per division are returned from USEF members, eight of which must be from relevant licensed judges, stewards, technical delegates or committee members.

2. Applicants for enrollment will not be considered unless the applicant served as a Learner judge at a minimum of three Licensed Competitions in the Arabian division, under a minimum of three different Federation/AHA Registered Arabian judges, within a three-year period preceding application. A copy of the Learner Judge Evaluation Form shall be submitted to the Federation and to AHA.

3. Applicants for enrollment will not be considered unless the applicant has attended a Federation/AHA Judges' School, and successfully passed all phases of an examination at this School within one year preceding application.

4. All Arabian judges must attend and successfully complete all requirements of a Federation/AHA Judges' Seminar at least once every three years, by seminar or other means of education as determined by the Education/Evaluation Commission or the Judges and Stewards Commissioner's Office.

5. At the request of the USEF Licensed Officials Committee (LOC), the Education Evaluation Commission (EEC), or the AHA Judges and Stewards Commissioner's office, a judge may be required to attend a Seminar outside of his regular rotation.

6. All Judges must satisfactorily complete a written exam once every three years with a minimum score of 85%; National/Regional judges must earn a score of 90% to maintain N/R status with AHA.

7. No applicant will be considered for promotion unless he has adjudicated in at least two Licensed Competitions with an Arabian Division, with a total of five (5) days judging (6 hour minimum each day) during the past four years in the division in which he is applying, verified by stewards' reports.

GR1044 Carriage Pleasure Driving Judges

1. No application will be considered unless and until 15 forms which actually evaluate the applicant per division are returned from USEF members, eight of which must be from relevant licensed judges, stewards, technical delegates or committee members.

2. Applicants for enrollment will not be considered unless they are
   a. licensed by the American Driving Society, or
   b. have successfully completed a training program planned by the Federation and/or ADS.

4. For an applicant in the Driving Divisions who already holds Registered status with the American Driving Society,

the Licensed Officials Committee shall have the option of granting Registered status.

5. The Committee will require judges who do not officiate at one USEF Licensed Competition OR ADS recognized Pleasure Competition with 15 classes or more within five years after obtaining a license or for any five-year period thereafter, to re-apply for a license.

6. All Carriage Pleasure Driving Judges must attend a Federation/ADS Carriage Pleasure Driving Judges' seminar, and receive a score of 85% or better on judges' written examination at least once every three years.

7. No applicant will be considered for promotion unless he has adjudicated in at least two USEF Licensed Competitions or two ADS recognized Pleasure competitions during the past three years, as verified by technical delegates' reports.

GR1045 Combined Driving Judges

1. No application will be considered unless and until 15 forms which actually evaluate the applicant per division are returned from USEF members, eight of which must be from relevant licensed judges, stewards, technical delegates or committee members.

2. Applicants for enrollment will not be considered unless they are
   a. licensed by the FEI or the American Driving Society, or
   b. have successfully completed a training program planned by the Federation and/or ADS, or
   c. have competed internationally as a driver for at least five (5) years, completed at least five (5) International Competitions, must have apprentice judged at least three (3) times and received positive evaluations at least three (3) times at three (3) Advanced Level competitions under three (3) different judges.

3. All Combined Driving Judges must attend a Federation/ADS Combined Driving Judges' seminar, and receive a score of 85% or better on judges' written examination at least once every three years.

4. For an applicant in the Driving Divisions who already holds Registered status with the American Driving Society, the Licensed Officials Committee shall have the option of granting Registered status.

5. The Committee will require judges who do not officiate at one Licensed Competition within three years after obtaining a license or for any three-year period thereafter, to re-apply for a license.

6. No applicant will be considered for promotion unless he has adjudicated in at least two Licensed Competitions during the past three years in the Combined Driving division, verified by technical delegates' reports.

GR1046 Combined Driving Course Designer

1. No applicant will be considered unless and until fifteen (15) forms which evaluate the applicant per division are returned, eight (8) of which must be from the current list of USEF Combined Driving Judges, Technical Delegates, and Course Designers, and the remaining obtained from members of the USEF Driving Committee, Combined Driving organizers, or USEF members who are Combined Driving competitors.

2. Minimum eligibility requirements for enrollment in the training program as an Apprentice.
   a. Must have competed at the Advanced level at four (4) or more USEF-licensed Combined Driving events, or
   b. Have instructed at least two (2) drivers who meet this requirement or
   c. Show evidence of practical experience with Combined Driving at the Advanced level.
   d. Must have designed courses at the Preliminary level or above at a minimum of two (2) different sites.
   e. Must receive a minimum score of 85% on the written open-book Combined Driving Course Designers' Examination, which will be administered to applicants for enrollment in the training program.

3. Registered Combined Driving Course designers must be the Course Designer at a minimum of one (1) course during a three-year period.

4. Combined Driving Course Designers must attend a USEF or FEI Combined Driving Course Design course once every three years and receive a minimum score of 85% on the closed-book written examination given at the conclusion of the course.

5. Minimum eligibility requirements to receive Registered "R" status.

   a. Complete a USEF or FEI Combined Driving Course Design course.

   b. Receive a minimum score of 85% on the closed-book written examination given at the conclusion of said course.

   c. Complete apprenticeship with two different USEF or FEI Course Designers at two events at the Intermediate level or above.

GR1047 Combined Driving and Carriage Pleasure Driving Technical Delegate

1. No application will be considered unless and until fifteen forms with an evaluation of the applicant per division are returned from members of the Federation, eight of which must be from relevant licensed judges, stewards, technical delegates or committee members.

2. Applicants for enrollment in the Carriage Pleasure Driving or Combined Driving Divisions will not be considered unless they:

   a. are licensed by the FEI or the American Driving Society, or

   b. have successfully completed a training program planned by the Federation and ADS, or

   c. have competed internationally as a driver at least five (5) years and completed at least five (5) international Competitions, must have apprentice TD'd at least three (3) times and received positive evaluations at least three (3) Advanced Level competitions under three (3) different Technical Delegates.

3. For an applicant in the Driving Divisions who already holds Registered status with the American Driving Society, the Licensed Officials Committee shall have the option of granting Registered status.

4. All technical delegates must attend a Federation technical delegates clinic at least once every three years.

5. All technical delegates must take a technical delegates' examination once every three years and must receive a mark of 85% or better before their license is renewed.

6. Any technical delegate who fails to meet the clinic requirement will not have his license renewed and will have to reapply for his status.

GR1048 Connemara Judges

1. In the Connemara Division, no application will be considered unless and until ten forms with an evaluation of the applicant have been received by the Federation. Of those ten, five must be recommendations received from Federation licensed officials and/or current Federation Connemara Committee members.

2. Applicants must serve as a learner judge at a minimum of two Federation licensed competitions, under a minimum of two different Federation Connemara Judges within five years preceding application.

3. Applicants must attend a Federation Connemara Judge's clinic and pass an examination with a score of 85% or better within five years preceding application.

4. No applicant will be considered for promotion unless he has judged at least two Federation licensed Connemara divisions within a five year period preceding application to "R" status.

5. Registered and Recorded Connemara judges do not have officiating requirements but are required to attend a Federation judges' clinic at least once every four years and pass an examination every two years with a score of 85% or better to retain their license. *BOD 1/17/15 Effective 12/1/15*

GR1049 Dressage Judges

1. No application will be considered unless and until 15 forms which actually evaluate the applicant per division are returned from USEF members, at least 12 of the 15 must be from licensed Dressage Judges, Dressage or Eventing technical delegates or members of the Federation Dressage Committee.

2. Applicants must complete the current training program of the Federation Dressage Committee, approved by the Federation Licensed Officials Committee. Information on application procedure and on the current program is available from the Federation. If otherwise eligible, currently licensed, or retired, foreign FEI Dressage judges may apply

for Federation Senior (S) Dressage judge classification and are exempted from participation in any Federation training program for judge licensing or promotion.

3. All judges must attend a Federation judges' clinic at least once every three years.

   a. Recorded and Registered Dressage judges must attend a national level clinic.

   b. Senior Dressage judges must attend a National and an International Level clinic. In the event that an (S) judge's clinic requirement falls due in a year when there is no International level clinic, the deadline will automatically be extended to the following year. (Exception: FEI-licensed dressage judges who attend an FEI judges clinic at least once every three years are required to attend a Federation judges' clinic only once every five years).

4. Dressage judges must judge four Licensed Dressage competitions, Regular Competitions (with open or breed-restricted Dressage divisions) and/or Eventing Competitions every two years or the license will not be renewed. This is a rolling schedule and the two years resets each December 1st (the beginning of the USEF competition year). Regular competitions with breed-restricted Dressage Divisions must be less than 50% of the total number of competitions required to renew the license.

5. Dressage judges must also take a separate open-book written examination every three years and receive a mark of 85% or better before their license is reissued.

6. Applicants for change of status must complete the current training program of the Federation Dressage Committee, approved by the Licensed Officials Committee. Information on application procedure and on the current program is available from the Federation Office.

7. Any judge licensed by the Federation to judge Dressage classes must be a current member in good standing of the United States Dressage Federation (USDF).

GR1050 Dressage Sport Horse Breeding Judges

1. No application will be considered unless and until 15 forms which actually evaluate the applicant per division are returned from USEF members, eight of which must be from relevant licensed judges, stewards, technical delegates or committee members.

2. Applicants must complete the current training program of the Federation Dressage Committee, approved by the Federation Licensed Officials Committee. Information on application procedure and on the current program is available from the Federation Office.

3. All judges must attend a Federation judges clinic at least once every three years. In the event that a Dressage Sport Horse Breeding clinic requirement falls due in a year when there is no Dressage Sport Horse Breeding clinic, the deadline will automatically be extended to the following year. 4. The Committee will require judges who do not officiate at one Licensed Competition within three years after obtaining a license or for any three-year period thereafter, to re-apply for a license. This is a rolling schedule and the three years resets each December 1st (the beginning of the USEF competition year).

5. Dressage Sport Horse Breeding judges must take a separate open-book written examination every three years and receive a mark of 85% or better before their license can be renewed.

6. Any judge licensed by the Federation to judge Dressage Sport Horse Breeding (DSHB) classes must be a current member in good standing of the United States Dressage Federation (USDF).

GR1051 Dressage Technical Delegates

1. No application will be considered unless and until fifteen forms with an evaluation of the applicant per division are returned from members of the Federation, 12 of which must be from the current roster of Dressage judges or technical delegates or current members of the Federation Dressage Committee.

2. Applicants to become a Dressage Technical Delegate must complete the current training program of the Federation Dressage Committee. The program must also be approved by the Federation Licensed Officials Committee.

Information on the application procedure and on the current program is available from the Federation office.

3. All technical delegates must attend a Federation Technical Delegates clinic at least once every three years.

4. In order to maintain his/her license, a Registered (R) Dressage Technical Delegate must have attended a Federation Dressage/DSHB Pony Measurement Certification clinic where certification testing to measure ponies for dressage or DSHB is conducted. Recorded (r) Dressage Technical Delegates must attend a Federation Dressage/DSHB Pony Measurement Certification clinic prior to January 1, 2011 where certification testing to measure ponies for dressage or DSHB is conducted.

5. Federation Dressage/DSHB Pony Measurement Certification clinics must include a live measurement evaluation (including a practical and written examination), which must be passed with a minimum score in each section of 75% or better. In addition, in order to obtain a passing score in the practical examination, the person being evaluated must receive scores of "5" or above in every category.

6. Once measurement certification is required, a Dressage Technical Delegate who fails the measurement certification examination will not have his/her license renewed the next membership year and will have to attend another clinic and pass the measurement evaluation before applying to have his/her license reinstated at his/her original status.

7. All technical delegates must take a technical delegates' examination once every three years and must receive a mark of 85% or better before their license is renewed.

8. The Committee will require those technical delegates who do not officiate at a minimum of three Licensed Competitions within three years after obtaining a license or any three-year period thereafter, to re-apply for a license. This is a rolling schedule and the three years resets each December 1st (the beginning of the USEF competition year).

9. A Registered (R) or Recorded (r) Dressage Technical Delegate must be a current member in good standing of the United States Dressage Federation (USDF). Only Dressage Technical Delegates who are current Participating Members of the United States Dressage Federation may officiate at USEF/USDF Regional and National Dressage Championships.

GR1052 Eventing Judges

1. No application will be considered unless and until 15 forms which actually evaluate the applicant per division are returned from USEF members who are Licensed Eventing Officials or current members of the Federation Eventing Committee.

2. Applicants must meet minimum requirements and complete the current training program of the Federation Eventing Committee approved by the Federation Licensed Officials Committee. Information on application procedure and the current program is available on the USEF website www.usef.org and also from the Federation Office.

3. Eventing judges must judge at three Federation Recognized/Endorsed Eventing Competitions every three years or the license will not be renewed.

4. All Eventing judges must attend a Federation/USEA Eventing judges' clinic and receive a score of 85% or better on an Eventing judges written examination at least once every three years.

   a. In the event that a Registered judges' and technical delegates' clinic requirement is due in a year when there is no Registered level clinic, the deadline will automatically be extended to the following year.

   b. Eventing Judges who do not hold a Federation Dressage Judge's license must also attend a national level Dressage Judges clinic once every three years or a Dressage for Eventing clinic especially organized for this purpose.

5. Eventing applicants for change of status must meet minimum requirements and complete the current training program of the Federation Eventing Committee, approved by the Licensed Officials Committee. Information on application procedure and on the current program is available on the USEF website www.usef.org and also from the Federation Office.

GR1053 Eventing Technical Delegates

1. No application will be considered unless and until fifteen forms which actually evaluate the applicant per division are returned from Federation Licensed Eventing Officials or current members, 12 of which must be from the current roster of Eventing technical delegates, Eventing judges, or current members of the Federation Eventing Committee.

2. Applicants to become an Eventing technical delegate must meet minimum requirements and complete the current training program of the Federation Eventing Committee. The program must also be approved by the Federation Licensed Officials Committee. Information on the application procedure and on the current program is available on the USEF website www.usef.org and also from the Federation office.

3. All technical delegates must attend a Federation technical delegates clinic at least once every three years. Any technical delegate who fails to meet the clinic requirement will not have his license renewed and will have to reapply for his status.

4. All technical delegates must take a technical delegates' examination once every three years and must receive a mark of 85% or better before their license is renewed.

5. The Committee will require those technical delegates who do not officiate at a minimum of three Recognized/Endorsed Competitions within three years after obtaining a license or any three-year period thereafter, to re-apply for a license.

6. Eventing technical delegate applicants for change of status must meet minimum requirements and complete the current training program of the Federation Eventing Committee approved by the Licensed Officials Committee. Information on application procedure and on the current program is available on the USEF website www.usef.org and also from the Federation office.

GR1054 Eventing Course Designers

1. No application will be considered unless and until 15 forms which actually evaluate the applicant per division are returned from USEF members who are Licensed Eventing Officials or current members of the Federation Eventing Committee. (See GR1057.4 below for additional requirements for Eventing Show Jumping Course Designer.)

2. Applicants for status as an Eventing Course Designer must fulfill the requirements for such status recommended by the Federation Eventing Committee and approved by the Federation Licensed Officials Committee.

3. Cross Country Course Designers.

   a. Recorded or Registered Cross Country Eventing Course Designers must be the Eventing Cross Country Course Designer at a minimum of three horse trials every three years.

   b. Eventing Cross Country course designers must attend a continuing education clinic and receive a passing score of 85% or above on a written exam once every three years.

4. Show Jumping Course Designers

   a. No application will be considered unless and until the USEF Licensed Officials Committee has received written recommendations from two "R" Eventing Technical Delegates and two riders who have officiated/ridden over jumping courses designed by the applicant and from the Eventing Show Jumping Course Advisor, stating that they believe that the applicant has demonstrated the knowledge necessary to design suitable courses and should be issued a license by the Federation. These evaluations will help fulfill the requirement of GR1057.1.

   b. Eventing Show Jumping Course Designers must officiate at a minimum of two separate Events at the Intermediate, Advanced or FEI two star or higher event every three years to maintain the license.

   c. Eventing Show Jumping Course Designers must attend either a continuing education USEF Jumping Course Designer clinic or a clinic given by the Eventing Jumping Course Advisor at least once every three years.

GR1055 Friesian Judges

1. No application will be considered unless and until ten forms which actually evaluate the applicant per division are

returned from USEF members, one of which must be a recommendation from a member of the Federation Friesian Committee.

2. Applicants for enrollment in the Friesian Division must learner judge at least three Federation Licensed Competitions, under a minimum of three different Friesian judges within a three-year period preceding application. Exception: If a judge is already licensed as a Registered (R) or Recorded (r) judge in the Andalusian, Arabian, Hackney, Morgan, National Show Horse, American Saddlebred, or Welsh divisions, he/she may apply for a Friesian license without learner judging but must attend the USEF Friesian Judges Clinic within a three-year period preceding application.

3. All persons applying for enrollment or re-enrollment must have attended a Federation Friesian Clinic within three years preceding application.

4. All Friesian Judges must attend a Federation Friesian Judges Clinic every five years and receive a passing score of 85% or better on a written exam administered every two years.

5. The Committee will require Friesian judges who do not officiate at one Licensed Competition within five years in the Friesian division after obtaining a license or for any five-year period thereafter, to re-apply for a license.

6. No applicant will be considered for promotion unless he has adjudicated in at least two Licensed Competitions during the past five years, verified by stewards' reports.

GR1056 Hackney Judges

1. No application will be considered unless and until 15 forms which actually evaluate the applicant per division are returned from USEF members, eight of which must be from relevant licensed judges, stewards, technical delegates or committee members. The applicant will not be considered unless and until questionnaires are approved by at least three (3) of the current Federation Hackney Pony Committee and should be familiar with the breed (i.e., breeding, training, showing, etc.)

2. Learner judge a minimum of 6 classes to include at least one class in the Harness Pony, Hackney Pony (Cob Tail), Pleasure (Show or Park or Country) and Roadster Pony sections at two Federation Licensed Competitions in the Hackney Division within a three-year period preceding application.

   a. If a judge is already licensed in the Roadster, American Saddlebred or Saddle Seat Equitation divisions, he/she may add an additional license in the Hackney division by enrolling as per GR1059.1 and learner judging a minimum of 6 Hackney classes to include at least one class in the Harness Pony, Hackney Pony (Cob Tail), Pleasure (Show or Park or Country) and Roadster Pony sections.

3. All persons applying for enrollment or re-enrollment must have attended a Federation judges' clinic within two years preceding application.

4. No applicant will be considered for promotion unless he has adjudicated in at least two Licensed Competitions during the past five years in the Hackney division, verified by stewards' reports. The applicant will not be considered unless and until questionnaires are approved by at least one-third of the current Federation Hackney Pony Committee.

5. Judges must take a written examination every two years and receive a passing score of 85% or better to maintain their license. The completed examination must be returned to the Federation within thirty days of receipt.

6. All licensed Hackney judges must attend a Federation judge's clinic at least once every five years.

7. All Federation judges holding a Hackney card must be a current member in good standing with the American Hackney Horse Society.

GR1057 Hunter Judges

1. Learner Permit. Applicants for the Hunter license must apply for a learner judge's permit through the Federation Licensed Officials Committee. (Exception: individuals currently licensed in at least one of these divisions: Hunter/

Jumping Seat Equitation, Hunter Breeding, or Jumper). Specific requirements are as follows:

   a. Hunter learner permit applicants must be a minimum of 21 years old at the time of application.

   b. Learner Permit applicants must have been an active competitor as either a rider, trainer, handler, breeder or coach in these divisions at USEF licensed competitions within the last four years.

   c. Learner Permit applicants must attend a Federation Hunter clinic within two years preceding application. *BOD 1/17/15 Effective 12/1/15*

   d. The completed application form along with the fee must be returned to the Federation Licensed Officials Department.

   e. No application will be considered unless and until 10 forms which actually evaluate the applicant are returned from USEF members, three (3) of which must be from relevant licensed judges, stewards, course designers, or committee members.

   f. If the learner judges permit application is approved by a sub-committee composed of a minimum of three members of the Licensed Officials Committee, the applicant may enter the learner judges training program.

   g. The learner judge's permit will expire three years from the date of issuance.

   h. The Learner judge must still apply for individual competitions through the Federation Licensed Officials Department.

   i. If a permit application is denied, the applicant may reapply after one year.

2. Recorded Judge

   a. Complete six full days of Learner judging at a minimum of two Federation Licensed Competitions, under a minimum of two different Federation Registered Hunter judges. Applicant must Learner judge at least two complete "A" Rated Conformation Hunter Horse sections or two Pony Hunter divisions that include a model. (Horse or Pony Hunter Breeding classes will also count towards meeting this requirement.) Attendance at the Hunter Breeding Clinic or learner judging one Hunter Breeding section may be substituted for one conformation section or for a Pony Hunter division with a model. These requirements must be fulfilled within a three-year period preceding application.

   b. Applicants in the Judges Mentor Program must meet the requirements set forth by the National Hunter Committee and/or USHJA Officials Education Committee and be approved by the Federation Licensed Officials Committee. Information on application procedure and on the current program is available from the Licensed Officials Department in the Federation office.

3. No application will be considered unless and until 15 forms which actually evaluate the applicant per division are returned from USEF members, eight of which must be from relevant licensed judges, stewards, course designers, or committee members.

4. The Committee will require judges who do not officiate at one Licensed Competition within three years in the Hunter division after obtaining a license to apply for an officiating extension.

5. All persons applying for enrollment, re-enrollment or promotion must have attended a Federation judges' clinic within two years preceding application.

6. Recorded judges must attend a Federation judges' clinic at least once every two years.

7. Registered judges must attend a Federation judges' clinic at least once every four years.

8. In the Hunter Division, an applicant for promotion must have judged three or more Licensed Competitions during the past three years in the Hunter division. In addition, the applicant for promotion must apprentice judge with a minimum of three Registered ('R') Hunter Judges at three or more separate 'National' or 'Premier' rated competitions. Registered Hunter judges that the applicant apprentice judges with must fill out an evaluation form on the applicant seeking promotion.

9. Any judge officiating USEF Open (not restricted to a breed) hunter and/or jumper classes must be a Senior Active member in good standing of the United States Hunter Jumper Association, Inc.

GR1058 Hunter Breeding Judges

1. Learner Permit. Applicants for the Hunter Breeding license must apply for a learner judge's permit through the Federation Licensed Officials Committee, following the requirements of GR1060.1. (Exception: individuals currently licensed in at least one of these divisions: Hunter, Hunter/Jumping Seat Equitation, or Jumper.)

    a. Hunter Breeding learner permit applicants must be a minimum of 21 years old at the time of application.

    b. Learner Permit applicants must have been an active competitor as either a rider, trainer, handler, breeder or coach in these divisions at USEF licensed competitions within the last four years.

    c. The completed application form along with the fee must be returned to the Federation Licensed Officials Department.

    d. No application will be considered unless and until 10 forms which actually evaluate the applicant are returned from USEF members, three (3) of which must be from relevant licensed judges, stewards, course designers, or committee members.

    e. If the learner judges permit application is approved by a sub-committee composed of a minimum of three members of the Licensed Officials Committee, the applicant may enter the learner judges training program.

    f. The learner judge's permit is valid for and will expire three years from the date of issuance.

    g. The Learner judge must still apply for individual competitions through the Federation Licensed Officials Department.

    h. If a permit application is denied, the applicant may reapply after one year.

2. Specific requirements are as follows:

    a. Learner judge evaluations must be received from all judges with whom applicant officiates. Learner judge will receive one point for every horse that he/she judges at Federation Licensed Competitions. Once the learner judge earns a total of ten (10) points at a minimum of two (2) separate shows with at least two (2) different judges total, he/she may apply for 'R' Hunter Breeding status.

    b. A Recorded "r" Hunter judge with five or more years of judging experience, may apply for a Hunter Breeding license after learner judging two complete Hunter Breeding sections at two Federation Licensed Competitions under two different Federation Hunter Breeding judges within a three-year period preceding application.

    c. A Registered "R" Hunter judge with a minimum of five years judging experience may apply his/her Hunter Breeding Guest judging towards his/her learner judging requirements.

3. All persons applying for enrollment or re-enrollment must have attended a Federation judges clinic within two years preceding application.

4. No application will be considered unless and until 15 forms which actually evaluate the applicant per division are returned from USEF members, eight of which must be from relevant licensed judges, stewards, course designers, or committee members.

5. Applicants approved in the Hunter Breeding Division shall automatically receive Registered status.

6. The Committee will require judges who do not officiate at one Licensed Competition within five years in the Hunter Breeding, Pony Hunter Breeding, or Arabian Sport Horse Divisions after obtaining a license to attend a Hunter Breeding Clinic within the current or previous year before their license can be renewed.

7. Hunter Breeding Judges must attend a Federation Hunter Breeding judges' clinic at least once every five years.

GR1059 Hunter/Jumping Seat Equitation Judges

1. Learner Permit. Applicants for the Hunter/Jumping Seat Equitation license must apply for a learner judge's permit through the Federation Licensed Officials Committee. (Exception: individuals currently licensed in at least one of these divisions: Hunter, Hunter Breeding, or Jumper.) Specific requirements are as follows:

    a. Hunter/Jumping Seat Equitation learner permit applicants must be a minimum of 21 years old at the time of application.

    b. Learner Permit applicants must have been an active competitor as either a rider, trainer, handler, breeder or coach in these divisions at USEF licensed competitions within the last four years.

   c. Learner Permit applicants must attend a Federation Hunter/Jumping Seat Equitation clinic within two years preceding application. *BOD 1/17/15 Effective 12/1/15*

   d. The completed application form along with the fee must be returned to the Federation Licensed Officials Department.

   e. No application will be considered unless and until 10 forms which actually evaluate the applicant are returned from USEF members, three (3) of which must be from relevant licensed judges, stewards, course designers, or committee members.

   f. If the learner judges permit application is approved by a sub-committee composed of a minimum of three members of the Licensed Officials Committee, the applicant may enter the learner judges training program.

   g. The learner judge's permit will expire three years from the date of issuance.

   h. The Learner judge must still apply for individual competitions through the Federation Licensed Officials Department.

   i. If a permit application is denied, the applicant may reapply after one year.

2. Recorded Judge

   a. Learner judge at least ten Equitation classes from the following list: Open Equitation, Federation Medal, Federation Pony Medal, Federation Adult Equitation, ASPCA Maclay, USEF Talent Search, or WIHS. Classes must be at a minimum of two Federation Licensed Competitions, under a minimum of two different Federation Registered Hunter/Jumping Seat Equitation Judges. At least one competition must have "A" rated Hunter sections. These requirements must be fulfilled within a three-year period preceding application.

   b. Applicants in the Judges Mentor Program must meet the requirements set forth by the National Hunter Committee and/or USHJA Officials Education Committee and be approved by the Federation Licensed Officials Committee. Information on application procedure and on the current program is available from the Licensed Officials department in the Federation office.

3. No application will be considered unless and until 15 forms which actually evaluate the applicant per division are returned from USEF members, eight of which must be from relevant licensed judges, stewards, technical delegates or committee members.

4. All persons applying for enrollment, re-enrollment or promotion must have attended a Federation judges' clinic within two years preceding application.

5. Recorded judges must attend a Federation judges' clinic at least once every two years.

6. Registered judges must attend a Federation judges' clinic at least once every four years.

7. The Committee will require judges who do not officiate at one Licensed Competition within three years in the Hunter/Jumping Seat Equitation division after obtaining a license to apply for an officiating extension.

8. In the Hunter/Jumping Seat Equitation Division, an applicant for promotion must have judged three or more Licensed Competitions during the past three years in the Hunter/Jumping Seat Equitation Division. In addition , the applicant for promotion must apprentice judge Hunter/Jumping Seat Equitation classes with a minimum of three Registered ('R') Hunter/Jumping Seat Equitation Judges at three or more separate 'National' or 'Premier' rated competitions holding Hunter/Jumping Seat Equitation classes. Registered Hunter/Jumping Seat Equitation judges that the applicant apprentice judges with must fill out an evaluation form on the applicant seeking promotion.

GR1060 Hunter, Hunter/Jumping Seat Equitation Course Designers

1. Hunter Course Designer Apprentice Program: To enroll in the Hunter Course Designer Apprentice Program, the following requirements must be met:

   a. Must have verifiable experience designing hunter/equitation courses at USEF Regional I, Regional II, Local and non-rated competitions

  b. Submit application for enrollment, along with appropriate fees, into the Program

  c. The USEF Licensed Officials Committee will review the application and approve or decline for the Program, with input from the USHJA Course Designer's Task Force considered. The application may be reviewed either by a sub-committee, composed of a minimum of three members of the Licensed Officials Committee, or at a full meeting of the Committee

2. Recorded 'r' status: To be eligible to apply for licensing as a Recorded 'r' Hunter Course Designer the following requirements must be met within two years after being approved into the Hunter Course Designer Apprentice Program:

  a. The Apprentice must work at all competition days at a minimum of four USEF-licensed National or Premier rated competitions assisting at least three different "R" Hunter Course Designers at three different locations within two years from the date of approval. Permission to apprentice must be obtained in advance from the Competition Managers and course designers

  b. At the beginning of each competition, the Apprentice must present the course designer with an evaluation form, which the course designer will complete and submit directly to the USEF following the competition

  c. Attend a USEF Hunter Course Design Clinic

  d. No application will be considered unless and until 10 evaluations are returned from members of the USEF / USHJA, five of which must come from relevant comparable discipline licensed judges, stewards, course designers or committee members

3. Registered 'R' status: To be eligible for promotion to a Registered 'R' status, the individual must:

  a. Hold a Recorded 'r' Hunter Course Designer's license for at least two years (24 months)

  b. Have served as the official Hunter Course Designer of record at a minimum of five National or three Premier horse shows during or within the previous two years

  c. No application will be considered unless and until 10 evaluations are returned from members of the USEF/USHJA, five of which must come from relevant comparable discipline licensed judges, stewards, course designers or committee members

4. To maintain his/her license, a 'r' Hunter Course Designer must attend a USEF Hunter Course Designer's clinic at least once every three years and a 'R' Hunter Course Designer must attend a USEF Hunter Course Designer's Clinic at least once every five years.

5. All applicants and licensed Hunter Course Designers must be a Senior Active in good standing of the United States Hunter Jumper Association, Inc.

GR1061 Jumper Judges

1. Learner Permit. Applicants for the Jumper license must apply for a learner judge's permit through the Federation Licensed Officials Committee. Specific requirements are as follows:

  a. Jumper learner permit applicants must be a minimum of 21 years old at the time of application.

  b. Applicants must demonstrate experience in the Jumper Division in the past three years, e.g. trainer, competitor, or official. They must also submit recommendations from a minimum of two Registered (R) Jumper judges.

  c. Learner Permit applicants must attend a Federation Jumper clinic within two years preceding application. *BOD 1/17/15 Effective 12/1/15*

  d. The completed application form along with the fee must be returned to the Federation Licensed Officials Department.

  e. No application will be considered unless and until 10 forms which actually evaluate the applicant are returned from USEF members, three (3) of which must be from relevant licensed judges, stewards, course designers, or committee members.

  f. If the learner judges permit application is approved by a sub-committee composed of a minimum of three members of the Licensed Officials Committee, the applicant may enter the learner judges training program.

   g. The learner judge's permit will expire three years from the date of issuance.

   h. The Learner judge must still apply for individual competitions through the Federation Licensed Officials Department.

   i. If a permit application is denied, the applicant may reapply after one year.

2. Recorded Judge.

   a. Learner judge forty classes including four full days in the Jumper Division with a minimum of two different Federation Registered Jumper judge at a minimum of four Federation Licensed Competitions offering $2,500 or more in prize money in their Jumper Division.

   b. The learner judge must have no other duties or responsibilities at the competition where he/she is fulfilling his/her requirements.

   c. Learner judges must demonstrate to the Registered Jumper Judge their ability to keep a jumper scorecard and also to operate the timing equipment.

   d. These requirements must be fulfilled within a three-year period preceding application.

3. No application will be considered unless and until 15 forms which actually evaluate the applicant are returned from USEF members, eight of which must be from relevant licensed judges, stewards, technical delegates or committee members.

4. All persons applying for enrollment, re-enrollment or promotion must have attended a Federation judges' clinic within two years preceding application. Persons applying for enrollment must also pass a written examination, administered in conjunction with the Clinic, with a mark of 85% or better.

5. A Recorded (r) Jumper judge must take a written examination every two years and receive a mark of 85% or better before his/her license can be renewed.

6. A Registered (R) Jumper judge must take a written examination every four years and receive a mark of 85% or better before his/her license can be renewed.

7. Registered (R) Jumper Judges that have held 'R' status over 20 years, upon 2/3 vote of the National Jumper Committee at a properly noticed meeting, may receive the title "Master." The person may only be nominated for this "Masters" status by at least three currently sitting members of the National Jumper Committee.

8. Recorded ("r") jumper judges must attend a Federation Jumper Clinic at least once every two years.

9. Registered ("R") jumper judges must attend a Federation Jumper Clinic at least once every four years.

10. The Committee will require judges who do not officiate at one Licensed Competition within three years in the Jumper division after obtaining a license to apply for an officiating extension.

11. No applicant will be considered for promotion unless he has adjudicated in at least two Licensed Competitions during the past three years in the Jumper division, verified by stewards' reports.

12. Foreign FEI Jumper Judges may apply to the Licensed Officials Department for a USEF Registered Jumper Judge card by fulfilling the following requirements:

   a. Attend a USEF Jumper Judges' Clinic,

   b. Successfully complete the Jumper Judges written exam with a score of 85% or higher, and

   c. Obtain approval from the National Jumper Committee.

13. Any judge officiating Federation Open (not restricted to a breed) hunter and/or jumper classes must be a current member in good standing of the United States Hunter Jumper Association, Inc.

GR1062 Jumper Course Designer

1. No application will be considered unless and until ten questionnaires are returned from members of the Federation, two of which must come from members of the Federation Jumper Committee.

2. Prerequisites for Recorded ("r") status program:

a. Applicants must have assisted as a Jumper Course Designer at a minimum of three Rating 1 or higher licensed Jumper competitions, under a minimum of two different Jumper Course Designers within the current year and/or previous three years.

    1. Experience can be with a Federation "R" Jumper Course Designer or a current FEI Level 2*, 3*, or 4* Jumper Course Designer.

    2. Each Applicant must receive verification in writing from the Course Designer that, at each competition, the Applicant has assisted with all aspects of course design and building throughout two or more days of competition.

b. Exemption from the requirements in 1065.2a will be given for any Applicant who has served as the Jumper Course Designer of record (listed in the prize list) at a minimum of 5 licensed Rating 1 or higher competitions within the previous 3 years.

3. Requirements to obtain Recorded 'r' status:

a. Upon receiving verification from the USEF Licensed Officials Department that the prerequisites listed above have been completed, the Applicant will apply to a Federation "R" or current FEI Level 2*, 3*, or 4* Jumper Course Designer and the Competition Manager for permission to work as an apprentice course designer.

b. The Applicant must work at a minimum of three USEF Licensed Rating 1 or higher Jumper competitions, with a minimum of three days at each, under the supervision of a minimum of two different Federation "R" or current FEI Level 2*, 3*, or 4* Jumper Course Designers within the previous three years. These Course Designers will certify whether or not they believe that the applicant has demonstrated the knowledge necessary to design suitable courses and be issued an 'r' license by the Federation.

c. Preceding application but within the current or previous two years, Applicants will be required to attend a Course Design Clinic (Federation or FEI) and must also have taken and receIt ived a passing score on the Federation Jumper Judges Examination. The Examination is sent to the Applicant after the application has been received by the Federation and upon verification that Recorded ("r") requirements have been completed.

4. All Applicants for a license, or for promotion, must have attended a Federation or FEI Course Design Clinic within the two years prior to application. Attendance at an FEI Course Design Clinic, with the Course Director's recommendation for the promotion of the applicant, must be documented prior to submission of any application to the FEI, for either licensing or promotion.

5. All licensed Course Designers will be required to attend a Course Design Clinic (Federation or FEI) every three years to maintain their 'r' license and five years to maintain their 'R' license. (Exception - "R" Course Designers who also hold their FEI Jumping Course Designer license).

6. All applicants who hold an Equine Canada Jumper Course Design card will be given the same status for The Federation.

7. Any individual currently licensed by the FEI as 3*or 4* Course Designer for Show Jumping, with approval of the Federation National Jumper Commit tee, is eligible to become a "R" USEF Course Designer for Show Jumping without having to apprentice, take a clinic, or exam.

8. To be eligible to apply for promotion to 'R' Jumper Course Designer the individual must have:

a. held a 'r' for two years,

b. designed courses at a minimum of 8 Level 1 or higher competitions and a minimum of 2 Level 2 or higher competitions, (verified by steward's reports) and

c. have apprenticed with two FEI Level 3 (I) Course Designers for classes of $25,000 or more and received their recommendations as to the applicant's knowledge and experience to build competitions at the $25,000 Level.

9. To be eligible to apply for enrollment as an FEI Candidate Course Designer, the individual must be a Registered "R" USEF National Course Designer and must have fulfilled the following requirements:

a. have held a 'R' license for a minimum of 2 years;

b. have apprenticed with a minimum of two different FEI Level 3 (I) Course Designers for a total of not less than 6 days of competition;

c. have been the Course Designer (as indicated in the prize list or Stewards Report) for a minimum of three competitions offering a minimum of $25,000 in prize money conducted at the National Standard or higher

d. obtain letters of recommendation from,

1. a minimum of two different management groups with competitions offered at the International (or FEI) Standard,

2. two FEI Level 3 (I) Course Designers with whom the applicant has apprenticed, and

3. a minimum of 3 different High Performance athletes familiar with the applicant's work in National Standard events.

e. Following approval for the promotion the applicant must be passed for promotion at an official FEI Course Design clinic.

10. All licensed Course Designers must be a current member in good standing of the United States Hunter Jumper Association, Inc.

GR1063 Certified Jumper Schooling Supervisor

1. No application will be considered unless and until a minimum of a total of 10 evaluations from current Category I Stewards, Jumper Judges, FEI Stewards for Jumping, FEI Jumping Judges, or Eligible Athletes as defined by USEF, are received.

2. Applicants must be 21 years of age or older, must be Senior Active Members of USEF, and must also demonstrate experience in the Jumper Division within the past three years.

3. Applicants must complete the Certified Jumper Schooling Supervisor Training Program of the USEF Jumper Committee approved by the USEF Licensed Officials Committee prior to submitting their application. Information on the application procedure and the Training Program (which consists of a training session and apprenticeships) is available on the USEF website www.usef.org and also from the USEF Office.

4. Maintenance of Status - To maintain Certification, Schooling Supervisors must officiate at a minimum of four competitions and attend a Training Session every four years.

5. FEI Stewards for Jumping are eligible to serve as Certified Jumper Schooling Supervisors.

GR1064 Morgan Judges

1. No application will be considered unless and until 15 forms which actually evaluate the applicant per division are returned from USEF members, eight of which must be from relevant licensed judges, stewards, technical delegates or committee members.

2. All applicants must attend two AMHA judge's schools, every day of the first school and two consecutive days of the second school and serve as a learner judge in the Morgan division at a minimum of one Licensed competition within a two year period preceding application and receive a passing score of 85% to be eligible for enrollment. A copy of the Learner Judge Report shall be submitted to the Federation Licensed Officials Department.

Exceptions:

a. recorded "r" Federation licensed judges from any discipline other than Morgan must attend two AMHA judge's schools, every day of the first school and two consecutive days of the second school within two years preceding application and receive a passing score to be eligible for enrollment.

b. Registered "R" Federation licensed judges from any discipline other than Morgan must attend two days of an AMHA judges' school within two years preceding application and receive a passing score to be eligible for enrollment.

3. Judges licensed in the Morgan Division and all persons applying for enrollment, re-enrollment or promotion must take an examination and receive a passing score in order to fulfill the judges' clinic and/or judges' school requirement.

4. Recorded ("r") Morgan judges must attend a Federation/AMHA judges' school at least once every three years.

5. Registered ("R") Morgan judges must attend a Federation/AMHA judges' school at least once every five years or attend a judges' clinic once every five years at the AMHA convention.

6. No applicant will be considered for promotion unless he has adjudicated in at least two Licensed Competitions during the past three years in the division in which he is licensed, verified by stewards' reports.

7. All Registered (R) and Recorded (r) Federation judges holding a Morgan card must be a current member in good standing of the American Morgan Horse Association.

GR1065 National Show Horse Judges

1. No application will be considered unless and until 15 forms which actually evaluate the applicant per division are returned from USEF members, eight of which must be from relevant licensed judges, stewards, technical delegates or committee members.

2. Learner judge at a minimum of two Federation Licensed Competitions, under a minimum of two different Federation National Show Horse judges, within a two-year period preceding application.

   a. If already a licensed judge in the Hackney, Roadster, Morgan, American Saddlebred, Saddle Seat Equitation, or Arabian divisions he/she may obtain a National Show Horse license by enrolling as per the respective division requirements and Learner judging a minimum of five classes in the National Show Horse division at a Federation Licensed Competition.

      1. Registered (R) judges in the American Saddlebred or Arabian divisions are not required to complete any Learner judging prior to applying for a license in the National Show Horse division.

3. All persons applying for enrollment or re-enrollment must have attended a Federation National Show Horse judges' clinic within 2 years preceding application.

4. Judges must attend a Federation National Show Horse judges' clinic at least once every four years and receive a passing score of 85% or higher on a written examination every four years.

5. National Show Horse Judges do not have officiating requirements, but will be required to complete the clinic and exam requirements or the license will not be renewed.

6. No applicant will be considered for promotion unless he has adjudicated in at least two Licensed Competitions during the past three years in the National Show Horse division, verified by stewards' reports.

GR1066 Paso Fino Judges

1. Judges in the Paso Fino Division must be at least 25 years of age.

2. Ten forms which actually evaluate the applicant must be received from USEF members. Of those ten, five recommendations must be from USEF licensed officials and/or current USEF Paso Fino Committee members.

3. Applicants for enrollment in the Paso Fino Division will not be considered unless they are licensed as a Certified Judge by the Paso Fino Horse Association, attended a PFHA/Federation clinic within three years preceding application, and passed an open book written exam administered at the clinic on USEF General Rules and responsibilities, receiving a score of 85% or better. If individual does not receive a passing score then he/she is required to attend another PFHA/Federation clinic and take an examination at the clinic.

4. Recorded (r) or Registered (R) judges who hold a Certified Judge (C) PFHA license are required to attend a PFHA/Federation clinic at least once every two (2) years.

5. Recorded (r) or Registered (R) judges who hold a Senior Certified (SC) PFHA license are required to attend a PFHA/Federation clinic at least once every three (3) years.

6. Recorded (r) or Registered (R) judges are required to take a written exam to be administered once every three (3) years and receive a score of 85% or better before their license is renewed. The exam will be administered to all Paso Fino judges starting in the 2008 competition year and then to all judges every three years thereafter. If an individual does not receive a passing score on the examination then he is required to attend another PFHA/Federation clinic and take an examination at the clinic.

7. The Committee will require judges who do not officiate at one Licensed Competition within three years in the Paso Fino division after obtaining a license or for any three-year period thereafter, to re-apply for a license.

8. An applicant for promotion must have adjudicated in at least six Federation Licensed competitions in the past three years where a minimum of 100 horses competed, verified by stewards' reports.

9. Applicants for change of status must have completed a written exam administered by the Federation on USEF General Rules and responsibilities to USEF within past two years and received a score of 85% or better.

10. All Registered (R) and Recorded (r) USEF Judges holding a Paso Fino card must be a current member in good standing with the Paso Fino Horse Association.

GR1067 Reining Judges

1. In the Reining Horse Division, a judges' application will not be considered unless and until ten forms which actually evaluate the applicant are returned from USEF members; three evaluation forms must be from USEF/USA Reining approved judges.

2. An applicant for enrollment in the Reining Division must be a current USA Reining approved judge and must comply with the requirements of Chapter 10.

3. In order to maintain their status, Reining judges must be on the USA Reining approved judge's list. Reining judges must have attended any USEF/USA Reining approved Reining Judges school at least once every two years, or in the event that a school not be held within that timeframe, be granted a waiver until the next available approved Reining Judges school.

4. The Licensed Officials Committee shall have the option of granting Registered status.

5. Reining judges must officiate Reining classes at a Licensed Regular, Local or Reining Competition or FEI Reining Event at least once every five years or this license will not be renewed. The LOC will consider officiating at USA Reining events as fulfillment of this requirement on a case-by-case basis.

6. No applicant will be considered for promotion unless he has adjudicated in at least two Licensed Competitions during the past three years in the Reining division, verified by stewards' reports.

GR1068 Roadster Judges

1. No application will be considered unless and until 15 forms which actually evaluate the applicant per division are returned from USEF members, eight of which must be from relevant licensed judges, stewards, technical delegates or committee members.

2. Learner judge a minimum of two days at two Federation Licensed Competitions under a minimum of two different Federation licensed Roadster judges within a three year period preceding application.

   a. If a judge is already licensed in the Hackney, American Saddlebred or Saddle Seat Equitation divisions, he/she may add an additional license in the Roadster division by enrolling as per GR1071.1 and learner judging a minimum of 5 Roadster classes.

3. All persons applying for enrollment or re-enrollment must have attended a Federation judges' clinic within two years preceding application.

4. All Recorded and Registered judges must attend a Federation Roadster Judges' Clinic at least once every five years. Clinics to be held each year and shall be conducted with the American Saddlebred and Saddle Seat clinics together in one day.

5. Judges must take a written examination every two years and receive a passing score of 85% or better to maintain their license. The completed examination must be returned to the Federation within thirty days of receipt. Judges who do not pass the examination on their first attempt will have the opportunity to re-take the exam one additional time.

6. No applicant will be considered for promotion unless he has adjudicated in at least two Licensed Competitions during the past three years in the Roadster division, verified by stewards' reports.

7. All Federation judges holding a Roadster card must be a current member in good standing of the American Road Horse and Pony Association.

GR1069 American Saddlebred Judges

1. No application will be considered unless and until 15 forms which actually evaluate the applicant per division are returned from USEF members, eight of which must be from relevant licensed judges, stewards, technical delegates or committee members.

2. Learner judge a minimum of four days at two Federation Licensed Competitions, under a minimum of two different Federation Registered (R) American Saddlebred Horse judges, within a three-year period preceding application.

   a. If a judge is already licensed in the Hackney, Roadster or Saddle Seat Equitation divisions, he/she may add an additional license in the American Saddlebred division by enrolling as per GR1072.1 and learner judging a minimum of ten American Saddlebred classes.

   b. In addition to Conflicts of Interest outlined in GR1012.4, Learner Judges in the American Saddlebred Division may not learner judge with someone who trains a horse owned by him, his cohabitant, or a member of his family, a farm/ranch/syndicate/partnership/corporation/business in which he, his cohabitant or a member of his family controls.

3. All persons applying for enrollment or re-enrollment must have attended a Federation judges' clinic within two years preceding application.

4. Registered and Recorded American Saddlebred Horse judges must attend a Federation judges' clinic at least once every five years. Clinics will be held each year and shall be conducted together in one day. Clinic will replace written exam. An open book test may be required as part of the clinic.

5. No applicant will be considered for promotion unless he has adjudicated in at least two Licensed Competitions during the past five years in the American Saddlebred division, verified by stewards' reports.

6. Any judge officiating at Federation licensed American Saddlebred classes must be a current member in good standing of the American American Saddlebred Horse Association.

GR1070 Saddle Seat Equitation Judges

1. No application will be considered unless and until 15 forms which actually evaluate the applicant per division are returned from USEF members, eight of which must be from relevant licensed judges, stewards, technical delegates or committee members.

2. Learner judge a minimum of four days at two Federation Licensed Competitions, under a minimum of two different Federation Saddle Seat Equitation judges, within a three-year period preceding application.

   c. If a judge is already licensed in the Hackney, Roadster or American Saddlebred divisions, he/she may add an additional license in the Saddle Seat Equitation division by enrolling as per GR1073.1 and learner judging a minimum of five Saddle Seat Equitation classes.

3. All persons applying for enrollment or re-enrollment must have attended a Federation judges' clinic within two years preceding application.

4. Registered and Recorded Saddle Seat Equitation judges must attend a Federation judges' clinic at least once every five years. Clinics will be held each year and shall be conducted together in one day. Clinic will replace written exam. An open book test may be required as part of the clinic.

          SPONSORED BY HAGYARD EQUINE MEDICAL INSTITUTE || © USEF 2016

5. No applicant will be considered for promotion unless he has adjudicated in at least two Licensed Competitions during the past five years in the Saddle Seat Equitation division, verified by stewards' reports.

GR1071 Shetland Pony Judges

1. No application will be considered unless and until 10 forms which actually evaluate the applicant per division are returned from USEF members, five of which must be from relevant licensed judges, stewards, technical delegates or committee members.

2. All applicants applying for enrollment as a USEF licensed judge must have fulfilled all American Shetland Pony Club ASPC requirements for licensure and have attended an ASPC/USEF judges clinic within three years prior to enrollment. Applicant must receive an 85% or better on the USEF exam on general rules, responsibilities and Shetland Division and submit a report documenting ASPC Judging experience.

3. Applicants for enrollment will not be considered unless they are licensed by the ASPC as a Modern and Classic "R", are an ASPC and Federation member in good standing and have attended a ASPC/Federation clinic within three years preceding application.

4. Shetland judges do not have to meet officiating requirements to maintain this license.

5. Judges applying for re-enrollment must meet requirements listed herein and receive a passing score of 85% or better on the USEF exam on general rules, responsibilities and Shetland Division and have attended ASPC/USEF judges clinic within three years prior to reenrollment.

6. In order to renew this license, USEF Shetland judges must hold a current ASPC Modern and Classic "R" judges card, be a current member of ASPC and USEF in good standing, have attended a ASPC/USEF clinic within the past three years and must receive a score of 85% or better on the USEF exam on general rules, responsibilities and the Shetland Division.

7. No applicant will be considered for promotion unless he has adjudicated in at least two Licensed Competitions during the past five years in the Shetland division, verified by stewards' reports.

8. The exam must be administered to all licensed Shetland judges during the 2013 competition year and every three years thereafter.

GR1072 Stewards - Category 1, Category 2

1. Applicants to become a Category 1 or Category 2 Steward must complete the current Category 1 or Category 2 training program approved by the Federation Licensed Officials Committee. Information regarding the application procedure and requirements for acceptance into the training program are available from the Federation.

2. Application for Recorded status may be submitted following the completion of the apprentice and clinic requirements and after the Federation receives the Confirmation of Completion Form.

   a. The applicant will be given a written examination which must be completed and returned to the Federation within 30 days from the date of postmark. The applicant must receive a grade of 85% or higher or the application will be considered void.

   b. No application for Recorded status will be considered unless and until fifteen forms with an evaluation of the applicant are returned from members of the Federation.

      1. Category 1 applications: eight of the fifteen evaluations must be from licensed hunter/jumper officials, of those two must be from R Category 1 stewards.

      2. Category 2 applications: eight of the fifteen evaluations must be from relevant licensed judges, and/or stewards.

3. Clinics:

   a. Recorded and Registered Category 1 stewards must attend a Category 1 Federation Stewards clinic at least once every four years.

b. Recorded and Registered Category 2 stewards must attend a Category 2 Federation Stewards clinic at least once every four years.

c. Any steward who fails to meet the clinic requirement will not have his license renewed and will have to reapply for his status.

d. Applicants to the Category 1 training program must complete the on line applicant clinic on the USEF website prior to beginning their apprentice work.

e. Applicants to become a Category 1 Recorded steward must have attended a Federation Category 1 Steward clinic within the past 24 months from their date of application.

4. The Measurement Exam

a. Steward clinics must include a live measurement exam. Stewards who officiate at USEF competitions that hold divisions where measurement is required must pass the exam with a score of 85% or higher.

b. There will be 2 categories of stewards related to measurement.

1. Measuring Steward – one who has passed the measurement exam at a clinic with a score of 85% or higher.

a. May steward at any competition where their license qualifies.

b. At least one Measuring Steward must be hired at competitions that hold divisions where measurement is required.

c. Stewards scoring 93% or higher on the measurement exam will be exempt from taking the measurement exam at their next required clinic, but will be required to pass the measurement exam at the subsequent required clinic. Exception: If said Steward has had measurement errors which require action by the LOC or the Hearing Committee, they may be asked to perform additional testing prior to the next required clinic where they are scheduled to test for measurement.

2. Non-measuring Steward – one who chooses not to take the measurement exam or who receives below 85% on the measurement exam. This steward:

a. May officiate alone at breed or discipline competitions that have no divisions which require measurement.

b. May officiate on a multi-steward panel at a competition with breed or discipline divisions requiring measurement, provided the competition has already hired a measuring steward.

c. May not measure any animal at any USEF rated competition.

3. A Non-measuring Steward may attain Measuring status upon successful completion of a Measurement Exam offered at a Steward's clinic.

4. Measurement appeals: A Steward who scores a 93% or higher on the measurement exam will be certified to measure for measurement appeals. Only Stewards certified to measure may be called upon for a measurement appeal.

5. Written examination

a. Registered and recorded Category 1 and Category 2 stewards must take the corresponding Category 1 or Category 2 Federation stewards' examination once every (3) three years and must receive a mark of 85% or higher before their license is renewed.

b. The method of administration will be decided by the Federation Licensed Officials Committee.

6. Continuing Education:

Registered and Recorded Category 1 and Category 2 stewards must complete yearly continuing education as required by the Federation Licensed Officials Committee. These continuing education modules along with corresponding quizzes will be offered on the United States Equestrian Federation website and must be taken and passed with a score of 85% or higher. Failure to complete this requirement will prevent a steward from renewing their license.

7. In order to officiate Federation Licensed AHA approved competitions that are restricted to Arabians and Half/Anglo Arabians, stewards must meet Federation licensing requirements and must also have passed the AHA approved Arabian stewards test, and also attended a special session for AHA approved Arabian stewards at a Federation

stewards clinic.

8. Officiating requirements:

    a. The Licensed Officials Committee will require Registered and Recorded Category 1 Stewards who do not officiate at a minimum of three licensed Hunter/Jumper competitions within (3) three years after obtaining a license for any three year period thereafter, to re-apply for a license.

    b. The Licensed Officials Committee will require Category 2 stewards who do not officiate at a minimum of three Licensed competitions in the C2 group within three years after obtaining a license or for any three-year period thereafter, to re-apply for a license.

9. Promotion Procedures.

    a. Applicants for promotion must have taken an examination and receive a mark of 85% or higher within the past 24 months.

    b. Category 1

        1. No recorded Category 1 steward will be considered for promotion unless the applicant has officiated as a Category 1 steward in at least ten (10) licensed Hunter/Jumper competitions. Recorded Stewards who wish to apply for Registered status must fulfill this requirement within five (5) years as verified by stewards' reports.

        2. An applicant for promotion to Registered status as a Category 1 Steward must have documented experience of having served as the Certified Jumper Schooling Supervisor or an apprentice schooling supervisor at four classes offering $25,000 or more.

        3. No application for promotion will be considered unless and until fifteen forms with an evaluation of the applicant are returned from members of the Federation. Of the 15 evaluations eight must be from licensed hunter/jumper officials, of those two must be from R Category 1 stewards.

    c. Category 2

        1. No recorded Category 2 steward will be considered for promotion unless the applicant has officiated as a Category 2 steward in at least five (5) Licensed competitions in the Category 2 group during the past three years, verified by stewards' reports.

        2. No C2 applicant steward under 25 years of age will be considered for promotion unless he has served as a Recorded Category 2 steward for at least two years (24 months).

        3. No application for promotion will be considered unless and until fifteen forms with an evaluation of the applicant are returned from members of the Federation. Of the 15 evaluations eight must be from relevant licensed judges and/or stewards. *BOD 9/29/15 Effective 12/1/15*

GR1073 Vaulting Judges

1. In the Vaulting Division, no application will be considered unless and until nine forms with an evaluation of the applicant are returned from members of the Federation, three of which must be licensed Vaulting judges or members of the Vaulting Committee.

2. Applicants for enrollment in the Vaulting Division will not be considered unless they are:

    a. licensed by the FEI in Vaulting, or

    b. licensed by the American Vaulting Association, or

    c. have successfully completed a training program for vaulting judges approved by Federation and the AVA.

3. All Vaulting Judges must attend the Federation/AVA Judges Forum each year or AVA Judges Training sessions of equal hours.

4. Vaulting judges must hold a current AVA judges' card and must judge at least one Licensed Competition once every five (5) years or the license will not be renewed.

5. No applicant will be considered for promotion unless he has adjudicated in at least two Licensed Competitions during the past three years in the division in which he is licensed, verified by stewards' reports.

GR1074 Vaulting Technical Delegates

1. No application will be considered unless and until nine forms, with an evaluation of the applicant, are returned from members of the Federation, three of which must be licensed Vaulting Judges or members of the USEF Vaulting Committees.

2. Applicants for enrollment as Vaulting Technical Delegates will not be considered unless they are:

   a. licensed by the FEI in the Vaulting division, or

   b. licensed by the AVA as a Vaulting judge, or

   c. have successfully apprenticed at a minimum of one USEF or FEI Vaulting competition within the two years prior to applying for the license.

   d. have attended an approved continuing education clinic for vaulting technical delegates within the two years prior to applying for the license.

3. Vaulting Technical Delegates must attend a Federation approved continuing education clinic for vaulting technical delegates at least once every four years; successful completion of a written exam may be required as part of the clinic requirement.

4. The Licensed Officials Committee will require Vaulting Technical Delegates who do not officiate at a minimum of one Licensed Vaulting Competition every five (5) years after obtaining a license to re-apply for a license.

5. Vaulting Technical Delegates must be members in good standing of the American Vaulting Association.

GR1075 Welsh Pony Judges

1. In the Welsh Pony Division, all applicants must have had experience breeding, training or showing Welsh ponies and must be recommended by the Welsh Pony and Cob Society of America, Inc. (WPCSA).

2. Applicants must complete three full days of learner judging in the Welsh division at a minimum of three Federation Licensed Competitions under a minimum of three separate Registered Welsh judges.

   a. Registered Hunter Judges may complete three full days of judging in the Welsh Division at a minimum of three Federation Licensed Competitions per GR1004.6 to fulfill their learner judging requirements.)

   b. Current approved WPCSA judges must complete a minimum of one full day of learner judging in the Welsh Division at a Federation Licensed Competition.

   c. Applicant must receive 10 recommendations, three of which must come from members of the Federation Welsh Committee.

3. Applicants must have attended a Federation judges' clinic within three years preceding application.

4. For an applicant in the Welsh Division who holds approved status with the WPCSA, the Licensed Officials Committee shall have the option of granting Registered status.

5. Licensed USEF Welsh judges must attend a Federation Welsh Judges Clinic every five years to retain their license.

6. Welsh judges must judge at least one Welsh division every five years or the license will not be renewed.

7. No applicant will be considered for promotion unless he has adjudicated in at least two Licensed Competitions during the past five years in the Welsh Pony division, verified by stewards' reports.

8. All Registered (R) and Recorded (r) USEF Welsh judges must be current members in good standing of the WPCSA.

GR1076 Western Judges

1. No application will be considered unless and until 15 forms which actually evaluate the applicant per division are returned from USEF members, eight of which must be from relevant licensed judges, stewards, technical delegates or committee members.

2. Learner judge at a minimum of two Federation Licensed Competitions, under minimum of two different Federation Western judges, within a two-year period preceding application. Judges holding Federation Reining Division license

and/or one or more national breed association judges card(s) are not required to learner judge.

3. Attend designated sessions at the International Equine Judges Seminar (IEJS), complete the USEF Western Judges technical training provided via the USEF website and interview with members of the National Western Committee. (Interviews may be conducted via teleconference)

    a. Persons holding a national breed association card with an association affiliated with the IEJS must attend designated sessions at the IEJS and interview before submitting an application for enrollment. (Interviews may be conducted via teleconference)

    b. All applicants for enrollment and reenrollment must also pass the rule book test with a score of 84% or better.

4. All persons applying for enrollment or re-enrollment must have attended the designated sessions at the IEJS and completed the USEF Western Judges technical training within one year preceding application.

5. Applicants approved in the Western Division shall automatically receive Registered status.

6. Registered judges must attend the designated sessions at the IEJS and complete the USEF Western Judges technical training at least once every six years.

7. Judges licensed in the Western division must take an examination and receive a score of 84% or better on the exam once every three years to maintain their license.

8. Western judges do not have officiating requirements, but will be required to complete the USEF Western Judges technical training and testing requirements or the license will not be renewed.

GR1077 Western Dressage Judges

1. No application will be considered unless and until 15 forms which actually evaluate the applicant for the Western Dressage division are returned from USEF members, eight of which must be from relevant licensed judges, stewards, technical delegates or Western Dressage Committee members.

2. Every applicant must be a current member in good standing of the Western Dressage Association of America. Once licensed, each judge must maintain membership in good standing of the Western Dressage Association of America.

3. Each applicant must complete the current training program of the Federation Western Dressage Committee, approved by the Federation Licensed Officials Committee. Information on the application procedure and on the current program is available from the Federation.

    a. An Accelerated Training Program (ATP) is authorized for a three-year period commencing with the effective date of this rule change. At the end of the three-year (36 month) period, the ATP ends and all applicants must follow the same licensing path.

    b. An eligible ATP applicant must complete all requirements of the ATP program in any order (judges seminar, on-line testing, apprentice judging) and submit a complete application form to the Licensed Officials Committee prior to the end of the three-year time period stated above.

    c. Complete details on the ATP are available from the USEF Licensed Officials Department.

4. Every Western Dressage judge must participate in and successfully complete all requirements of a Federation Western Dressage Judges' continuing education clinic at least once every three (3) years.

5. At the request of the USEF Licensed Official Committee, a judge may be required to attend a continuing education clinic, outside of his regular rotation or may be asked to complete additional testing.

6. All Judges must satisfactorily complete a written exam once every three years with a minimum passing score of 85%. The exam will be administered by USEF once in each three-year period.

7. No applicant will be considered for promotion unless he has adjudicated a minimum of 15 entries at each level in USEF Western Dressage classes. Of these 15 entries at each level, five (5) must have been at the highest test for the level.

CHAPTER 11 FEDERATION RECORDS AND AWARDS

SUBCHAPTER 11-A HORSE IDENTIFICATION AND RECORDING

GR1101 Horse Identification Number and Horse Identification Form

GR1102 Horse Recordings

SUBCHAPTER 11-B HORSE PASSPORTS AND DOCUMENTATION

GR1103 FEI Horse Passports

GR1104 National Passports

SUBCHAPTER 11-C OWNERSHIP AND COMPETITION RECORDS

GR1105 Transfer of Ownership

GR1106 Exhibitor Registration

GR1107 Change of Name

GR1108 Lease Registration

SUBCHAPTER 11-D HORSE OF THE YEAR AWARDS

AND NATIONAL CHAMPIONSHIPS

GR1109 General

GR1110 General

GR1111 National, Regional and Zone Awards

GR1112 USEF Championships

GR1113 Credit

GR1114 Winners

GR1115 Competition Year

SUBCHAPTER 11-E SPECIAL CONDITIONS

GR1116 Special Conditions

GR1117 Tabulation of Points

GR1118 Ties

GR1119 Disputes

GR1120 Awards

GR1121 Presentation

SUBCHAPTER 11-F AWARD SECTIONS

GR1122 Awards Sections

GR1123 Andalusian/Lusitano Division

GR1124 Arabian and Half/Anglo Arabian Divisions

GR1125 Carriage Pleasure Driving

GR1126 Connemara

GR1127 Driving, Combined

GR1128 English Pleasure

GR1129 Friesian

GR1130 Hackney

GR1131 Hunter and Equitation Divisions

GR1132 Pony Hunter Breeding and Hunter Breeding

GR1133 Jumpers

GR1134 Morgan Horse Division

GR1135 National Show Horse

GR1136 Paso Fino

GR1137 Reining

GR1138 Roadster

GR1139 American Saddlebred

GR1140 Shetland Division

GR1141 Vaulting

GR1142 Welsh Pony and Cob

GR1143 Western

GR1144 Western Dressage

SUBCHAPTER 11-G ZONE FINAL COMPETITIONS

GR1145 Zone Finals

CHAPTER 11 FEDERATION RECORDS AND AWARDS

SUBCHAPTER 11-A HORSE IDENTIFICATION AND RECORDING

GR1101 Horse Identification Number and Horse Identification Form

1. All horses competing in Federation licensed competitions must be properly identified. For all such competitions, entries for each horse must include either a Federation-issued Unique Horse Identification Number or a registration number from a Federation Recognized Affiliate. Additionally, a Federation Recognized Discipline Affiliate may require horses to be registered with their organization, and if so, the entry must also include that registration number.

2. The Federation will issue only one Unique Horse ID Number per horse. This Unique Horse ID number must subsequently remain with the horse in perpetuity, and shall not be changed for any reason, including upgrade from Unique Horse ID to a Recording, change of ownership, change of name, or death.

3. Prior to submitting an application for a new Unique Horse ID number, it is the owner's responsibility to verify the current ID status of a horse through a Horse Recording/ID search, (the assistance of Federation staff may be requested). Anyone who knowingly seeks to obtain an additional Unique Horse ID Number for a horse which has previously been issued one is subject to disciplinary action.

4. The Federation must be notified of any change of ownership and/or competition name of the horse.

5. Owners are requested to notify the Federation of corrections to previously submitted information, e.g., names, addresses, breed registration, pedigree, or markings.

6. A Unique Horse ID number can be upgraded to Federation recording. The Unique Horse ID Number will remain the same.

7. Applications for Unique Horse ID Numbers and/or recordings can be completed online at www.usef.org using the Horse application form which can also be downloaded. The ID application form is also available on request from the Federation office, and from competition management.

8. Competition management is responsible for notifying exhibitors in their prize lists of the Unique Horse ID Number requirement, and availability of Horse ID Number application forms.

9. There will be no charge for Unique Horse ID Numbers that are issued via the internet to members of USEF or its affiliates for: 1) horses that are life recorded, registered or otherwise identified or listed with a USEF discipline affiliate, or 2) horses registered with a USEF breed affiliate. Horses not meeting the above criteria must have a completed USEF Horse application indicating on the application the request for a Horse ID before a number will be issued. This form can be completed on the internet, free of charge, at www.usef.org.

GR1102 Horse Recordings

1. Using each horse's Unique Horse ID number the Federation maintains the only official record of winnings of horses at all Regular Competitions. To keep these records consistent, a horse should be recorded with the Federation in the same name of horse and owner under which it is exhibited at competitions. The Federation's horse recording records are not a title registry and the Federation does not decide, otherwise resolve, or become involved in ownership disputes.

2. Horses must be recorded in order to be eligible for National, Regional, or Zone Horse of the Year Awards (see GR1110), and to enter a USEF Show Jumping Ranking List class. (Exception: Horses entered in a USEF Show Jumping Ranking List class that are owned by a member of another National Federation and, have proof, in English, of current membership in good standing of their own National Federation, GR901.9, item 9.)

3. Horses must be recorded in order to be eligible to compete in USEF/USDF qualifying classes for dressage championships and will not be credited with qualifying for the Regional Finals for Dressage Championships until they are recorded in the name of the current owner or lessee of record and unless they are entered in qualifying classes under

their official recorded names and ownership. The responsibility for such recording rests entirely with the exhibitor.

4. Horses competing in divisions restricted to a particular breed may be recorded with the Federation under any name but if registered in a Breed Registry, the registered name must also be given.

a. To maintain breeding identification, exhibitors may not shorten horses' names by dropping registered prefixes.

5. Horse recording applications are available from the Federation office or online at www.usef.org. The recording fee is discounted for the life of a horse if applied for from birth to December 31st of year foaled; for horses one year of age (if applied for from January 1 to December 31 of the first year after foaling); and for horses two years of age (if applied for from January 1 to December 31 of the second year after foaling). For horses three years of age or older there is no discount for a life recording. A recording may also be activated on an annual basis, using each horse's Unique Horse ID number. Exception: Horses must be recorded for life to be eligible to receive FEI or National Passports. To qualify for the age discount, registration papers and/or other proof of age must be provided. The fees can be found on the horse recording application at www.usef.org.

6. A duplicate annual card or a duplicate life certificate will be issued for a fee.

7. Once a foal year has been submitted to the Federation office, the original date cannot be changed without a copy of the animal's breed registration papers or a signed statement from a veterinarian certifying the animal's age.

SUBCHAPTER 11-B HORSE PASSPORTS AND DOCUMENTATION

GR1103 FEI Horse Passports

1. Horses must be life recorded with the Federation. To be listed in the passport, the owner(s) of the horse must be active member(s) of the Federation. The passport application and applicable fee must be submitted by the recorded owner (agent's signature is not acceptable) for a specific horse.

2. FEI passport applications can be found on the Federation website or obtained from the Federation office. The horse's name on the passport must match its life recording with the Federation exactly.

3. Group-rate passports are available for Pairs and Teams of driving horses as follows:

a. For Pairs of two, three, or four horses and Teams of four, five, or six horses (all horses with the same owner), the first FEI Horse passport is issued for the current individual rate and each additional FEI Horse passport (up to six) is issued for 50% of the cost of the initial passport. To qualify for this group rate, the passport applications for all horses in the Pair or Team must be submitted (by the owner) simultaneously and clearly marked "Driving Pair / Horses" or "Driving Team / Horses."

b. If an existing Pair or Team has FEI Horse passports and a horse is replaced, the new horse will be issued an FEI Horse Passport at the current individual rate (see also GR1103.5 and .6).

4. Group-rate passports are available for Pairs and Teams of driving ponies as follows:

a. For Pairs of two, three, or four ponies and Teams of four, five, or six ponies (all ponies with the same owner), the first FEI Pony Passport is issued for the current individual rate and each additional FEI Pony Passport (up to six) is issued for 50% of the cost of the initial passport. To qualify for this group rate, the passport applications for all ponies in the Pair or Team must be submitted (by the owner) simultaneously and clearly marked "Driving Pair / Ponies" or "Driving Team / Ponies."

b. If an existing Pair or Team has FEI Pony Passports and a pony is replaced, the new pony will be issued an FEI Pony Passport at the current individual rate (see also GR1103.5 and .6).

5. In accordance with GR1105 and GR1107, any change of the horse's name, or ownership must be recorded with and the passport sent in to the Federation for processing.

6. Passports in need of change of ownership or nationality must be submitted to the Federation; applications and fee structure are available on the Federation website or obtained from the Federation office. The horse must be recorded with the National Federation of the new owner.

7. All passports sent to the Federation for processing will be reviewed for compliance with current FEI regulations including those for Equine Influenza.

8. Passports must be revalidated every four years. Applications are available on the Federation website or obtained from the Federation office.

9. Duplicate passports may be issued for lost or filled passports. The request for a duplicate passport must be signed by the owner of record, and in the case the passport is filled, the old passport must accompany the letter of request.

GR1104 National Passports

1. Federation National Passports are issued for a fee to Federation Life recorded horses and may be presented in lieu of FEI Passports only at those competitions for which approval of Federation National Passports has been granted by the FEI. (See GR1308.4)

2. Application must be made in writing by the owner (agent's signature is not acceptable) and must be accompanied by the applicable fee. Applications and fee structure are available on the Federation website or obtained from the Federation office.

3. Any change of name or ownership must be recorded with the Federation in accordance with GR1105 and GR1107. The passport must be submitted to the Federation for any changes. The fee for transfer of ownership from U.S. owner to U.S. owner in a National Passport payable at the time of the request.

4. Requirements for issuance and validation of National Passports are subject to current FEI regulations.

5. National Passports may be upgraded to the FEI Passport for a fee. An upgrade application must be submitted under the owner's signature (agent's signature is not acceptable) accompanied by the fee and the National Passport.

SUBCHAPTER 11-C OWNERSHIP AND COMPETITION RECORDS

GR1105 Transfer of Ownership

1. Ownership of a Federation recorded horse may be transferred during the year without affecting the animal's points provided proper authorization and fee are received by the Federation office. Authorization for transfer of ownership of a horse holding a lifetime recording with the Federation may be submitted in the form of the original Federation recording certificate or a proper bill of sale. Authorization must be signed by the previously recorded owner(s). Authorization for transfer of ownership of a horse holding an annual recording may be submitted in the form of a bill of sale signed by the previously recorded owner(s). If these documents are unavailable, a Federation transfer affidavit may be obtained from the Federation office which must be completed, signed, notarized and returned to the Federation office with proof of ownership. A horse will not be eligible to receive points under its new ownership until the conditions of GR1110 and GR1111 are met. The fees can be found on the horse transfer form at www.usef.org.

2. Authorization for transfer of ownership of a horse or pony that is or has been in possession of a Federation measurement card may be submitted in the form of a bill of sale signed by the previous owner or a copy of breed registration papers issued to the new owner. There is no fee to transfer ownership of a horse or pony possessing only a Federation measurement card.

3. Authorization for transfer of ownership within a family (as defined in GR123) may be submitted in writing and signed by the previous owner(s) and the new owner(s). There is no fee to transfer a horse/pony within a family.

GR1106 Exhibitor Registration

1. Entries may be made in a name other than that of an individual for Horse of the Year Awards, provided such name (Stable/Farm, Corporation, etc.) is registered with the Federation. Duplication of farm names is discouraged but not prohibited. Horses shown under a partnership, i.e., Smith & Smith, Jones & Jones, must be duly registered. All applications for registration of (Stable/Farm, Corporation, etc.) must be signed by each of the bona fide owners

and accompanied by the required fee. The fees can be found on the Farm, Corporation, Syndicate or Partnership Recording application at www.usef.org.

2. In order for points to count toward Federation Horse of the Year Awards, at least one owner, recorded as such with the Federation, must be a Federation Senior Active, Junior Active, or Life Member.

3. Additional owners (including members of the family of the owner) may be included at no extra fee. Authorization to include additional owners must be made in writing and must be signed by each bona fide owner and will be effective the day such authorization is received in the Federation office.

GR1107 Change of Name

1. The recorded name of a horse competing in divisions that do not require breed registration may be changed by submission of the original recording certificate to the Federation office accompanied by the required fee. The recorded name of a horse can also be changed by submitting the Horse Name Change Request form which lists the fee and can be found at www.usef.org.

2. The registered name of an exhibitor may be changed by submitting the original certificate to the Federation office accompanied by the required fee. The recorded name of a farm, corporation, syndicate, or partnership may be changed by submitting the original certificate to the Federation office accompanied by the required fee.

3. All name changes officially recorded with the Federation will be listed in equestrian.

GR1108 Lease Registration

1. The Federation encourages all lessors of horses competing in Federation competitions to register the lease with the Federation. A recorded horse must be shown under a lessee's ownership provided an official lease is registered with the Federation.

2. For points to count with respect to any recorded horse at a Federation competition, such agreement or lease registration form (provided by the Federation) and fees must be received by the Federation office on or before the first day of such competition. The lessee becomes the bona fide owner of the horse for the period of the lease (except for Owner classes) for Federation award purposes. The horse must be entered in the ownership of the lessee and must be shown in accordance with GR1110.

3. To be official, a certified copy of a lease agreement or a lease registration form must be submitted and registered with the Federation and must be accompanied by the required fee. The Horse Lease Form which lists the fee can be found at www.usef.org. Either document must contain a start and end date and be signed by the lessee and the lessor. If a lease is not renewed within 30 days of its expiration, a later renewal will require an additional fee. The lease registration with the Federation will then be effective the day the renewal is received by our office.

4. A written statement of termination must be submitted signed by the lessee and the lessor if the lease is terminated before the end date stated in the lease registration form.

5. The Federation does not accept agent signatures.

SUBCHAPTER 11-D HORSE OF THE YEAR AWARDS AND NATIONAL CHAMPIONSHIPS

GR1109 General

The Federation offers annual Horse of the Year Awards on a national, district, regional and zone level, in numerous divisions. The purpose of these awards is to encourage participation at Federation Licensed Competitions. In making the awards the Federation in no way implies that the winners are the best in their respective divisions (although they may well be) but certifies that these animals are properly recorded for competition purposes, and registered with the USHJA if competing for awards defined in GR1131, GR1132 or GR1133, are exhibited by the recorded owner, who must be a Federation Member, and USHJA Member if competing for awards defined in GR1131, GR1132 or GR1133, and acquired the greatest number of points during a given year.

GR1110 General

1. Points toward any Horse of the Year Award will not be credited until the applications and fees for the horse's recording, exhibitor's registration, transfer of ownership, name change or addition of owner(s) and owner's Senior Active, Junior Active or Life membership are received by the Federation office. Furthermore, points toward Horse of the Year Awards defined in GR1131, GR1132 or GR1133, will not be credit until the applications and fees for the horse's USHJA Horse Registration and the owner's USHJA Active or USHJA Life membership are received by the Federation or USHJA offices. Exception: Applications for Federation and USHJA Individual Membership and Horse Recordings submitted at Licensed Competitions:

   a. For Dressage Competitions, reference Bylaw 223, Section 1:

      1. Applications are considered effective on the date the application and dues are received by the Competition Secretary provided the application is signed and dated by the Competition Secretary on that same day.

      2. Applications completed online at the competition are effective the date the application is submitted.

   b. For all Competitions other than Dressage Competitions, reference Bylaw 221, Section 1:

      1. Applications are considered effective, for points and eligibility to compete only, on the start date of said Competition provided the application and dues are received by the Competition Secretary and the application is signed and dated by the Competition Secretary during the period of the Competition.

      2. Applications completed online at the competition are effective, for points and eligibility to compete only, on the start date of the Competition.

2. For points to count with respect to any competition, the required materials and fees must be received by the Federation office (or by the Competition Secretary - see below) on or before the first licensed day of such competition. Exception: Applications for Federation Individual Membership and Horse Recordings submitted at Licensed Competitions:

   a. For Dressage Competitions, reference Bylaw 223, Section 1:

      1. Applications are considered effective on the date the application and dues are received by the Competition Secretary provided the application is signed and dated by the Competition Secretary on that same day.

      2. Applications completed online at the competition are effective the date the application is submitted.

   b. For all Competitions other than Dressage Competitions, reference Bylaw 221, Section 1:

      1. Applications are considered effective, for points and eligibility to compete only, on the start date of said Competition provided the application and dues are received by the Competition Secretary and the application is signed and dated by the Competition Secretary during the period of the Competition.

      2. Applications completed online at the competition are effective, for points and eligibility to compete only, on the start date of the Competition.

3. A horse must be recorded with the Federation, and the name of at least one individual appearing on the horse recording certificate as owner must be that of an Senior Active, Junior Active or Life Member in good standing. If the horse is leased at the time of the competition, per GR1108, the lessee is considered the owner (exception all Owner classes) and must be a Senior Active, Junior Active or Life Member in good standing. If the recorded owner is a farm/stable, corporation or any name other than that of a person, refer to GR1106. For the purposes of accruing Federation points, the horse must be entered and shown in the ownership of an individual or entity, including a member of the owner's family, who is included on the Federation horse recording certificate. Effective date of ownership is the day written authorization is received by the Federation office.

4. If the owner, rider, animal, and trainer are all in good standing and an error occurs on the entry blank (i.e. the wrong USEF number is written, the old owner is written in error, the correct number but incorrect spelling is written, etc.), HOTY points may be awarded after review by the Federation.

5. No points can be credited toward an award unless the Federation recorded name and Horse Recording number of

the horse and the Federation recorded owner or lessee's name and membership number appears in the competition's records (i.e., result sheets or catalogue) as exhibited in the name of the Federation recorded owner or, if the horse is leased, under the ownership of the lessee as required under GR1108.

6. Failure to comply with the rules respecting eligibility for points will result in points not counting for Federation purposes and awards. Points standings are available on the Federation website, www.usef.org, and it is the responsibility of exhibitors to check standings and call to the Federation's attention any omissions or inaccuracies. As a service to members the Federation may from time to time advise exhibitors when points are not able to be counted, but the responsibility for checking standings and ensuring that eligibility requirements are met remains solely with the exhibitors.

GR1111 National, Regional and Zone Awards

1. All horses are eligible for National Awards, as long as all requirements of GR1110 are met. See GR1122-GR1144 for specific classes and divisions offered at the National level.

2. In the Arabian, Half/Anglo Arabian, Andalusian/Lusitano, Friesian and Morgan divisions, horses are eligible for Regional Awards in any region they compete. (Points will be awarded in the qualifying region stated in the prize list regardless of the owner's home region). Exception: In Friesian division, any points won at Nationals will count solely towards National Awards and not towards any Regional awards. In the Andalusian/Lusitano Division, any points won at the IALHA designated National Show will count solely towards National Awards and not towards any Regional Awards. In the Hackney, Roadster, and American Saddlebred divisions, points won at competitions in states contiguous to an exhibitor's home region, or in Canada if contiguous to an exhibitor's home region, will count in addition to any points won in an exhibitor's home region.

3. For purposes of distributing Regional Awards for the Andalusian/Lusitano, and Western divisions, refer to the Regional map in GR1123. For Friesian division, refer to Friesian Regional map in GR1129. For Arabian and Half/Anglo Arabian divisions, refer to Regional map in GR1124. For Hackney and Roadster divisions, refer to Hackney Regional map in GR1130. For the Morgan division, refer to Morgan Regional map in GR1134. For the American Saddlebred division refer to American Saddlebred Regional map in GR1139.

4. Horses are eligible for Zone Awards only within the home zone of the entry's recorded owner(s) exception Hunter Seat Equitation, the rider's home residence will be used. However, points won at competitions in states contiguous to an exhibitor's home zone, or in Canadian provinces if contiguous to an exhibitor's home zone, will also count if the state or Canadian province has been designated as provided below.

   a. Zone awards are offered in the following disciplines: Hunters, Jumpers and Hunter Seat Equitation. For Hunter, Jumper and Hunter Seat Equitation divisions for which zone awards are offered, each zone committee may designate one or more states and/or Canadian provinces contiguous to its zone in which to compete for zone points. Designated Canadian provinces that are contiguous to the zone will receive zone points for national Horse of the Year award sections and for USHJA Zone Horse of the Year award sections providing they conduct their classes under national Federation rules for these sections. For purposes of this rule as applied to hunter/jumper and equitation zone awards, the state of New Jersey which is a state land-locked within the zone will be treated as a part of either New York or Pennsylvania. Therefore if Zone 1 chooses New York as one of its contiguous states, New Jersey is also included. If Zone 3 chooses Pennsylvania as one of its contiguous states, New Jersey is also included.

   b. Zone committees must submit their designation of contiguous state(s) and/or Canadian provinces by August 1 annually, to be in effect for the next competition year. If no designation of contiguous states and/or Canadian provinces is submitted, it defaults to the previous year's policy.

5. For purposes of distributing Zone Awards, refer to Zone map.

6. An owner's residence at the time he applies for or renews his membership will be maintained throughout the

competition year and is considered his home district, region or zone for the purposes of counting points. For a Life Member, his residence on December 1st will be used for this purpose. If the recorded owner moves his residence during the year to a new district, region or zone, points can be accumulated in the new location provided the owner declares in writing to the Federation that the new district, region or zone will be his home district, region or zone. The declaration must be received by the Federation office on or before the first licensed day of a competition for points to be counted for that competition. See also JP101.

7. If the recorded ownership of the horse is transferred, valid points earned by the previously recorded owner will be retained in his home district, region or zone. Points are not transferable from one district, region, or zone to another.

8. Horses showing under multiple ownership involving more than one district, region or zone must have one home district, region or zone declared for the purpose of these Awards. This declaration must be made in writing to the Federation office by March 1st of the current year or within 30 days of receipt of horse recording application and must be signed by each bona fide owner. Effective date of declaration is the day the written authorization is received by the Federation office and for points to count, the declaration must be received by the Federation office on or before the first day of the competition. If only one owner is a Federation Member in good standing, this person's residency will automatically become the entry's home district, region or zone.

9. If the horse is recorded under the ownership of a registered farm, the residence of the farm's owner is the entry's home district, region or zone. If the owners of a farm reside in different districts, regions or zones see paragraph 8 above.

10. Exception to GR1111.8-1111.11: Arabian, Half/Anglo Arabian Division, Andalusian/ Lusitano, Morgan and Friesian Divisions; see GR1111.2.

11. Responsibility in fulfilling the requirements of the above Rules rests entirely with the exhibitor. As the competition entry blank is generally the source of information required in GR1110.5, care should be taken to fill out entry blanks correctly.

GR1112 USEF Championships

1. For rules governing the following Championships, see specific Rules as noted:
    a. Dressage Regional and National Championships: See DR127.
    b. Hunter Pony Championships: See HU181.
    c. Junior Jumper Prix des States. See JP151.3.
    d. Medal Championships: See EQ110, EQ117.12.
    e. Hunter Breeding Championships: See HU184.
    f. Junior Hunter Championships (see HU182).
    g. Eventing National Championships (See EV161-EV165).

GR1113 Credit

1. No credit will be given for classes where judging specifications are not in accordance with the Federation rules. Points will not count towards Horse of the Year Award competitions and classes will not be counted for division or section ratings.

2. No credit will be given in classes if less than three entries have shown and placed. Exceptions:
    a. Hunter Breeding, Pony Hunter Breeding.
    b. Hunter Classes, a minimum of three entries must have competed per HU130.
    c. At a National or Premier rated hunter/jumper competition where it is required that the division be held over two days, if there are less than three exhibitors the second day, Zone and National Horse of the Year points will still apply.

a. Andalusian/Lusitano

b. Friesians

c. Carriage Pleasure Driving (GR1125)

d. Hackney

e. Jumper Classes, a minimum of three entries must have competed per JP133.13.

f. Morgans

g. American Saddlebreds

h. Shetlands

i. Arabians (Exception: Championship classes based only on scores or high point awards are not awarded points.)

j. National Show Horse

k. Roadsters

l. Ladies Side Saddle Over Fences Class in the Hunter Division, see HU142.

m. Driving Combined (GR1127).

n. Western Dressage.

o. Welsh.

3. Credit will be given for the first six (6) placings only, regardless of the number of ribbons offered. Exception: in the Morgan and Hunter Breeding divisions where only the first four (4) place ribbons will receive points, and Hunter Divisions, where only the first eight (8) place ribbons will receive points in accordance with GR1131 when entries are 16 or higher. Ribbons must be awarded to 8th place in all hunter classes. Exception: in Bonus Point classes, Classics in the Hunter and Jumper divisions, National Show Horse Finals, Federation Zone Finals and jumper sections, Hunter Breeding Best Young Horse Class, Morgan In-hand Championship Classes. All model classes will receive 1/2 points. (Exception: Arabian, see GR1124)

GR1114 Winners

1. In all divisions, except Dressage and Open Jumper classes offering $25,000 and over, winners will be those horses which accrue the highest number of points or amount of prize money at Federation Licensed Competitions.

2. The Junior Jumper and the Amateur Owner Jumper winners will be those horses which earn the highest number of points based on a scale of one point for every dollar earned in their classification at Regular Competitions.

3. The Open Jumper Horse of the Year Award is based on money won in classes which comply with JP151.

4. Awards are made to the owner as shown in the Federation recording files, at the time the horse wins its last point in the competition. If the ownership of a horse is transferred, all district, region or zone points earned up to that date stand.

GR1115 Competition Year

1. Competition year for awards will be as follows: All breeds/disciplines will begin December 1 and end November 30. Exceptions: Paso Fino competition year will begin September 1 and end August 31; Hunter Breeding and Pony Hunter Breeding will begin January 1 and end November 30 (see HU184 and GR102).

2. If a competition is in progress on the last day of any qualifying period points or money won at said competition will be allowable in reckoning the year's total score.

3. Championship qualifying periods for the following Championships will appear on the Federation website.

Dressage Regional Championships

Hunter Pony Championships

Hunter Breeding Championships

4. Adult Hunter Seat Medal qualifying year begins December 1 and ends November 30.

SUBCHAPTER 11-E SPECIAL CONDITIONS

GR1116 Special Conditions

1. No credit will be given in any class that does not count toward a division or section rating (See GR314).

   a. Exceptions:

      1. In Hunter Classics Bonus Points will be awarded in horse's respective section.

      2. In cases which Juniors, Young Riders and Amateur Owners compete in a Combined class, prize money will be awarded in the horse's respective section.

      3. Hunter Seat Equitation classes listed as eligible classes in GR1131.13 will count for points even if the class does not count toward division or section rating.

2. Where the term Championship is omitted from a class title, the class that is open to all horses in a division or section that has the required specifications will be counted as the Championship. When Championships are awarded on a point basis, only the Champion and Reserve will receive points for a Horse of the Year Award. (Exception: Arabian, see GR1124).

3. Only classes held in accordance with HU142 will count toward Ladies Side Saddle Hunter.

4. Credit for the following will be applied as specified in Chapter 11:

   a. Andalusian/Lusitano Division will be applied as per GR1123.

   b. Arabian Division will be applied as per GR1124.

   c. Friesian Division will be applied as per GR1129.

   d. Hackney Division will be applied as per GR1130.

   e. National Show Horse Division will be applied as per GR1135.

   f. Morgan Division will be applied as per GR1134.

   g. Roadster Division will be applied as per GR1138.

   h. American Saddlebred Division will be applied as per GR1139.

   i. Shetland Division will be applied as per GR1140.

   j. Western Dressage Division will be applied as per GR1144.

GR1117 Tabulation of Points

Scores of all horses will be kept in the Federation office. Results from Federation Licensed Competitions will furnish the sole basis upon which the scores are figured, and the Federation tally thus derived will be the final authority in determining winners. Although the Federation uses its best efforts to insure that the points as recorded by the Federation on its web site and elsewhere are accurate, the Federation assumes no liability to anyone for any errors or omissions whatsoever. Anyone who uses these points for Federation purposes or for any other purpose is hereby notified that the Federation disclaims any and all liability and responsibility, including for negligence, with respect to these point tabulations and records.

GR1118 Ties

In the event of a tie, the Horse of the Year Award will be awarded to each competitor.

GR1119 Disputes

1. Points are final on December 15 (should the 15th fall on a weekend, the deadline will be set for the following Monday) following each competition year or 15 days following the end of the designated Zone competition year and in the Paso Fino Division points are final on September 15 following the competition year.

2. Any participant wishing to dispute a tabulation or qualification or disqualification must appeal the issue in writing specifying the reasons for disputing the tabulation or qualification or disqualification (the "Dispute"). Said Dispute must be received by the Federation by December 15 (should the 15th fall on a weekend, the deadline will be set

for the following Monday) following the competition year in question, except for the Paso Fino Division for which the deadline is September 15. A Dispute must be accompanied by the required fee which is not refundable. Disputes will be referred to the CEO or his designee for a ruling in the first instance, who will determine if the information which is provided in the Dispute is sufficient to alter the tabulation or qualification or disqualification. If the participant is dissatisfied with the CEO's or his designee's ruling, the participant may submit a written request for an appeal. An appeal must be accompanied by the required fee, which will be refunded if the appeal is upheld. Appeals will be referred to the Hearing Committee or a special committee appointed by the President, whose decision is final.

GR1120 Awards

1. Awards may be offered in any division or section recognized by the Federation. The Board of Directors will determine those classifications in which awards will be offered and should competition throughout the year in any way be so slight as not to warrant the giving of an award, such award may be canceled.
2. Any requests for new awards to be added must be received in writing in the Federation office by August 1 of the preceding year and approved by the appropriate committee.
3. Presentation of breed-specific awards will be made at venues most suitable to that breed or may be awarded at the Federation Annual Meeting.

GR1121 Presentation

1. Presentation of the Federation National Horse of the Year Awards will be made at the Federation's Annual Meeting, or other venue as approved by the Federation. The trophies awarded to the National Champions are perpetual trophies and remain in the possession of the Federation.
2. Presentation of the Federation District, Regional or Zone Horse of the Year Awards will be made at venues specified within each breed and discipline, as approved by the Federation, and the appropriate breed/discipline Committees.

SUBCHAPTER 11-F AWARD SECTIONS

GR1122 Awards Sections
Refer to Subchapters 11-C to 11-E for all general rules for all Award Sections.

GR1123 Andalusian/Lusitano Division
1. Eligibility. See GR1110.
2. Point Tabulation. See Rules GR1113-GR1119.

Started	10+	9	8	7	6	5	4	3	2	1
1st	10	9	8	7	6	5	4	3	2	1
2nd	9	8	7	6	5	4	3	2	1	
3rd	8	7	6	5	4	3	2	1		
4th	7	6	5	4	3	2	1			
5th	6	5	4	3	2	1				
6th	5	4	3	2	1					
7th	4	3	2	1						
8th	3	2	1							
9th	2	1								
10th	1									

  a. Full points will be awarded to Andalusian/Lusitano classes conducted at Federation Licensed competitions.

  b. Half points will be given in the following classes: Maiden horse, Novice horse, Limit horse, and Green horse.

  c. At Federation Licensed Regional level competitions, class entries will receive double points.

  d. At Federation Licensed National level competitions, class entries will receive triple points.

  e. Classes that are restricted to Maiden, Novice, Limit or Green riders/drivers are not counted.

  f. Combined Pure Andalusian and Half-Andalusian classes do not receive points, with the following exceptions: Junior Equitation, Showmanship, Western Trail, Western Riding, Doma Vaquera, Reining, Dressage, and working Equitation.

  g. Showmanship, Produce of Dam, Get of Sire, and Cobra of Mares classes do not receive points for Halter awards.

  h. Equitation and Showmanship only count toward Junior Exhibitor awards.

  i. Hunter Hack, Walk-Trot, Liberty, Musical Freestyle and Long Reining classes do not receive points.

3. Points received at the IALHA designated National Show will count solely towards National Awards and not towards any Regional Awards (see GR1111.2).

4. Regional Awards will be distributed according to the Regional Map.

5. National Awards will be presented at the Federation Annual Meeting.

6. Regional Awards will be presented at regional venues at the discretion of the IALHA Regional organizations, as approved by the Federation.

7. Award Categories. National and Regional awards will be awarded in the following categories:

  a. Andalusian/Lusitano Halter: Classes to count include stallions, mares, geldings, and Dressage Sport Horse In-Hand.

  b. Half Andalusian/Lusitano Halter: Classes to count include stallions, mares, geldings, and Dressage Sport Horse In-Hand.

  c. Andalusian/Lusitano English Pleasure (Open, Amateur, Junior Horse): Classes to count include Formal Saddle, Saddle Seat, Country, Hunt Seat, Pro-Am-for Open award, and Vintage Rider-for Amateur award)

  d. Half Andalusian/Lusitano English Pleasure (Open, Amateur, Junior Horse): Classes to count include Formal Saddle, Saddle Seat, Country, Hunt Seat, Pro-Am-for Open award, and Vintage Rider-for Amateur award)

  e. Andalusian/Lusitano Western Pleasure (Open, Amateur, Junior Horse): Classes to count include Western Pleasure, Pro-Am-for Open award, and Vintage Rider-for Amateur award)

  f. Half Andalusian/Lusitano Western Pleasure (Open, Amateur, Junior Horse): Classes to count include Western Pleasure, Pro-Am-for Open award, and Vintage Rider for Amateur award)

  g. Andalusian/Lusitano or Half/Andalusian/Lusitano Working Western (One Award Category): Classes to include Trail, Reining, and Western Riding.

  h. Andalusian/Lusitano Driving: Classes to count include Country Pleasure Driving, Show Pleasure Driving, Pleasure Driving, Formal Driving, and Traditional Type Carriage Driving.

  i. Half Andalusian/Lusitano Driving: Classes to count include Country Pleasure Driving, Show Pleasure Driving, Pleasure Driving, Formal Driving, and Traditional Type Carriage Driving.

  j. Andalusian/Lusitano Specialty (One Award Category): Classes to count include English Show Hack, Versatility English to Western, Versatility Driving to English, Native Tack & Attire, Heritage Tack & Attire, Fantasy Costume, Doma Vaquera, Best Movement, Dressage, Dressage Suitability, Dressage Hack, and working equitation.

  k. Half Andalusian/Lusitano Specialty (One Award Category): Classes to count include English Show Hack, Versatility English to Western, Versatility Driving to English, Native Tack & Attire, Heritage Tack & Attire, Fantasy Costume, Doma Vaquera, Best Movement, Dressage, Dressage Suitability, Dressage Hack, and Working Equitation.

  l. Andalusian/Lusitano Junior Exhibitor Horse: Based on the total of all points won in Andalusian/Lusitano Junior Exhibitor classes (including Equitation and Showmanship).

  m. Half Andalusian/Lusitano Junior Exhibitor Horse: Based on the total of all points won in the Half Andalusian/

Lusitano Junior Exhibitor classes (including Equitation and Showmanship).

8. Grand Champion Andalusian/Lusitano: Based on the total of all points won in all Andalusian/Lusitano categories.

9. Grand Champion Half Andalusian/Lusitano: Based on the total of all points won in all Half Andalusian/Lusitano categories.

ANDALUSIAN / LUSITANO REGIONAL MAP

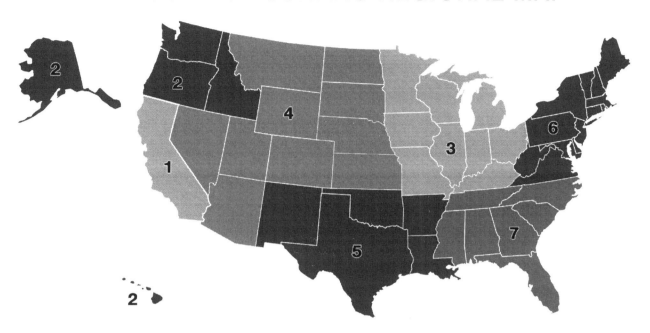

GR1124 Arabian and Half/Anglo Arabian Divisions

1. Eligibility. See GR1110.

2. Point Tabulation. See GR1113-GR1119. Points for all competitions will be awarded as follows.

Started	10+	9	8	7	6	5	4	3	2	1
1st	10	9	8	7	6	5	4	3	2	1
2nd	9	8	7	6	5	4	3	2	1	
3rd	8	7	6	5	4	3	2	1		
4th	7	6	5	4	3	2	1			
5th	6	5	4	3	2	1				
6th	5	4	3	2	1					
7th	4	3	2	1						
8th	3	2	1							
9th	2	1								
10th	1									

Full points shall be awarded to Arabian and Half/Anglo Arabian Breeding/In-Hand and Performance classes conducted at USEF Licensed Competitions.

3. Exceptions:

a. In Breeding and/or In-Hand Championship classes, points will be awarded to only Champion and Reserve.

b. In Breeding, In-Hand and Performance Championship classes based only on scores or high point awards are not awarded points.

    c. Half-points will be given in the following classes: Maiden, Novice, Limit and Green horse classes; no points will be awarded for Model classes.

    d. For additional restrictions, refer to GR314 Special Conditions.

4. At USEF Licensed Regional level competitions, class entries will receive double points; points will be awarded to fifth place in Breeding, In-Hand and Performance classes. Only those Top Five placings receive points, doubled. Regional Awards will be distributed according to the Regional map. Regional Awards will be presented at regional venues at the discretion of the AHA Regional organizations, as approved by the Federation.

5. At USEF Licensed National level competitions, class entries will receive triple points; points will be awarded to tenth place in Breeding, In-Hand and Performance classes. Only those Top Ten placings will receive points, trebled. Any points won at a National Championship (U.S., Youth and Sport Horse) will count solely towards National Awards and not towards any Regional Awards. National Awards will be presented at the Federation Annual Meeting.

6. Award Categories. National and Regional awards will be awarded in the following categories:

English Pleasure/Pleasure Driving—Open, Adult Amateur, Junior Exhibitor;

Country English Pleasure/Country Pleasure Driving—Open, Adult Amateur, Junior Exhibitor;

Hunter Pleasure—Open, Adult Amateur, Junior Exhibitor;

Western Pleasure—Open, Adult Amateur, Junior Exhibitor;

Working Western Horse—includes Trail, Reining, Working Cowhorse, Cutting and Western Riding, one award category;

Hunter— Regular Working; Green Working; Hunter Specialty (Hunter Specialty is one award category based on total number of points from ATR/JTR, AOTR, Horses 14.2 Hands and Under; and Working Hunter 2');

Specialty Horse—includes Park, English Show Hack, Ladies Side Saddle, Native Costume, Hunter Hack, Formal Combination, Informal Combination, Formal Driving, Roadster, English Trail, Versatility, Gymkhana, Carriage Pleasure Driving, Western Dressage, and Jumper, one award category;

Breeding/In-Hand—includes Stallions, Mares, Geldings for Arabians and Mares and Geldings for Half/Anglo Arabians, one award category;

Dressage—Open: Training Level; First Level; Second Level, Third Level, Fourth Level and FEI combined Level

Amateur: Training Level; First Level; Second Level, Third Level, Fourth Level, and FEI combined Level

Sport Horse - Sport Horse In-Hand, Sport Horse Under Saddle and Sport Horse Show Hack are combined. *BOD 6/30/15 Effective 12/1/15*

7. Overall Grand Champion Categories:

Purebred Arabian -based on the total of all points won in all Purebred Arabian categories.

Half/Anglo Arabian-based on the total of all points won in all Half/Anglo Arabian categories.

Arabian Gelding -based on the total of all points won in all Purebred Arabian categories.

Purebred Arabian Junior Exhibitor- based on the total of all points won in Arabian Junior Exhibitor classes (classes combined with amateur sections will not be counted).

Half/Anglo Arabian Exhibitor -based on the total of all points won in Half/Anglo Arabian Junior Exhibitor classes (classes combined with amateur sections will not be counted).

ARABIAN / HALF / ANGLO-ARABIAN REGIONAL MAP

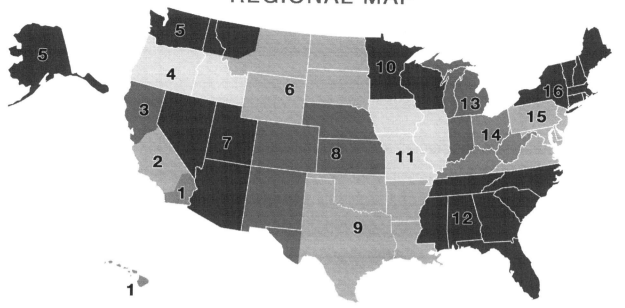

GR1125 Carriage Pleasure Driving

1. Eligibility. See GR1110.

2. Point Tabulation. See GR1113-GR1119. Points for all competitions will be awarded as follows:

Started	16+	15	14	13	12	11	10	9	8	7	6	5	4	3	2
1st	20	19	18	17	16	15	14	13	12	11	10	9	8	6	4
2nd	17	16	15	14	13	12	11	10	9	8	7	6	5	3	1
3rd	15	14	13	12	11	10	9	8	7	6	5	4	3	1	
4th	13	12	11	10	9	8	7	6	5	4	3	2	1		
5th	12	11	10	9	8	7	6	5	4	3	2	1			
6th	11	10	9	8	7	6	5	4	3	2	1				
7th	10	9	8	7	6	5	4	3	2	1					
8th	9	8	7	6	5	4	3	2	1						
9th	8	7	6	5	4	3	2	1							
10th	7	6	5	4	3	2	1								
11th	6	5	4	3	2	1									
12th	5	4	3	2	1										
13th	4	3	2	1											
14th	3	2	1												
15th	2	1													
16th	1														

The USEF Licensed Regional breed/discipline competitions will receive double points.

The USEF Licensed National Championship breed/discipline competitions will receive triple points.

3. Driving awards will be presented at the USEF Annual Meeting.

4. Award categories. Awards will be given in the following award categories:

    a. Carriage Pleasure Driving Single Horse, Carriage Pleasure Driving Pair Horses, Carriage Pleasure Driving

Tandem Horses, Carriage Pleasure Driving Multiple Horses (3 or more), Coaching Horses, Coaching Ponies, Carriage Pleasure Driving Single Pony, Carriage Pleasure Driving Pair Ponies, Carriage Pleasure Driving Tandem Ponies, Carriage Pleasure Driving Multiple Ponies (3 or more), and Driven Dressage at the Training, Preliminary, Intermediate and Advanced levels. (Exception: Concours d'Elegance)

    b. ½ Points will be awarded in any of the above classes with the following restrictions: Maiden, Novice, and Limit Horses and/or Drivers.

    c. The combination for a pair is made up of three horses or ponies; the combination for a four-in-hand is made up of five/six horses or ponies. The combinations must be declared before the first show of the competition year in which they are competing, and any substitution to this combination will constitute a new combination which will be awarded points as a new entry. No points from the original combination carry forward and a separate form is required. The form must be received in the Federation office two weeks prior to the start date of the competition in which they will be competing. Declaration forms are available at   http://www.usef.org/_IFrames/breedsdisci-plines/discipline/allcpdriving/forms.aspx.

5. The winner with the most points in all Carriage Pleasure Driving categories combined will be named the overall winner.

GR1126 Connemara

1. For eligibility see GR1110 and CO101.

2. Point tabulations. See GR1113-1119. Points will be awarded according to the number of horses defeated in a class for which the Federation has class specifications. Three points will be awarded for every horse defeated in a class at Federation Licensed Competitions. Championship In Hand classes will be awarded double points.

3. National awards will be presented at the USEF Annual Meeting.

4. Awards will be given in the following categories for horses participating in Connemara sections as described in Chapter CO:

    a. Purebred Connemara Mare- to include points earned in In Hand classes for purebred mares 3 years of age and older

    b. Purebred Connemara Stallion or Gelding-to include points earned in In Hand classes for purebred stallions or geldings 3 years of age and older

    c. Purebred Connemara Hunter- One award category

    d. Purebred Connemara Jumper- One award category

    e. Halfbred Connemara Hunter - One award category

    f. Halfbred Connemara Jumper - One award category

5. Awards will be given in the following categories for horses participating in either Connemara sections or open competitions provided USEF has received breed registration papers or verification from ACPS prior to December 15:

    a. Purebred Connemara Dressage

    b. Halfbred Connemara Dressage

    c. Purebred Connemara Eventing: awarded to purebred Connemaras competing in Beginner Novice through Training levels at Federation Eventing Competitions.

    d. Halfbred Connemara Eventing: awarded to halfbred Connemaras competing in Beginner Novice through Training levels at Federation Eventing Competitions.

    e. Purebred Connemara Jumper

    f. Halfbred Connemara Jumper

6. Special Awards

    a. McKenna Trophy: awarded to the highest ranking purebred or halfbred Connemara in Preliminary through

Advanced levels at Federation Eventing Competitions.

b. Clifden Trophy: awarded to the highest ranking purebred Connemara in the Regular Hunter Pony section or Green Hunter Pony section in Federation Hunter Competitions.

c. Seldom Seen Trophy: to be awarded to the highest placing purebred or halfbred Connemara ridden by a junior at USEF Dressage competitions.

GR1127 Driving, Combined

1. Eligibility. See GR1110.

2. Point Tabulation. See GR1113-GR1119. Points for all competitions will be awarded as follows:

If 16 or more competitors have started	15	14	13	12	11	10	9	8	7	6	5	4	3	2
1st	20	19	18	17	16	15	14	13	12	11	10	9	8	6	4
2nd	17	16	15	14	13	12	11	10	9	8	7	6	5	3	1
3rd	15	14	13	12	11	10	9	8	7	6	5	4	3	1	
4th	13	12	11	10	9	8	7	6	5	4	3	2	1		
5th	12	11	10	9	8	7	6	5	4	3	2	1			
6th	11	10	9	8	7	6	5	4	3	2	1				
7th	10	9	8	7	6	5	4	3	2	1					
8th	9	8	7	6	5	4	3	2	1						
9th	8	7	6	5	4	3	2	1							
10th	7	6	5	4	3	2	1								
11th	6	5	4	3	2	1									
12th	5	4	3	2	1										
13th	4	3	2	1											
14th	3	2	1												
15th	2	1													
16th	1														

The USEF National Championship Combined Driving classes will recieve double points.

3. National Awards will be presented at the USEF Annual Meeting.

4. Award Categories. Awards will be given in the following award categories:

a. Combined Driving Single Horse, Combined Driving Pair Horses, Combined Driving Four-In-Hand Horses, Combined Driving Single Pony, Combined Driving Pair Ponies, and Combined Driving Four-In-Hand Ponies.

b. Horses and ponies competing in combinations (Pair or Four-in-Hand) must be declared as a unit prior to the classes at the competition in which they plan to compete in order for points to accrue as a Pair or Four-in-Hand. Declarations are available at http://www.usef.org/_IFrames/breedsdisciplines/discipline/alldrivng/points.aspx. The unit for a pair is made up of three horses or ponies, the unit for a four-in-hand is made up of five horses or ponies. The units must be declared before the first show of the calendar year they are competing in, and any substitution to this unit will constitute a new combination and will be awarded points as a new entry.

GR1128 English Pleasure

1. Eligibility. See GR1110.

2. Point Tabulation. See GR1113-GR1119.

3. Points will be awarded as follows:

	First Place	Second Place	Third Place	Fourth Place	Fifth Place	Sixth Place
A Rating	36	28	26	24	22	20
B Rating	30	14	22	20	18	16
C Rating	26	20	18	16	14	12
Local	20	16	14	12	10	8

4. National Awards will be given in the following categories through 6th place:

   a. English Pleasure Saddle Seat

   b. English Pleasure Hunter Seat

   c. English Pleasure Driving

5. Classes not to count towards national awards include: Classes restricted riders or drivers with maiden, novice, or limit status, Classes designated as Amateur-Owner-Trainer, Horsemanship, Combined Hunter Seat and Saddle Seat classes, Walk/Trot classes, unrated classes per GR902.2, and classes listed in GR314.1.

GR1129 Friesian

1. Eligibility. See GR1110.

2. Point Tabulation. See GR1113-GR1119.

   a. Points for all eligible classes (See GR1129.3-GR1129.7) at Friesian competitions will be awarded according to the following chart:

Started	16+	15	14	13	12	11	10	9	8	7	6	5	4	3	2	1
1st	20	19	18	17	16	15	14	13	12	11	10	9	8	4	2	1
2nd	17	16	15	14	13	12	11	10	9	8	7	6	5	3	1	
3rd	15	14	13	12	11	10	9	8	7	6	5	4	3	1		
4th	13	12	11	10	9	8	7	6	5	4	3	2	1			
5th	12	11	10	9	8	7	6	5	4	3	2	1				
6th	11	10	9	8	7	6	5	4	3	2	1					
7th	10	9	8	7	6	5	4	3	2	1						
8th	9	8	7	6	5	4	3	2	1							
9th	8	7	6	5	4	3	2	1								
10th	7	6	5	4	3	2	1									
11th	6	5	4	3	2	1										
12th	5	4	3	2	1											
13th	4	3	2	1												
14th	3	2	1													
15th	2	1														
16th	1															

   b. Points for all eligible classes (See GR1129.3-GR1129.7) at IFSHA designated regional competitions will be awarded at double value.

    c. Points for all eligible classes (See GR1129.3-GR1129.7) at the IFSHA designated national competition will be awarded at triple value.

    d. Points for all eligible classes (See GR1129.3-GR1129.7) at Local competitions will be awarded 1/2 value.

3. National and Regional awards will be given in the following categories through 6th place:

    a. Friesian In Hand - To include points earned from all In Hand classes including open, amateur, masters, junior exhibitor, owner to lead, all horse genders, and all horse age groups.(Exception: Trail In-Hand-see Friesian Specialty Horse).

    b. Friesian Saddle Seat - To include all points earned in Saddle Seat (Country Pleasure, Pleasure, and Park) classes. All classifications of those classes (Open, Amateur, Owner to Ride) all rider age groups (adult or junior exhibitor), all horse genders, and all horse age groups.

    c. Friesian Hunter - To include all points earned in Hunter Pleasure & Hunter Hack classes. All classifications of those classes (Open, Amateur, Owner to Ride), all rider age groups (adult or junior exhibitors), all horse genders, and all horse age groups.

    d. Friesian Western -To include all points earned in Western Pleasure, e.g., all classifications of those classes (Open, Amateur, Owner to Ride), all rider age groups (adult and junior exhibitors), all horse genders, and all horse age groups.

    e. Friesian Driving - To include all points earned in all types of driving classes (Show Driving, Fine Harness, Country Pleasure Driving, Reinsmanship, Working, Turnout, Pleasure, and Sjees) all hitches (tandem, random, unicorn, single, pair, and four-in-hand), Obstacle (Timed, Pick Your Route, Gambler's Choice) all horse genders, all horse age groups, all classifications of those classes (open and amateur exhibitors) and all driver age groups (adult and junior exhibitor).

    f. Friesian Dressage - To include all points from Dressage Suitability, Dressage Hack, and Dressage Tests, all horse genders, all horse age groups, all classifications (open, and amateur exhibitors) all rider age groups (adult and junior exhibitors).

    g. Friesian Specialty Horse - One award category, based on the total number of points from Costume (Fantasy, Period, & Armor), English Show Hack, Liberty, Tandem riding, English and Western Trail, Drive and Ride, Drive, Ride and Jump, all Walk/Trot Classes (not to include Junior equitation classes or Lead line) Reining, Western Dressage and any rated Friesian class not mentioned in any previous category within this rule.

    h. Part-bred Friesian In Hand - To include points earned in all In-Hand classes in Open, amateur, masters, junior exhibitors, owner to lead, all horse genders, and all horse age groups, and all age groups. (Exception: Trail In-Hand-see Friesian Specialty Horse).

    i. Part-bred Friesian Saddle Seat - To include all points earned in Saddle Seat (Country Pleasure, Pleasure, and Park) classes. All classifications of those classes, (Open, Amateur, Owner to Ride), all rider age groups (adult or junior exhibitors), all horse genders, and all horse age groups.

    j. Part-bred Friesian Hunter - To include all points earned in Hunter Pleasure & Hunter Hack classes, all classifications of those classes (Open, Amateur, Owner to Ride), all rider age groups (adult or junior exhibitors), all horse genders and all horse age groups.

    k. Part-bred Friesian Western - To include all points earned in Western Pleasure, e.g., all classifications of those classes (Open, and amateur, Owner to Ride) all rider age groups (adult and junior exhibitors), all horse genders, and all horse age groups.

    l. Part-bred Friesian Driving - To include all points earned in all types of driving classes (Show Driving, Fine Harness, Country Pleasure Driving, Reinsmanship, Working, Turnout, Pleasure, and Sjees) all hitches (tandem, random, unicorn, single, pair, and four-in-hand), Obstacle (Timed, Pick Your Route, Gambler's Choice) all horse genders, all horse age groups, all classifications of those classes (open and amateur exhibitors) and all driver age groups (adult and junior exhibitors).

m. Part-bred Friesian Dressage - To include all points from Dressage Suitability, Dressage Hack, and Dressage Tests, all horse genders, all horse age groups, all classification (open, and amateur exhibitors) all rider age groups (adult and junior exhibitor).

n. Part-bred Friesian Specialty Horse - One award category, based on the total number of points from Costume (Fantasy, Period, & Armor), English Show Hack, Liberty, Tandem riding, English and Western Trail, Drive and Ride, Drive, Ride and Jump, all Walk/Trot Classes not to include Junior equitation classes or Lead line, Reining, Western Dressage and any rated Part-bred Friesian class not mentioned in any previous category within this rule.

4. Grand Champion Friesian is based on the total points won in all Friesian categories as specifically stated above in all categories.

5. Grand Champion Part-bred Friesian is based on the total points won in all Part-bred Friesian categories, as specifically stated above

6. Friesian Junior Exhibitor Award - To include points from all junior exhibitor classes (including but not limited to all performance, in-hand, equitation, and showmanship classes).

7. Part-bred Friesian Junior Exhibitor Award - To include points from all junior exhibitor classes (including but not limited to all performance, in-hand, equitation, and showmanship classes).

FRIESIAN REGIONAL MAP

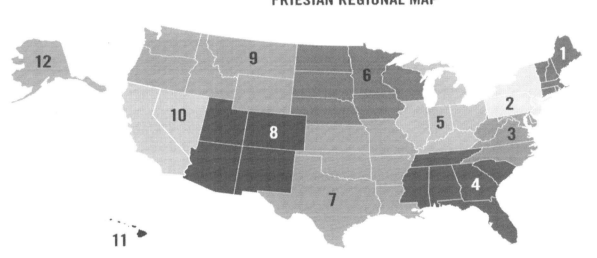

GR1130 Hackney

1. Eligibility. See GR1110.

2. Point Tabulation. See GR1113-GR1119. Points for all competitions will be awarded as follows:

First	Second	Third	Fourth	Fifth	Sixth
20	12	8	4	2	1

The Kentucky State Fair World's Championship Horse Show will receive *triple* points.

3. Regional Awards will be distributed according to the Hackney Regional map.

4. National Awards will be presented at the Federation Annual Meeting.

5. Regional Awards may be presented at an appropriate venue within each region as approved by the Federation. 6. Award Categories. A National Award will be given for the category of Hackney Horse. National & Regional Awards will be given in the following categories: Open Hackney Pony, Amateur Hackney Pony, Open Harness Pony, Amateur Harness Pony, Show Pleasure Pony Driving, Hackney Roadster Pony (shares one award with Open Roadster Pony),

Amateur Hackney Roadster Pony (shares one award with Amateur Roadster Pony), and Junior Exhibitor Hackney Roadster Pony (shares one award with Junior Exhibitor Roadster Pony). See GR1138.6.

HACKNEY REGIONAL MAP

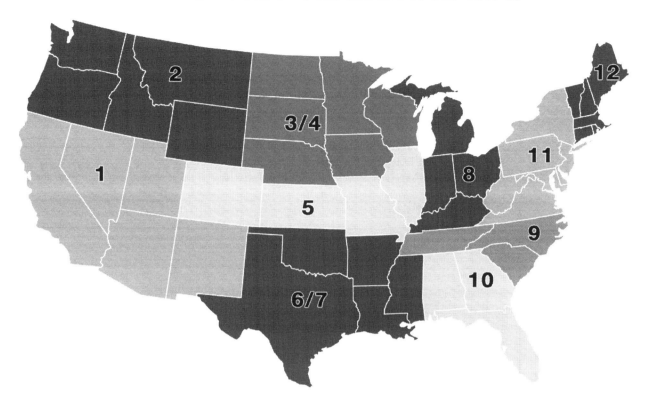

GR1131 Hunter and Equitation Divisions

1. Eligibility

   a. Points toward any Horse of the Year Award for the Hunter Division will not be credited until the applications and fees for the horse's recording, exhibitor's registration, transfer of ownership, name change or addition of owner(s) and owner's Senior Active, Junior Active or Life membership are received by the Federation office. Furthermore, points toward Horse of the Year Awards for the Hunter Division will not be credited until the applications and fees for *the horse's USHJA Horse Registration,* the owner's USHJA Active or USHJA Life membership are received by the Federation or USHJA offices. Exception: Applications for Federation and USHJA Individual Membership and Horse Recordings submitted at Licensed Competitions.

   b. USHJA Zone points toward any Hunter Seat Equitation Division Rider of the Year Awards will not be credited until the applications and fees for the horse's USHJA registration, and rider's USEF and USHJA's active membership are received by the Federation or USHJA offices. Exception: Applications for Federation and USHJA Individual Membership and USHJA Horse Registration submitted at Licensed Competitions.

2. Point Tabulation. See GR1113-GR1119.

3. In the Hunter division, points are calculated according to the Increment system. In "C" and "B" rated sections, points are determined by the number of horses that compete in the section; in "A" rated sections, points are determined by both the rating of the competition (based on scheduling restrictions of HU158) as well as the number of horses that compete. Exception: National awards for First and Second Year Green Hunter, High Performance and Performance Working Hunter, Green Conformation Hunter, and Regular Conformation Hunter will be calculated using

two systems towards two separate sets of national awards. The national Money Won Awards will be based on the money won by each horse in their respective section. The national Points Awards will be calculated according to the Increment System. Both money won and points won in hunter classics and the international hunter derby will be included. The money won and points won in the USHJA International Hunter Derby will only be awarded towards a declared Hunter section for HOTY points if a horse competes in the declared section a minimum of 5 times during the competition year.

4. All Hunter competitions are required to offer the minimum number of classes and amounts of prize money listed in GR313 for each approved Hunter section. If sections are canceled or entries are insufficient to award all prize money offered then only money offered to the number of places awarded must be distributed. All Hunter competitions must state their Increment rating clearly on the cover of the prize list. A maximum of $5,000 in Hunter Classic, USHJA International Hunter Derby and/or USHJA National Hunter Derby prize money can count as part of the required $24,000 in prize money, including add back money if any, that must be paid in order to maintain a "Premier" rating. If an add-back is offered, the minimum required prize money for that section must be guaranteed, and the add-backs must be clearly indicated in the prize list. Premier competitions offering add back must offer a minimum of $18,001 and must pay a minimum of $24,000. Exception: if sections are cancelled or entries are insufficient to award all prize money, then additional money not awarded must be pooled and redistributed 60% to the champions, and 40% to the reserve champions of the remaining "A" rated hunter sections.

5. Hunter Division Increment Chart:

Base points per section rating:

Rating	"C"	"B"	"A"	"AA"
1st	10	15	20	25
2nd	6	10	15	20
3rd	4	8	12	16
4th	3	6	9	12
5th	2	5	8	11
6th	1.5	4	7	10
7th	1	3	6	9
8th	.5	2	5	8

Total Prize Money in Rated Hunter Sections

Regional II competitions	N/A
Regional I competitions	N/A
National competitions	$5000 and over
Premier competitions	Competitions paying $24,000 and over including add-back money if any.

6. Points are calculated according to the Hunter Division Increment System utilizing a combination of the base points for each placing at each level of section rating and adding one point for each entry that competes in the first performance class except in High Performance Hunter, 3'6" Performance Hunter, and 3'3" Performance Hunter where individual classes may be entered in which case the points will be calculated by the number of entries that competed in each individual class (see HU102). In the under saddle classes points will be calculated on the number of horses entered. Points for competitions offering add-backs will be determined in the Federation Office when results

and amount of prize money paid are received.

7. Bonus points for Hunter Classics will be awarded according to HU143.9.

8. Number of entries. The number of entries for the Hunter Division is determined by the number of entries that compete in the first performance class of the section, except in sections where individual classes may be entered in which case the number of entries will be determined by the number of entries that competed in each individual class (see HU104). In the under saddle classes the number of entries will be determined by the number of horses entered. Sections may not be split if there are less than 40 entries. Sections may be split if there are 40 but less than 50 entries. Sections must be split if there are more than 49 entries. Competition management must post within 12 hours of the completion of the class, in a prominent place on the competition grounds, the number of entries that compete in the first performance class of each rated Hunter section, signed by the officiating Judge.

9. Hunter Division Section champions will be awarded 2.0 times the total 1st place point value of the first class in that section toward any National Horse of the Year point award based on points earned. Section reserve champions will be awarded 1.2 times the total 1st place value of the first class in that section towards any National Horse of the Year award based on points earned. Exception: For National Horse of the Year awards that are based on money won, Section Champions in the First and Second Year Green Hunter, High Performance Working Hunter, Green Conformation Hunter, Performance Working Hunters 3'3", Performance Working Hunters 3'6", and Regular Conformation Hunter will be awarded dollars equal to 10% of the total prize money offered for each respective section towards National Horse of the Year awards. Reserve Champions will be awarded dollars equal to the amount of 5% of the total prize money for each respective section.

10. Hunter Division Section Awards
    a. Awards are offered from USHJA for the following at the Zone level:
       Children's Working Hunter Ponies, Children's Working Hunter Horses, Adult Amateur Working Hunter 18-35 Years Old, Adult Amateur Working Hunter Over 35 Years Old, Pre-Green Hunter, Small Hunter and Thoroughbred Hunter.
    b. The USHJA shall determine the Zone and/or Stirrup Cup HOTY points to be awarded for its USHJA Hunter Championships, Finals and Classes. The USHJA shall notify the Federation and publish the point scale to be utilized on the USHJA website a minimum of 120 days prior to the start of each event.

11. Hunter Division Section awards are offered for the following at the Zone from USHJA and National levels from the Federation:
    a. Green Conformation Hunter, Green Working Hunter - First and Second Year, Regular Conformation Hunter, High Performance Working Hunter, Performance Working Hunters 3'3", Performance Working Hunters 3'6", Small Green Pony Working Hunter, Medium Green Pony Working Hunter, Large Green Pony Working Hunter, Small Pony Working Hunter, Medium Pony Working Hunter, Large Pony Working Hunter, Small Junior Working Hunter 15 yrs. & under, Small Junior Hunter 16-17 yrs., Large Junior Working Hunter 15 yrs. & under, Large Junior Working Hunter 16-17 yrs., Amateur Owner Hunter - 18-35 Years Old and Over 35 Years Old, Ladies Side Saddle, Amateur Owner 3'3" 18-35 Years Old and Over 35 Years Old, Small Hunter, and Junior Hunter 3'3".
    b. The USHJA shall determine the National HOTY points to be awarded for its USHJA Hunter Championships, Finals and Classes. The USHJA shall notify the Federation and publish the point scale to be utilized on the USHJA website a minimum of 120 days prior to the start of each event.

12. Grand Champion Horse of the Year Awards are based on National points and are offered for the following Hunter sections:
    a. Amateur Owner Hunter: awarded to the horse with the most points from the rider age sections of Amateur Owner 3'6"
    b. Amateur Owner Hunter 3'3": awarded to the horse with the most points from the rider age sections of Amateur Owner 3'3"

   c. Junior Hunter 15 Years & Younger: awarded to the horse with the most points in the 15 & Under rider age section of the 3'6" Junior Hunters

   d. Junior Hunter 16-17 Years: awarded to the horse with the most points in the 16-17 rider age section of the 3'6" Junior Hunters

   e. Pony Hunter: awarded to the pony with the most points from the small, medium and large Regular Hunter Pony sections

   f. Green Hunter Pony: awarded to the pony with the most points from the small, medium and large Green Hunter Pony sections

   g. Conformation Hunter: awarded to the horse with the most points from the Regular Conformation and Green Conformation Hunter sections

   h. Green Working Hunter: awarded to the horse with the most points from the 1st year and 2nd year Green Hunter sections.

   i. High Performance Working Hunter: awarded to the horse with the most points from the High Performance Working Hunter section

13. USHJA Zone Rider of the Year Hunter Seat Equitation Division Awards.

Unless USHJA Zone Committees submit their specifications by August 1, the following specifications will apply for the Age Group Equitation Hunter section:

   a. Awards are offered for the following at the Zone level: Equitation 14 and under, Equitation 15-17, Adult Equitation 18-35 and Adult Equitation 36 and over.

   b. Points will be awarded in accordance with the Hunter Seat Equitation Increment Chart.

1st	20
2nd	15
3rd	10
4th	6
5th	5
6th	4
7th	3
8th	2

   c. Section champions will be awarded 2.0 times the total 1st place point value. Section reserve champions will be awarded 1.2 times the total 1st place value.

   d. Equitation that is offered by age and then combined at the competition will be awarded points and points will be credited to the correct age groups in the appropriate section. Classes restricted in any other way than outlined above will not count for points (i.e. Amateur/Owner Equitation; Equitation classes that are not offered in the prize list split by age; and all medal classes).

   e. Equitation 14 and under and Equitation 15-17 classes to be shown over a course of not less than eight fences and the fence heights cannot exceed 3'6" and wings are optional.

   f. Adult Equitation 18-35 and Adult Equitation 36+ classes to be shown over a course of not less than eight fences and the fence height cannot exceed 3'3".

   g. The USHJA shall determine the Zone and/or Stirrup Cup HOTY points to be awarded for its USHJA Equitation Championships, Finals and Classes. The USHJA shall notify the Federation and publish the point scale to be utilized on the USHJA website a minimum of 120 days prior to the start of each event.

14. For the purposes of the USHJA Zone awards, ribbons won in any "A" or "B" rated section will receive B points. For the purposes of the USHJA Zone Equitation awards, ribbons won at any competition will receive points per GR1131.12b. USHJA Zone Awards will be distributed according to the Zone map.

15. Presentation of the National Horse of the Year Awards will be made at the Federation Annual Meeting.

                   SPONSORED BY HAGYARD EQUINE MEDICAL INSTITUTE || © USEF 2016

16. Presentation of the USHJA Zone Horse of the Year Awards will be made at Zone meetings at the discretion of Zone Committees and auspices of Zone Committees, only after approval of the USHJA.

ZONE MAP

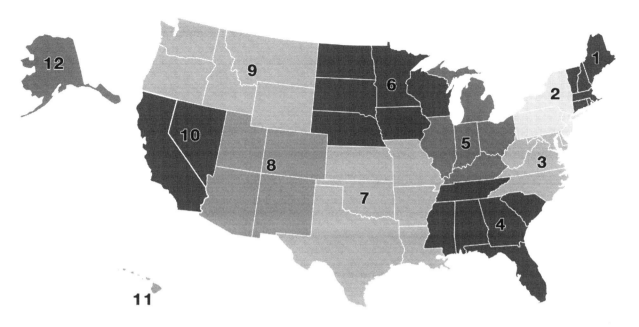

GR1132 Pony Hunter Breeding and Hunter Breeding

1. Eligibility- Points toward any Horse of the Year Award will not be credited until the applications and fees for the horse's recording, exhibitor's registration, transfer of ownership, name change or addition of owner(s) and owner's Senior Active, Junior Active or Life membership are received by the Federation office. Furthermore, points toward Horse of the Year Awards will not be credit until the applications and fees for *the horse's USHJA Horse Registration,* the owner's USHJA Active or USHJA Life membership are received by the Federation or USHJA offices. Exception: Applications for Federation and USHJA Individual Membership and Horse Recordings submitted at Licensed Competitions.

2. Hunter Breeding Awards are offered for the following at the Zone level from USHJA and National level from the Federation: Hunter Breeding Yearling, Hunter Breeding Two-Year-Old, and Hunter Breeding Three-Year-Old. Point Tabulation, see HU184.4.

3. The horse accumulating the most National points out of the Yearling, Two-Year-Old and Three-Year-Old Hunter Breeding (horse) sections will be awarded the Grand Champion Hunter Breeding Award.

4. Pony Hunter Breeding awards are only offered at the Zone level from USHJA for the following: Pony Hunter Breeding Yearling, Pony Hunter Breeding Two-Year-Old, Pony Hunter Breeding Three-Year-Old. Point Tabulation, see HU186.5.

5. Presentation of the National Horse of the Year Awards will be made at the Federation Annual Meeting.

6. Presentation of the USHJA Zone Horse of the Year Awards will be made at Zone meetings at the discretion of Zone Committees and auspices of Zone Committees, only after approval of the USHJA.

7. USHJA Zone awards will be distributed according to the USHJA Zone map.

8. The USHJA shall determine the National, Zone and/or Stirrup Cup HOTY points to be awarded for its USHJA

Hunter Breeding Finals and Classes. The USHJA shall notify the Federation and publish the point scale to be utilized on the USHJA website a minimum of 120 days prior to the start of each event. *BOD 1/17/15 Effective 12/1/15*

GR1133 Jumpers

1. Eligibility.

Points toward any Horse of the Year Award will not be credited until the applications and fees for the horse's recording, exhibitor's registration, transfer of ownership, name change or addition of owner(s) and owner's Senior Active, Junior Active or Life membership are received by the Federation office. Furthermore, points toward Horse of the Year Awards will not be credit until the applications and fees for the horse's USHJA Horse Registration, the owner's USHJA Active or USHJA Life membership are received by the Federation or USHJA offices. Exception: Applications for Federation and USHJA Individual Membership and Horse Recordings submitted at Licensed Competitions.

2. Point Tabulation. See GR1113-GR1119. Children's and Adult Jumper USHJA Zone Horse of the Year Awards and Pony, 5-Year Old, 6-Year Old, and 7/8-Year Old Jumper National and USHJA Zone Horse of the Year Awards will be based on the following:

Exhibitors	3-8	9-15	16-25	26+
1st	15	20	25	30
2nd	10	15	20	25
3rd	5	10	15	20
4th	4	5	10	15
5th	3	4	5	10
6th	2	3	4	5

*Determined by the number of entries that competed (see JP135.13) in the class.

3. The Junior Jumper, Amateur Owner Jumper, U25 and Young Rider Jumper Horse of the Year Awards will be based on one point for every dollar won in their classification at Regular Competitions.

4. The Open Jumper Horse of the Year Award will be based on money won in classes which comply with JP150, classes of $25,000 or more. One point for every dollar won will be awarded.

5. Award Categories. National awards will be given in the following categories: Low Junior, Junior, Low Amateur Owner, Amateur Owner, Open, Pony, YOUNG RIDERS. Zone Horse of the Year Awards will be given by USHJA in the following categories (see JP118 for Zone specifications): LOW JUNIOR, JUNIOR, CHILDREN'S, ADULT, LOW AMATEUR OWNER, AMATEUR OWNER, PONY, YOUNG RIDERS, U25 and Thoroughbred Jumper. *BOD 9/29/15 Effective 12/1/15.*

6. USHJA Zone awards will be distributed according to the Zone map.

7. National Awards will be presented at the Federation Annual Meeting.

8. Presentation of the USHJA Zone Horse of the Year Awards will be made at the discretion and auspices of Zone Committees, only after approval of the USHJA.

9. The USHJA shall determine the National, Zone and/or Stirrup Cup HOTY points to be awarded for its USHJA Jumper Championships, Finals and Classes. The USHJA shall notify the Federation and publish the point scale to be utilized on the USHJA website a minimum of 120 days prior to the start of each event.

GR1134 Morgan Horse Division

1. Eligibility. See GR1110.

2. Point Tabulation. See GR1113-GR1119. In-hand classes will accrue points in all age group classes as listed below. Junior and Senior Champion and Reserve Champion ribbons will receive double points; Grand Champion and Reserve In Hand will receive triple points.

SPONSORED BY HAGYARD EQUINE MEDICAL INSTITUTE || © USEF 2016

3. All other restricted classes will count 1/2 points (Maiden, Novice, Limit, Green Horse classes and classes held at Local competitions).

4. In all other classes points will count as follows:

First	Second	Third	Fourth
20	12	8	4

Points in all Championship Performance classes will be scored as follows:

Champion	Reserve	Third	Fourth
40	24	16	8

Local competitions will receive half points.

5. Categories. National and Regional awards will be given in the following:

    a. ENGLISH PLEASURE - Open, Amateur, Junior Exhibitor;

    b. WESTERN PLEASURE—Open, Amateur, Junior Exhibitor;

    c. PLEASURE DRIVING—Open, Amateur; Junior Exhibitor;

    d. CLASSIC PLEASURE SADDLE;

    e. CLASSIC PLEASURE DRIVING;

    f. PARK - Saddle and Harness

    g. HUNTER PLEASURE—Open, Amateur, Junior Exhibitor;

    h. IN-HAND;

    i. CARRIAGE-Classes offered in the CP rules of the USEF rule book will count towards this award. Exception: Concours D'Elegance; Classes which are restricted (number of ribbons won; number of ADS and/or USEF Carriage Pleasure Driving competitions completed; number of years of competition experience; entry status: maiden, novice, limit; driver status: junior, adult, professional, amateur, maiden, novice, limit; horse status: maiden, novice, limit, size, age, sex) will count as half points;

    j. DRESSAGE—Training, 1st Level, Second Level through Fourth Level;

    k. ROAD HACK;

    l. VERSATILE MORGAN—Jumper, Parade, Roadster, Reining, Trail, Cutting, Working Hunter O/F and U/S, Hunter Hack, Bridle Path Hack and Western Dressage.

6. Grand Champion Morgan Horse is based on the total of all points won in all Morgan categories.

7. For purposes of distributing Regional awards the following map will be used: Region 4 - Alabama, Florida, Georgia, Mississippi, Tennessee; Region 10 - Delaware, District of Columbia, Maryland, North Carolina, South Carolina, Virginia.

8. National Horse of the Year Awards will be presented at the Federation Annual Meeting.

9. Regional awards will be presented at a place determined by each AMHA regional organization. Or if no regional organization exists, by a committee of Morgan club presidents selected by and chaired by the AMHA regional director of that region.

10. All Federation members receiving awards must also be members of AMHA prior to the presentation of the awards.

MORGAN REGIONAL MAP

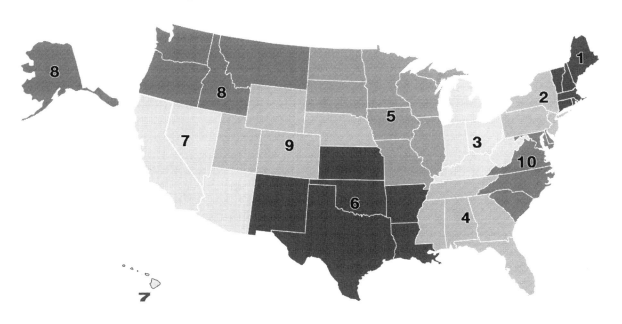

GR1135 National Show Horse

1. Eligibility. See GR1110.

2. Point Tabulation. See GR1113-GR1119.

Points for all competitions will be awarded as follows:

Started	10+	9	8	7	6	5	4	3	2	1
1st	10	9	8	7	6	5	4	3	2	1
2nd	9	8	7	6	5	4	3	2	1	
3rd	8	7	6	5	4	3	2	1		
4th	7	6	5	4	3	2	1			
5th	6	5	4	3	2	1				
6th	5	4	3	2	1					
7th	4	3	2	1						
8th	3	2	1							
9th	2	1								
10th	1									

Championship classes will receive double points; NSHR District classes will receive double points; NSHR National Finals classes will receive triple points.

3. Awards will be given on a National basis.

4. Categories. National awards will be given in the following categories: English Pleasure, Pleasure Driving, Three-Gaited, Five-Gaited, Fine Harness, Country Pleasure, Hunter Pleasure, Show Hack, Western Pleasure.

5. National Horse of the Year Awards will be presented at the Federation Annual Meeting.

SPONSORED BY HAGYARD EQUINE MEDICAL INSTITUTE || © USEF 2016

GR1136 Paso Fino

1. Eligibility. See GR1110.

2. Point Tabulation. See GR1113-GR1119. Points will be awarded according to the number of horses beaten in a class for which the Federation has class specifications. Exception: In Equitation classes no points will be awarded. 3 points will be awarded for every horse beaten in a class at a Federation Regular Competition. 1 point will be awarded at Federation Local Competitions. Championship classes will be awarded double points.

3. Award Categories. National awards will be given in the following categories:

   a. Fino

   b. Performance

   c. Pleasure

   d. Specialty

   e. Amateur

   f. Junior exhibitor-based on the total of all points won in junior exhibitor classes (exception: equitation and horsemanship)

   g. Sub-junior-based on the total of all points won in sub junior classes (exception: equitation and horsemanship)

4. Grand Champion Paso Fino- based on the total of all points won in all Paso Fino categories.

5. National Horse of the Year Award will be presented at the Federation Annual Meeting.

GR1137 Reining

1. Eligibility. See GR1110.

2. Point Tabulation. Points will be awarded according to the number of horses beaten in a class. A rated competitions will award 2 points for every horse beaten; B, C, and Local rated competitions will award 1 point for every horse beaten in the class. Championship classes will be awarded double points.

3. Award Categories. National Awards will be given in the following categories: Open, Non-Pro/Adult Amateur, Junior Exhibitor;

4. National Horse of the Year Awards will be presented at the Federation Annual Meeting.

GR1138 Roadster

1. Eligibility. See GR1110.

2. Point Tabulation. See GR1113-GR1119. Points for all competitions will be awarded as follows:

Started	6+	5	4	3	2	1
1st	6	5	4	3	2	1
2nd	5	4	3	2	1	
3rd	4	3	2	1		
4th	3	2	1			
5th	2	1				
6th	1					

The Kentucky State Fair World's Championship Horse Show will receive triple points.

3. Regional Awards will be distributed according to the Hackney Regional Map.

4. National Awards will be presented at the Federation Annual Meeting.

5. Regional Awards will be presented at an appropriate venue within each region.

6. Award Categories. National and Regional Awards will be given in the following categories: Roadster Horse Under Saddle, Roadster Horse To Bike, Amateur Roadster Pony, Junior Exhibitor Roadster Pony, Open Roadster Pony (shares one award with Hackney Roadster Pony). See GR1130.6.

GR1139 American Saddlebred

1. Eligibility. See GR1110. All horses must be registered American Saddlebred Horses, and owners must be members of the American Saddlebred Horse Association.
2. Point Tabulation. See GR1113-GR1119. Points for all competitions will be awarded as follows:

GR1139 American Saddlebred

1. Eligibility. See GR1110. All horses must be registered American Saddlebred Horses, and owners must be members of the American Saddlebred Horse Association.
2. Point Tabulation. See GR1113-GR1119. Points for all competitions will be awarded as follows:

Started	6+	5	4	3	2	1
1st	6	5	4	3	2	1
2nd	5	4	3	2	1	
3rd	4	3	2	1		
4th	3	2	1			
5th	2	1				
6th	1					

    a. The Kentucky State Fair World's Championship Horse Show will receive triple points.

    b. The UPHA/American Royal National Championship Horse Show will receive double points for qualifying classes and triple points for the Championship and/or Stake classes.

    c. The Saddle and Bridle Hunter Classic Final and Saddle and Bridle Shatner Western Final held at the St. Louis National Charity Horse Show will receive triple points.

3. Regional Awards will be distributed according to the American Saddlebred Regional Map.
4. National Awards will be presented at the Federation Annual Meeting.
5. Regional Awards may be presented at an appropriate venue within each region as approved by the Federation.
6. Award Categories. National and Regional awards will be given in the following categories: Three-Gaited Park Horse, Open Three-Gaited American Saddlebred, Amateur Three-Gaited American Saddlebred, Junior Exhibitor's Three-Gaited American Saddlebred, Open Five-Gaited American Saddlebred, Three Gaited Park Pleasure, Amateur Five-Gaited American Saddlebred, Junior Exhibitor's Five-Gaited American Saddlebred, Adult Three-Gaited Show Pleasure Horse, Junior Exhibitor Three-Gaited Show Pleasure, Five-Gaited Show Pleasure Horse, Country Pleasure English Horse, Country Pleasure Western Horse, Show Pleasure Driving Horse, Country Pleasure Driving Horse, Country Pleasure Hunter Horse, Open Fine Harness, Amateur Fine Harness.

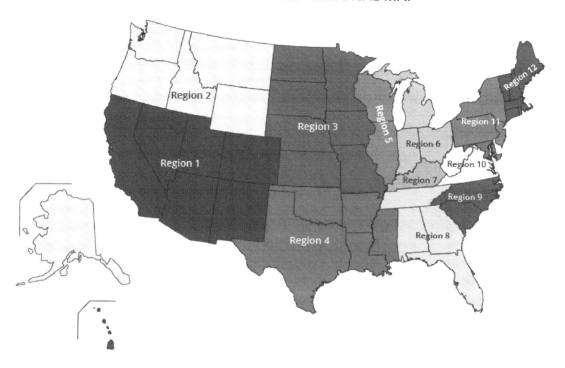

GR1140 Shetland Division

1. Eligibility. See GR1110.
2. Point Tabulation. See GR1113-GR1119. Points for all competitions will be awarded as follows:

Started	10+	9	8	7	6	5	4	3	2	1
1st	10	9	8	7	6	5	4	3	2	1
2nd	9	8	7	6	5	4	3	2	1	
3rd	8	7	6	5	4	3	2	1		
4th	7	6	5	4	3	2	1			
5th	6	5	4	3	2	1				
6th	5	4	3	2	1					
7th	4	3	2	1						
8th	3	2	1							
9th	2	1								
10th	1									

Local competitions will receive half points.

3. Award Categories.

   a. A National High Point Award will be given for Shetlands participating in Shetland sections as described in Chapter SP.

   b. An Overall Open Competition High Point Award will be given for Shetlands participating in open Dressage, Carriage Pleasure Driving, Combined Driving or Hunter divisions.

4. National Horse of the Year Awards will be presented at the Federation Annual Meeting.

GR1141 Vaulting

1. Eligibility. See GR1110.

2. Points are based on the following:

To be eligible for an award, a horse must have participated in a minimum of three USEF recognized vaulting competitions. Only horses that carry the same vaulter/s for all classes in a division are eligible. The horse must receive a qualifying average horse score of 6.000 or greater. Only the highest average horse score for each award category in a competition will be converted to points for this program. The sum of the three highest point totals (one from each competition) will be used to determine award winners in each category. Points will be used to determine awards only in the competition year in which they are earned.

3. Award Category. A National High Point Award will be given in the following categories: Individual Vaulting Horse, Pas de Deux Vaulting Horse, and Team Vaulting Horse.

4. Presentation of the National Horse of the Year Awards will be made at the Federation Annual Meeting.

GR1142 Welsh Pony, Cob and Half Welsh

1. Welsh Pony Awards are offered for the following at the Regional and National level
   a. Welsh Pleasure Sections A&B, 12.2 hands & Under (to include English and Western Pleasure)
   b. Welsh Pleasure Sections B over 12.2 hands but not exceeding 14.2 hands (to include English and Western Pleasure)
   c. Welsh Pleasure Sections C&D (to include English and Western Pleasure)
   d. Welsh Pleasure Sections A&B- Adult to Ride (to include English and Western Pleasure)
   e. Welsh Pleasure Driving, Sections A&B
   f. Welsh Hunter Sections A&B 12.2 hands & Under
   g. Welsh Hunter Section B over 12.2 hands but not exceeding 14.2 hands
   h. Welsh Hunter Sections C&D
   i. Welsh Hunter Sections A&B- Adult to Ride

2. Half/Part-Bred Welsh Awards are offered for the following at the Regional and National level:
   a. Half/Part-Bred Welsh Pleasure
   b. Half /Part-Bred Welsh Hunter

3. Full points shall be awarded to classes within the Welsh division conducted at A, B, and C rated competitions. Model classes will receive half points.

4. Points are based on the following:

	First	Second	Third	Fourth
A Rating	20	12	8	4
B Rating	10	6	4	2
C Rating	5	3	2	1

Championship points will be scored as follows:

	Champion	Reserve
A Rating	40	24
B Rating	20	12
C Rating	10	6

5. For the purposes of Regional awards, ribbons won in any A or B rated section will receive B points. Regional Awards will be distributed according to the Regional map.

6. Presentation of the National Horse of the Year Awards will be made at the Federation Annual Meeting.

7. Presentation of the Federation Regional Horse of the Year Awards will be made at Regional meetings at the discretion of Regional Committees.

WELSH REGIONAL MAP

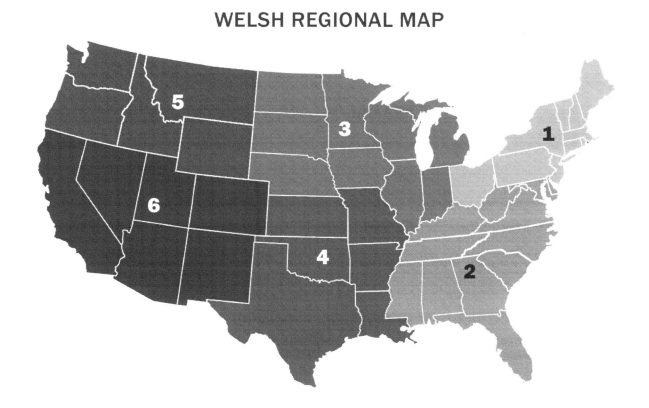

GR1143 Western

1. Eligibility. See GR1110.

2. Point Tabulation. Points will be awarded according to the number of horses beaten in a class. A rated competitions will award 2 points for every horse beaten; B, C, and Local rated competitions will award 1 point for every horse beaten in the class. Championship classes will be awarded double points.

3. Award Categories. National and Regional Awards will be given in the following categories:

TRAIL—Open, Adult Amateur, Junior Exhibitor;

WESTERN PLEASURE—Open, Adult Amateur, Junior Exhibitor.

4. For purposes of distributing Regional Awards refer to the Regional map in GR1123.

5. National Horse of the Year Awards will be presented at the Federation Annual Meeting.

GR1144 Western Dressage

1. Eligibility: See GR 1110.

2. Point Tabulation: See GR 1113-1119.

Full points will be awarded to all Western Dressage classes conducted at USEF licensed competitions, as well as Breed restricted competitions and competitions holding open Western Dressage classes. Points in all classes will be awarded as follows. They are awarded on the scores of rides versus placings. Scores are achieved through a horse and rider combination, (unit).

3. Award Categories:

• Intro Tests (1-4)

• Basic Tests (1-4)

• Level 1 Tests (1-4)

• Level 2 Tests (1-4)

• Level 3 Tests (1-4)

Level Score	60.00-64.99%	65.00-69.99%	70.00-74.99%	75.00%+
Introductory	1	2	3	4
Basic	1.5	3	4.5	6
Level 1	2	4	6	8
Level 2	2.5	5	7.5	10
Level 3	3	6	9	12

SUBCHAPTER 11-G ZONE FINAL COMPETITIONS

GR1145 Zone Finals

Information on zone finals/championships is available from USHJA.

SPONSORED BY HAGYARD EQUINE MEDICAL INSTITUTE || © USEF 2016

CHAPTER 12 COMPETITION OFFICIALS, EMPLOYEES, AND VOLUNTEERS

SUBCHAPTER 12-A COMPETITION OFFICIALS

GR1201 Licensee - Operation of Competition

GR1202 Manager

GR1203 Competition Secretary

GR1204 Veterinarian

GR1205 Course Designer

GR1206 Farrier

GR1207 Designated Competition Office Representative

SUBCHAPTER 12-B COMPETITION EMPLOYEES AND VOLUNTEERS

GR1208 Ringmaster

GR1209 Timekeeper

SUBCHAPTER 12-C DUTIES OF COMPETITION MANAGEMENT IN GENERAL

GR1210 General

GR1211 Appointment of Officials and Employees

SUBCHAPTER 12-D DUTIES CONCERNING COMPETITION RECORDS

GR1212 Prize Lists

GR1213 Entries

GR1214 Results

SUBCHAPTER 12-E DUTIES CONCERNING FACILITIES

GR1215 Stabling

GR1216 Facilities

SUBCHAPTER 12-F DUTIES CONCERNING ENFORCEMENT OF FEDERATION RULES

GR1217 Rules

GR1218 Protests, Charges and Violations

CHAPTER 12 COMPETITION OFFICIALS, EMPLOYEES, AND VOLUNTEERS

SUBCHAPTER 12-A COMPETITION OFFICIALS

GR1201 Licensee - Operation of Competition

The Licensee of a Licensed Competition is responsible for the operation of the competition. The Licensee may appoint a Show Committee of at least three responsible people who must be available at all times to act in executive capacity. It is the duty of the Licensee to enforce all the rules of the Federation from the time entries are admitted to the competition grounds until their departure.

GR1202 Manager

1. An individual acting in this capacity is required to be a Senior Active Member of the Federation. In addition, any individual acting as the manager of a hunter and/or jumper Open (not restricted to a breed) competition must be a Senior Active member in good standing of the United States Hunter Jumper Association, Inc. The competition manager of a Federation- licensed/USDF-recognized competition must be a current USDF Participating or Group member in good standing at the time competition recognition is granted and on the date of the competition.

2. Licensed Competitions should exercise extreme care in the selection and appointment of a competition manager for the mutual benefit of committees, exhibitors and spectators. Any member of a Show Committee who performs the duties assigned herein to the competition manager, in lieu of an appointed manager, is in fact the responsible officer within the meaning of these rules and must be so named in the prize list. A thorough knowledge of the rules of the Federation is one of the requisites of a person serving as a competition manager.

3. Any competition manager who violates or knowingly permits violation of the rules of the Federation at his competition is subject to disciplinary action by the Committee on Charges, Protests and Hearings in accordance with Chapters 6 and 7.

4. A manager cannot serve as judge, steward or technical delegate of his own competition. A member of a manager's family cannot officiate as judge, steward or technical delegate at said manager's competition.

5. A manager or secretary of a Dressage Competition or an organizer of an Eventing Competition may not compete as rider or handler in his/her own competition. However, he or she may show Hors de Concours if he or she designates an assistant in charge while he or she is showing. This does not absolve the manager's or secretary's duties and responsibilities.

6. A manager of a Dressage Competition must be present throughout the competition he/she is managing while classes are underway. However, he or she may leave the competition grounds if he or she designates an assistant manager in charge during the time of his/her absence. This does not absolve the manager's duties and responsibilities.

7. The manager of a Level 3, Level 4 or Level 5 Dressage Competition must be eligible according to the criteria listed in DR126 and listed in the Dressage Levels chart posted on the USEF website.

GR1203 Competition Secretary

1. An individual(s) who processes entries or performs such other duties as assigned by the Board of Directors, the Show Committee and manager. A secretary of a Dressage Competition may not serve as judge or compete as rider or handler in his/her own competition. However, he or she may show Hors de Concours if he or she designates an assistant in charge while he or she is showing. This does not absolve the secretary's duties and responsibilities. An individual acting in this capacity must be an Individual Senior Active member of The Federation.

2. The secretary of a Level 3, Level 4 or Level 5 Dressage Competition must be eligible according to the criteria listed in DR126 and listed in the Dressage Levels chart posted on the USEF website. The competition secretary of a Federation- licensed/USDF-recognized competition must be a current USDF Participating or Group member in good

standing at the time competition recognition is granted and on the date of the competition.

GR1204 Veterinarian

1. The official veterinarian shall be a licensed graduate of an accredited veterinary school in good standing in his/her state of practice, be familiar with the current USEF Equine Drugs and Medications Rules and have experience in equine veterinary practice. He/she shall not rule on soundness in classes in which he/she or a family member may have a horse or pony entered or measure any horses or ponies in which a conflict of interest exists due to personal or family interest in the equine. The official veterinarian may be a competitor and the competition will still be in compliance with the requirements of GR1211.4 (Exception: Eventing). Veterinary emergencies shall take precedence over competing.

2. He shall render complete veterinary service to visiting International Teams and feature attractions; the cost of drugs, x-rays, laboratory procedures and expendable equipment is to be paid for by the competition or as otherwise provided prior to the competition. The examination and treatment, except when requested by the judge, of all other horses in the competition shall be on a private practice basis.

3. The veterinarian shall assist management in all matters pertaining to the health and welfare of the animals in the competition.

4. The official veterinarian's decision, if requested by the judge as to the serviceable soundness of a horse (i.e., whether the horse shows evidence of lameness, broken wind, or complete loss of sight in either eye), will be final for the purpose of awarding ribbons in the class for which he has been called.

5. The official veterinarian, if called upon by the judge, will act as consultant in regard to structural faults, defects and blemishes in areas which might impair a horse's activity and durability. Having received the benefit of the veterinarian's consultation, the judge will then place the horses in question at his own discretion, based on their relative merits in light of the entire class specifications.

6. The veterinarian will immediately, after leaving the ring, file a statement of his findings with the competition secretary, setting forth therein the number and title of the class, the number of the horse, the date and time of day. The veterinarian must have his certificate of finding read and signed by the steward of the competition on duty during the particular class.

7. Examination of a horse in the ring by a veterinarian must be done as inconspicuously as possible and in such manner as not to draw public attention thereto. Cooperation of judges to this end is required.

8. It is the duty of the veterinarian to assist the steward/technical delegate in the measurement of any animal requiring measurement in accordance with the rules of the Federation. (See Chapter 5, Chapter HU (HU168-HU179).

9. Veterinarian(s) for Federation Licensed Endurance rides must be selected a) from a list of Federation Endurance Committee approved veterinarians, or b) from the FEI list of Contact and Event Veterinarians in the Endurance Category. Refer to EN113 for Personnel and Qualifications and Duties.

GR1205 Course Designer

1. The Jumper course designer is responsible for laying out the course, building the obstacles and for the measurement of the course. An "R" license is required to officiate alone for all classes offering $25,000 or more in prize money. An "r" license is required to officiate any competition with a Jumper rating 2 or higher. To obtain recognition as a course designer, an individual must apply to the Federation for recognition. (See GR1062).

2. The Jumper Course Designer, or his designated representative, must be present during all Jumper classes for which he has responsibility for the courses during a licensed competition and be available to report to the judge at any time that the course is ready in all respects.

3. The Hunter course designer, or his designated representative, must be present at all sessions of a competition and be available to report to the judge at any time that the course is ready in all respects. The Hunter course designer

is responsible for the correctness of the course and must give consideration to any suggestions made by the judge. Copies of the courses must be given to the judges. The Hunter course designer must be a Senior member of USEF and must be knowledgeable in the rules relating to the Hunter classes being offered. At non-breed restricted USEF Licensed Competitions the hunter course designer must also be a Senior Active member of USHJA.

4. A minimum of a "r" Hunter course designer license is required to officiate alone at a National or Premier rated Hunter/Jumper competition with a Hunter class offering up to $4,999 in prize money. A "R" Hunter course designer license is required to officiate in any class at an National or Premier licensed Hunter/Jumper competition with a Hunter class offering $5,000 or more in prize money.

5. Eventing Course Designer.

   a. A course designer, a member of a course designer's family, or a Course Advisor at Eventing Competitions shall not compete at the following competitions: Three Day Events, National Championship Horse Trials, competitions being used for Federation selection purposes, and similar competitions designated by the Eventing Committee when the Course Designer or Course Advisor is officiating.

GR1206 Farrier

A farrier cannot officiate in any class in which he is an exhibitor. He must report promptly when called to the ring to make repairs during a class.

GR1207 Designated Competition Office Representative

1. A Designated Competition Office Representative need not be appointed at all competitions. It is at the discretion of the Steward/Technical Delegate to appoint one if the circumstances so require. Some examples that may require the Steward/Technical Delegate to appoint a Designated Competition Office Representative are:

   a. Large competition grounds or eventing courses that may cause an extraordinary amount of time to reach the competition office.

   b. Many arenas that require the Steward's/Technical Delegate's attention.

   c. Special classes that require the Steward/Technical Delegate to remain at the schooling area.

   d. A large number of entries at the competition, which may cause many trips to the competition office for collection of the Drugs and Medications Report Form.

2. Further the Designated Competition Office Representative must be a Federation Senior Member and an office staff person mutually agreed upon by the Competition Management and Competition Steward/Technical Delegate.

3. The Designated Competition Office Representative will be responsible to collect, date, sign, and issue receipt for all the Medication Report Forms submitted. Additionally, all Medication Report Forms are to be given to the Steward/Technical Delegate on a daily basis. It is the Steward's/Technical Delegate's sole responsibility to inspect, sign and return all the Medications Report Forms to the Federation office.

SUBCHAPTER 12-B COMPETITION EMPLOYEES AND VOLUNTEERS

GR1208 Ringmaster

A ringmaster cannot officiate in any class of a competition in which he or a member of his family or any of his clients is an exhibitor.

GR1209 Timekeeper

A timekeeper cannot officiate in a class in which a member of his family or any of his clients is competing (Exceptions: Jumper classes, Dressage Classes and Eventing Competitions). See also GR831.1 and GR833.

SUBCHAPTER 12-C DUTIES OF COMPETITION MANAGEMENT IN GENERAL

GR1210 General

Apply annually to the Federation for dates for the competition.

1. Medal Classes.

    a. Competitions offering Hunter/Jumping Seat Medal classes must offer at least three additional classes under Federation rules suitable for those competitors who are eligible to compete in the Medal. These classes do not have to be Equitation classes.

    b. Competitions cannot restrict cross entries between Medal classes.

    c. NOTE: Permission to hold a Medal class will not be granted to more than one, one day Licensed Competition held on consecutive days with the same management at the same location.

    d. Following the holding of the Federation Hunter/Jumping Seat, the Federation Adult Equitation Class and/or the Federation Pony Medal Class, Competition Management shall forward to the Federation a total amount representing the $10 per entry in each class.

    e. Following the holding of Federation Saddle Seat Medal and Saddle Seat Adult Amateur Medal classes, Competition Management shall forward to the Federation a total amount representing the $15 per entry in each class. BOD 1/17/15 Effective 12/1/15

2. National competition grounds must have a level surface area for measurement (when there are divisions that require measurement) in accordance with GR507.

3. See that animals required to be measured are correctly measured by the rules and order the measurement of any horse whose height or length of foot is protested by an exhibitor.

4. Competition management shall place a minimum of one sharps container per each competition, whether or not stabling is provided. Additionally, at least one sharps container per fifty occupied stalls for the disposal of needles and other disposable sharp instruments in convenient locations in barns housing competition horses. It is competition management's responsibility to replace such containers when full and dispose of them properly. Competition management may fine any individuals including trainers, owners, exhibitors, or their agents up to $100 for improper disposal of needles or other sharp disposable instruments. Competition management will place a notice of this requirement either in its prize list or on a specific handout given to trainers on check in at the competition. If local law has different requirements, local law will prevail. Competitions failing to comply with placing the required number of containers on the show grounds will be considered in violation of the rules and may be subject to penalty as determined by the CEO or his designee and/or the Hearing Committee.

5. Competition Management is required to submit a Post Competition Report, along with the appropriate fees, to the Federation, postmarked or electronic date stamped within 10 calendar days after the close of the competition. Fees must be submitted by cashier/company/personal check, money order, credit card or wire transfer; cash will not be accepted as proper payment. For purposes of this rule, a Post Competition Report shall include all appropriate fees and the following properly completed forms: a Post Competition Report Form, Membership Applications and Horse Recording Applications. A fine of $100 will be imposed on any Competition Management which fails to submit any appropriate fees with the Post Competition Report postmarked or electronic date stamped within 10 calendar days after the end of the competition. Competition Management disputing that the fee/fine is properly owing may appeal in writing to the Federation within 30 days of the date of the notice of outstanding fees and fines. The Federation's CEO or his designee will consider the appeal and may waive part or all of the fine upon a finding of good cause why the payment was not submitted in a timely fashion and/or a finding that extreme hardship results from the automatic penalty.

6. If required by management, premiums of the competition will be paid to all competitors that have provided Social Security numbers, Federal ID numbers or Tax Identification numbers to the competition secretary. It is the sole

responsibility of the competitor to provide the competition secretary with accurate payee information, including Social Security number, Federal ID number, or Tax Identification number, payee name and address. The above mentioned premiums must be paid within 30 days of the last day of the competition to competitors whose accounts with the competition are current. Pay other indebtedness of the competition within 30 days of the invoice date. A fine of $100 will be imposed on any Competition Management which fails to pay any competition fees/fines to the Federation within 30 days of the notice of the fees/fines owing. A Competition Management disputing that the fee/fine is properly owing may appeal in writing to the Federation within 30 days. The Federation's CEO or his designee will consider the appeal and may waive part or all of the fine upon a finding of good cause why the payment was not submitted in a timely fashion and/or a finding that extreme hardship results from the automatic penalty.

7. If competition management fails to pay invoices owing within 45 calendar days from the date on the invoice, the Federation will levy a fine of $50 for each month the invoice remains outstanding.

8. Collect $8 fee in all classes for the Equine Drugs and Medications Program, except where prohibited by law. (See GR407).

9. It is a violation for Competition Management to assess and/or collect a drug enforcement fee in excess of, or in addition to, that specified and required by GR407.2 of these rules, unless said assessment is approved in writing by the Federation in advance, and then only under the terms and conditions set forth.

10. It is a violation for Competition Management to withhold from the Federation any or all of the drug fees collected in accordance with GR407.3, for any purpose, including to defray the expenses incurred providing stalls, passes, and other items to the Federation drug testing personnel, as required by GR407.4 and .5.

11. At the Federation's request, a competition must furnish entry blanks, judges' cards, class sheets or any other documents within the time requested by the Federation. These records must be kept on the competition grounds during all sessions of the competition. These records must be retained for three years.

12. Be responsible for the construction of courses.

13. Collection of a Mandatory Participation Fee

   a. Federation International Discipline Associations and Recognized Affiliate Associations, as defined in GR204.1a and .b, may require a Licensee to collect fees from exhibitors and remit such fees to the applicable association, unless the Federation objects to such fees in writing.

   b. A Licensee may also agree with any Federation Alliance Partner, as defined in GR204.2, to collect a mandatory participation fee from exhibitors and remit such fees to the applicable association only if the following terms and conditions are met. Only one mandatory participation fee may be collected and it must be charged to all exhibitors. No other mandatory fees may be collected on behalf of a Federation Alliance Partner or other entity, except as described in (a) above.

      1. Association must be a member in good standing of the Federation and the Federation Recognized Affiliate(s) representing the breed/discipline competing at competitions where the fees are to be assessed.

      2. Association must apply for and obtain permission from the Federation, in accordance with procedures published on the Federation's website, no less than one hundred twenty (120) days prior to the start of the competition.

      3. Association, upon approval from the Federation, must provide a Licensee with a copy of the Federation Approval Letter prior to collection of fees.

      4. Association fees must be listed separately from Federation, International Discipline and Recognized Affiliate fees on entry blank and all amounts collected must be disclosed to the Federation and reported on the post competition report and are subject to all post-competition reporting requirements.

   c. Licensee shall not collect non-USEF fees unless they have received approval based on the conditions stated above in GR1210.13.b.

14. It is the responsibility of competition management to hire officials. It is the responsibility of the Licensed Official to

ensure that he/she is properly qualified and in good standing with the Federation to officiate. Special, and Guest officials' cards must be applied for in accordance with GR1010-1011, GR1016, GR1026-1027, GR1030.

15. For all Federation competitions holding Dressage classes, remit to the Federation with post-competition report the required fees for use of Federation copyrighted Dressage Tests, as specified on the post-competition report.

16. No manager or representative of the manager may hold a prize money class without distributing the prize money.

17. To ensure that Federation Member Reports and Judge Evaluation Forms are publicly displayed and available for Federation members during the entire competition. Ensure that an announcement is made via the competition's public address system at least once each session, pertaining to the availability of said forms.

18. Specific duties of Dressage Competition Management are listed in the Dressage Levels chart posted on the USEF website.

GR1211 Appointment of Officials and Employees

1. Obtain the necessary Special, and Guest cards for judges, course designers, stewards and technical delegates.

2. Judges.

    a. Hire the necessary judges and officials for the operation of the competition and to see that they are properly qualified.

    b. If a competition finds it necessary to substitute a judge for one who is officially designated in the prize list and/or catalogue and who is unable to serve due to circumstances beyond his control, the restrictions of GR1304.2-.12 and GR1304.21-.24 shall be non-effective.

    c. Furnish the judges in each class a scorecard containing exact class specifications. (Exception: only the percentage of conformation must be noted for rated Hunter classes.) Fence heights must be noted for all unrated classes. Method of breaking ties in Jumper classes must be included.

3. Stewards/Technical Delegates.

    a. Appoint and identify in the prize list and catalogue one or more licensed Federation Stewards licensed to officiate in the divisions and sections for which the competition is approved who shall be present at each session of the competition. A technical delegate must be appointed for Eventing Competitions, Dressage Competitions and Regular and Local Competitions offering "open" Dressage Division classes (i.e., classes which are not limited to certain breeds) or classes above Third Level. (Exception: A Category 2 or Combined Category steward may officiate through Fourth Level in the Andalusian, Arabian, Friesian, Morgan or other breed-restricted Divisions at regular or local competitions, only if classes are not part of an "open" Dressage Division.) If required to officiate, a Dressage Technical Delegate must be present and officiate for all Dressage classes held on the day(s) which he/she is in attendance. If no other classes except Dressage are held on a licensed day of a breed-restricted regular or local competition, a steward does not need to be present in addition to the Dressage Technical Delegate.

    b. If a competition finds it necessary to substitute a steward or technical delegate for one who is officially designated in the prize list and/or catalogue and who is unable to serve due to circumstances beyond his control, the restrictions of GR1304.14 and/or GR1304.25 shall be non-effective.

    c. Competitions are urged to engage a steward for each ring when classes are held simultaneously and to select individuals who are well versed in the divisions being offered.

    d. With the exception of Hunter/Jumper competitions (see GR1211.3e), competitions using more than three performance areas simultaneously must have at least two stewards on duty. Dressage arenas do not count as a performance area. If more than six performance areas are used simultaneously, at least three stewards must be on duty. When three stewards are officiating, one steward will not be subject to the provisions of GR1035.1 and will be eligible to serve as steward for a fourth consecutive competition run by the same governing body, Board of Directors or Licensee.

e. A Hunter/Jumper competition using up to four performance areas simultaneously must have at least one Steward on duty. When five or more performance areas are in use simultaneously, there must be two Stewards on duty. A competition using four performance areas simultaneously that had more than 500 horses competing the previous year must have two Stewards on duty. If more than eight performance areas are used simultaneously, then at least three Stewards must be on duty. A competition in its first year of operation must have two Stewards on duty if there are more than three performance areas in use simultaneously and three stewards on duty if there are more than eight performance areas in use simultaneously. When there is more than one steward required, the licensed Stewards must designate one as the Senior Steward for that competition and must notify competition management.

f. For each competition day that a Dressage Competition schedules 300 or more rides (including Dressage and DSHB entries), the competition must have at least two Dressage Technical Delegates on duty. When only one competition ring is in session, only one Dressage Technical Delegate need be present on the grounds. Dressage Competitions holding both a national competition and a CDI must have a separate Dressage Technical Delegate in addition to the FEI Chief Dressage Steward.

g. At all competitions using more than one competition ring, management must provide a hand-held communication device (i.e. walkie-talkie or cell phone) to at least one steward or technical delegate.

4. Veterinarians.

a. Every competition with rated or non rated division(s) or sections must have a qualified veterinarian present throughout the competition if the previous year's competition's entry number was 300 horses or greater. See individual breed/discipline rules that may require a lower threshold than listed above. At a multi-breed competition, the lowest threshold will prevail.

b. The previous competition entry number shall be determined by the amount of Federation fees paid to the Federation. Exception: For Dressage Competitions, the number of horses competing the previous year shall determine if a veterinarian must be present on the grounds or on call.

c. Competitions without a qualified veterinarian present throughout the competition must have a written agreement with a veterinarian to be on call.

d. First year multi-day competitions with "A" rated divisions must have a veterinarian present throughout the competition. Exception: First year multi-day Breed or Multi-breed restricted competitions with "A" rated divisions must have a veterinarian either on call or on the grounds throughout the competition. All other first year multi-day competitions and first year one-day competitions must have a written agreement with a veterinarian on call.

e. At competitions where the official veterinarian is on call, the prize list must include the time period when the veterinarian will be available to conduct measurements. This information must also be posted in the show office. If the veterinarian is required to measure at any time other than as stated in the prize list, the owner is responsible for paying veterinarian fees.

5. Qualified Medical Personnel.

a. Qualified medical personnel with no other duties and with appropriate medical equipment, as required by their certifying State or EMS Region, must be present during all scheduled performances at all competitions and during all paid scheduled schooling sessions over fences, including one (1) day prior to the start of the competition if applicable, and during all scheduled performances.

1. Qualified medical personnel is a currently certified or licensed EMT, or Paramedic, Certified First Responder, or a Physician or Nurse trained in pre-hospital trauma care and currently certified or licensed in their profession under applicable law where the competition is held. (Exception: Eventing - see EV113.5).

2. A Physician or Nurse trained in pre-hospital trauma care is a Physician or Nurse who is currently certified in Advanced Trauma Life Support (ATLS), Basic Trauma Life Support (BTLS), Pre-hospital Trauma Life Support

(PHTLS), or who has First Responder or comparable certification. Comparable certification requires review and written approval in advance by the Safety Committee. (Exception: Eventing - see EV113.5)

3. It is strongly recommended that EMTs and/or Paramedics be used to fill this position. Medical personnel must not exceed the scope of their practice.

4. A fine of $750 per day will be imposed on Licensed Competitions failing to comply with this rule.

5. All medical personnel must be readily identifiable and the area where they are available must be designated and readily accessible.

6. Unless prohibited by Federal, State or local law, this person must furnish the Steward(s) or TD(s) with a copy of his/her report(s), or assist these officials with documenting any findings and treatment for all injuries sustained in competition or on the competition grounds.

b. Competitions using more than three performance areas simultaneously must have at least one additional person who is CPR-certified to assist the medical personnel of record for that competition. The additional person may have other duties related to the competition provided they can be immediately available to respond to an emergency. This person must be identified to officials and staff. Dressage arenas do not count as performance areas. If more than six performance areas are used simultaneously there must be at least two additional people who are CPR-certified to assist the medical personnel of record for that competition. Hunter and Jumper competitions using four or more rings simultaneously must have, in addition to the qualified medical personnel of record, one additional person who is at least First Responder certified present during all performance sessions.

c. An operational telephone and/or other emergency call priority system must be provided by the competition. Management must post in the office and by the telephone and/or the emergency call equipment, emergency telephone numbers plus directions to the competition which could be quickly relayed to the off site responder.

d. Additionally, during the time period as defined above, an ambulance must be on the competition grounds or on call.

e. All competitions must have in place prior to the start of the competition, an accident preparedness plan and in conjunction with the plan make the necessary arrangements for an ambulance to be on the grounds or on call.

1. Competition management is responsible for ensuring that all competition officials and competition staff are advised of the accident preparedness plan and that it is distributed accordingly.

2. Said plan shall be given to the Steward or Technical Delegate prior to the start of the competition.

3. The Steward or Technical Delegate shall submit a copy of said plan to the Federation along with his/her Steward or Technical Delegate report.

4. A fine of $750 per day will be imposed on Licensed Competitions failing to either have an ambulance on the grounds or on call.

6. Safety Coordinator

a. All Licensed Competitions must appoint a Safety Coordinator, who shall oversee the establishment and coordination of medical and veterinary services. This person may have other roles or duties in relation to the competition except:

1. The Safety Coordinator may not serve as Judge at the competition.

2. The Safety Coordinator may not compete as a rider, driver, vaulter, longeur, or handler at the competition.

b. Duties of the Safety Coordinator. The Safety Coordinator shall:

1. Oversee provisions for the safety and welfare of exhibitors, horses and spectators.

2. Oversee the implementation of the Accident Preparedness Plan (GR1211.5).

3. Hold a meeting with Competition Management and Medical Personnel to ensure that parties are aware of the requirements of the Accident Preparedness Plan.

4. Provide Medical Personnel with a map of the competition grounds which includes plans for vehicle access to

competition/warm-up areas and stabling.

     5. Have his name and contact information posted along with the required emergency information at the competition.

7. Farrier

    a. Every competition that offers a Hunter division or section with a National rating must have a farrier qualified in those divisions or sections offered at that competition on competition grounds and available during all performances (Exception: "A" rated Welsh competitions).

    b. Competitions restricted to Arabians, Morgans, Hackneys, Roadsters, American Saddlebreds or National Show Horses must have a qualified farrier on competition grounds and available during all performances. (Exception: Arabian competitions restricted to sections exempt from shoeing regulations are not required to have a farrier on the grounds).

    c. A farrier must be on the grounds or on call at all other competitions.

8. It is required that all Licensed Competitions must have a 'Competition Secretary', i.e. a secretary who is a Senior Active Federation member, present in the competition office during the competition.

9. Specific requirements for staff and officials for Dressage Competitions are listed in the Dressage Levels chart posted on the USEF website.

SUBCHAPTER 12-D DUTIES CONCERNING COMPETITION RECORDS

GR1212 Prize Lists

1. A copy of the prize list must be received by the Federation Office at least thirty (30) days prior to the competition. Prize list must be forwarded by mail with proof of delivery or submitted electronically via e-mail, with staff confirming receipt. If the prize list is not received thirty (30) days prior to the competition, the competition will be invoiced as outlined in GR1212.2. Copies also must be forwarded to the Federation steward or technical delegate and to the judges.

2. If the prize list is not received thirty (30) days prior to the competition, the Federation shall levy a fine of $200. If the fine is not paid, it shall be added to the amount of dues for the ensuing year and future competition dates will not be awarded until both penalty and dues have been paid. For the second consecutive offense, the competition will be suspended.

3. If management disputes that the prize list was not timely filed or that the above fine is not properly owing, it may appeal in writing to the Federation within 30 days of management's receipt of the Federation's notice of fine, specifying the grounds for the appeal. The Federation's CEO or his designee, a special committee appointed by the President or the Hearing Committee will consider the appeal and may waive a part or all of the fine upon a finding of good cause why the prize list was not timely filed and/or a finding that extreme hardship results from the automatic penalty. See Chapter 9 for requirements regarding prize lists.

GR1213 Entries

1. The name of any exhibitor whose fees are not negotiable must be reported in writing to the Federation within 90 days of the close of the competition. (See GR913).

2. If there is a closing date, the competition must acknowledge all entries made by that date.

3. Ensure that no entry will compete until or unless the exhibitor and the rider, driver, or handler and trainer, or agent(s) of such person(s), have signed an entry blank, including all post entries. In the case of a rider, driver or handler under 18, his/her parent or guardian, or if not available, the trainer, must sign an entry blank on the minor's behalf.

4. Have available applications for amateur status. If a rider or driver in amateur classes does not possess current amateur certification, the secretary must require the individual to complete the necessary application (see GR1307).

5. Collect and remit promptly to the Federation and its applicable Recognized Affiliate Associations as defined under

Bylaw 222, Section 1 (1) and 1 (2), the Show Pass fee, if applicable, as provided in GR205 and GR206 for each rider, driver, handler, owner, lessee, agent and trainer who is a non-member and participates in any Regular Competition, Eventing Competition at the Preliminary Level or above, Dressage Competitions, Combined Driving Competitions at the Advanced Level or above, Endurance and Vaulting Competitions who has not produced a valid Federation membership card or copy thereof. Lessees are considered owners in connection with this membership requirement. In the event of an entry under multiple ownership, where no owner is a Member, only one owner need pay a Show Pass fee.

6. When classes or divisions are recognized by The Federation under the same competition number, duplicate Federation fees (drug, Show Pass, etc.) may not be charged to exhibitors, regardless of whether different competition secretaries officiate in these classes or divisions. See GR407.

7. Ensure that riders, driver, handlers, vaulters, longeurs, owners, lessees, agents and trainers who are not members as required by the provisions of Bylaw 203, are not allowed to participate in Regular Competitions, Eventing Competitions at the Preliminary Level or above, Driving Competitions at the Advanced Level or above, Dressage Competitions, Endurance and Vaulting Competitions unless all provisions of .1-.6 (above) are met.

8. Ensure that every rider, driver, longeur, and vaulter in a non-breed-restricted event in an FEI recognized discipline has complied with GR828.

9. Eliminate without waiting for a protest to be made, a competitor who has made an entry of horse, rider or driver that is ineligible.

10. If management accepts unpaid entries, it thereby subjects the competition to the provisions of GR913.

11. A number card for each competitor must be provided. For Dressage: A separate number must be issued for each horse/rider combination (DR126.1j(4)). For Dressage Sport Horse Breeding: One number must be issued for each horse showing In Hand. A separate number must be issued to each entry (combination of horses) showing in group classes. Entries in Materiale and Under Saddle classes must be issued a separate number only if the rider did not also show the same horse in hand (DR207.8).

GR1214 Results

1. All competition results and other data as specified by USEF in the license agreement may be electronically transmitted to USEF within 10 days following a Licensed competition including all corrections, changes and additions to the prize list. All results must meet the criteria and format of the Federation result template as published by USEF and must be submitted as outlined in the license agreement. A fee may be assessed for any required data not received electronically. Full results are defined as the names and Federation numbers of all horses, riders and owners in all classes. In the event of an entry under multiple ownership, only one owner need be a Member or pay a Show Pass fee. The competition is responsible for listing either the active member or the person that paid the Show Pass fee in the results. (Exception GR901.9). For all Jumper Classes offering $500 or more in prize money (including add back) the competition must submit the following in addition to the above: the number of horses competing in the class, the Level under which the class was conducted, the identification/recording number for each horse in the class, and the placings with the money paid out to each placed entry. For Young Jumper classes the first round fault scores for each entry must also be included. For classes with $25,000 or more in prize money a copy of the starting order (showing the rider) and judges card(s) are required. At Jumper Rating 4 or higher competitions, results must include faults of each round in jumper classes held at 1.40m or above. Results must include faults from each round of Pony Jumper classes. Results for Dressage Competitions and Regular or Local competitions holding open Dressage or Dressage Sport Horse Breeding classes must include the Federation and USDF membership and identification/recording numbers for all owners, riders, handlers and horses for whom this information is required for the competition. This material is needed in order to include the winnings of exhibitors in the Federation's permanent records.

2. The secretary of each Federation Licensed Competition must, within 10 calendar days of the competition, send to the Federation, either electronically or by mail with proof of delivery, a list of judges, stewards, technical delegates and competition officials, as well as the names and addresses of all ribbon winners, the amount of money won if applicable, and number of entries in the Federation Medal classes and USEF/USDF dressage qualifying and championship classes, the first place winners of all other Equitation classes.

3. Competitions offering Medal classes must make a complete report to the Federation in order that Federation memberships can be checked and credit given winners. Names and addresses of all ribbon winners and the numbers of entries in a class must be included.

4. If the competition fails to file a full set of results postmarked within 10 calendar days of the closing of the competition, the Federation will levy a fine of $250. If the fine is not paid, future competition dates might be retracted or not awarded. The competition has the right to request a waiver of this fine, provided they can show good cause.

5. If management disputes that the results were not timely filed or that the above fine is not properly owing, it may appeal in writing to the Federation within 30 days of management's receipt of the Federation's notice of fine, specifying the grounds for the appeal. The Federation's CEO or his designee, a special committee appointed by the President or the Hearing Committee will consider the appeal and may waive a part or all of the fine upon a finding of good cause why the application was not timely filed and/or a finding that extreme hardship results from the automatic penalty.

6. Within 30 days of the deadline for filing any report or paperwork required under the Rules, the Federation must notify the Official Competition Contact responsible for filing such report or paperwork in the event that it has not been received.

7. The Federation must be notified of any retirement ceremony held at any Licensed Competition. See GR812.

SUBCHAPTER 12-E DUTIES CONCERNING FACILITIES

GR1215 Stabling

1. At Level 3, Level 4 and Level 5 Dressage Competitions, and competitions offering "A" rated hunter sections, overnight stabling, on the competition grounds, must be provided for any accepted and confirmed entry in a section held on multiple days that has requested and paid for the stall(s) by the closing date of entries.

2. Stalls provided must be of sturdy construction, in good condition and safe for horses and ponies. The recommended minimum dimensions for box stalls for horses are 9' wide by 9' deep by 7' high or comparable square footage. It is essential that the covering over the stalls is weatherproof. Prize list must specify type of stabling and whether stall doors will be provided.

3. At competitions which offer overnight stabling, adequate lighting must be provided.

4. It is recommended that at Level 4 and Level 5 Dressage Competitions, and at competitions with an A rated division provide, upon request of the official competition veterinarian, a suitable area, protected from the elements, secured from public view, adequately lighted, with adequate electrical supply and running water, to serve as a first aid station for the emergency treatment of ill and injured horses.

5. Additional stabling requirements for Dressage Competitions are listed in the Dressage Levels chart posted on the USEF website.

GR1216 Facilities

1. Convenient and ample water facilities must be provided.

2. Adequate and sanitary toilet facilities must be provided.

3. All competition grounds (where there are divisions that require measurement) must have a level surface area for measurement in accordance with GR507.

4. Food must be provided on the grounds.

5. A secretary's office with adequate personnel and proper communication between secretary, announcer, in-gate, each ring and stables must be provided.

6. Proper schooling and exercise areas must be provided. See Rules GR834-GR838.

7. Subject to local law and contract requirements, any owner or trainer stabled on the grounds of a competition must be permitted to haul in hay, grain and bedding, meeting management's specifications as published in the prize list, for his own use, and use any farrier or veterinarian of his choice.

8. Directions to the competition grounds must be posted outside the competition office so that directions can be relayed to the EMS.

9. Before the first day of competition, competition management must post the name, address, and telephone number of the closest veterinary emergency and surgical facility. The competition management must have notified and obtained assurance that such facility can handle competition related emergencies. The name, address, and telephone number of this facility must be posted in the same location as the telephone and/or other emergency call priority system.

10. Lighting at sunrise and sunset that provides full and complete visibility is a requirement for the competition ring and schooling area. Horses may not be required to be exhibited in the competition ring or schooled in the designated warmup areas before the official hour of sunrise or after the official hour of sunset unless lighting is provided that assures full and complete visibility.

11. Competition management is required to make an effort to provide the best possible footing in competition and warm-up areas. Provisions must be made (by having on hand proper equipment and scheduling sufficient breaks in the schedule) to maintain the footing in those areas, e.g. by dragging, watering, and raking, if necessary, throughout the competition.

12. Additional requirements for Dressage Competitions regarding facilities, services and amenities are listed in the Dressage Levels chart posted on the USEF website.

SUBCHAPTER 12-F DUTIES CONCERNING ENFORCEMENT OF FEDERATION RULES

GR1217 Rules

1. Each Licensed Competition must have a copy of the current Federation Rule Book available for reference at all times during the competition.

2. Enforce all rules of the Federation from the time entries are admitted to the competition grounds until their departure.

3. Comply with and enforce the 1979 Horse Protection Act. Copies of this law and lists of associations that provide D.Q.P.s can be obtained from the Federation office.

4. Prevent manual poling with unauthorized poles, or the abuse of a horse anywhere on the grounds and to see that GR844 and GR839 are rigidly enforced.

GR1218 Protests, Charges and Violations

1. Receive and act upon protests and charges in accordance with Chapter 6 and report whatever action is taken to the Hearing Committee.

2. It is within the jurisdiction of a Licensed Competition to disqualify a person and/or his entries and to cause him to forfeit his winnings and ribbons at that competition and for cause to have the horses removed from the grounds without being held for damage. All such disqualifications must be reported to the Federation.

3. Any Licensed Competition which allows a person not in good standing to judge, serve as steward or technical delegate, manage, exhibit, ride, drive, or participate in any manner after due notice has been received from the Secretary of the Federation, is liable to suspension or expulsion from the Federation. See GR704.

4. In the event that any person participating at a competition commits an offense or violation described in Chapter 7,

the Directors of the Competition may in their discretion disqualify that person and/or his entries from further participation in their competition only (See GR908). Any such offense must be reported to the Hearing Committee for whatever further action is deemed necessary.

5. Report in writing to the Federation any act on the part of any person named in GR701 deemed prejudicial to the best interests of the Federation. Matters to be so reported include withdrawal by an exhibitor of his horses from the competition grounds, or from the competition after it has commenced, without permission.

6. Report in writing to the Federation within ten (10) days of the close of the competition the names and addresses of exhibitors and horses that were eliminated or disqualified from the competition for a rule violation and reasons for said elimination or disqualification.

SPONSORED BY HAGYARD EQUINE MEDICAL INSTITUTE || © USEF 2016

CHAPTER 13 COMPETITION PARTICIPANTS AND ASSOCIATED INDIVIDUALS

SUBCHAPTER 13-A RESPONSIBILITIES

GR1301 General

GR1302 Duties

GR1303 Conduct

GR1304 Regulations Governing Showing Under Judges, Stewards and Technical Delegates. See also GR107 for definition of Client

GR1305 Elimination & Withdrawal from Classes & Competition

SUBCHAPTER 13-B AMATEURS AND PROFESSIONALS

GR1306 Professional/Amateur Status

GR1307 Amateur Status

SUBCHAPTER 13-C MEMBERSHIP AND DOCUMENT REQUIREMENTS

GR1308 Membership and Document Requirements

GR1309 Presidential Modifications for the Dressage Division

SUBCHAPTER 13-D COMPETITION DISPENSATIONS

GR1310 Dispensations

GR1311 Para-Equestrian Eligibility/Classification

GR1312 Applying for a Dispensation Certificate

GR1313 Applying for Para-Equestrian (PE) Classification

GR1314 Hearings/Protests

GR1315 Definition of Terms

SUBCHAPTER 13-E RETURN TO COMPETITION

GR1316 Accidents Involving Competitors

CHAPTER 13 COMPETITION PARTICIPANTS AND ASSOCIATED INDIVIDUALS

SUBCHAPTER 13-A RESPONSIBILITIES

GR1301 General

1. Knowledge of and compliance with the rules of the Federation.
2. Obtain Federation membership or pay a per-competition Show Pass fee if competing at Federation member competitions. (See GR202 and GR205-GR206.)
3. Obtain Federation Amateur Certification and measurement cards where required. (See GR1307, GR501, and HU168.).
4. Any member or non-member who fails to pay sums owing to the Federation or who makes payment for fees to the Federation which is not negotiable will be notified by the Federation of his or her indebtedness and warned that unless settlement is made within two weeks he or she will automatically be fined the sum of $250 to be paid to the Federation; and further, that he or she and any horses owned by him or her and any horses and/or persons for which payment has not been made or for which the non-negotiable sums have been paid will automatically be barred from taking any part whatsoever in Licensed Competitions until payment or settlement is made of the total indebtedness to the Federation. Publication of the suspension will be published on the Federation's web site.
    a. If any individual affected by GR1301.4 disputes that the amounts in question are owed or unpaid, he or she may request a review of these issues by the Hearing Committee provided his or her written statement specifying the grounds for the review is received at the Federation's office within said two week period accompanied by a fee of $100., which will be refunded if the dispute is settled in favor of said person.
    b. In the event a person makes non-negotiable payment for fees to the Federation on three or more occasions, he or she is, after a hearing, subject to further disciplinary action. In addition, any future payments made to the Federation, must be submitted in the form of a certified check, cashier's check, money order, or valid credit card.
5. Every person participating in any competition licensed by the Federation is subject to the Federation Bylaws and Rules including the provisions of Chapters 6 and 7 and is responsible under the rules for their own acts and failures to act and for the acts and failures to act of their agent or agents whether or not they or their agent or agents have signed an entry blank.
6. Dogs are not permitted to be loose on competition grounds and must be held on a leash or otherwise restrained. Individuals must not lead dogs on a leash while mounted. Dog owners are solely responsible for any damages, claims, losses or actions resulting from their dogs' behaviors. Dog owners failing to comply with this rule will be issued a Yellow warning card may be subject to penalty under Chapters 6 and 7.
7. Minors who do not have a valid driver's license which allows them to operate a motorized vehicle in the state in which they reside will not be permitted to operate a motorized vehicle of any kind, including, but not limited to, golf carts, motorcycles, scooters, or farm utility vehicles, on the competition grounds of licensed competitions. Minors who have a valid temporary license may operate the above described motorized vehicles as long as they are accompanied by an adult with a valid driver's license. The parent(s), legal guardian(s), or individual who signs the entry blank as a parent or guardian of a minor operating a motorized vehicle in violation of this rule are solely responsible for any damages, claims, losses or actions resulting from that operation. Violations of this rule will be cause for sanctions against the parent(s), guardian(s) and/or trainer(s) who are responsible for the child committing the offense. Penalties may include exclusion of the child, parent(s), guardian(s), and/or trainer(s) from the competition grounds for the remainder of the competition and charges being filed against any of the above individuals in accordance with Chapter 6. Wheelchairs and other mobility assistance devices for individuals with disabilities are exempt from this rule.
8. In the event of an acute and serious injury to or illness of a horse on competition grounds when the owner or trainer

of the horse or agent of the owner is not present, after reasonable effort to contact that individual has been made, competition management, in consultation with a licensed equine veterinarian, may authorize the provision of emergency veterinary treatment of the horse. If competition management so authorizes treatment under the provisions of this rule, competition management and veterinarian are not liable for any resulting costs, damages, losses, claims or actions arising directly or indirectly from the treatment of the horse.

GR1302 Duties

1. Every exhibitor, rider, driver, handler and trainer or his/her agent(s) must sign an entry blank (see GR404 and GR908.2). In the case of a rider, driver or handler under 18, his/her parent or guardian, or if not available, the trainer, must sign an entry blank on the minor's behalf.

2. Every exhibitor, rider, driver, handler, and trainer or his agents must provide on the competition entry blank, all information required under Federation rules. Exhibitors are responsible for their own errors and those of their agents in the preparation of entry blanks.

   a. The following credentials must be made available to Competition Management. Competitions may, at their discretion, confirm any of the below electronically with the Federation Office:

      1. Original or copies of Federation membership cards, Exemption: Applications completed at the competition. The member will retain the pink copy of the membership application form which, when properly signed by Competition Secretary, is valid for 45 days from the date signed or until the membership card is received from the Federation.

      2. Copies of Federation Measurement cards;

      3. Federation Amateur Certification;

      4. Federation horse recordings for USEF/USDF qualifying classes for dressage championships and USEF/USDF Dressage Championships (see DR127.2).

      5. Registration papers showing proof of ownership or a copy of the registration papers with a Certificate of Eligibility to Show issued by the American Saddlebred Registry for horses entered in classes restricted to American Saddlebreds must be submitted either with entry form at the time of making entry or submitted to the show office before show numbers will be released (or an affidavit completed). If a copy is sent with the entry form, the copy of registration papers will be returned when exhibitors pick up their numbers, if requested by the exhibitor. Original or copies of United States Hunter Jumper Association, Inc., membership card, if applicable.

   b. Exhibitors are urged to submit photostatic copy of all required credentials with their entry blanks. (Exception: measurement cards, see Rules GR502.1 and HU168.1).

   c. If an exhibitor does not submit the proper membership documentation to the competition and the competition cannot verify such information, (with the exception of Federation measurement cards) the exhibitor will be responsible to pay a $30 Show Pass fee which is non-refundable.

GR1303 Conduct

Exhibitors' attention is directed to Chapter 8 which includes rules pertaining to conduct at Licensed Competitions.

GR1304 Regulations Governing Showing Under Judges, Stewards and Technical Delegates (See also GR107 for definition of Client)

Refer solely to GR1304.16 for rules pertaining to showing under judges in the Reining Division. Refer solely to GR1304.21-26 for regulations and restrictions for Hunter/Jumper/Hunter Seat Equitation Judges and Category 1 Stewards. See also GR1038, GR107, and GR301. Refer to GR1304.22 for rules pertaining to competing under Organizing Committees, Officials: Stewards, Ground Jurors, Veterinary Judges and Technical Delegates in the Endurance Division. See also GR1038 for restrictions on Judges.

1. An exhibitor, coach or trainer may not serve as a judge, steward or technical delegate at any competition in which he/she exhibits, whether or not the classes are conducted under Federation rules. See also GR1038.1. A licensed judge may officiate at the special competition, provided he/she is not or does not have a client participating in the special competition.

2. No member of a judge's family, nor any cohabitant, companion, domestic partner, housemate, or member of a judge's household nor any of the judge's clients, employers or employees or employers of a member of the judge's family may compete as trainer, coach, exhibitor, rider, driver, handler, owner, lessor or lessee in any division, or Dressage class (Arabian, Morgan, Western Dressage and Hunter divisions in any competition) unless the relationship is terminated 30 days prior to the competition. For purposes of this rule included as employers are any individuals, corporations, partnerships, foundations, trusts or non-profit organizations and shareholders owning five or more percent of the stock of any corporation which employs the judge or a member of the judge's family, and any officers, directors and partners of any corporation or partnership and officers, directors or trustees of any trust or foundation or non-profit organization which employs the judge or a member of the judge's family. The hiring of a judge to officiate at Licensed Competitions shall not constitute employment for purposes of this rule.

3. No judge's trainer nor any of the judge's trainer's clients may compete as trainer, coach, exhibitor, rider, driver, handler, owner, lessor or lessee in any Division or Dressage class (Arabian, Morgan, Western Dressage and Hunter divisions in any competition) unless the relationship is terminated 30 days prior to the competition.

4. No horses trained by a member of the judge's family may compete in any division or Dressage unless the client/trainer relationship is terminated 30 days prior to the competition. Stud fees, retiree board and broodmare board excluded. Exception: American Saddlebred and Hackney classes where requirements that nominations or qualifying be accomplished in advance of the competition (i.e. Futurities, Sweepstakes, Classics, etc.) and the Roadster USTA Classic class, a judge may be substituted in that class for the officially appointed judge who has a conflict. Such substitution shall not affect the restrictions referred to in GR1304.2-.4 on the substituted judge.

5. No horse that has been sold (American Saddlebred division or leased) by a judge or by his/her employer within a period of 90 days (Morgan and Paso Fino 30 days) prior to the competition may be shown before that judge.

6. No horse that has been trained by a judge within the period of 30 days (American Saddlebred, Hackney and Roadster Divisions, 90 days) prior to the competition may be shown before that judge.

7. No one may show before a judge who has received or has contracted to receive any remuneration for the sale, purchase or lease of any horse to or from, or for the account of the exhibitor within a period of 30 days (Welsh Division 90 days) prior to the competition unless the sale or purchase has been made and fully consummated at public auction.

8. No one may show before a judge who boards, shows or trains any horse under the exhibitor's ownership or lease, within a period of 30 days prior to the competition. Stud fees, retiree board and broodmare board excluded.

9. No one may show before a judge who has remunerated the exhibitor for the board or training of any horse for competition purposes within a period of 30 days prior to the competition. Stud fees, retiree board and broodmare board excluded.

10. No one may show before a judge from whom he has leased a horse unless the lease terminated 90 days (Morgan, Paso Fino 30 days) prior to the competition.

11. No rider may compete in an Equitation class before a judge with whom his or her parent, guardian or instructor has had any financial transaction in connection with the sale, lease, board or training of a horse within 30 days of the competition unless the sale or purchase has been made at public auction.

12. No rider may compete in an Equitation, Dressage or Western Dressage class before a judge by whom he has been instructed, coached or tutored with or without pay within 30 days of the first day of the competition. The conducting of clinics or assistance in group activities such as Pony Clubs, Saddle Seat Young Rider Team and/or Saddle Seat World Cup Team, unless private instruction is given, will not be considered as instruction, coaching

or tutoring. Exception: Carriage Pleasure Driving - A judge may officiate over entries (competitors and/or animals) who attended group clinics at the competition if the clinic is open to all competitors and animals entered, the clinic is advertised and available to all possible entrants, and during the clinic the judge does not drive any animal that is entered in the competition.

13. No one shall approach a judge with regard to a decision unless he first obtains permission from the Show Committee, steward or technical delegate who shall arrange an appointment with the judge at a proper time and place. No exhibitor has the right to inspect the judge's cards without the judge's permission.

14. No member of a steward or technical delegate's family, nor any cohabitant, companion, domestic partner, housemate, or member of a steward or technical delegate's household, nor any of the steward or technical delegate's clients may take part as a trainer, coach, lessor, lessee, exhibitor, rider, driver, handler or vaulter at a competition where the steward or technical delegate is officiating. In addition, the trainer or coach of a Steward or Technical Delegate, or an individual from whom the Steward or Technical Delegate has purchased or leased a horse within 30 days, may not participate (as rider, driver, owner, trainer or coach) at a competition where the Steward or Technical Delegate is officiating. Technical Delegates and Stewards may not officiate unless the client, trainer or coach relationship is terminated at least 30 days prior to the competition.

15. If a horse or person is presented to a judge that the judge knows is ineligible to compete under these rules, the judge may advise the ring steward that he/she believes the entry to be ineligible and request that the entry be excused, or the judge may proceed to judge the entry and file a charge under Chapter 6, alleging a violation of this Rule. If a judge has any doubt as to the eligibility of any entry, he/she should judge the entry and file a charge alleging the violation.

16. In the Reining Horse division, a horse may not be shown under a judge if that judge has been owner, trainer or agent of that horse within the previous 90 days, or if said horse is ridden by a member of his/her family or by an employee of said judge. If such a horse is entered in a competition, its entry fee shall be refunded and it is not to be exhibited. A judge may not show to another judge whom he/she has judged or judged with within five days nor may he/she judge another judge under whom he/she has shown or judged with within five days. Volunteer USA Reining approved judges utilized for equipment inspection are excluded from the five day requirement.

17. Competition Restrictions on Judges:
   a. A judge may not be an owner of any interest in a horse (including but not limited to syndicate and partnership shares).
   b. A judge may not be a trainer, coach, exhibitor, rider, driver, halter handler, steward, technical delegate, lessor, lessee or manager at any Federation Licensed Competition at which he/she is officiating, including unrated classes. Exception:
      1. in the Eventing division and in the Dressage division, except for Dressage Sport Horse Breeding classes, horses may be shown Hors de Concours in classes where the owner is not officiating. (See GR1038.1)

18. A steward or technical delegate cannot own or operate any business (i.e. tack shop, braiding business, etc.) at the same competition where he/she is officiating.

19. In the Endurance Division, the other subdivisions in this Rule are applicable unless they conflict or create an ambiguity when read in conjunction with this subdivision. In that case and at all times involving competing within the Endurance Division, the following rule applies:
   a. A Veterinary Judge may not examine horses in competition in which he/she has an ownership interest, are owned by his/her nuclear family members or his/her spouse or children, are owned by his/her cohabitants or significant others or other persons within his/her household, or are owned by a client from whom he/she received 10% or more of his/her gross income or income benefit in the current or prior year or for whom he/she performed work on this horse in the past 30 days;
   b. A Technical Delegate, Ground Juror or Steward may not involve him/herself in objections, complaints or other

formal disputes involving horses in which he/she has an ownership interest or which are owned under any of the other examples listed above for Veterinary Judges;

    c. Extended or nuclear family or household cohabitants or significant others or horses owned by him/her or members of the event Organizing Committee will be allowed to compete in said event, but such relationships should be disclosed in posted announcements at the event or orally at the pre-ride briefing; and,

    d. These exceptions do not inhibit or prevent a competitor or other authorized person from asserting such conflict of interest or other issues relating to bias for scrutiny and consideration at the event. However, any such complaint or objection must be raised pursuant to applicable rules or regulations for the event and in a timely manner or they are deemed waived. This Rule is intended to set parameters to allow a Veterinary Judge, Steward, Ground Juror and Technical Delegate to perform his/her duties at rides and should be construed in all cases to provide that flexibility.

20. The provisions of sections .2-.19 of this rule notwithstanding, an Eventing Judge or Combined Driving Judge may officiate on the Ground Jury of an Eventing or Combined Driving competition when a competitor(s) or horse(s) listed in those sections is/are entered, under the following restrictions

    a. The Judge must notify the Technical Delegate and the Organizer of the conflict prior to the start of competition. If the conflict is discovered after the start of competition the competitor(s) or horse(s) must either withdraw from competition or participate Hors de Concours (H.C.).

    b. The Judge may not judge any of the tests for the Section in which of the affected competitor(s) or horse(s) are competing. For decisions regarding disqualification, elimination or penalties, the Technical Delegate will assume the role of the Ground Jury.

    c. If an Inquiry or Protest is lodged from the Section in which the affected competitor(s) or horse(s) is/are competing, the Judge must excuse himself from the process and the Technical Delegate will assume the role of the Ground Jury.

    d. There are no restrictions on a Judge if a competitor(s) or horse(s) listed in GR1304.2-.22 participates in the Competition H.C.

21. When you are officiating as a Judge in the Hunter or Hunter Seat Equitation divisions:

    a. You may not be a competitor, coach, trainer, rider, handler, lessor, lessee, or manager at the same competition. However, you may compete as a rider in jumper classes that you are not judging.

    b. You may not have any ownership interest in a horse (including but not limited to syndicate and partnership shares) competing in a class in which you are officiating in the Hunter or Hunter Seat Equitation Divisions including unrated classes. However, such horse may compete in Jumper classes at the same competition.

    c. A member of your family may compete in Jumper classes at the same competition.

22. When you are officiating as a Judge in the Hunter or Hunter Seat Equitation divisions, none of the following may compete as a trainer, coach, competitor, rider, owner, handler, lessor or lessee in either the Hunter or the Hunter Seat Equitation divisions in a class in which you are officiating at that competition, unless the relationship is terminated, or the transaction is completed, at least 30 days prior to the competition:

    a. A member of your family.

    b. A member of your household or housemate.

    c. A cohabitant, companion, or domestic partner.

    d. An employee. Catch Riders and Independent Service Providers (defined below) are not employees for purposes of this rule.

        1. Catch Rider: An individual who is engaged, for remuneration or as a volunteer, to compete on a horse(s) owned by another with whom they have no current business relationship regarding the ongoing training, care, custody or control of the horse.

        2. Independent Service Provider: An individual who performs a service(s) for another and the payer has the right

to control or direct only the result of the work and what will be done and how it will be done. The Independent service provider controls the details as to how the service is performed.

   e. A client.

   f. Your trainer.

   g. A client of your trainer.

   h. An entity that employs you or a member of your family, which includes individuals, corporations, partnerships, foundations, trusts, non-profit organizations, and any shareholder owning five or more percent of the stock, if any.

   i. A horse trained or shown by you or by a member of your family.

   j. A horse sold by you or by your employer.

23. When you are officiating as a Judge in the Jumper division at a competition:

   a. No member of your family may compete in a Jumper class you are judging. However, said family member may compete in jumper classes you are not judging, as well as in the Hunter and Hunter Seat Equitation Divisions.

   b. No horse in which you have any ownership interest may compete in a Jumper class you are judging. However, said horse may compete in jumper classes you are not judging, as well as in the Hunter and Hunter Seat Equitation Divisions.

   c. You may compete as a rider in jumper classes of $25,000 or more that you are not judging.

24. When you are officiating as a Hunter or Hunter Seat Equitation Judge at a "special" competition as described in GR301.2, that is also held in conjunction with a licensed competition:

   a. You may not compete as a competitor, coach, or trainer in the "special" competition. However, you may compete as a competitor, coach, or trainer in the non-special part of the competition.

   b. You may not have a client compete in the "special" competition. However, you may have a client compete in the non-special part of the competition.

25. When you are officiating as a Category 1 (C1) Steward at a competition:

   a. You may not be a competitor, coach, rider, handler, lessor, lessee, trainer, or manager at the same competition.

   b. You cannot own or operate any business (i.e. tack shop, braiding business, etc.) at the same competition.

   c. None of the following may compete as a trainer, coach, competitor, rider, owner, handler, lessor or lessee at that competition, unless the relationship is terminated at least 30 days prior to the competition:

      1. A member of your family.

      2. A member of your household or housemate.

      3. A cohabitant, companion, or domestic partner.

      4. An employee.

      5. A client.

      6. Your trainer.

      7. A client of your trainer.

      8. An entity that employs you or a member of your family, which includes individuals, corporations, partnerships, foundations, trusts, non-profit organizations, and any shareholder owning five or more percent of the stock, if any.

      9. A horse trained by you or by a member of your family.

      10. A horse sold by you or by your employer.

      11. A person for whom you have or are scheduled to receive any remuneration involving a horse sale, purchase, (unless at public auction), lease, or board (stud fees, retiree or broodmare board excluded).

26. Other Hunter/Jumper Regulations and Restrictions:

   a. If a judge believes (but is not certain) that a horse or person presented to him is ineligible to compete under these rules, the entry should be judged, an investigation should occur and, if substantiated, the judge should file a charge alleging the violation.

b. Sixty days prior to the first day of a competition through 30 days after the last competition day, no horse or rider that has been trained by a judge or a judge's employee or agent may show before a judge officiating at any of the following competitions:

1. National Junior Hunter Finals.

2. National Pony Hunter Finals.

3. All USEF Hunter Seat Equitation Medal Finals (USEF Jr. Medal, ASPCA, USEF Pony)

4. USEF Show Jumping Talent Search Finals.

5. Washington International Horse Show Equitation.

6. No one shall approach a judge with regard to a decision unless he first obtains permission from the Steward, who shall arrange an appointment to meet with the judge at a proper time and place. The Steward shall be present for the meeting.

c. No competitor has the right to inspect a judge's card without the judge's permission.

d. No rider may compete in an equitation class before a judge by whom he has been instructed, coached, or tutored (with or without pay) within 30 days of the competition. Conducting clinics or assistance in group activities such as Pony Clubs, unless private instruction is given, will not be considered as instruction, coaching, or tutoring.

e. No rider may compete in an Equitation class before a judge with whom his parent, guardian, or instructor has had any financial transaction in connection with the sale, lease, board, or training of a horse within 30 days of the competition unless the sale or purchase was been made at public auction.

f. The hiring of a judge to officiate does not constitute employment under this rule.

GR1305 Elimination & Withdrawal from Classes & Competition

(See also GR118)

1. No exhibitor may withdraw horses from a Licensed Competition after it has commenced, or remove them from the competition grounds, without the permission of the competition secretary.

2. If an exhibitor voluntarily removes a horse from the ring without the permission of the judge, the Show Committee will disqualify the exhibitor and all his entries from all future classes at that competition and all prizes and entry fees for the entire competition will be forfeited.

3. Any horse leaving the ring without the exhibitor's volition is deprived of an award in that class. See also division rules for other causes of elimination.

4. All horses competing in USEF/USDF Regional Dressage Championships classes must remain on the competition grounds from the time of entry to the grounds and for the duration of their USEF/USDF Regional Dressage Championship classes. (See DR127.7) If required to remain overnight, horses must be stabled on the competition grounds.

SUBCHAPTER 13-B AMATEURS AND PROFESSIONALS

GR1306 Professional/Amateur Status

1. Amateur. Regardless of one's equestrian skills and/or accomplishments, a person is an amateur if after his 18th birthday, as defined in GR101, he has not engaged in any of the activities identified in paragraph 4 below.

a. In the Dressage Division, individuals are only eligible to compete as amateurs from the beginning of the calendar year in which they reach age 22, see DR119.3.

b. For Amateurs in Jumper Sections, see JP118.

c. For Amateurs in Hunter Sections, see HU106.

d. For Amateurs in Eventing, see EV Appendix 3-Participation in Horse Trials.

2. Remuneration. Remuneration is defined as compensation or payment in any form such as cash, goods,

sponsorships, discounts or services; reimbursement of any expenses; trade or in-kind exchange of goods or services such as board or training.

3. Permitted activities by Amateur. An Amateur is permitted to do the following:

a. Accept reimbursement for actual expenses associated with conducting classroom seminars for a not-for-profit organization, therapeutic riding programs, or programs for charitable organizations approved in advance by the Federation.

b. Act as a camp counselor when not hired in the exclusive capacity as a riding instructor; assist in setting schooling fences without remuneration; give instruction or training to handicapped riders for therapeutic purposes.

c. Appear in advertisements and/or articles related to acknowledgement of one's own personal or business sponsorship of a competition and/or awards earned by one's owned horses.

d. Accept prize money as the owner of a horse in any class other than equitation or showmanship classes.

e. Accept prize money in Dressage.

f. Accept a non-monetary token gift of appreciation valued less than $300 annually.

g. Serve as an intern for college credit or course requirements at an accredited institution provided one has never held professional status with the Federation or any other equestrian National Federation. In addition, one may accept reimbursement for expenses without profit, as prescribed by the educational institution's program, for the internship. In the Hackney, Roadster, American Saddlebred, Saddle Seat Equitation, Morgan, Andalusian/Lusitano, Friesian, Arabian, and National Show Horse Divisions, college students may also accept a stipend during the internship served under this paragraph. At the request of the Federation, an Amateur shall provide certification from the accredited educational institution under whose auspices a student is pursuing an internship that he is undertaking the internship to meet course or degree requirements.

h. Write books or articles related to horses.

i. Accept remuneration for providing service in one's capacity as a: presenter or panelist at a Federation licensed officials' clinic, competition manager, competition secretary, judge, steward, technical delegate, course designer, announcer, TV commentator, veterinarian, groom, farrier, tack shop operator, breeder, or boarder, or horse transporter.

j. Accept reimbursement for any bona fide expenses directly related to the horse (i.e. farrier/vet bills, entries). Travel, hotel, equipment, and room and board are not considered bona fide expenses.

k. Entries for non-under saddle classes in amateur sections at hunter, jumper or hunter/jumper competitions, must be paid either (i) directly to the competition by the Amateur or by the Amateur's family or (ii) by someone whom the Amateur or the Amateur's family reimburses within 90 days of the last day of the competition for which entries were paid.

l. Accept educational competition or training grant(s).

4. Professional based on one's own activities. Unless expressly permitted above, a person is a professional if after his 18th birthday he does any of the following:

a. Accepts remuneration AND rides, exercises, drives, shows, trains, assists in training, schools or conducts clinics or seminars.

b. Accepts remuneration AND gives riding or driving lessons, showmanship lessons, equitation lessons, trains horses, or provides consultation services in riding, driving, showmanship, equitation, or training of horses.

c. Accepts remuneration AND acts as an employee in a position such as a groom, farrier, bookkeeper, veterinarian or barn manager AND instructs, rides, drives, shows, trains or schools horses that are owned, boarded or trained by his employer, any member of his employer's family, or a business in which his employer has an ownership interest.

d. Accepts remuneration AND uses his name, photograph or other form of personal association as a horseperson in connection with any advertisement or product/service for sale, including but not limited to apparel, equipment or property.

e. Accepts prize money unless permitted in paragraph 3d or 3e above.

f. Rides, drives or shows any horse that a cohabitant or family member or a cohabitant or family member's business receives remuneration for boarding, training, riding, driving or showing. A cohabitant or family member of a trainer may not absolve themselves of this rule by entering into a lease or any other agreement for a horse owned by a client of the trainer.

g. Gives instruction to any person or rides, drives, or shows any horse, for which activity his cohabitant or another person in his family or business in which his cohabitant or a family member controls will receive remuneration for the activity. A cohabitant or family member of a trainer may not absolve themselves of this rule by entering into a lease or any other agreement for a horse owned by a client of the trainer.

h. Accepts remuneration AND acts as an agent in the sale of a horse or pony or accepts a horse or pony on consignment for the purpose of sale or training that is not owned by him, his cohabitant, or a member of his family, a farm/ranch/syndicate/partnership/corporation/business in which he, his cohabitant or a member of his family controls.

i. Advertises one's equestrian services such as training or instruction.

j. Accepts remuneration AND acts as an intern, apprentice, or working student whose responsibilities include, but are not limited to, riding, driving, showmanship, handling, showing, training or assisting in training, giving lessons/coaching and/or schooling horses other than horses actually owned by him.

k. Accepts remuneration in excess of rental fee for use of a facility, ring or school horses.

l. Accepts remuneration for such use AND uses commercial logoed items while on competition grounds unless expressly permitted by applicable division rules.

5. Professional based on one's own activity along with another's. A person is also deemed a professional after his 18th birthday, if he accepts remuneration for his spouse, family member, or cohabitant engaging in any activity enumerated in 4 a-l above. For the purposes of this rule, the term cohabitant is defined as any individuals living together in a relationship, as would a married couple, but not legally married.

6. Violations of Amateur status. After an investigation as to proper status has been initiated, and upon request by the Federation and to the satisfaction of the Federation, an Amateur shall submit verifiable proof of Amateur status, including but not limited to a bill of sale for any horse(s) the Amateur is competing in classes restricted to Amateur Owners. If the Federation deems such proof insufficient, then the Federation may initiate proceedings under Chapter 6.

a. Any individual found to have knowingly assisted in the violation of the Amateur rule may also be subject to proceedings in accordance with Chapter 6. See GR1307.

7. Questions about whether you are an Amateur or Professional. For specific inquiries, email amateurinquiry@usef.org.

GR1307 Amateur Status

1. Only active Federation members may obtain amateur status. Every person who has reached his/her 18th birthday and competes in classes for amateurs under Federation rules must possess current amateur status issued by the Federation. (Exception: This is not required for Opportunity classes except for the Dressage Division. If Opportunity classes are offered at Dressage Competitions or Regular/Local Competitions with "Open" Dressage classes and are restricted to amateurs, riders are required to have amateur status with the Federation). This status must be available for inspection or the competitor must have lodged with the competition secretary, at least one hour prior to such class, an application for such status provided by the Federation. Amateur status will be issued only on receipt of the application properly signed and is revocable at any time for cause. Foreign riders requesting Federation Amateur status, must be a Junior, Senior or Life Competing Member of the Federation (Exception: Equine Canada members in possession of current EC membership may sign for USEF Amateur status on a show by show basis at no cost). Any person who has not reached his/her 18th birthday is an amateur and does not require amateur status. *BOD 9/29/15 Effective 12/1/15.*

2. An amateur continues to be such until he/she has received a change in status from the Federation. Any amateur who wishes to be re-classified on the grounds that he/she has engaged or is planning on engaging in activities which would prevent him/her from continuing to remain an amateur must notify the Federation in writing.

3. There is no fee for amateur status for Senior Active or Life Members. Such status will expire on November 30th.

4. If a person violates or does not comply with the above, he/she will not be eligible to compete in amateur classes and will not be entitled to an award in such classes and will be deemed guilty of a violation within the meaning of Chapter 7 in the event he/she does compete.

5. In the event a person is found to be a professional as a result of a protest or charge made in connection with a competition, all awards won by such person in amateur classes at such competition and subsequent competitions shall be forfeited and returned to the competition and the person shall be subject to further disciplinary action. The holding of an amateur card does not preclude the question of amateur standing being raised by a protest or charge.

6. The trainer may be subject to disciplinary action if an exhibitor who shows as an amateur is protested, and that protest is sustained by the Hearing Committee, and it is determined that the trainer had knowledge of their professional activities.

   a. Any changes of status from professional to amateur, or vice versa, will be published on the Federation's web site.

7. An exhibitor who engages a person to ride, drive or show in halter in any amateur class and then remunerates such person beyond the extent to which such amateur is entitled as provided above in GR1306 will be subject to disciplinary action under Chapter 7.

8. Any person who under these rules is a professional and knowingly and falsely represents himself/herself to be an amateur by declaring or maintaining current amateur status issued by the Federation, and any person who violates any of the provisions of this rule will be subject to disciplinary action under Chapter 7.

9. A professional continues to be such until he/she has received amateur status by a vote of the Hearing Committee. Any professional who wishes to be reclassified as an amateur on the grounds that he/she has not engaged in the activities which made him/her a professional within the last twelve months must notify the Federation in writing.

   a. Such person shall submit to the Hearing Committee an amateur reclassification request which is supported by:

      1. A notarized letter signed by him/her outlining the horse related activities (using specific dates) which made said person a professional and outlining the activities performed within the twelve month period (or longer) since professional activities have ceased,

      2. Two or more notarized letters from any Senior Active Federation members stating the relationship with the applicant and outling the applicants activities for the one year period preceding such written notification advising and testifying that the applicant has not engaged in any activities which would make him/her a professional as outlined in GR1306 during that period,

      3. A processing fee of $50,

      4. Sign and declare amateur status on a current USEF membership application. The burden of proof of proving amateur status is on the applicant. The Hearing Committee may call for and/or consider any and all further evidence and facts which it deems pertinent. The decision of the Hearing Committee on the reclassification request shall be final.

   b. Any changes of status from professional to amateur, or vise versa, will be published on the Federation's website.

10. Please contact the Federation office for information regarding international/professional licenses.

SUBCHAPTER 13-C MEMBERSHIP AND DOCUMENT REQUIREMENTS

GR1308 Membership and Document Requirements

1. To be eligible to participate as a rider, driver, owner, handler, vaulter, longeur, lessee, agent, coach or trainer at Regular Competitions, Eventing Competitions at the Preliminary Level or above, Combined Driving Competitions

at the Advanced Level, Dressage, Endurance and Vaulting Competitions, persons must be Members of the Federation as provided in GR202 or if not a member, must pay a Show Pass fee as provided in GR206 (for exceptions see GR901.9). Exception: Applications for Federation Individual Membership and Horse Recordings submitted at Licensed Competitions:

a. For Dressage Competitions, reference Bylaw 223, Section 1:

    1. Applications are considered effective on the date the application and dues are received by the Competition Secretary provided the application is signed and dated by the Competition Secretary on that same day.

    2. Applications completed online at the competition are effective the date the application is submitted.

b. For all Competitions other than Dressage Competitions, reference Bylaw 221, Section 1:

    1. Applications are considered effective, for points and eligibility to compete only, on the start date of said Competition provided the application and dues are received by the Competition Secretary and the application is signed and dated by the Competition Secretary during the period of the Competition.

    2. Applications completed online at the competition are effective, for points and eligibility to compete only, on the start date of the Competition.

c. Lessees are considered owners in connection with this membership requirement. When an entry is under multiple ownership, only one owner need be a Member or pay a Show Pass fee. When an entry is under a minor's ownership and training, the parent who must sign will be exempt from the Federation Show Pass fee. Only a parent will be exempt from the Federation Show Pass fee if signing as coach for his/her minor child.

2. Memberships completed at the competition must be forwarded to the Federation office within ten (10) days of the close of the competition as part of the full competition results, which are defined in GR1214. The member's copy of the application is valid for 45 days or until the membership card is received from The Federation.

a. The following credentials must be available to Competition Management and the Federation steward/technical delegate. Competitions may, at their discretion, confirm any of the below electronically with the Federation office:

    1. Amateur Status.

    2. Copies of Junior Hunter and pony measurement cards.

    3. Federation membership cards or a copy thereof, Exception: Applications completed at the competition. The member will retain the pink copy of the membership application form which, when properly signed by the Competition Secretary, is valid for 45 days from the date signed.

    4. Federation horse recordings for USEF/USDF qualifying classes for dressage championships (see DR127.2), and USEF/USDF Dressage Championships (see DR127.2).

    5. A copy of the registration papers showing recorded ownership or a copy of the registration papers with a Certificate of Eligibility to Show issued by the American Saddlebred Registry for horses entered in classes restricted to American Saddlebreds unless the competition, at their discretion, confirms registration electronically with the American Saddlebred Registry or the Canadian Livestock Records Corporation.

    6. A copy of the registration papers showing proof of ownership or copy of the registration papers issued by the American Hackney Horse Society and/or the Canadian Hackney Society for ponies and horses entered in classes restricted to Hackney Horses and Hackney Ponies.

    7. Non-U.S. citizens (as defined by GR901.9) and Foreign Competitors (as defined by GR828.4) must provide proof, in English, of current membership in good standing in their respective National Federation, or hold current membership in good standing with USEF.

    8. For all horses competing in Young Jumper classes a copy of the registration papers issued by a Breed Registry (or other means of identification issued by the Federation providing proof of age and identity) must be checked by the horse show office.

    9. Originals or copies of United States Hunter Jumper Association, Inc., membership card, if applicable.

b. If an exhibitor does not submit the proper membership documentation to the competition and the competition cannot verify such information, (with the exception of Federation measurement cards) the exhibitor will be responsible to pay a $30 Show Pass fee which is non-refundable.

3. Participation of non-US citizens in non-breed-restricted national competitions in the US.

   a. Non-US citizens who are not current members of USEF as provided in GR202 must either provide proof, in English, of current membership in good standing in their own National Federation, or must pay a registration fee as provided for in GR206 (for exceptions see GR901.9.)

   b. In any discipline, owners and trainers who are non-US citizens and who have a current letter of permission/good standing from their own federation, are exempt from Federation membership requirements per Art. III, Sect. 3. Under this rule, non-US citizens must provide proof to competition management of current permission/good standing from their own federation in order to be exempted from Federation membership requirements.

   c. Foreign Competitors (non U.S. citizens) who participate in Federation amateur classes, in any discipline, must be in possession of a Federation Amateur Card and must be a Junior, Senior, or Life Competing Member of the Federation. (Exception: Equine Canada members in possession of current EC membership may sign for USEF Amateur status on a show by show basis at no cost). However, non U.S. citizens who are not competing in Federation amateur classes are not required to become Federation Members if they provide proof, in English, of membership in good standing in their own National Federation.

4. U.S. Competitors competing in their own country in an FEI-sanctioned event, not requiring an FEI Passport, must present a valid USA National Passport or a valid FEI Passport. Exception: Endurance Minor Events.

GR1309 PRESIDENTIAL MODIFICATIONS FOR THE DRESSAGE DIVISION

In the Dressage Division, competitors will not be allowed to compete with modifications unless a copy of their Federation Presidential Modification letter is provided to the competition secretary by the beginning of the competition.

SUBCHAPTER 13-D COMPETITION DISPENSATIONS

GR1310 Dispensations

1. Dispensation Certificate. Any individual with a diagnosed permanent physical disability wishing to compete in a Federation licensed competition with a compensatory aid and/or adaptive equipment must obtain a Dispensation Certificate from the Adaptive Sports Committee. Upon the Committee's approval, a Dispensation Certificate will be issued by the Federation. The Dispensation Certificate will list all compensatory aids and adaptive equipment allowed the individual while competing. Other compensatory aids or special equipment not specifically listed on the Dispensation Certificate are not allowed. A copy of the Dispensation Certificate must be included with the individual's entry. The competition manager or secretary shall include a copy attached to all applicable scoring sheets for the judge's reference. For instructions on how to apply for the Dispensation Certificate, please refer to GR1312. Also see GR1315 for definitions of terms used in this section. (Exception: Dispensation certificates are not required for Breed or Multi-breed restricted or Hunter competitions or classes; Equitation Division classes, Carriage Pleasure Driving Division, or the Open Western Division).

2. In circumstances that fall outside of the dispensation program, a Presidential Modification may be considered. Please refer to GR152 and Bylaw 332.1.f.

GR1311 Para-Equestrian Eligibility/Classification

In order for an individual to compete in USEF licensed Para-Equestrian Competitons, he/she must have a diagnosed, permanent physical disability as determined by the USEF Para-Equestrian Classification System. The individual will be Para-Equestrian eligible (PE eligible), possess a USEF classification card for up to National level competition (USEF PE), or possess and FEI PE Card for Qualifying and International level competition. See GR142 for the definition of Para-Equestrian and GR1315 for additional definitions).

GR1312 Applying for a Dispensation Certificate

1. Applications for a Dispensation Certificate can be obtained from the Federation (via the USEF website or the USEF office) and are reviewed on a continuing basis throughout the year by the Adaptive Sports Committee. Only applications submitted along with supporting medical documentation will be considered. The Adaptive Sports Committee may request additional supporting evidence from the individual regarding his/her medical status or regarding the aid/equipment which he/she requests dispensation for. The Adaptive Sports Committee will render an opinion (approval of all or some of the aids requested or denial of the dispensation) and the individual will be notified by the USEF in a timely manner.

    a. The Dispensation Certificate will be issued annually upon re-application, and remains in effect until the end of the competition year or until he/she receives a change in status from the Federation, whichever is earlier. Any individual who wishes to make changes to his/her Dispensation Certificate must notify the Federation in writing and obtain written approval. Certification is revocable at any time for cause.

    b. Applications should be submitted in order to allow 30 days for the Adaptive Sports Committee to render a decision regarding the dispensation status.

    c. There is no fee for a Dispensation Certificate.

    d. The individual must be a member in good standing with the USEF.

GR1313 Applying for Para-Equestrian (PE) Classification

1. The individual will request classification from the USEF. Applications may be found on the USEF website or at the USEF office. Once the USEF office receives the application, they will contact the USEF classification coordinator.

    a. Until such time that the classification is scheduled, the individual will be considered Para-Equestrian Eligible (PE Eligible) as determined by the USEF classification coordinator.

    b. PE Eligible individuals may participate in competition using the self-classification system for local and regional competitions.

2. The USEF classification coordinator will assist in scheduling a classification with one of the USEF Classifiers. There is no fee for the classification, though if the individual requests a classification to be scheduled at their convenience, all expenses for the classifier will be paid for by the individual.

3. The classification will result in a Profile and a Grade based on the FEI Profile system. The Profile will remain with the individual for as long as their physical disability remains constant with no need for re-classification. If the individual has a fluctuating medical condition or if his/her function changes, the profile may change with future re-classifications. The Grade will be based on the specific discipline.

4. Upon classification, the USEF will issue a USEF Classification Card. This card will outline the individual's profile and grade, indicate any compensating aids/adaptive equipment that may be used in USEF PE competition and the expiration date of the classification.

5. For USEF licensed PE competitions, the individual will send in a copy of their Card with their competition entry. The individual will also be responsible for carrying their card throughout the show for review by the TD or Steward as necessary.

6. When change in status occurs (i.e. change of compensating aids/adaptive equipment), written request for a change will be submitted to the USEF office.

7. The USEF Classifier will determine the renewal period for classification. For those with disabilities with no expected change in functional status, the classification will have no expiration. For those with fluctuating conditions or conditions expected to change, either by deterioration or improvement there will be indicated on the card an expiration and expected time for re-classification. It is the individual's responsibility to apply for re-classification through the USEF at least 45 days and at most 90 days prior to the expiration date. It is also the individual's responsibility to apply for re-classification if a major change in status (i.e. resulting from a surgery or therapy which causes

significant functional improvement) occurs.

8. Upon receipt of an FEI PE Card for Qualifying and International competition, the FEI card will take the place of a USEF PE Classification Card and may be used for USEF licensed PE competitions.

9. Classification status can be challenged by a USEF PE competition official, competitor or trainer with the potential for re-classification occurring at that event.

GR1314 Hearings/Protests

1. Any individual whose application for a Dispensation Certificate or a Para-Equestrian Classification has been denied may request a hearing by the Hearing Committee or by such individual or committee as it may designate to review said decision. The request must be in writing and mailed to the Hearing Committee within ten (10) days from receipt of the decision sought to be reviewed.

   a. The hearing shall be after ten (10) days notice to all parties concerned. The notice shall contain a brief statement of the facts reporting the position of the Federation and shall specify the time and place at which the hearing is to be held. The person requesting said hearing may attend and bring witnesses, sworn statements or other evidence on his or her behalf. Upon the written request of a representative of the Federation or of the person requesting the hearing, there shall be furnished before said hearing any evidence to be introduced, the names of witnesses and the substance of their testimony.

   b. The decision of the Hearing Committee or the person or committee designated to preside at said hearing shall be final.

   c. Protests or charges brought in connection with an individual's Dispensation Certificate status or Para Equestrian Classification status shall be handled in accordance with the provisions of Chapter 6.

GR1315 Definition of Terms

1. Diagnosed permanent physical disability - An individual with a medical condition resulting in functional limitations affecting their ability to participate in equestrian sport and diagnosed by a medical doctor. The condition is not reasonably expected to improve and may, in fact, be one that worsens over time. The condition should be easily objectively measurable in scope, either by physical examination by a medical professional or with medical testing. An example may include a limb amputation, paralysis, weakness due to a neuromuscular condition or hearing or vision loss.

2. Compensating aid and/or adaptive equipment - Allowance for an alteration in performance, an alteration of dress or alternate piece of equipment which allows the individual with a disability to perform the requirements of the competition. The aid or equipment assists in equalizing the functional ability of the individual and should not give the individual an undue advantage. The aid/equipment must be deemed safe for the competitor and the horse and is subject to review by the TD and/or judge at each event. Examples:

   a. Saluting with the nod of the head only when taking a hand off of the reins would be unsafe.

   b. Use of paddock boots and smooth leather half chaps rather than tall boots if wearing tall boots is unsafe for a rider with leg dysfunction.

   c. Allowance to not wear gloves for the individual with abnormal sensation in the hands.

   d. Use of 1 or 2 whips to cue the horse for an individual with impaired use of his/her legs.

   e. Use of a golf cart to survey a course prior to driving for the individual who is unable to walk.

   f. Use of quick release equipment for carriage driving.

For additional examples, please see USEF booklet entitled, Guidelines for USEF Dispensation and USEF Classification Systems found on the USEF website.

3. Dispensation

   a. Dispensation Program - The Federation encourages competition amongst all individuals, including those with a diagnosed permanent physical disability. For those individuals wishing to compete in a Federation licensed competition and who require compensating aids and/or adaptive equipment to do so, a Dispensation Certifcate may be granted. The purpose of the dispensation is to aid those with limited function by allowing the use of aids/equipment which will result in more equal function. These aids/equipment should not give the individual with a disability an advantage over his/her competitors.

    b. Adaptive Sports Committee: An interdisciplinary group representing the equestrian disciplines, the medical field, competitors, and the USEF who is charged with the review and/or approval of dispensation applications. (Bylaw 503.3)

4. Para-Equestrian (PE)

    a. USEF Para-Equestrian (PE) Classification System - The USEF has chosen to adopt the FEI Profile System for classification for individuals with disabilities. This system provides a means to assess an individual's functional abilities and impairments to determine which Grade they will compete in amongst individuals with similar levels of function. There is a minimal level of impairment required in order to qualify for the FEI Profile System. In the system, an individual with a permanent measurable physical disability is assessed by a USEF or FEI approved classifier. As a result of the assessment, the classifier will determine eligibility and then assign the individual a Profile. The Profiles are grouped into Grades based on the discipline in which the individual will be competing. For example, an individual who has minor impairment of the Left arm and leg after a stroke would likely be given a Profile 15. If they compete in dressage, they would compete in Grade III. If they choose to compete in Carriage Driving, they would compete as a Grade II.

    b. FEI Profile System - Amongst individuals with disabilities, there are many different types of impairments. To provide meaningful competition for these individuals it is necessary that those of similar levels of impairment compete together. The "Profile System" fulfils this criterion. It is a System of tests administered by trained and certified Physical Therapists or Physicians. It is based on the classification systems used in other sports for individuals with disabilities and has been tested for reliability and validity in its application in equestrian sport.

5. Profile - an individual is given one of 42 profiles based on their level of function as assessed by a USEF or FEI Classifier. The Profiles are versatile but tight, easy to use and understand. The locomotor Profiles are not disability (diagnosis) specific, but are based on the ability of the functioning part(s) of the body. The Profile is considered permanent except in the case of a diagnosis that has a reasonable expectation of change, such as with progressive Multiple Sclerosis.

6. Grade - the grouping of profiles within a discipline. In Dressage, there are 5 grades (Ia, Ib, II, III, and IV). In Carriage Driving there are 2 Grades (I and II). A Grade is made up of several profiles, grouping Para-Equestrians of similar level of function. The lower number Grades (i.e. Grade I) is made up of Para-Equestrians with a more significant level of impairment, whereas the higher number Grades (i.e. IV) identify those Para-Equestrians with a lesser impairment. The Grade determines which tests a rider rides and against whom the Para-Equestrian will be competing. In National and International competition, medals/placement is awarded in each Grade.

7. Para-Equestrian (PE) Eligible - an individual with a permanent measurable physical disability who has entered into the classification process but has not yet been classified by a USEF or FEI Classifier. The USEF Classification Coordinator will determine PE Eligible status. This individual may compete in Para-Equestrian classes at the local or regional level, but may not medal.

8. USEF Para-Equestrian (USEF PE) - a classified Para-Equestrian carrying a USEF Classification card indicating their Profile, Grade, and compensating aids/adaptive equipment. These individuals may compete up to the National level of USEF licensed PE competitions.

9. FEI Para-Equestrian (FEI PE) - a Para-Equestrian carrying an FEI Classification Card indicating their Profile, Grade and compensating aids/adaptive equipment. This individual may compete Nationally and in Qualifying trials. To achieve this classification, the individual will need a classification by two FEI Classifiers, at least one from outside

of their home country. There is a fee to the FEI for application and renewal for the FEI PE Classification Card. Individuals must request renewals through the National Federation.

10. USEF Classifier - a Physical Therapist or Physician who has been trained and certified by the USEF to classify individuals using the FEI Profile System. A USEF Classifier may classify Para Equestrians up through a National level competition.

11. FEI Classifier - a Physical Therapist or Physician who has been trained and certified by the FEI to classify Para-Equestrians using the FEI Profile System. An FEI classifier may classify Para-Equestrians through to the International level (i.e. Paralympics and World Games). FEI Classifiers are designated as 'I' (International) or 'O' (Paralympic and World Games).

12. USEF Classification Coordinator - the lead USEF Classifier responsible for assisting individuals through the classification process and establishing PE Eligible status.

13. Para-Equestrian (PE) Self-classification - When it is difficult due to logistics to complete a classification by a USEF or FEI Classifier, an individual may choose to classify themselves based on the USEF Classification System. Using the stick figures and definitions for trainers, a profile will be determined. (see Guidelines for USEF Dispensation and USEF Classification Systems) This will in turn determine a Grade depending on the individual's particular discipline. The self-classification is a means to begin competition based on the individual's self evaluation of their level of function. This will be allowed for local or regional USEF licensed competition only. At this status, an individual may compete at a Grade lower than their functional status determines. Once National competition is attempted, an official classification must be completed.

14. Classification Card - The card issued to a Para-Equestrian indicating the Para-Equestrian's Profile, Grade, Compensating Aids/Adaptive Equipment and expiration of the classification. USEF issues the USEF Classification Card and the FEI issues the FEI PE Classification Card.

SUBCHAPTER 13-E RETURN TO COMPETITION

GR1316 Accidents Involving Competitors

1. This rule pertains to accidents involving competitors at Federation-Licensed or endorsed competitions.

2. In the event of a fall/accident where the competitor is apparently unconscious or concussed, he/she is precluded from competing until evaluated by qualified medical personnel as defined in GR1211.5. If the competitor refuses to be evaluated, he is disqualified from the competition.

3. A Time-Out may be called under paragraph 2 above in accordance with applicable division rules.

4. Unconsciousness/Concussion. If qualified medical personnel determines that a competitor has sustained unconsciousness or a concussion, he/she must be precluded from competing until cleared to compete under paragraph 6 below.

5. Medical Suspension. Any competitor who is determined ineligible to compete under any of the preceding paragraphs will be placed on the Federation Medical Suspension List that will be posted on the Federation's website.

6. Return to Competition.

    a. Seniors - In the event that a competitor is determined ineligible to compete under one of the preceding paragraphs, the competitor shall submit to the Federation, a signed release, which includes criteria established by the Federation from time to time, completed by a licensed physician in order to be eligible to once again compete in Federation-Licensed or endorsed competitions.

    b. Juniors: In the event a Junior competitor is determined to be ineligible to compete under one of the preceding paragraphs, the following apply:

        1. No loss of consciousness but with brief symptoms of concussion e.g. confusion, loss of memory, altered mental state (all symptoms of concussion must have resolved within 15 minutes both at rest and exercise)

– minimum 7 days mandatory suspension. The day of injury counts as the first day of the suspension period.

2. Any loss of consciousness, however brief, or symptoms of concussion persisting after 15 minutes – minimum 21 days mandatory suspension. The day of injury counts as the first day of the suspension period.

3. Notwithstanding the above, riders who have established a baseline neurocognitive skills level through a Federation approved testing program e.g. IMPACT test, may return to competition after 7 days upon submission to the Federation of certification that they have passed an exam establishing that they have suffered no impairment of that level. In addition, they must submit clearance as required in a above.

4. All other riders may, at the expiration of the mandatory suspension, return to competition by complying with the requirements of a above. *BOD 1/17/15 Effective 12/1/15*

7. For all competitors evaluated pursuant to this rule, the Steward or Technical Delegate shall submit a properly completed Accident/Injury Form, and, if applicable, any corresponding signed release to the Federation Director of Competitions by 6:00 p.m. on the day following the last day of the competition.

8. Refusal of Entry. Competitions shall refuse entries of any competitor who is on the Federation Medical Suspension List unless he submits to the Federation a properly signed release as described in paragraph 6 above. Any competitor on the Federation Medical Suspension List is responsible for not competing in any further Federation-Licensed or endorsed competition until they are removed from the medical suspension list.

9. Substitution. Not withstanding any other provisions of the rules herein, if an entry is accepted prior to the time the competitor was added to the Federation Medical Suspension List , a substitute competitor may be named.

10. Refund. Not withstanding any other provisions of the rules herein, for any competitor who appears on the Federation Medical Suspension List, a Federation-Licensed or endorsed competition shall refund the entry fees and Jumper nominating fee, if applicable, less office fee.

CHAPTERS AL TO WS

WHICH DESCRIBE THE CLASSES FOR ALL DIVISIONS, TOGETHER WITH DEFINITIONS AS TO APPOINTMENTS. Entries in various classes are judged on some of the following qualifications:

Appointments (equipment)	Handiness (promptness)	Soundness
Breed Character	Manners	Speed
Brilliance	Performance	Substance (strength)
Color	Presence (style)	Suitability
Conformation (build)	Quality (finesse)	Type

The particular qualifications for each class are hereinafter set forth and in each class the order of precedence indicates how the emphasis is to be placed in adjudication.

Class specifications included in division rules are mandatory.

Any class described herein may be confined to exhibitors within a desired area by prefixing "LOCAL" to the class title and clearly describing the area involved (e.g., "Open to horses owned and stabled within...miles of the competition grounds" or "Owned by residents of the Town of ...").

Entry fees, trophies or cash awards must always be indicated. If classes not included herein are offered, extreme care should be exercised in the proper wording of the specifications.

Table of Yards, Feet and Meters

1	inch	=	0.025 m		1.00 m	=	3 ft.	3 ins.
1	foot	=	0.30 m		1.10 m	=	3 ft.	7 ins.
2	ft.	=	0.61 m		1.20 m	=	3 ft.	11 ins.
1	yard	=	0.91 m		1.30 m	=	4 ft.	3 ins.
4	ft.	=	1.22 m		1.40 m	=	4 ft.	7 ins.
4	ft. 3 ins.	=	1.30 m		1.50 m	=	4 ft.	11 ins.
4	ft. 6 ins.	=	1.37 m		1.60 m	=	5 ft.	3 ins.
4	ft. 9 ins.	=	1.45 m		1.70 m	=	5 ft.	7 ins.
5	ft.	=	1.52 m		1.80 m	=	5 ft.	11 ins.
5	ft. 3 ins.	=	1.60 m		1.90 m	=	6 ft.	3 ins.
5	ft. 6 ins.	=	1.68 m		2.00 m	=	6 ft.	7 ins.
6	ft.	=	1.83 m		3.00 m	=	9 ft.	10 ins.
6	ft. 6 ins.	=	1.91 m		4.00 m	=	13 ft.	1 ins.
7	ft.	=	2.13 m		5.00 m	=	16 ft.	5 ins.
8	ft.	=	2.44 m		6.00 m	=	19 ft.	8 ins.
9	ft.	=	2.74 m		7.00 m	=	22 ft.	11 ins.
10	ft.	=	3.05 m		8.00 m	=	26 ft.	3 ins.
15	ft.	=	4.57 m		9.00 m	=	29 ft.	6 ins.
20	ft.	=	6.10 m		10.00 m	=	32 ft.	10 ins.
10	yds.	=	9.14 m		25.00 m	=	82 ft.	
25	yds.	=	22.86 m		100.00 m	=	328 ft.	
50	yds.	=	45.72 m		1000.00 m	=	3281ft.	
10	yds.	=	91.44 m					
1000	yds.	=	914.40 m					

Conversion

Yards to Meters, multiply by .9144

Meters to Yards, divide by .9144

Feet to Meters, multiply by .3048

Meters to Feet, divide by .3048

M

N

Made in the USA
Lexington, KY
09 July 2016